THE PLIGHT
OF A POSTMODERN HUNTER

EDITED BY DAVID PARRY

CHINGIZ AITMATOV
MUKHTAR SHAKHANOV

London 2015

CULTURAL FIGURES REFLECT ON THE WORKS OF M. SHAKHANOV

Mukhtar Shakhanov is one of the most significant writers ever to have emerged from Kazakhstan. As Ambassador Extraordinary and Plenipotentiary of the Republic, his work is unrivalled. Honours culminating in equally becoming the National Poet of the Kyrgyz Republic. Further plaudits include his chairing of "Intellectuals Union of the Turkic World" and "Best Poet in the World among Turkic-Speaking Peoples". Indeed, Shakhanov's academic titles range from Professor and Doctor of Sciences, to Academician in 22 universities across the globe. Most significantly, Shakhanov holds a Nobel gold medal (dedicated to the 100th anniversary of the Nobel Prize), along with the highly prestigious Albert Einstein gold medal, awarded by the California Academy of Sciences (USA). His name has also been entered in the Golden Book of the United Nations. As a contributor to Global Text and a vigorous defended of minority rights, Shakhanov is an honorary citizen of more than 40 cities.

The poetic vision of Shakhanov is comparable with the vision of people endowed with a cosmic sense of existential harmony and historical continuity between past, present and future. His poetry is derived from personal experience, as well as the ethical learning rooted in traditional stories. As such, he focuses on those perennial values that elevate our existence.

Federico Mayor,
Director-General of UNESCO (1999)

He is the carrier of new way of thinking. There has never been such a significant poet in Central Asian literature before him.

To verify this, read his epic novel (written as poetry) "Cosmic Formula of Punishing Memory or Mysterious Eruptions by Genghis Khan". Indeed, no poet of the 20th century has stepped into the 21st century on this clearly planetary level apart from Mukhtar Shakhanov.

Chingiz AITMATOV

As a poet, Mukhtar Shakhanov is the active conscience of our addled era. As such, he is unlikely to be appreciated by political authorities, although I am proud he is my friend.

Rasul GAMZATOV

So significant is the attention paid by UNESCO to Shakhanov's poetry, it is tantamount to a recognition of the fact current social and philosophical thought in Central Asia has reached new heights. Primarily, it must be said, due to perceptions of poetry as indisputable achievements within world literature - which remind us of the consciousness and intuition required to fight against negative developments in civilization generated by the 20th century.

Hans Peter DUERR
Nobel Prize Laureate

"Delusion of civilization" by M. Shakhanov is an epochal poem, rich in prudence and nobility – as is his foremother steppe. It is the voice of the Earth, which raised itself in defense of the human soul. This is a new genre of spiritual ecology. As such, this book is written from the heart of a former tractor driver, who knows all the "scars and wrinkles" of the soil - its thirst for human intimacy. This book is also authored from the perspective of an outstanding intellectual whose love for national traditions has grown as universal as our common great motherland.

I dare say, this book is a spiritual instrument of patriotism for all humankind. Hence, there is something gentle, kind, and sad, about the old swan-song of Mukhtar's brave ancestors. Those who for six months fought to the death to protect Grand Otrar - famous worldwide for its philosophers and rich library, from the hordes of Genghis Khan.

Yevgeny YEVTUSHENKO

His Holiness Pope John Paul II expresses to you sincere gratitude for the philosophical and poetic reflection on the current state of culture and civilization as a whole, which is reflected in your works, and hopes that it will serve as a more effective protection of universal spiritual values, such as high morality, justice, peace and equality between peoples. As a sign of respect and honour, His Holiness sincerely prays to heaven to bless you and your family.

Cardinal Angelo SODANO,
Secretary of State of His Holiness, the Pope
(Vatican City, September 11, 2001)

Shakhanov is a poet-philosopher who continually contributes to our understanding of modern civilization with his irresistible style. That's why we elected him a member of our academy. Notably, his works "Delusion of civilization" and "Cosmic formula of punishing memory" presents moral principles for human existence from a completely different incarnational stance - by succinct poetic-scientific and philosophical interpretation. This extraordinary author, who squeezes large plots within novels into two three-verse lines, gives us high hopes for new possibilities in the poetic word throughout our digital age.

Michael BAKHMUTSKY,
Academician, President of the International
California Academy of Sciences,
Industry, Education and Arts (USA)

Shakhanov, as an outstanding poet of our time, is always at a universal level. He represents a completely secular, enlightened form of humanism, in which East and West are connected. For example, Shakhanov's poem "Delusion of civilization" - which is an outstanding poem-epopee about moral anxieties - penetrates like a fireball from the depths of Central Asia into the "black holes" of Western European space.

UNESCO praised poetry by Shakhanov as the current height attained by verse in our modern world.

Friedrich HITZER

Being a champion and defender of the honour of humanity, Mukhtar Shakhanov, with his usual perspicacity of thought, vulnerable sensibility, and powerful poetic words, tries to show the imminent danger of falling off accepted morality into a circle of permissiveness.

Moreover, Shaklanov's concept of a new type of people "computer-headed half-humans" rejecting spirituality and focused on one-sided knowledge, shocked us Japanese. I congratulate his people for having such an outstanding poet.

Daisaku IKEDA

The epic poem "Delusion of civilization" can be considered as one of the outstanding examples of modern poetry. Mukhtar Shakhanov is not only as a poet of planetary-level thinking but also a philosopher and strong moralist. A writer who condemns and denounces the decline of indigenous culture for the sake of building a consumer-based future, while fearing a naked society deprived of spiritual virtues.

Furthermore, his Beautiful style, as well as his presentational skills, make this novel-in-verse a work of global importance. Easily meeting requirements of the highest aesthetics.

Doudou DIENE
Director of the Department of UNESCO (1999)

Frankly speaking, Shakhanov has no equal among our contemporary poets in Europe.

Roberto CHIULI

In 1989, together with a friend Mukhtar (Shakhanov) I worked in the Supreme Soviet of the USSR. Then, many people did not know the truth about the events of December ... The great merit of Mukhtar was that he first told our whole world the truth of these December events and made the Kremlin chimes listen to him.

Askar AKAYEV
Former President of the Kyrgyz Republic

Too serious burdens have been fated to him - speaking out against the CPSU and its power structures SSC (State Security Committee) and MIA (Ministry of International Affairs), in order to defend the honour of trampled youth in Kazakhstan. I remember Andrei Sakharov once told me about him with admiration...

David KUGULTINOV

God grant that each poet would serve his nation as Mukhtar Shakhanov.

John ASHBERY,
American poet

Mukhtar Shakhanov was the civil conscience of his time. We know he stubbornly engaged in the restoration of justice regarding December 1986 events in Alma-Ata. The authorities in Moscow, as well as here, continuing to resent it. And we, the followers of the poet, firmly declare if merely one hair falls from Shakhanov's head, then the whole world will immediately raise their voices in his defense.

Andrei VOZNESENSKY
(Extract from the poetry evening at the Palace of Lenin in Alma-Ata, 1990)

The true meaning of poetry (as universal resonance) is established within the works by Mukhtar Shakhanov. Indeed, any lack of spirituality and morality is the target of M. Shakhanov.

Naguib MAHBUZ,
Nobel Prize Laureate

Poets cannot be silent, since they are responsible for everything. M. Shakhanov's epic poem "Delusion of civilization" (The Saga of morals in our age) proves it to us. Written in the same breath, this phenomenal work - due to its position on the doorstep of our third millennium - is the voice of a poet-citizen of the Planet!

... The role of culture is invaluable in the life of an individual, nation, humanity. Additionally, the worst thing in this line of reasoning is when it results in - "civilized savagery and spiritless education." That's the fear! That is where the trouble befalling humanity, lies! In which case, this book is the textbook from where we must start.

Bakhtiyar VAGABADZE,
National Poet of Azerbaijan

Works by Mukhtar Shakhanov such as "Delusion of civilization" and "Cosmic formula of punishing memory" (Mysterious Eruptions by Genghis Khan) are poetic reflections on our world's moral and ethical condition. Both of these philosophical poems not only left a deep impression on me, but also raised questions about the future of humanity. M. Shakhanov is one of the spiritual pillars of the 21st century.

James H. BILLINGTON,
Professor, Director of the Library of Congress USA

Shakhanov at poetry is Aitmatov at prose. Apparently, their creative union produced two wonderfully wise things written in collaboration - a book Dialogue "The Plight of a Postmodern Hunter" (Confession at the end of the century) and a philosophical drama "Night of memories about Socrates, or the Court on the skin of a foolish person", wherein the global problems of our 20th century are raised.

Revelations by the poet-philosopher of the East, Mukhtar Shakhanov, in the poem "Delusion of civilization" anticipate ideas and concepts indicated by thinkers of our time – A. Toynbee, F. Fukuyama, S. Huntington, K. Jaspers. Yet, his intellectual and poetic reflections on the crisis of world culture on the threshold of the 21st century, point to the spiritual and philosophical concerns of Eurasian peoples.

Rustan RAHMANALIYEV
Academician of the Academy of California,
Doctor of Social Sciences and History

I was able to stage a performance of "Mysterious Eruptions by Genghis Khan" based on the novel "Cosmic formula of punishing memory" in an Uzbek theater. The Shakespearian scope of this work stirred up and turned around all my ideas about the social regeneration of the world and its historical contradictions. As a result, it took more than a year to implement the director's intention on our stage, according to the content of the drama.

And I'm doubly pleased that another extraordinary spiritual height has been reached by Central Asia on a global scale.

Karim YULDASHEV,
Director, Honored Worker of Culture
of the Republic of Uzbekistan

I had the great pleasure of translating "Delusion of civilization" into Bulgarian, which the newspaper "Friendship" gave five stars - all causing an unprecedented interest among readers. This suggests Shakhanov succeeded in touching the most urgent and topical issues of our day. Issues concerning everyone, in spite of religion and nationality, in his poetic novel.

Christine ARBOVA

I had the great pleasure of translating into Czech Mukhtar Shakhanov's book "The Power of Words". I think Mukhtar is one of the major poets of the 20th century.

Kamil MARZHIK,
Czech poet

The performance of works by Mukhtar Shakhanov such as "Night of memories about Socrates" (co-authored with Chingiz Aitmatov) and "Mysterious Eruptions by Genghis Khan" had great success in two Baku theatres. I must say the role played by this poet is highly significant - not only in the Turkic world, but across the entire world of poetry.

Polad BULBULOGLU,
Chairman of TyurkSOI,
Minister of Culture of Azerbaijan (1997)

"Delusion of civilization" by Mukhtar Shakhanov, in my opinion, is a significant feat in the poetic world. In this regard, I want to heartily congratulate the Kazakh people on their outstanding new exponent of indigenous destiny and aspiration.

Vladimir JANIBEKOV
Pilot-Cosmonaut of the Russian Federation,
Hero of the Soviet Union

If I had been lucky enough to make a second trip into space, I would have picked works by Chingiz Aitmatov and Mukhtar Shakhanov to read.

Zhugderdemiydiyn GURRAGCHA,
first cosmonaut of the People's Republic of
Mongolia

Mukhtar Shakhanov is a great spiritual reformer of the 21st century.

S. K. TRESSLER,
Minister of Culture, Sports, Tourism and
Youth Affairs of the Islamic Republic of Pakistan

Published in United Kingdom
Hertfordshire Press Ltd © 2015

9 Cherry Bank, Chapel Street
Hemel Hempstead, Herts.
HP2 5DE, United Kingdom

e-mail: publisher@hertfordshirepress.com
www.hertfordshirepress.com

THE PLIGHT OF A POSTMODERN HUNTER
CHINGIZ AITMATOV & MUKHTAR SHAKHANOV ©

English

Edited by David Parry
Epilogue by Vladimir Korkin
Cover design by Aleksandra Vlasova
Typesetting All Well Solutions

This edition is Mukhtar Shahanov's authorized reprint of Walter May translation of "The Plaint of the Hunter Above the Abyss" book initially published by Atamura in 1998.

British Library Catalogue in Publication Data
A catalogue record for this book is available from the British Library
Library of Congress in Publication Data
A catalogue record for this book has been requested

ISBN 978-1-910886-11-3

AN INTRODUCTION TO POSTMODERN WANDERING

Perhaps life in London never really changes. A perception which may explain why British kids sing the nursery rhyme *Oranges and Lemons* about growing up in this Capital of contrasts. They are ageless lyrics, after all, which accurately describe the cultural realities behind living here. Unlike, Paris, the "City of Light", Rome, the "Eternal City", or Moscow, the "Second Byzantium", our "Old London Town" is a place where the sweet and sour experiences of Shakespearean theatre, spiteful gossip, ruthless commerce, poetry, world music, skulduggery, and intrusive public surveillance, mix together as commonplace. It is a "planetary" location, they say, wherein differing classes, as well as a multiplicity of migrants, interact, shop, and travel - on a daily basis. Nothing new there, of course, except that in a city where everyone lives on top of everyone else, the affluent go home to delightful "Greater London" residences, whereas the poor congregate inside lemony "Inner City" tower blocks. Reflecting, even in these postmodern times, the words of this rhyme when it continues, "When will you pay me, say the bells of Old Bailey?" - testifying to rampant social inequality (both then and now) as characteristic of our metropolis. Indeed, the bells of "Old Bailey" endlessly sound around our central criminal court for broker and bankrupt alike. Alleviated, perhaps, by the sweeter bells of Shoreditch when their chimes reply - fortunes may be made, dreams realised, and Ladies clad in department store remainders can still rub shoulders with High Fashion "toffs".

A vibrant dialectic reminiscent of deliberations within this revived and renamed English language edition of **The Plight of a Postmodern Hunter** by Chingiz Aitmatov and Mukhtar Shakhanov. An epistolary volume by two giants of Global Text, which brazenly bridges the literary divide between Central Asia and Europe. And as such, this weighty tome is an invigorating joy to read. Not simply due to the fact Aitmatov and Shakhanov – two lifelong friends and colleagues, adopt an almost deconstructive methodology in their endless sifting of documents and anecdotes (a sorcerous practice leading into the numinous core beneath all phenomena), but equally because they each hail from ageless Turkic environments: the former from Kyrgyzstan and the latter from Kazakhstan. Cultural contexts clearly placing them outside the usually stilted confines of Anglo-American academia, or for that matter, received colonial attitudes towards existence generally. Hence, this volume has a surprisingly avant-garde appeal. Particularly if we recall postmodernism - as a late-20th-century movement in the arts, history, and criticism, - reacted against an increasingly conformist modernity, whilst simultaneously encouraging a rejuvenation of traditionalist tendencies within cultural commentary.

Stated so, this series of pre-recorded letters has an openly sceptical stance towards accepted interpretations of social discourse. Gleefully meandering, as it does, through the sensuality and mysticism of the Steppes. Themes additionally expounding a restless (nevertheless deeply human), need to wander across unending panoramas of speculation: be they in magical Samarkand, the city-museum of Bukhara, or the flower-drenched outskirts of Bishkek. At times, therefore, this book makes a magisterial impression on its readers: akin possibly, to Joyce, or Faulkner, at their best. Certainly, on a personal level, I occasionally felt overwhelmed by the rarefied phenomena, political intrigues, and breadth of content inside these covers. A feeling, moreover, making me remember London itself has a multi-layered history. Beginning as a Roman settlement named "Londinium" way before England was born. Only later developing into "Ludenwic" when Anglo-Saxon invaders seized these streets as their own. Before it eventually transmuted into the "Port of London" where cultural fusion, accompanied by international trade, were always the underlying secrets of this city's wealth. Yet, the value of such enriching cultural memories are often taken for granted in Great Britain, along with the importance of indigenous identity. All subjective narratives, no doubt, even though these types of archetypal recitation are ignored at our communal peril.

Thus, it comes as little surprise if such learned Ex-Soviet pundits prove quick to contend any people robbed of their sense of place and purpose speedily falls into ennui, ethical dislocation and psychological torpor. Tragic occurrences Aitmatov and Shakanov have witnessed personally, not to mention through their work as highly respected intellectuals. In which case, we Brits seem far too blasé about a small Island housing innumerable playwrights, novelists, ghosts, liverymen, and the very Mother of Parliaments. Elements of a nation's Species Being, which Aitmatov and Shakanov vigorously defend. Truly, they stress, Central Asia can boast, alongside Europe, of a glorious past. Albeit in dramatically different states of preservation. However, without an insistent continuity between penmanship and metaphysical vagrancy, betwixt adventuring and reportage, any sense of enduring orientation sadly disappears. An attitude making this historically significant work more attuned to "reconstructive experimentalism" than Romantic diatribe. Unarguably, every chapter links pedestrians to pilgrims, as well as a flâneur to a stalker. Analogous, maybe, to the candle lighting us "to bed", before the chopper tries to "chop off" our heads? Be that as it may, in our mind's eye we can visualize striding around royal castles, Dickensian lanes, and bronze statues guarding Big Ben (especially of Iceni warrior-Queen Boudica, whose freewheeling war chariot perpetually guards Parliament against its foes), at the same time as Aitmatov and Shakhanov interweave enchanting fable and forgotten phenomena into previously unsuspected vistas. Twin storytelling activities bringing to the forefront of public imagination, once again, an age-old association of fearless writers with valiant voyeurs - as these street artists re-engage with controversial ideas animating, and reanimating, earlier generations. Concepts, for example, ranging from zombism, two fanged fish, priest-magicians, groaning swans, psychic vampirism, congenital sadism, the grim reality behind phrases like "hair-brained", all the way to why people would hide a human skull in a jug. For wanderers are on the march. Imitating the epic hero Manas as he ceaselessly battles forward - no matter how painful the surrounding scenery. Trooping, and likewise refusing to abandon their own knightly search for better roads to travel. In addition to mapping recovered territories and detailing new visions of the landscape.

Observations boding extremely well for this groundbreaking publication in its new lease of life. Although, at the same time begging questions such as "Was Dr. Samuel Johnson correct in saying when a man is tired of London, he is tired of life; for there is in London all that life can afford"? Assuredly not! Looking back, exactly the same sentiments must have permeated other "planetary" locations in their own day: places like Otrar, Konye-Urgench, or Sarai. Despite the "Freudian" slip of "afford" - since any contemporary equivalent to these megacities needs to resist William Blake's financially insightful retort "Hell is a city much like London". Hinting, as he intended, that every city across the globe can easily slip into an overly gentrified caricature of itself! Either way, this astonishing book by Aitmatov and Shakhanov evidentially displays a sizable number of pleasant postmodern "oranges" to its readers, while remaining stoically mindful that audiences can learn a great deal from lost, or potential, "lemons".

David Parry
London 2015

CHİNGIZ AITMATOV * MUKHTAR SHAKHANOV

THE PLIGHT
OF A POSTMODERN HUNTER

HERTFORDSHIRE PRESS

THE THIRST FOR REVELATION
(PROLOGUE)

If one does not deal with words carefully, I would even say sparingly, if one wastes them (like water flowing all day and night without any measure), neither weighing up each syllable nor comprehending every invaluable life-giving meaning, then they inevitably lose their vital strength. Indeed, human society from the earliest days of its emergence, has understood that a man whose "word" means nothing is quite worthless.

To speak with one's whole soul means to live, "squared" - as it is expressed in mathematics. Maybe this is why, I remember how, in my childhood, I chanced to hear one respected elder from our village saying: "Now, there is nobody to talk with!" At that time, this was a surprise for me. What had happened to our wise man? There were so many people around him, yet he felt lonely and saddened! Only later, did I understand his need for heartfelt conversation with people as experienced as himself: with those who understood the value of words and their deeper morphology. Dare one say, with those who know how to listen and appreciate qualitative discourse?

Relatedly, the way this book emerged as an item in your hands is very interesting. It was born after my conversations with Mukhtar - and their ensuing revelations. Truly, one of us spoke the Kazakh tongue, whilst the other Kirghizian (they belong to the same language family), although this didn't depreciate either the form, or content, of our deliberations. Unlike the aforementioned white-headed elder, therefore, we experienced the frisson of genuinely conversing with a colleague. Thus, these essays may rightly be called "an exchange of innermost thoughts via magnetophone, or a book of delayed replies derived from magnetic tape". So confessed, during the flow of our discussions there were moments when we both fell captive to our own personal dispositions. A largely unsurprising occurrence! Yet, we decided not to "comb out" these predilections, since they were spontaneously present within our natural intercourse: a dialogue often coloured by opposing emotional responses. Neither did we choose to hide any instance of gladness, or disappointment, encountered along this daily path: a road only our dear ones know about. Rather, we embraced these disruptions between free conversation and a written account.

Now, I think it would be fitting, for the sake of our overseas readers, to say a few words about my co-author and comrade. After all, there have been two Mukhtars in my life. The first of them, the great writer Auezov, who showed such fatherly care for me, and was my teacher: my leader. The second, Mukhtar Shakhanov, as a long-standing friend and tutor. Admittedly, as far as I can judge, Shakhanov, is one of the outstanding poets of Central Asia. Moreover, he is a man who attracts my attention due to his inquisitive manner of thinking. Binding himself, as he does, to inherited sources of Eastern wisdom, while recognizing the sensibilities of the West. As such, he is not to be blamed by those beyond the boundaries of his own land for any lack of familiarity with his work. An imbalance hopefully corrected by this book-dialogue, which will grant foreign literati access to his many-faceted poetry, as well as slacking the lyrical thirsts of curious intercontinental readerships.

At this juncture, one extra comment needs to be added. The popularity of Mukhtar Shakhanov in Kazakhstan equates with, one might say, that of a national hero. A cultural characteristic starting to emerge when the poet was a popular tribune-member in those tragic days of December, 1986. At that time, Kazakh youth spontaneously arose against the empire of a totalitarian regime. Albeit protesting in a climate wherein secret prohibitions were introduced against the publication of any news regarding social upheaval. Still, despite ominous threats against his life, it was Shakhanov who raised his voice as a poet and a fighter for national freedom. Undertaking serious efforts to attain the release and the re-habilitation of innocent, repressed, citizens.

One more attendant factor leading to our debate demands comment. Namely, the remarkable coincidence of circumstances knitting together its composition. Already, for several years, Shakhanov had been an envoy of Kazakhstan to Kirghizstan. Hence, we frequently met, trying to comprehend the rapidly changing world around us, along with our individual sense of identity. As a result, these tentative jottings have been made manifest. Maybe they will shed some light on current global issues for both our friends and our new audiences!

Chingiz Aitmatov.

CONTENTS

FOUR MOTHERS
OR
AN AWARENESS OF ONE'S MOTHERLAND

My birthplace is the village of Sheker. From the crest of the Manas Mountains, there flows down, drop pressed on drop (in a hurly-burly current) a white-foamed pale blue river into this community. It is named the Kurkureu - and that title suits it well, for its meaning is "thunderous". In itself, this river is a vital source of life. Yet, still further away, I recall catching sight of Sheker, and my heart trembled: my breath barely sufficed when my eyes directly meet the ice-caps of Manas-Ata, gleaming in the sun's bright rays.

Your fate, similar to a loss of memory requiring restoration, tells us a man on his hard, long, road, must remain aloof. Apart from his own Mother - the one who brings children to life - there are four others: as if they were four wings outstretched. There's Mother Earth - our essence, and the core of our core, there's Mother Tongue - which comes from our forebears. Then there's Mother Custom - a kindly and generous light, which shines and warms us through the generations - ever bright! There's also Mother History - however hard it seems - with bitter distresses, torments, oppressions continuous!..
An unconscious wind blows above unconscious, dead, dust. O'er those who forgot their four Mothers - let their memory rust. Those folk who four Holy of Holies could not protect well. Can they ever expect a bright prosperous future? Well, there are four Mothers - the fate of the faithful and true. Those who live, truly live for them, and rightfully so, they do. Those who die, give their lives for them - and willingly too!

SHAKHANOV. No matter how a changeable fate bears us mortals on the waves of Life, to various places, and to various lands, only one thing retains its everlasting attraction for us - the place we call "the land of our fathers". No matter where we are, we return again and again (even if only in our thoughts), to this not very large spot on the world's wide planetary space. To that single spot on which, as Kazakhs and Kirghizians express it so vividly, a drop of our blood dripped from our umbilical cord. Assuredly, this is the beginning of the world for all of us. The initially determined point of our habitat, along with our love for it. Although in quite recent times we have tried to convince ourselves, in the spirit of song-slogans, that

"My address is not a house, nor street –
My address is the Soviet Union complete!"

Postulated so, is there anyone on earth in whose consciousness an image of his fatherland does not live? Even if that image is just of a wild free-flowing river, the banks of which are trodden still - as when one stood barefoot on them as a boy. Sometimes one even longs to hear the croaking of frogs in the rushes and reeds, or the barking of a dog in a village's quiet eventide...

I was privileged, dear Chingiz, to be with you in your birthplace, in the village of Sheker. Now it is a famous spot in the Talas valley. For many of your admirers, that village is an interesting place worth seeing. Yes, it is really a fairy nook in the mountains.

We travelled together to Sheker in a car, and I noticed how agitated you were, and how that emotion was reflected on your face. Sitting beside you, I guessed what feelings were troubling your soul - sometimes sad ones, sometimes happy memories of childhood. I thought each rise and fall, each hill and dale, on our way, were asking, as it were; "You have not forgotten me, have you?" It must be so, that the nature of your native village has formed your character as a writer. Your creative ability grew up there, even in those meadows - and thanks to them you penetrated deeply into the surrounding countryside, falling in love with it, whole-heartedly.

It seemed to me if some unknown power suddenly tore it out of your memory, you would merely add to a mediocre phalanx of ordinary writers with no special talents.

Sheker surprised me with its unusual character as a village (in many ways almost a town), in its outstanding features. Even from a distance, one could catch glimpses of its houses: unusually impressive for such areas, along with a school, a club-house, and a shop or two.

Many of its inhabitants came running out to meet us. Everyone wanting to shake your hand, and welcome you back.

***

AITMATOV.   Yes, it must be so - the fate of a person from the very start, is laid down by his native land. The place where one was born and grew up. It is important to be able to take into one's soul whatever is found there and, like a bee gathering nectar, to collect these memories and pour them into One's heart.

I remember in my childhood, at times of great gatherings among wise old men, they watched us youngsters at play. From time to time, they teased us saying: "Well, which of you can enumerate without a mistake the names of your forefathers to the seventh generation?"

We momentarily fell silent, then, each of us in turn recited by heart the names of his seven forebears. God save us, if we missed only one! ... Later, I understood in the old greybeard's trick there was a hidden, deeper, sense. So, from early childhood, our consciousness imbibed an understanding of our personal genealogy: of our ties with past generations; who were our nearest and dearest. Along with those who are more distant ... When I was a child, I knew by heart the recitation: "I am of the tribe of Sheker. My father was Turekul, and his father was Aitmat, his father was Kimbildi, his father was Konchuzhok ... and so on and so forth.

My grand-father Aitmat was a jack-of-all trades: carpenter, smith, and an excellent tailor. Additionally, he skillfully played a three-stringed komuz.*

Furthermore, he was a fine singer. He had three daughters and two sons. The daughters were named Aimkul, Karakiz and Gulyaim, while the sons were - Turekul and Riskulbek.

Any village, like an organism, lives according to its own laws. The most significant of them being respect for all elders. Hence, this knowledge of one's forebears to the seventh generation is fundamental. The essence of the matter lies in this - each one must place himself in the future ranks of these seven predecessors. What will his successors think of him? Supposing he is the grandson of a horse thief? Most likely, an unenviable position to be in!

We grew up absorbing these simplicities from our elders as a strictly logical philosophy. Up till nowadays, I respect this glorious custom of knowing one's seven grandfathers - "Zheti Ata". By the way, medical men assert the blood of our forebears (up to the furthest seventh generation) is similar in its composition. If, therefore, not knowing who his forebears were, a man marries some close relative, it may have bad consequences for his descendents. In which case, our wise old men, pasturing cattle, and composing proverbs, got right to the roots of our Being.

Why, for example, do strong, energetic people populate America? The generally accepted opinion is that with the discovery of this continent, thither streamed representatives of many different ethnological sources. They married among themselves - and also with the local population. Blood-streams were mixed, renewed, and genetically rejuvenated. Not for naught do those living in America today name that place the "new world" - and their native lands "old".

***

SHAKHANOV. Once a lad from the Zhambyl region came looking for me. He explained, his younger brother had studied in an Alma-Ata Institute and that, "We have one female relative. Unexpectedly, the two of them fell in love. My young brother told me he would marry her regardless of family opinion. Furthermore, if permission was withheld, he would commit suicide. That was that! He did not want to hear any argument to the contrary. Of course, we all got together and tried to convince him he was in the wrong. With the very best of intentions, we argued with him and we quarreled with him, but all to no avail. At last, having thought things over, we decided to ask for your help. If there is anybody in this world to whom he might listen, then it will be you! Primarily because he reads your poems, knowing many of them by heart - and loves them. We beg you to make him take a more sensible view of things, or, if nothing else, to write a couple of lines demanding he see sense!" So pleaded this young man. Adding with a sigh there was no other way.

I was in an awkward position. Obviously so. If one tugs too hard on a cart, one can break it! Tug harder still - you'll lame the bullock pulling it! There was no doubt these two young people loved each other deeply and passionately. But what can one do with the customs of our forebears, since they do not permit marriage with a close relation? Up to the seventh generation? Exclude them or push them apart? Will that break their great feeling for each other? If it does, maybe all the rest of their lives they will regret it? After all, such great love comes only once in a lifetime. It's extremely hard to know how to reply to these tortuous conundrums.

Finally I said to him, "Your brother is in his first course of studies. Let him delay his marriage till the end of the course. It would unsurprising if by this time he had not cooled down a little. People are often mistaken in these matters, confusing attraction for real love! If, however, by the end of his studies their feelings for each other have not changed, it means true love lies there and they should be together forever!"

My decision, maybe, lacked a Solomonic touch, although I could not find anything else to say that might be of help to the young man...

Chingiz, do you remember the Third All-Union Meeting of Young Writers in Moscow, in 1969? For us, who were young back then, it was a great honour to meet and speak with you, an already famous master of the word. I did not know you personally, even though I immediately took to you - as a Kirghizian: as my elder brother. A person close to me in spirit. Possibly, this was why I decided to approach you and start a conversation. I even introduced you to a young Yukagir writer, Semyon Kurilov. Interestingly, Konstantin Fedin spoke in his address of Kurilov's novel "Khanido and Khalerkha". And, in his capacity as President of the Writers' Union Council, praised this work. Other participants at the meeting also appreciating it highly. Later, through the director of "Zhalin" publishing house, Kaldarbek Naimanbayev and I took part in further publications of that novel. Indeed, it was translated into our Kazakh language by the famous journalist Minbai Ilesov. Alas, as the fates will have it, Semyon Kurilov, a most talented and clear-headed writer, died soon after.

This novel of Kurilov's was a kind of historic manuscript about Yukagirs: who numbered at that time, as far as I remember, just over six hundred people all in all! By the way, I might mention that among the

Yukagirs, and other peoples of a limited number, there was a custom whereby a host ceded his wife, as a mate, to his guests.

***

AITMATOV. Yes, I had heard about that. A shocking condition for a tribe to be in! Extreme behavior, indeed!

***

SHAKHANOV. For us it appears extreme and rather wild, yet for those living on the tundra, or the taiga, such practices were no idle amusement, nor a display of immorality. Instead, numerically small ethnic groups (some of whom could be counted on ones fingers), explored every means necessary to renew their tribal gene pool as they battled for survival. Contrarily, we know marriage between close relations approaches incest, leading to the appearance of congenitally inferior offspring: along with the potential degeneracy of a nation. Its complex. Clearly, customs like naming seven generations of predecessors formed a part of our people's consciousness, albeit **a** fundamentally patriarchal preoccupation.

In addition, if we consider how a young married woman, upon seeing an elderly man approaching her on the street, never crosses his path, but backs away and bows respectfully, we see a healthy cultural continuity. Or again, how she never names her husband and his relations straight out! What delicacy! Each a tradition honouring our elders and their experience of life!

***

AITMATOV. At the same time, however, a certain irony is found there. In our village, for instance, how many bewildering names have they thought of for their husbands' brothers: both old and young! One practice was to name kinsfolk by their occupation. They called a miller "brother of the grindstones", whilst someone's lanky, tall, brother was jokily nick-named "head-in-the-clouds". Atop this, one fellow in Sheker, a stuck-up youngster, found himself spoken of as "spudger" (little sparrow). All causing these young wives to whisper "Spudger is coming!" Curiously, each man got his name according to received image and merit.

***

SHAKHANOV. A tale circulates among our folk in relation to this: From the opposite side of the river, in the rushes, a wolf attacked, and wounded, a young sheep. A married woman, coming for water, frightened the wolf away. On seeing the dying sheep, she took out a knife, sharpened it on a stone, and cut the poor thing's throat, so as to put it out of its misery. Returning home, she wanted to tell her husband's relatives what had happened, but suddenly remembered they had names she must not say - Ozenbai (ozen is a river), Kamisbai - (kamis means rushes), Kaskirbai (kaskir is a wolf),- Koyshibai - (koy is a sheep) and Kayrakbai (kayrak is a stone for sharpening), so how could she mention all these names? Impossible! She thought a little! It was hard for her, yet she wanted to tell her story. Finally she decided to tell it like this. "On the other side of the wet babbling one, the howling one fell upon the bleating one. I took my cutting one, rubbed it on a rough-edged one; and cut the throat of the poor bleating one!"

All her cleverness originating in the "steppeland academy" wherein she took to heart the ways of ancient vagrant shepherds. For example, if someone starts building a house, all those living nearby, according to custom, named "asar" come to help. If there is a feast, or if there is a funeral, for the villagers, it is a common joy or sorrow. Keeping distant is considered shameful.

Relatedly, I had an uncle, on my mother's side, named Iskak. He was a kindly fellow, who had never harmed anyone in his life. If he passed along the street on his horse, and saw a big stone on the roadway, he stopped, dismounted, and threw it to the wayside. Idlers, watching him saying: "He does that so others won't stumble over it!"

These regions had taught him a generosity of spirit. His selfless reactions forming an extra case in point. Every spring, he noticed, the river Badam overflowed its banks. The only bridge being regularly washed away, leaving folk living on both sides of the river cut off from each other. For his part, Isak had a nag which could easily swim across with him, although this did not satisfy my uncle. Thinking of other's needs before his own, and without any call for assistance, he went to his orchard and cut down some old trees with his axe. His aim focused on building a new bridge by himself. When looking at him, those standing round felt ashamed, until, finally, the whole village joined him in this labour.

He was a good fellow, one of the best. A preserver of folk traditions and customs. Dying, nonetheless, that autumn of a serious disease. However, before his end he called me to him, to speak with me:

"Well, you see, my bright one," he murmured as his voice weakened, "I am starting along the road from which there is no return, the way taken by our forefathers ... so, I want to speak to you about one thing ... I know you wish to become a poet, my dearest. That sacred gift is rare, and only he who does not sully its beauty can ever be happy. The all-powerful word recognizes only pure thoughts. Therein lies its strength. If you get led off the path, and are attracted by the deceptive glitter and gleam of life, then, in revenge, your words will lose their magical power!" Gazing at the ceiling, he momentarily lay silent, afterwards adding: "I have a last request to beg of you. I do not know whether you will be able to fulfill it, or not. Try to keep your away from alcohol. I do not insist on this, and you may even ignore my entreaty completely. Either way, be powerful in what you do! Probably, I shall be with you but a couple of days more. If during that time you decide this era is such there is no reason to differ from others, don't promise me anything. I shall not feel offended. Even though my hope for you is to learn moderation when drinking!"

"My dear uncle there's nothing to think over," I replied, "If you want, I will give you my word here and now. Rest assured of that!"

"That's good, my dear chap," he said, affectionately, "May you be happy!" His eyes filled with tears, and he became quieter. He took my hand and pressed it between his own lean, veiny, hands: "Now I feel calm, regret nothing, and give my soul to the Lord!" Unsurprisingly, within two days he met his end, leaving this transitory world.

On the other hand, my mother Umsin Aitbaikizi, quitted this world when she was eighty-five, in 1994: just when I came to you in Kirghizia on diplomatic service. You knew her personally, and she often regaled you in our home. Thinking back, this dear old lady gave birth to thirteen children, although only I remain out of all of them. Assuredly, whenever I had to go with mother on a trip, she always prepared three dishes for us - flat cookies, home-made horse-sausage, and dried milk-cheese.

At that time I often travelled to Moscow to various kinds of meetings. Mindful of this, she wrapped up my favourite tidbits, and put them in my travelling bag. Truly, my mother could neither read nor write a word. Yet, she treated Yevgeny Yevtushenko with special respect. Maybe because he translated her son's poetry and held out a helping hand in difficult times, or perhaps because of the general deference he enjoyed among our many surrounding friends.

"Try some of the tasties from our village. My mother gave them to me for you!" I said with pride, and began to lay out tidbits on the table, much to his delight.

"Your mother remains the personification of all those living in a Kazakh village!" Yevgeny Aleksandrovich said to me on one occasion.

Often in Moscow, I met with your old DagestanI friend Rasul Gamzatov, and with David Kugultinov. In those days the Deputies of the Supreme Council lived in special apartments set apart for them in the hotel "Moscow".

Once, going into my apartment I opened the refrigerator and saw, to my surprise, it was quite empty. I had managed to guess who had raided my refrigerator, when the telephone rang. I took up the receiver and heard the well-known laughter of David Nikitich:

"Did you recognize our hand-writing?" he enquired. In your absence Rasul and I paid you a visit! Listen, you yourself kept inviting us to your aul! Now we have tasted your mother's delicacies and no one can say we didn't appreciate those tasty village tidbits". We both laughed.

Chuckles allowing me to recall that my mother used to buy confectionery and biscuits with her monthly pension. Exiting the village shop, her pockets were always full of sweets! She had only to go outside the house for neighbouring children to practically assault her on all sides. As they chattered, Mama began to give them all a sweet in turn, making the cacophonous kiddies very happy.

A mental digression evoking a trip I made to the Guryev region (now named Atyrau), many years ago. Once there, I got acquainted with Ravil Sherdabayev, who later became my good friend. From him

I learned the sad fate of Makhambet Utemisov. Later, on the basis of this report, I wrote a short, fretful, poem. When my visit ended, the Balakshin regional authorities awarded me the title of "Honorary Fisherman." Local custom obliging them to leave sixty or seventy kilograms of fish for me as a gift! Its peculiarity laying in the fact almost a quarter of this present was in caviar.

With hindsight, the hospitality of the villagers was second to none. They even accompanied me to the airport. When I was seated in the plane, the First Secretary of the Regional Party Committee, Orinbasar Erkinov, placed a bag beside me!

"Don't forget to take it when you leave the plane!"

"But what is it?" I asked in surprise, seeing the huge parcel.

"It's caviar from the fish they gave me to you. Some fifteen to twenty kilos, I'd say, packed with genuine care!"

Ten days later my mother went to Shimkent. Provoking, for some inexplicable reason, my wife to peer into our refrigerator and discover the meagre remnants of this caviar.

"Most likely it's you being too generous" said my wife reproachfully.

"What are you niggling me? I don't go near the fridge, as well you know." Ominously, our housemaids were unsettled.

As fate would have it, the secret of this disappearance was quickly solved. Returning home from work one evening, my neighbour, an elderly Russian woman, came up to me and said very gratefully:

"Mukhtar, we thank you very much! Oh, how we enjoyed your present! Such an expensive giveaway! Where can we poor pensioners hope to find the wherewithal to buy it? We shall be economical with it I assure you, and it will last us half a year" - and she burst out smiling. Initially, I could not understand a word of what she said:

"What you are trying to tell me?"

"Oh, I'm speaking of that big cup of black caviar, which you sent to us via your mother. We are so grateful to her and to you!"

Later in the week, I heard similar words of gratitude from several other neighbours. It turned out my mother had shared caviar in big cupfuls among needy neighbours: giving a big dish to those who had a special liking for it before she went to Shimkent.

When mother came back to our village, we wanted to rebuke her a little. However, she brushed all our words aside with laughter, replying:

"They say in our villages - "It's better to share what's good, than be loaded down by food!" What would you have done with so much caviar? *It* would have gone bad in the end and been wasted!

Mama did not give way to our influence though she lived for many years in town, where people were not in the habit of greeting strangers as they pass by, nor call on friends, without a special invitation. In spite of everything, she kept her village courtesies: maintaining the psychology of country people whose generosity of spirit and rapid responses to need were always evidenced.

Chingiz, dear friend, in spite of sweet memories, lets return to our original conversation. In the village of Sheker there is a secondary school named after your father, Turekul Aitmatov. At the entrance, one may still see a remarkable statue of him. A work by the renowned sculptor Turginbai Sadikov. As a figure, it appears to solidify both the fate and tragedy of our intelligentsia in the 30's. Your father, a Kirgizian government official was, after all, repressed and eventually executed.

AITMATOV. Yes, they were bitter times! Back then, my father studied at the Institute of Red Professorship, whereas, our whole family (including my mother Nagima Khamzayevna), lived in a hostel. I, the eldest of four children, being nine years of age, while the youngest, Roza, was only six months old.

In August-September 1937, there were two articles published in "Pravda" - "Bourgeois Nationalists", and "Political errors of the Central Committee of the Communist-Bolshevik Party of Kirghizstan." As a result of these publications, leaders of the Republic, one after another, were placed on a black-list. Among many others on this list, my father's name was mentioned. Fully aware, therefore, that dark clouds were gathering above our heads, he told mother: "Return home with our four children. If I am arrested as an enemy of the people, they won't give you any peace. Also, orphaned youngsters are automatically sent to some Children's Home where they change their family names. Groundless accusations and vile lies are difficult to defend against. Even so, I shall live on and tell you about my situation through personal letters'. When we left Khazan Station, my father ran as long as he could after the train, waving his hand in farewell. Maybe he already felt in his heart there was little chance of seeing us again, and that he would be parted from those he held most dear in life - his wife and his children.

For seven days and nights we travelled. The train taking us through Orenburg, Saratov, and the endless steppes of Kazakhstan. Finally, however, in the middle of the night, we arrived at Maimak station. My whole life is refracted within that memory. An incident without a spark of white light. A night full of unadulterated fears. The next day, sitting on uncle Subanbek's cart, and scarcely alive, we got home to Alimbek, in Sheker.

The last letter we received from my father, hastily written on a Moscow post office paper, has been kept to this day. Every line breathes his alarm at the thought they may arrest him at any moment. Again and again he repeats to his wife she should take care of us children: the apples of his eye. He regurgitates his conscience is clear, that he is in no way guilty, firmly reiterating these assertions were worth nothing.

He was arrested on December 1st in Moscow. Soon afterwards being taken back to Frunze, and thrown into prison.

Upon returning to our native land with the stamp "A family hostile to the people", many friends began to leave us. Should one be offended by such an action in those hazardous times? Anyway, more often than not, we found it necessary to copiously thank those relatives and close friends, who were courageous enough to offer us shelter.

Shockingly, our relations did not escape repression either. Grandfather Aitmat, for example, and Birimkul were blood brothers. Birimkul had three sons - Alimkul, Ozibek, and Kerimbek. Alimkul was a few years older than my father. He worked as Chairman of the Sheker Village Council. We heard, a month later, they had arrested Alimkul, as the elder brother of an "Enemy of the people". At times like these, fate hurls down one torment following another. After Alimkul's arrest, Ozibek, working as a militia-man, was likewise arrested and thrown into prison as a relative of an "Enemy of the people."

The youngest son of my grandfather, Riskulbek (on returning from Moscow), found himself excluded from the Pedagogical Institute where he studied. He lived in our aunty Karakiz-azhye's house. Early one morning, I suddenly saw my mother and Karakiz-azhye weeping. They said Riskulbek had been arrested at midnight. Thus, our family, in the shortest of time periods, had been deprived of all four men. Only women and young children remained.

SHAKHANOV. If one reads stories from those times it seems not a single village escaped having "Enemies of the people". Often being arrested on simply ridiculous charges. They were shot straightway, or thrown into prison, or a labour-camp for many years. Did you hear how they arrested the father of a famous scientist - the Academician Rustan Rakhmanaliyev - a literary specialist close to you and deeply connected with your creative work?

AITMATOV. No, I haven't heard that story!

SHAKHANOV. Somebody gave Rustan's father some tobacco, holding out a scrap of newspaper for him to make a cigarette. When he started smoking, an unknown man appeared from nowhere and ordered Rustan's father to pinch out his cigarette. Unwrapping the newspaper, he found a scorched portrait of Stalin! Do you see what kind of traps they laid? What ingenious tricks? But, I interrupted you. Please continue your account.

AITMATOV. Well, Alimkul died in prison. Ozibek sent news he was a convict, labouring in an Ak-Tyuz lead mine. Unsurprisingly, during the war years, letters ceased altogether. Later on, whenever a postal rider came, we all stood wide-eyed and anxiously waited, since there might be news of father, or of his brothers. The postman, however, did not want to stay near us, and got away again as quickly as he could...

On one occasion, we received a letter from Riskulbek. It was written in the Kirghizian tongue. In which case, it was unlikely to have been censored.

Mama read it to us aloud. Heartbreakingly, he asked about each one of us, how we were getting on, and about the fate of his brother Turekul. Equally, he wrote about himself, saying: "They have taken us to work on a new railway line not far from the Manchurian border. It is cold there. I got an infection in both my kidneys. Each man has his given task. If he does not fulfill it, he gets no food. As soon as I started to lift heavy loads, my kidneys began to ache. Because of this - and chronic hunger - I am growing thin: looking half dead. Can you guess what happened next? I shriveled up still smaller! Children, if it is possible, send me at least half-a-pood* of oatmeal, and maybe I shall last out another five or six months.

The fate suffered by Riskulbek touched us to the very depths of our souls. Without delay, Mama and aunty Karakiz set about preparing oatmeal and roasting a "talkan".**

As the day dawned next morning, mama shouldered the bag containing food and set out on foot for the regional centre post-office.

We do not know whether Riskulbek received the parcel or not, we scarcely expected a reply. Most probably he died in an alien land.

Meanwhile we lived as before, in Sheker. Beneath the roof of our father's young sister Karakiz-azhye, and her husband, Dosalyzhezde. Their house stood on the bank of a big irrigation ditch and had two modest rooms. They lived in the first one, whilst we did in the second. Overall, Dosaly was a very kind and generous man. Additionally, he was a born hunter. Often, we watched him saddle his steed, sling a gun over his shoulder, and dashingly gallop into the horizon. Accompanied, as he always was, by two borzois, to search for prey in the hills. If I recall correctly, his home was spread with bear-skins, wolf-hides, and lynx-skins. If his hunt was successful, he returned home merrily. Calling out to us all by our names, beginning with aunt Karakiz. He was one of the bright images of our uneasy and restless childhood.

SHAKHANOV. Hemingway said once: "To be a great writer one needs talent, knowledge, and an unhappy childhood!" It is interesting Chingiz that in your childhood you did not dream of becoming a writer? You wanted to be a driver of some machine, a lorry or a car. You spoke about this, it seems, with a correspondent from "Lenin Youth" years ago. A man who eventually became the well-known writer and dramatist, Raikan Shukurbekov. That interview was published on July 5th, 1935. As an article, it is in the Tashkent archives edited by Sharmen Usubaliyev, while Abdildazhan Akmataliyev included it in his book. I have a part of the text here and would like you to hear it:

"When Chingiz was seven, he became distinguished through his clean and diligent character. At home, he read and played alone, taking responsibility for himself. As such, I chatted to him for more than an hour. He was used to reading, and answering freely, without the slightest hesitation.

"What do you want to be when you're grown up?"
"I want to be a chauffeur!"
"And where is your Papa?"
"He's in Moscow!"
"What is he doing there?"

"He is studying. This children's corner he made for me. Papa and Mama teach me all the time. I listen carefully to what they tell me! I myself decided that when I am old enough I shall be a chauffeur!"
"What playthings have you got?"
"I have many things. Now I need a motor-car. Papa promised to buy me one soon, in Moscow. He will find me one there I am sure!"

This interview was printed under the title: "Chingiz dreams of becoming a chauffeur". The author himself adding:
"Chingiz's dreams, without doubt, could have come true!" How could he have known, after all, that a lad, dreaming of becoming a car-driver, would be a world-famous writer instead?
AITMATOV. In those days private automobiles were a rarity indeed. Nonetheless, in our dreams, my companions and I sat at the wheel of a car. Not only me, but all my young contemporaries dreamed of this - a seat at the steering-wheel!
After the arrest of my father, the folk in our village even feared to pronounce his name. Only Mama and aunt Karakiz-azhye kept our memories of him alive. Privately, Mama showed us photographs of father, his documents, and badges. Most of all, however, we were taken up by his stamps. Having pressed them to the pad, we then found some paper, and stamped his name in Latin letters: "Aitmatov. T."
Wise old Karakiz-azhye (though she was illiterate) highly esteemed my father throughout her life. In 1964, dying from a painful disease, she said to us:
"I am grateful to the whole four of you! Ah, how young your father was when he left us! If he had not occupied such a high post, but lived

like others in our village, he would probably have survived." Uttering those words, she burst out crying...

At the start, they sent us false reports: "He has been sentenced to 10 years imprisonment, without any right to correspond with family members!" So, we counted every day during those long years of waiting. Indeed, we all continually looked towards the road -- living with the hope of seeing him again.

On one single occasion, I overheard a straightforward conversation about our father. A blind old man entered our house, holding on to his son. I remember how he spoke to Mama:

"They arrested me along with Turekul. We both shared the same cell in prison and went through every type of torture imaginable. They blinded me in the process! Gowever, Turekul is alive. Justice triumphs. Don't lose hope Nagima!"

My mother immediately wrote several letters to the Ministry of Internal Affairs, one after another, although nothing definite was returned in reply. This went on for ten years.

SHAKHANOV. Not long ago, we had a spirited conversation with your younger sister Roza, and this is what she told us:

"Chingiz studies at the Institute achieved excellence. They wanted to award him a post-graduate studentship, even though the question arose; "Why should the son of an enemy of the people receive a Stalin stipend? Yet, he didn't give up. On free days, he worked on the railway to earn a little extra money: loading coal and logs. Although, the money he received he did not spend, instead, in winter, he came to see us and brought us all clothes and gifts. I remember receiving a warm coat with a big fur collar. I can't describe how pleased I was. I had never owned such an expensive coat before! To Ilgiz, studying in Moscow, he sent his own coat, fully repaired and cleaned. Curiously, there were several internal pockets in it, and in each one he had placed a five-rouble note! He obviously had in mind the idea that a student would put his hand in his pockets and find them; and be glad.

In 1957 we received information from the Ministry of Internal Affairs: "For a reply to your question about Aitmatov T. you should appear personally before the Committee." I can't say how excited Mama was. Her heart nearly beat out of control. Now and then she went to Chingiz's bed, where he lay ill with a high temperature, to tell him. Hearing the news, he wanted to accompany her, but his legs would not support him. It remained for me to go with her.

"Your father," she said, "must be in Siberia. A number of prisoners are returning from there nowadays. Poor Turekul, how glad he will be to see you so grown up, along with Chingiz and Ilgiz, and forming a real family again. You and Lucia have grown up into respectable young people! What about your father, however? When arrested he was only thirty four, but this year he'll be fifty five! For twenty one years we have not seen him -yes, twenty-one years. It is easy to say, yet to live through it all? Well, all right, if he is safe and sound ... They say many of the men who went to Siberia got married there ... Maybe he did so too? One has got to live somehow! My God, I am trembling all over! How could my heart hold any happiness for them!?

I listened to Mama, and saw the tears in her eyes. My God! What a majestic heart! Yes! Let him have another wife, if only he is hale and hearty! In her, one observed the mighty power of true love, not desiring anything for herself, just for her beloved!

For our Mama, plain speaking was natural. It made her younger than her days and genuinely impressive. This may be why her attitudes, her outlook, raised her a head higher than most other people in our village. There was nothing hidden in her. A trait many men considered attractive and the reason they showed such an interest in her. Repelling these attentions, she always thought there could be none among them more handsome than Turekul, or more generous than Turekul, or cleverer than Turekul. She was completely devoted to him and spent all her lifetime waiting for her one and only husband to return. Her respect and esteem for him, for his good deeds - which she remembered with satisfaction - colouring every moment. Furthermore, she poured each of these noble sentiments into our hearts: counting herself unusually happy, and lucky to be so, and act so.

At last, we reached the Ministry of Internal Affairs. At the entry stood a soldier on guard, with his automatic. Mama handed him a note.

"You come on!" he said to her, "But you stay here!" he said to me. A short while passed, and then Mama reappeared, scarcely able to stand. A sharp pain stabbed through my heart. Her reactions making me tremble. As tears streamed down her cheeks, her lips trembled. Instantaneously, I took her by the arm. In her wearied condition, she stretched out before me a sheet of paper, unable speak one word. There I read:

CERTIFICATE.

Concerning the accusation against AITMATOV TUREKUL, before his arrest on December 1st, 1937, a student at the Red Institute of Professorship. This matter was reviewed by the Military Board of the Supreme Court of the USSR on June 15th, 1967.

The sentence of the Military Board of November 5th 1938, in relation to AITMATOV T. in view of new circumstances developing, has been abolished, and the affair closed in the absence of any further criminal actions.

Therefore AITMATOV T. is rehabilitated posthumously.

Signed: Assistant to the Chairman of the Military Board of the Supreme Court of the USSR. Colonel of Justice M. Rusakov.

That cursed paper! Bringing us the blackest news, it smashed to pieces in one minute all of the hopes which had nourished us - and given us some strength, beforehand. Over the course of twenty one years we had forced ourselves to keep positive. Now, along with Mama, I fell lifeless. I became soft and flabby, like a dead fish thrown up against the shore. I assisted her as best I could, even though utterly exhausted. We both wandered back on to the street. The whole world lost its sense, and our joy in life had flown away. I looked closely at Mama, and saw she had changed somehow. She had grown pinched, gone pale: her shoulders slumping down listlessly. Oh, Allah! She lived through the course of many long years with transparently deceptive hopes that Turekul would return - if not today, then tomorrow. This hope gave her daily strength, helping her to overcome all kinds of difficulties. My poor Mama - what did she not go through!

I too wanted to cry out aloud on the street. I wanted to complain about the injustice, which like a curse, had hung over the whole family for many years. To protest against our fate. However, if I did, it would only deepen the sorrow of my poor dear Mama, who could scarcely walk. Thenceforth, I kept control of myself by will-power and repressed my inner shrieking.

When we reached home, supporting each other all the way, we entered and stood motionless, not holding back our tears any longer.

"Well, what then, daughter of mine? What has happened has happened!" murmured Mama, as if gathering herself together a little. Let us not tell Chingiz straightway about his father's death. You never know, he may take to his bed - and such a shock will not help him in recovering from his sickness.

A little later, along came aunt Kara-kiz with presents from our village: with parcels and portmanteaus. Mother asked us to invite her back when Chingiz had recovered.

When Mama carefully and gently explained to her that her brother was officially no longer in this world, our aunt's heart almost stopped dead. Having given way to her sorrow and yearning for her dear brother (feelings which had for over twenty years gnawed away at her soul), she went round to each one of us, pressing us closely to her breast, lamenting and crying.

Oh, if only relatives everywhere could be as sympathetic as she was!

Afterwards the whole Aitmatov family congregated in Sheker. There, within the home of Kerimbek, in commemoration of these four victims of enormous injustice - Turekul, Alimkul, Ozibek and Kerimbek, we arranged commemorative feasts for our relatives.

All the same, Mama could not resign herself to the death of our father. Even though she said nothing aloud, deep inside her heart there survived a warm little hope, that, maybe, he was still alive somewhere? Perhaps this was the actual background to the circumstances following. Along with those who settled in Sheker, during the Great Patriotic War, came a Greek woman (from the Caucasus) called Aivazidi. She claimed clairvoyant skills and told fortunes from coffee-grounds in cups. Strangely, people began to say all her prophecies came true, one after another, prompting Mama to see her.

"Your husband was in prison. You have four children. Life is hard for you, yet you will live here another ten years. Your eldest son will take you to the city. His name will be famous, known everywhere!" she intoned.

"And my husband? Is he alive and when will he return?" asked Mama.

"Your husband is very far away. You will meet him after many, many years!"

Answered so, this woman, not wishing to deprive mother of all hope, hinted that they would meet each other on the other side".

AITMATOV.   In any event, the fortune-teller acted very humanely!

SHAKHANOV.   Not far from the Kazakh town of Akmola, in those days, was a special camp named ALGIR (Akmola Lager for the Women of Traitors to their Motherland). In that camp the wives of well-known representatives of literature and art, of high government workers and Party officials, such as Turar Riskulov, Saken Seyfullin, Beymbet Mailin, Temirbek Zhurgenov, Uzakbai Kulimbetov, Sultanbek Kozhanov and Zhanaidar Sadibakasov were imprisoned.

Oddly enough, this outpost of hell was situated at about forty to fourty five kilometres from Akmola, and consisted of twenty six separated camps. The primary demand on those secondary "traitors to the Motherland" - brought from all corners of the Soviet Union - being to admit their husbands had been traitors. Thereafter, signing a paper refusing all future contact with them. If they did this their fate might be softened a little. Of course, this was the time when the evil activities of the mobile-gas-chamber men from the NKVD (National Committee for Internal Affairs) reached its utmost limit: taking children away from their parents and lodging them in Children's Homes. Usually, in rural locations cut off from all contacts with their mothers and fathers, thereby uprooting entire families.

So said, even in such hellish times close friends who valued life - Saken Seyfullin, and Ilyas Dzhansugurov, were able to preserve for their successors priceless manuscripts written by our great teachers. Keeping them safe inside holes in the ground, or hiding them within their pillows. In those days a monumental achievement.

Once Gabit Musrepov told me he went to this ALGIR lager and met the wife of Beymbet Mailin. Apparently, she said to him:

"The lager sheep I take out to pasture myself. Alternatively, I can sit from dawn till dusk in a prison cell. Surely, it's much better to be out on the steppe and weep my sorrows in open spaces? Being in the wilds of Nature makes everyone feel lighter."

On closer inspection, this ALGIR lager allowed about twebty two thoudand women to languish as partial "traitors to their motherland". If your Mama had not found a place for you in the village, and hidden herself out there in the wilds, maybe she too would have suffered a similar, bitter, fate.

AITMATOV.   Anything could have happened in those days ... When I studied in school, one kindly teacher told me; "Never drop your eyes when your father's name is mentioned!" Such wise advice comforted me in difficult times and remained in my memory throughout the rest of my life.

His words meant "Your father was not an enemy of the people!" and warmed up my childish soul.

SHAKHANOV.   Let us return again to the story of your sister Roza.

Aitmatov.

"In 1975, she went to Talas on business.

An unknown woman came up to her, and greeted her, asking:

"Are you Chingiz Aitmatov's sister, by any chance?"

"Yes, that's right, I am!"

"I learned by chance of your coming, which is why I, myself, prepared to come and seek you out in Frunze!"

Before continuing this anecdote, I need to briefly digress. As a writer, this period brought floods of letters to me from all corners of the Soviet Union: as well as from abroad. The majority of them consisting of complaints made by people in deep despair about their allotted accommodation, and asking for my support against unjust local authorities. A few even asked for my proactive assistance in purchasing expensive imported medicines. Most likely, they were penned because it was well-known I too had suffered wild injustices since childhood. Hence, people used to attach themselves to me, especially when I visited geographically distant regions. They even handed members of my family letters requesting: "Kindly ask Chingiz to consider this plea! Assuredly, no one in the Soviet Union will refuse to listen to him!" At times, both I and my family tried to avoid such people if we could. So, when my sister met this woman, she initially took her for one of those petitioners. Anyway, the story unfolds as follows .....

"No, no!" the woman persisted, intuiting my sister's dismissive attitude, and making haste to reassure her, "No, I was looking for you, because your father Turekul was in the same prison cell as my brother!"

When this mysterious woman pronounced my father's name, any pretense at reserve escaped my sister and she poured out question after question:

"Where is your brother? Is he alive?" She couldn't hold back.

"Alive! But seriously ill, and in hospital. The doctors have given him only a limited number of days to live. He wanted very much, if possible, to meet your brother Chingiz. However, I read in the papers he is in America at present, which is why I was anxious to meet you!"

Scarcely any additional conversation was required. My sister unhesitatingly went with this woman to the hospital, even though they arrived at an unsuitable time. "Quiet hour!" Nevertheless, the medical sisters (having asked permission from the doctor in charge), soon brought her brother back on to the ward: holding his limp arms for safety. His name was Tanirberdi Alapayev.

Apparently, one could see at a glance he was a patient and introverted man. Along with the brutal evidence that this heavy sickness had withered him away: undercutting all his reserves of strength. Every heavy breath seemingly causing his shoulders to rise and fall uncomfortably. Resultantly, after a few mutual courtesies, he began to look fix his stare on my sister – staring, and then quietly weeping:

"You have the same features as Turekul!" he groaned. "Now I may die in peace. God has shown mercy on me!" Despite his laboured breathing, he unexpectedly continued with his story: "I was working in the Komsomol in those days, whereas my brother, Uzakbai, held the position of Chairman on the board on a collective farm. The times were such that - if one raised one's head, the label "An enemy of the people" was applied! Without any reason, therefore, my brother was arrested, and a little while later, I too suffered the same fate - being cast in prison.

Irrational accusations flew around: "Your brother is a traitor to his country! With whom has he been plotting? What counter-revolutionary affairs has he been planning? What foreign propaganda has he been spreading? Come on – speak up!" In this manner, they questioned me about everything. Issues that even in my most terrible dreams I had never imagined. All the while mercilessly beating me.

At first, I stood against it. Yet, resistance drove my interrogator into a rage. He struck me in the face with the butt of his gun. Seeing some of my teeth were knocked out - I dropped down, half alive on the floor of the cell. Eventually, coming to myself again, I lay on the cold, blood-bespattered, cement. When I found enough courage to open my eyes, I could six or seven other people with unshaven beards. Each one of them was emaciated by hunger, fatigue and beatings. In the corner, stood one bedstead, while sitting on his haunches a good-looking young fellow was wiping the blood off my face.

"Get up, my dear man! Come and lie on this bed" he said, managing to drag me to the corner, and lifting me up on the frame. I soon learned all my cell-mates shared this bed. Today, it was his turn, so no one objected. All I knew, however, was that being saved from the cold damp cement was a real relief. Besides, the vacant looks of those around me were strangely dull, as if they were afraid to even speak with one another in the cell. Still, as the hours of incarceration passed, we all became better acquainted, whilst my "Good Samaritan" told me he was called Turekul Aitmatov. Moreover, on hearing I was from Talas, he was weirdly comforted. It made us real brothers. Upon listening to the circumstances which brought me there, he quietly advised:

"You have not committed any crime apart from being very young. You are only here because of your brother. Be on guard. Look out for yourself! Don't let the inquisitors lead you on! Don't give any one away! Hold fast! Don't surrender! Sooner or later they will release you! But we politicos - that is another matter. They may shoot us!" he added in hollow tones, lowering his eyes.

From a grey prison pillow-case, he had made a kind of bag. Inside, the black thread stitched "Chingiz, Ilgiz, Talas" the name of the place close to our hearts. Sadly, he didn't have enough thread to finish the final "s", leaving an unnatural gap. Remaining aloof, nonetheless, his well-educated, cultured, clean-bodied persona spoke volumes. This was seen by everyone straight away. It was expressed in his words and actions. A piece of soap, for example, and a tooth-brush told the world he was determined to keep his standards high.

One night, secretly from the others, he whispered in my ear:

"They have hung the fifty eighth statute on me. All meaning, I was deprived of the right to correspondence. So, I have one request. The first, and maybe the last. If you ever get away from here, seek out in Sheker my family. Let them know I am no enemy of the people. That's slander. My eldest son Chingiz is a very sensitive and responsive lad - especially to unfairness in life. And there is so much of it here, but how is he to know? When we lived in Moscow, he saw on the street a healthy youngster, with fists like hammers, cruelly beating an old man. He came running to us back home, on the point of tears, and affirmed: "That is terrible. It is so painful, you know!" Well, then - have a heart-to-heart talk with him, I beg you. Try to influence him (as far as you can) that I am not an enemy of the people. Explain to Chingiz if I do not return, he must stand in my place as family elder. Give him this bag as a memento of me! Telling him semiotics will reveal my destiny. If they do not sentence me to be shot, but send me to Moldovanovka Camp, it will contain - through the militia-Men - soap. If Siberia, it will have a comb. If I place a tooth-brush within it, this means they have sent me to serve out my sentence in the Urals somewhere. Farewell, my dear friend. If I don't have enough luck to meet you again in this world, we'll certainly meet in the next!

With tears in my eyes, I swore to fulfill all of his requests. Then, sure enough, they took Turekul away. Two days later, an official came into the cell and asked: "Does anything here remember Aitmatov?" Sensing something bad, I inquired what had happened. He pointed his finger skyward, grinning: "His soul is now flying free in heaven!" My knees nearly gave way beneath me. I felt half-dead, or possibly half-alive. I handed him Turekul's tunic and cap. The sewn bag I kept, deciding to pass them on to his children when I could.

A few days later, as a member of a traitor's family, I was sentenced to ten years in Sverdlovsk goal. May God be my witness when I say during these ten years I kept the sewn bag with the names of Turekul's sons embroidered within it! The inner pocket of this loose-padded prison body-warmer housing his comb, tooth-brush and all. Yes, I promised to hand them over to his eldest son. Imagining Chingiz to be a shapely twenty year old lad, with the same kind of features as his father.

But, as they say; "A human head is merely a ball in the hands of Allah!" Thus, my fate turned out otherwise. Ten years onwards, they did not allow me to go to my native land, but lengthened my sentence. On top of which, they chose the wildest Siberian waste as my home. Well, at least it was no longer prison, though I had to endure enforced isolation. Truly I was free to move about, and work in the area. Circumstances even permitting me to marry a Tatar girl and start a family. Maybe I had lost all hope of ever returning home, or perhaps I had drunk the home-brew of sorrow too deeply? Either way, the Devil himself had tricked me! May God forgive my thoughtlessness, I finally threw Turekul's old prison body-warmer into the river, with his things still in the inner pocket! Neither will the spirit of your father forgive me easily! I do not say these things lightly. As coincidence will have it, that same day, when I was re-shoeing a horse in the local stable, she kicked hard enough to knock me unconscious. Two ribs were broken, and half a lung was crushed. Thereby, I became a cripple in one hour. Since then, I have lingered in hospital, or at home (across the years but always in bed), while now, as you can see, death is waiting for me on the threshold.

At the end of the day, they allowed me to return to my native land. For that, I praise Kruschev a thousand times over. Immediately, I thought of work, took my wife, and, as if on wings, almost flew back to Talas. Once here, I was embraced by my relatives and all of my tormenting sadness wafted away. I asked the villagers about Turekul's family. They told me they had returned to Frunze. When I heard this, I began to suffer again in the depths of my soul. Equally, my sickness began to pester me once more and I experienced distress in breathing. For a long time I felt old aches and pains, till they eventuallt calmed down. Yet, much water has flown under the bridge since then ... and the have years rolled by.

Curiously, I firmly believed the day would come when, as if by a stroke of lightning, my memory and energy would be renewed. Albeit laid up in hospital through that same illness! At one point, a young fellow lay beside me for several days, burying himself in a book. When he left his bed to get extra medicine, I took a look at his book. It was a collection of works by Chingiz Aitmatov, under the title of "Mother's Land" I read through a few lines:

> *"Father, I know not where you lie buried, therefore,*
> *I dedicate this to you, Turekul Aitmatov.*
> *Mother, you brought us all up alone, we four,*
> *I dedicate this to you, Nagima Aitmatova. "*

These words were threaded like coral beads on a necklace.

Lastly, when I saw on the book-folder a portrait of Chingiz, with his stern look of reserve, I was instantaneously reminded of his father. Indeed, I saw before me the living image of Turekul, still languishing in his cement cell in Frunze prison: with his hand-sewn bag, with the embroidered names inside, and finally the Siberian waste taiga. In that moment, my ears began to ring the urgent tones of his last request to me.

"Yes, this is indeed Turekul's son, my dear friend!" I cried to myself, pressing the book to my chest, unable to hold back tears.

What sin I was hiding - I even scorned myself at that moment! It felt as if I was burned by cold metal in a furious frost. I had not fulfilled the last request of a man who had stretched out a helping hand to me, and trusted me. Right away, I had one desire - I should write a letter to Chingiz, and tell him everything, and ask his forgiveness for my weakness of mind: for not keeping his father's last word. More than once I hastened to do so, but each time could not come to a real decision on the matter.

Not long ago, this confessed, I heard a chance remark by a doctor to my sister:

"His strength will last about another month!" Unsurprisingly, I have had little sleep or rest ever since. How can I go to that other land, not having paid my debt to Turekul? If I chance to meet him there, he is sure to ask me why I, Taniberdi, did not keep my word. After all, he had only asked me to pass a few small presents to his son, and I couldn't even do that, it seems. How then shall I be able to look him in the eye? Therefore I asked my sister: "Do you wish me to go in peace to that other land? If so, lead me to Turekul's relatives. I have decided to go down on my knees before them, and beg their pardon. Clearly, God has seen my tears! Take off from me, dear sister, this heavy load of sin." And the old man wailed like a child.

"Do not cry so! In what are you really guilty? Surly, the guilt lies with Time if anywhere. May it be cursed for its injustices" In this way, she tried to comfort the poor old man. But I fail to check myself as well. Disturbed by the image of an emaciated old man, already standing on the threshold dividing life and death (who had been a witness of my father's last days), I too embrace him and give way to my innermost feelings.

This is the last news I have of my father. It arrived in 1975. By that time Mama was already four years buried.

SHAKHANOV.   In the damp autumn of 1938, in foothills not far from Bishkek, in a spot known as Chon-Tash, (situated near the rest-home of the National Committee for Internal Affairs) I saw how they secretly carted off - on a few wagons - a large group of people, then shot them With Jesuitical foresight, they had prepared some specially dug-out ditches to bury them. This was witnessed from a hidden place, occupied by a guard named Abikan Kidiraliyev, who worked in the rest-home. For many years after that, old man went to this place where innocent men were murdered, and recited memorial prayers for them. As an elder, he also had a daughter, named Byubyura. She was born in 1928, meaning she is your contemporary. Well, then, the old man strictly ordered Byubyura: "Remember, daughter, hold fast in your mind, that in this place many people are buried. If God grants good times to come again, you can reveal them to the people!" When Kirghizstan stood on the road to democracy, and took up independence, auntie Byubyura wrote a letter to the Committee of State Security, describing what she had heard from her father. A young lad, Bolot Abdrakhmanov, acting as leader of the Committee, and ignoring the objections of his colleagues, placed the honour of his uniform above all else. Hence, he organized an exhumation. In the vicinity of this unspeakable tragedy, they found the remains of one hundred and thrity seven bodies. Among the remains, three pages of a half-decayed condemnation were discovered - in accordance with which your father Turekul Aitmatov had been shot. Archive records made it possible to confirm that your father's fate had been shared by such outstanding sons of the Kirghiz people as Dzhusup Abdrakhmanov, Osmonkul Aliyev, and Sidik Chombashev...

These soils of bitterness and sorrow they eventually named Ata-Beyit (Grave of our fathers). At a funeral ceremony of reinternment with all due honours, the President of the Republic, Askar Akayev, was present and, having flown in from Luxemburg, you were there too: making a memorial speech. According to the general opinion of those who took part, along with other witnesses, there was not one person who was not deeply moved. Then, by a special decree of the President, November 25th was declared a Memorial Day for all victims of repression. We were all united at that ceremony. An endless flood of people passed before us. Groups of young students proudly held up a portrait-banner, from which there looked out a man in the bloom of life, with pitch-black hair, with a thoughtful look on his features. An image seemingly giving to all around a warm feeling - this was Turekul Aitmatov. At that time he was twice as young you are presently, but had already suffered so much, and achieved high fame.

AITMATOV. Yes, the discovery of the document condemning my father to death, found among the remains of one hundred and thrity seven murdered men, became, for me, a turning point within my soul. What a wonder, Mukhtar, after fifty three years - which turned to dust even some of the bones of the slain - those three sheets of paper did not decay: lying in the inner pocket of my father's padded prison jacket! There is a God on Earth! Though late, justice triumphed. Let not fate condemn anyone, whoever it may be, to suffer such sleepless nights as descended upon our family!

SHAKHANOV. Chingiz, if you have no objections, let us return once again to the story of your sister Roza!

AITMATOV. Until her very end, she took care of Mama - probably because she was the eldest daughter and because there was some special spiritual nearness between them. Additionally, she read every line I wrote, even articles and interviews. Tangentially becoming well-informed on contemporary Soviet and world literature.

When I was awarded the Lenin Prize, she experienced it as an enormous honour, not only for the Kirghizian people, but also for the entire peoples of Central Asia. In those days this Soviet award meant a recognition of merit, the recipient of which became a respected savant in his lifetime. Exceptionally prestigious, this Prize in the sphere of literature had only been awarded to one single representative of Central Asia before: the Kazakh - Mukhtar Auezov.

Indeed, the day when this award was conferred on me, dignity was restored for the Aitmatov family. Republican newspapers devoted whole columns to my achievements. From everywhere, a flood of congratulatory letters and telegrams arrived. Ironically, not having the slightest idea of our existence previously, Party leaders and officials (of various levels) congratulated us by telephone, or made a special visit. On the streets, in the shops, as well as in cultural and educational establishments, there were conversations about my work. Yet, Mama suddenly fell sick, and was taken to hospital. So, Roza went to Osh bazar to buy fresh herbs for her. On the way, she heard (on the street-bus), a Kirghiz man of about fifty, thick-set, with sweeping moustaches, say prouldy to a young fellow beside him: "You see, the Kirghizian folk have once again shown, through Chingiz, that we are a worthy people!" These words filled her with an unusual pride. Had we not, only yesterday, been named, "Enemies of the people?" O God, O God, now we deserve a festival on our street!"

Mama always carried in her hand-bag a photo of father, along with one of myself and Ilgiz. When in hospital she placed that photo beside her.

When I arrived back from Moscow, leaders of the republic, and relatives came to meet me. Having sent her husband Esenbek to collect me, I too visited Mama. She was hardly able to rise from her hospital bed (her legs were badly swollen). What tears of joy there were, pure and bright, like a bejeweled mountain stream, when we were all reunited! For the first time in many years, Mama breathed freely, as if no traces remained from those endless frightful days and sleepless nights. In a phrase, she knew these celebrations were a spiritual triumph for Turekul!"

SHAKHANOV. I see you are disturbed! Very well, then, we'll talk about something else. Do you remember when we travelled to Sheker village? When you gave an interview to the correspondent from Russian Television, Vladimir Fyodorov? We were accompanied by Omarbai Narbekov and Daulletbek Shadibekov (along with two other class-mates of yours) to the ravine of the river Kurkureu? A stormy river, bursting down from the mountains, after which it floods among green rushes full of curative fragrances ... We all enjoyed these sights, I recall you stepping up to me saying: "You see there, on the Manas peak, a cloud has now perched? Just watch - in ten or fifteen minute's time, there will be a heavy rainstorm here, yet it won't last long!

At first, I thought that you were joking. Could such an innocent-looking cloud grow as furious? Would not the wind just waft it away? Hardly had I finished wondering such things, when a sudden breeze blew, lightning flashed, thunder roared, and down came pouring rain! In one moment everything around us changed into a rain sodden scene beneath the pattering drops.

Unintentionally you had introduced us to your resonance with the land. Your native country wherein, down to the last nuance, you knew its nature.

Chingiz, I remember another amusing story: In Bishkek, in 1995, there was a meeting of three brotherly Republics: the Prime Ministers of Kazakhstan, Uzbekistan, and Kirghizstan meeting together; Akezhan Kazhegeldin, Abdikashim Mutalov, and Apas Dzhumagulov. These government leaders discussed common problems regarding energetics, the gas industry, and also health care, finally coming to a mutual agreement on cooperation.

Towards the end of this diplomatic gathering, I invited guests to the Kazakhstan Embassy. On the way there I phoned you from the car to say: "The heads of three Republics do not meet every day! Would you not like to take supper with us?" Interestingly, the atmosphere at the festive board was lively, no matter what we discussed. Most of all, we laughed over your story on the history of "donkey-breeding', based on your student days at the Dzhamby Livestock Technical Institute. At the climax of this tale, I was summoned to the telephone by our Alma- Ata, Minister of Foreign Affairs, Kasimzhomart Tokayev, and so I missed the end of your story. When I returned, everyone around the table was laughing hysterically. Till this day I regret I didn't hear the whole story through.

AITMATOV. In order for the essence of this amusing, half-tragic, story to be understood, I must make a small digression at the start. The fact is, during the years of my father's repression, and in the war-years which followed, I lived most of the time with my aunt Karakiz. For some reason or other, she had pinned her hopes on me to become a great man of some kind - a Party organizer, a lawyer-prosecutor, or something of this kind. As far as she was able, she even tried to arrange matters in such a way that I should study in the city. She gave me her very last groats, and prepared for me a veritable store of fried oat-meal: my favourite.

And see what a joke life played on me!

Parallel with daily lectures went practical work. Going through the course of lectures on "Horse-breeding" and "Sheep-breeding", we went on to "Ass-breeding". At first we all laughed, joking ironically: "Here's a rarity - the Ass! What's more, do we not have enough of these studies already"? In fact, it turned out otherwise! We soon learned a flop-eared braying ass tribe would lead us into discord. Anyway, our teacher was a Russian. A strict old fellow. Albeit an expert on his subject of horse-breeding and a man who had been evacuated to Kazakhstan from blockaded Leningrad. However, lacking a suitable establishment for practical work - the Professor usually took us students to Zhambil cattle-market, "Atshabar". On Sundays, a place where a world-shattering hubbub actively reigned all round. Obviously, folk from the nearest villages came, those from Talas too, to buy and sell cattle of all kinds. In the crowd, skilfully making tricky deals, went the middle-men; keen-eyed. For our part, we students managed to pick out a donkey with very long ears to suit our lesson. The Professor then began questioning us, following the previous days lecture:

"Student Aitmatov", he called, setting his eyes on me, "What can you tell us about this well-bred creature? What part did it play in the civilization of man?"He did not have to wait long, as I immediately answered:

"This beast was first found spread across the continents of Africa and Asia. At present, they are met with in Syria, Kashmir, Tibet,

Turkmenia, Uzbekistan, Kazakhstan and Kirghizia, as well as in Mongolia. Basically asses are used as domestic beasts of burden. As you see for yourself, they differ from other beasts in the length of their ears, also having long skinny tails. Moreover, they are nurtured twelve months before birth ... ". And here, half way, I stopped dead - suddenly recognizing the owner of the chosen ass! He was the neighbour of my uncle Dosala and aunt Karakiz, from the village. Puzzled, eyes lowered, and greatly surprised, he had noticed how I, standing by his ass, had passionately recited his animal's whole pedigree! I was ready to fall through the earth. My voice gave way ... But how could the Professor understand all this?

"Student Aitmatov, why have you paused? Conclude your answer! In what does the grey donkey before us differ from other asses? Borne from confusion, even sweat appeared on my brow ... Sensing upon his return to Sheker, that this respected old man would tell the entire village about the students with whom I had been studying in the city, who had made, as it were, a mock of him and his long-eared donkey!..

Towards the end of the fourties, in the village, they specially valued professions such as magistrates, public prosecutors, and militia-men. There was even a couplet about it, which goes like this:

"May your husband serve as militia-man, see!
May you drink a cup of tasty Indian tea!"

My relations, my aunt and uncle too, were very proud I still studied in town. They counted on my taking up a respected profession, and on my return, God grant it so, that I should break through to high rank! During vacations, they begrudged me nothing. Further, they tried to feed me well, and gave me their last kopeks. On hearing the story of my aunt Karakiz's neighbour and his ass, however, they did not know whether to laugh, be cross, or cry...

When I finally came home on holiday, Karakiz sadly looked at me and sighed:

"Some people are saying you are only learning about silly donkeys in town! How is one to understand such things, my dear? Have you not found a better subject to study? If they only want to teach you about asses - well, we have them here, plenty of them in the village!

To this day, I remember how ashamed I felt. How much I longed to justify myself before my kindly relatives who constantly dreamt of some wonderful goal for me in the future.

Their simplicity of soul, their childish naivety is so characteristic of our people, and by the way, is one of those attitudes learned in that same "steppeland Academy", of which we previously spoke.

SHAKHANOV. Once you brought with you to my home your friend Seitali Bekmambekov. It was in the blessed days of summer, when, supping our fermented-milk kumis with great enjoyment, and remembering past days, we started up a long and interesting conversation.

AITMATOV. Yes, in the war years, all who could take up arms, set off for the front. In the village, only old men, women and children remained. Thirteen and fourteen-year-olds became our main stay. The chairman of the kolkhoz, himself, torn to pieces by new tasks and cares, took the children out of school, and set them working. I became a postman for two whole villages for a while, and worked in Sheker and Archagul. Receiving a "lift", Seitali became director of the school.

Those who could read and write (more or less) and knew elementary arithmetic, very soon became teachers of the others themselves.

SHAKHANOV. One time, on meeting, Seitali told me a lot about you.

"Although Chingiz and I already had an occupation, when spring came, and the days became warmer, we participated in all kinds of farm duties. Just like our class-mates, in particular Toktosun, Bayizbek, and Alimbek, we could be seen working everywhere. We got up at dawn showered, and worked till sunset.

Once, the Board of the kholkhoz chose Chingiz to lead us as jobbing porters. Sending each of us to Maimak Station to fill huge sacks with grain. Every day, seated on a cart behind two lazy bullocks, we transported them to and fro. Reaching our reception point beneath the burning rays of an afternoon sun. The leader of the storage point,

Naumenko, could see us coming from far away. He always greeted us with a fraternal smile. Speaking Russian fluently, Chingiz would often converse with him. A very useful thing! Additionally, I recall Chingiz being much stronger than me. When he loaded a heavy sack on his shoulders, and went up the plank-way, I took pride in his labours. More so, since most of the sacks were just pulled along by others as they climbed up the mountains of grain.

Having finished this business, we returned to the village again. On our homeward journey the bullocks moved more energetically, so we had races with one another, on the empty carts.

Having eaten some simple food on the long road back, we too felt bolder, and even began to sing. Yet, Chingiz was inseparable from the Russian classics! Sometimes he took it upon himself to retell these stories to us, and did so passionately.

If I am not mistaken, it was in 1944, when I came to see Chingiz - he was at home alone, and was very glad to see me.

"Seitali, I have to travel to the district centre, Kirov, to pay back some loans. It is a long way to go, and to travel with money and rather dangerous. What if we two go together? The cart is ready.

Although I was tied up with work at school, I could not refuse my friend. The following day at noon, after questions here and there, we found the Bank we needed, watered our bullocks and fed them, then sat down ourselves to chew some maize pancakes. A bit later a black-haired, broad-shouldered young fellow of medium height came up to us and asked:

"Well, my lads, what are you doing here, eh?"
We explained everything to him.
"Whose son are you, brother?" he asked, turning to Chingiz.
"I'm Turekul Aitmatov's son!" he responded, and before he could say another word, the young lad gave a shout:
"Ah, yes!" he cried, "My dear fellow, you are and (with tears in his eyes) he hugged Chingiz tightly.
"I am your uncle Kozhomkul. I'm the Chief of the District Savings Bank. Turekul helped me to stand on my feet. All my life I shall feel obliged to him ..."

He lived, so he said, along with his family, in one of the rooms at the Bank. Indeed, he showed us the way: sitting on the cart without further ado, and inviting us in as his guests. He took the money from us, and gave us a stamped receipt. The following day he saw us off, and said:

"Here, buy yourself some clothes or something you need. This is all I can spare at the moment, my dear lad!" and with that he stuffed a wad of notes into Chingiz's pocket. That same year Chingiz and I went to Zhambyl. Uncle Kozhomkul's bank-notes gave him no rest. Going through the bazaar "Atshabar", choosing carefully, we bought two high-collared tunics, leather belts and breeches, and caps with red stars. Having changed into them in a secluded spot, we went to the Red Army".

Equally, I remembered another story relating to the days of his youth. We met by chance with a fellow named Musa Kasimov, who studied at the Agricultural Institute as a junior student. He was a fine story-teller. He told me some yarns about those days when Chingiz was a young veterinary worker on a farm run by the Kirghizian Scientific Research Institute of Cattle-breeding.

AITMATOV.   Yes, in 1956, leaving for the Gorky Literary Institute, I relinquished my duty there to that same Musa Kasimov.

SHAKHANOV.   It is interesting - Musa found in a drawer inside your writing table, two scientific works; both written in Russian. One of them was fully typed, while the other in manuscript. The articles were entitled: "Is a triple milking sufficient?" and "Maize in cattle-food rations". These works Musa kept for forty years as a precious relic. "Maybe Chingiz would like to have them back again, or if not, just take a look at them?" he said to me not long ago, handing me the copies. He went on to tell me more of you and your work.

"Chingiz first came to the farm as a technical cattleman: introducing great changes into the breeding line (many of which we had not ever heard of) before occupying himself with their extended implementation. Yet, in the middle of the 1950's, in Kirghizia, there were no cows specially bred for their pedigree. It wasn't until years later that pedigree bulls from the Leningrad Region were brought to us. As a result of this practice, newborn calves speedily showed an improvement, producing better quality milk with a higher fat-content. Additionally, I remember he worked like a Trojan to ameliorate horse-breeding techniques.

In general, I didn't entertain the slightest doubt Chingiz would become a famous writer; of academic classics, not to mention of scientific cattle breeding.

AITMATOV.   People close to one are always complimentary. Who can know what will be? Fate is impartial for all. Let us talk about you now!

Remember, not long ago you and I, along with the dramatist Kaltai Mukhamedzhanov, visited Tashkent. On our way we stopped at your native region of Southern Kazakhstan, to pay homage to the spirit of Khodzha Akhmed Yasavy. Afterwards, we visited his mausoleum in Turkestan, named by Moslems across the globe as "a second Mecca". We were then entertained by your young relations Serik Seitzhanov, Alimzhan Kurtayev and Kuanish Aitakhanov. Indeed, we listened enchanted to their attractive story-telling about Otrar, Aristanbab, and holy Turkestan. Taking up their words about Otrar, you then began to sing in blank verse about the valorous deeds of knights. Prompting me, involuntarily, to grasp how close and firm were the ties binding you to your native land. Your poem, in its turn, made a deep impression on me.

SHAKHANOV. Chingiz, this poem speaks of tragic events in the history of my own land. My father knew other ancient poems, both long and short, although written in Arabic, accompanying these ancient tales. To a certain degree he too was a mullah:

> *"Join the farm-workers in their frays –*
> *With your whips drive out*
> *Mullahs and Beys!"* –
> *So sang the poet …*

Compelled by that policy, my father was forced to quit his native land. He travelled to his married daughter Izyet, in the village of Kaskasu, in the district of Tole-bi. I was a child in those days; not more than forty days old.

Sadly, my father left this world when I was nine years old. In my memory, as if preserved in stone, I recall how he used to sit me on his knee and tell me of my brave forefathers, boldly fighting their foes during the time when Otrar was heroically defended. All intended, possibly, to foster in me a child's spiritual love towards his native land.

Sometimes mother doubted his motives: "He is too small - will he not understand what you tell him" "But, he must understand!" answered my father, "And if he doesn't, it will be the worse for him. A tree which doesn't put down deep roots lives a short life!"

Similar to damage caused by an unending flood was the onslaught wreaked by the troops of Genghis-Khan: a man who aimed to conquer the whole world. Certainly, the outstanding cities of Central Asia, with their gleaming minarets reaching up to the heavens, fell beneath his conquering warriors within a few day. They simply swamped them in hordes. Kings and Princes, scared by his ferocious forces, opened up the gates of their cities to them. Otrar alone, for half a year, did not surrender to the enemy. Otrar alone stood to the death before this storm: not bowing its noble head.

Genghis-Khan gave an order. "Let no male seed remain in Otrar!" All of his men, except the one who betrayed them, meeting a heroic finale.

This was the story my father was never tired of telling me. The story of the unbendable legendary Kair-Khan, and of the tragedy of the young knight who betrayed him - serving as a lesson for me I suppose. Thanks to one tale repeatedly told by my father, I unearthed a proud joy in life: though it had a tragic end. In truth, "The best education is the education of the innermost feelings of man!"

Perhaps, it was even the case that my father nourished in me from early childhood a love of this land of my forebears, along with my respect for him. An attitude determining my life path. As such, his principles have always adhered to me like an unchangeable rule. Let's take another example: I don't know why, but my father never had his hair cut before noontide.

You may find it strange to hear I too have never had my hair cut before noon. Most likely because there is nothing very exceptional about that, or simply due to the fact I follow my father habit. Sometimes, oddly enough, it caused me personal difficulties. On flying to America a few years ago (it was a mid-day flight), I remembered I must shave before leaving. However, I had no time to do so. Yet, how could I break this ingrained habit taught to me by my father in youth? It was impossible! So I flew to another continent unshaven!

In 1992, in accordance with a request made by the citizens of Otrar, I was to appear one evening to recite my best creative works. A reading offered, as fate would have it, at the warmest time of year. Pitilessly, the sun blazed down, the air was dry, and I trembled with the heat. Almost three thousand of my countrymen met me at the outskirts of our region: roughly thirty kilometres from the centre. Mature men who remembered my sire, along with esteemed young mothers in white head kerchiefs. Looking back, I was embraced so heartily it seemed I would never escape them. Local poets endlessly read their lines, the whole steppe echoed with songs, and folk-dancers pirouetted with temperamental cries.

Three old women, who had between them sewed a neck-amulet of white silk and gold thread, (with a pinch of Otrar soil within), placed it round my neck with these words:

"Wherever you go, son of ours, let your sacred native soil defend you!" All my life I have received many presents, as a sign of respect from my native folk - even in far distant land they have offered me gifts, but not one of them ever moved me like that amulet: with a pinch of native soil!"

AITMATOV. In connection with your story I remember in olden times our forebears, leaving their native land, bound up a pinch of soil, and tied it to their belts. Also, when a warrior went to war, his wife, or beloved one, left a crust of bread for him to eat. Warriors kept those crusts, believing the old folk saying: "Those who taste home-made food will return safely!"

SHAKHANOV. Chingiz, my friend, I'll tell you the lesson of a tale which ancient historical memories have taught me.

I have a countryman named Sergey Tereshenko. His Kazakh speech, full of folk-sayings, is envied by other Kazakhs. A few years ago, he worked in the Komsomol Youth Organization as the head of the Shimkent Local Party Committee. Later, he became Chairman of the Council of Ministers of the Republic. In addition, Sergey's father led a large concern in the Tyulkubas region. He was a Hero of Socialist Labour, a deeply respected person. In a word or two, he and his father were people who had profound roots in their native soil.

Well, the first Mongolian cosmonaut, Zhugderdemidiyn Gurragchu is also our friend. By the way, he collects your books. "If I fly again in the Cosmos", he is quoted as saying, "I shall surely take with me some of Aitmatov's works!"

This may be why I originally invited the cosmonaut to my native home. Anyway, while making my way back, I called on Sergey Tereshenko.

"Show Otrar to our Mongolian friend, and the ruins of other cities, wiped from the face of the earth by his predecessors. Maybe this will incite him to some other kind of meditation!" said Sergey with a grin.

In my excitement, I did not pay much attention to the subtext hidden within his words, but a little later I had to reconsider it.

At last, we stepped onto the soil of Otrar. The governor of the region welcoming us gleefully. Towards evening, there was a pre-planned meeting with guests in the newly-constructed Palace of Culture: named after Al-Farabi. Before my homeland trip, I had been told by some friends of mine, Kanzhigit Sizdikov and Abilkasim Kulumbetov, that a resolution had been taken to bestow on me the title of "Honoured Citizen of Otrar." I thought of my cosmonaut friend instantly. At that time, a "tradition" was developing, whereby a cosmonaut (having flown around the world) was given the title of "honoured citizen" of the spot where he, or she, had landed.

As a case in point, our Almati Sewing Factory bears the name of the first Soviet woman cosmonaut - Tereshkova, while we are equally proud of streets bearing the personal name Gagarin, Titov and Nikolayev. Anxiously, I thought, if Gurragchu (in honour of his first visit to South Kazakhstan) was given the appellation "Otrar" who would object? After all, in ideological spheres, such an action would be evaluated as friendship between two peoples, even though in ancient times they had been enemies.

But the previous leader of the region, Mukhamedkasim Shakenov, was confused and pushed into saying:

"Mukhtar, your motivation I share wholeheartedly... However, let's discuss this suggestion with local elders!"

It was early spring ... The steppe grew green, spreading blissfully under the sun's rays. Therefore, we all strolled together with Gurragchu into the ruins of Otrar itself. Truly, one could scarcely believe these stony remains were once a handsome town known on the Silk Road to be a blossoming centre of culture and trade: with a thriving population of about sixteen thousand. Undoubtedly, ignorant people would not believe the story they had laid-on running water in their homes back then.

In its day, Otrar had been the home of Abu nasr al-Farabi, and a whole galaxy of wise men - historians, philosophers, doctors, astrologers and scientists. It was a glittering hub of civilization.

Regardless, it was utterly destroyed and then laid waste by Genghis-Khan's warriors. Moreover, in cruel, collective, memory, the thought of pregnant women having their abdomens slashed open, whilst little babies were tossed in the air to be caught on a spear-tip, still lingers. The remaining witnesses to those atrocious events being the broken ruins of this devastated town lying there in the sunshine.

As I held a mental dialogue with this dead town, we went down to the green meadow beneath where carpets were already spread out, and long, low, tables sported noisy copper samovars.

With hindsight, who could have foreseen that long after the days when Genghis-Khan cut away the very roots of a people we, their descendants, accompanied by one of his descendants, might become indivisible friends: sitting together without the slightest hostility towards each other?

Soon, some elders rode up and hastily dismounted. Apprehensively, I saw among them the much respected Musabek Azhibekov, Kutum Ordabayev and Adikham Shillerkhanov – wise, highly esteemed old men, who had written manuscripts about the Southern Region and exercised their wits on historical contortions.

Having greeted us, they led me aside

"Mukhtar-zhan, you have approached the leaders of this region with a special request. Your friend and guest, the Mongolian cosmonaut - we shall honour as befits our traditions. Yet, regarding your request to make him an honoured citizen of Otrar ... well, if his distant forbears had not caused such carnage here, our city would still be standing. Its sacred buildings continuing to thrill our hearts with their holy blue minarets. And what of the forty-two other towns in Sidar, which were wiped off the face of the earth? Admittedly, you may ask wherein lies Gurragchu's guilt in all of this? Assuredly, we ourselves are aware that he is in no way to be blamed. But, to our minds, Gurragchu bears some responsibility for the evil done by his forbears due to his veins containing the bad blood of his predecessors. However slight its traces may be. Now, it is not in accord with our custom to bear grudges. Yet, to wipe them out as if they never occurred, betrays ancestral memory. You must ponder on this, and then act!

Without another word, these three elders mounted their steeds and rode off. At that moment, I suddenly seemed to come to myself. My God, how could I, named as a poet, be so reckless in my judgement before these venerable men - in truth, preservers of the historical memory of my own folk? I remembered my father. It seemed I had not really reached the essential value behind his legends of Otrar. Although, here, in the mouths of these three wise men, this truth spoke anew!

Later, when I confessed my conversation with the elders to Gurragchu, he sincerely answered me and said:

"Therein lies your happiness, my dear poet. In your village you have such elders, who do not permit false steps along historical paths to the past, but preserve their national memory!"

AITMATOV. Unarguably paradoxical! And all concurring with received wisdom when it states a man must check his steps in decisive events. Particularly, I suppose, if he is not to damage his successors – whether, In fact, this is true or not. I wonder if Genghis-Khan thought about these things, as he set out to conquer half the World: did he pause at the sea of blood he was shedding? Maybe, it was just the opposite - the instincts of this planetary conqueror overwhelming his mental conceptions? Yet, centuries have passed since that era. It goes without saying, of course, Gurragchu was in no way responsible for any of this mayhem - as our elders clearly understood. However, history moves in mysterious ways all the same. Moreover, he who ignores historical memory can, it seems, devolve into a maniac.

If one merely leafs through the yellowed pages of passed epochs, how many are the clashes recorded between peoples! Do we have the right, if we follow historical memory, to blame the whole Mongolian people, for the chaos of Genghis-Khan, or the whole of the German people for the horror of Hitler? For instance, there was in its time a Hundred Years War between England and France even though neither Englishmen nor Frenchmen denounce each other nowadays, nor break their relations.

On reflection, enclosure in the narrow bounds of historical memory is not always the best course for a nation. Contrariwise, completely forgetting the past can cause a spiritual loss within the soul.

Wisdom consists in being able, perhaps, in the fullness of time, to balance up these weights correctly: if judged according to our universal humanity. That is why the so-called "steppe Academy" is so named - because, taking on itself the experience of the past, it teaches us to live consciously - thinking about the future, and observing recognized principles of human society.

SHAKHANOV. I remember, back in my childhood, how older people who stared at the setting of the sun used to say: "The greater part of life has gone, and only the lesser part is left!" A sentiment which haunted me, along with a parable I knew:

Once, in olden times, on the banks of the Syr-Darya, there lived a rich Bey. Unluckily for him, a great flood swept across the land and washed all his riches and cattle away. The Bey, however, could swim, and so saved his life. Crawling onto the bank, therefore, soaked and shivering, but still up to his knees in watery slime, he stood trembling and prayed: "O God, grant me worthily to live out my days!" Having noticed him, a young and self-willed, fellow laughed at the words of this elder. "Old man," he said, "your days were passed threescore- and-ten ago. Everything you gathered in life has been taken from you, and nothing left. Oh, what worthiness words you speak?" and with that he whipped his steed and rode off.

In this ever-changing world, is there truly anything really lasting?

Time passed by, and a terrible drought fell upon the land. Having become a merciless Bey, the previously young, bold, fellow, was left with just one horse - to whose reins he clung, weak with hunger. His cattle died of thirst, his relations too, and he himself set off wandering in search of food and drink. Hungry, unhappy, he roamed down to the banks of Syr-Daria; at last noticing some smoke nearby. When he came closer he saw a yurta, and there a woman opened the door to him, took him inside, and seated him in the place of honour. Immediately understanding that her guest was ravenous, she set some food before him, while her children played merrily with knuckle-bones, there on the floor.

"Eat, and rest, dear guest. Soon your host will come home" said the woman, and then got on with her work about the yurta.

After a while, there stepped into the yurta the same old man whom he had seen before, and, unsurprisingly, they recognized each other. After supper, they began to converse:

"When you mocked me, and went on your way - I went on mine, and came down the river bank to this village. Here they took me in, fed me, warmed me, and helped me to survive. As for the mistress of this yurta, she was a widow. In time we got together, lived and raised cattle: growing prosperous again in the process and fed by our flock. I then prayed to God once again that I might worthily live out my days. My prayer was heard, which is why I bless Allah a thousand times, and one. Riches today may disappear tomorrow. You made a great mistake, my dear fellow. Now you must be convinced, surely, that an unworthy action, deliberately done, calls forth long-sounding echoes: reminding a man of his errors."

That parable, Chingiz, I repeated from the beginning to the end, because we, travelling the same road, sooner or perhaps later, will approach the age when we shall beg Allah to prolong our days, so that we may go on living worthily on this earth.

AITMATOV.   In this you are right, for it is well to remember the old saying: "The greater part of life has gone, only the lesser is left!"

For every mortal being on this earth, there comes a time when he must ask fate to worthily live out his remaining days. God grant he does not come deflated by bad actions, but has successfully overcome all kinds of testing trials.

SHAKHANOV. From the moment of a man's birth, and the attainment of reason, to the full formation of his character, his teacher - at one and the same time severe, yet kindly disposed towards him, is his mother land;

Uncomely, the thorn-bush 'mid the shifting sand,
Blooms all to itself beneath scorching rays.
For why? Don't ask - that is the law of the land –
To live in the desert, knowing no sorrowful days.

The others in grass-land have faded long ago,
Have burned in flames, have died in the throes of thirst.
Only the thorn-bush here can lord it so –
It sends deep roots in search of water first.

They penetrate through sand, to where the moisture lies,
And only they know how to seek it out.
And if there's a blizzard? Still another dies.
The sand-hills in the blast then fly about.

The sand then mixes with the racing clouds.
The sun has gone, the darkness howls and rings.
One's heart just shrinks before death's saddening shrouds,
And all that lives, from fear runs off, takes wings.

But tumble-weeds go rolling like a ball,
And gives themselves to blind and mad free-will.
The homeless plant can stay nowhere at all.
Where does it fly? To goodness? Or to ill?

In the desert of life, amid work and days,
We are condemned such bitter lessons to learn –
To be like a tumble-weed, no roots always,
To fly off careless, where no roadways turn?

Or stand before the hurricane, breast to breast,
To meet another, not thinking to run away?
To overcome all - and only then find rest –
There's no other plan, from now till that last far day!

AITMATOV. Yes, people are such.

There is another old legend which goes: Once a young lad was taken prisoner by enemies, and sold into slavery in a foreign land. Time passed, and the bold young jigger began to forget the land which had brought him up, and even his parents themselves. He became used to this strange land, and finally, thanks to his great patience and wisdom, and strength of will, to became a local ruler. More years passed by and this ruler grew old. Yet, one day, a caravan on its long route from his homeland, started burning a clump of wormwood as it passed. The scent of this bitter plant, plucked from a distant land, brought back to the ruler memories of long forgotten childhood days, when he, being a lad, serenely gathered wild tulips on his native steppeland. Tears came into his eyes, and his heart winced from a deep, unbearable, yearning for that old homeland of his. Nothing could hold him down any longer - no local power attained, no glory, nor riches ... Hastily he mounted his horse, to return to his Fatherland.

To love one's native land does not necessarily mean to remain forever there, not casting an eye on the wide world around. Shut up in a single place one can never blossom, nor develop all one's various gifts in several directions.

For instance, youths from your Otrar, or from my Sheker, have at last flown over the whole Earth. One wants to get an education, another to get overseas experience in some profession. Our forebears said; "When you are on your horse, get to know the world!" Yes, this is wonderful! While one is young, full of strength and energy, learn, become enlightened, and find out how people live in foreign lands!

All the same, wherever you have been, whatever you may have seen, your native land remains for you the one and only destination. Just keep up your contacts with it spiritually, and you will be worthy to go on through life. Thusly, foreign soil, foreign air, and foreign water can never take the place of one's motherland.

Yes, we are tied to our native land by innumerable, invisible threads. I am fully of your opinion, that to every man, apart from his own mother, there should be four more holy mothers. Yet his native motherland is the most majestic of them all:

To us, the self-conceit of other people, convinced they can live without any connection to their motherland is strange: especially when they think that their country cannot survive without them. Just the opposite is true, of course. The sacred land of our forefathers will live and flourish with or without us, whereas our spirit, without our native land, will not fly very high, nor achieve great ends. Truly, while our motherland lives we too remain alive!

THE WARMTH OF SHINING STARS
OR
A HANDFUL OF SOIL

What deep feelings, memories of our forebears call forth, about those who went not so very far away when they left us! Especially if one takes into account that we shall eventually be with them again ... To know and to remember is essential, and to throw a handful of soil onto their graves - that is the binding thread!

What blindness, to look - and not to recognize!
Those non-understanders - are they not to blame?
It's a crime - not to want to know, and be wise!
Was it so? 'Twas so! That account we must claim!

AITMATOV. My misfortune. All the time I have dreams ceaselessly, I scarcely close my eyes, and in a moment I am the prisoner of dreams. I wake before dawn, yet do not understand what kind of punishment this is, which I myself must permanently bear.

At times, in dreams, I visit great people, whom I have never met, but of whom I have heard something or other. Then it happens I pass on to them those hidden things, which are not known to anyone, no, not to a single living person. Visions.

I confess they happen so often, those alarming and unusual dreams, that I even consulted my doctors about it. Their opinions were one and the same - there is no reason for alarm, all is in order! So again I go to sleep, and almost immediately I am loaded down by all kinds of transparent pictures and events.

SHAKHANOV. I think those dreams have a real pre-history, but I will take the risk of slightly frightening you. Dreams, as Rodger Zhelyazni has said, "Are transparent curtains, dividing us from the day: each dream also being a well of Time!" They are forms of self-purifying for the spirit. He who sees no dreams, also sees no reality. Dreams are given to creative people - they are a conversation with the forces of world-creation. So, who knows, perhaps the inspiring secret of your creative work lies hidden in eternal dreams, which you translate into literature.

Be pleased with dreams!

What then do we say of the light of falling stars! But, surely the farewell blaze of dying planets only reaches us a million years later!

So it is with people. When they say farewell forever to this earthly life, and fly off into infinity and forgetfulness, many of them remain to us in our memory - living, bright, unfading stars! Maybe some of those stars which have left us go to another world, and from there light up your dreams with unseen, uncapturable light? An illumination predestined for you, as if it were a sign of hope, sent from Eternity, which you succeed in exchanging with it, without knowing how. With previously non-existent great projects and beautiful visions; breaking up into potholes this transitory world - you hear someone's call, and you echo it for future generations.

AITMATOV.   In what you have said there lies a portion of truth, and also a tinge of humour. Concerning Homer and his creative works - "The Iliad" and "The Odyssey" Plato once said: "That poet educates the whole of our Hellas!" Great poets are teachers of the people. Who knows, if their aspiration to create good in the world were not passed over to those living now, our fate, maybe, would have turned out otherwise?

If we speak of starry personalities, then the first bright star to illuminate my life was Mukhtar Auezov, and this is how it happened ...

I was a student at that time in the Frunze Agricultural Institute named after Skryabin. Those were days of stormy discussions, scientific disputes, and the sharpest polemics concerning the epic "Manas". All our people took this heroic epic as a great historical creation of the folk of Kirghizia. However, when, in accord with the "spirit" of those times, questions arose on the correspondence of this epic with the principles and canons of socialist realism, most people sided with official pronouncements. What else could one do – Stalin's ideology demanded works, without exception, should blame our misfortunes on the rich, and describe the needful existence of the poor. As a result of this - the mutiny of the humiliated against those wealthy, exploiting, and dominating rulers, became acceptable.

Some good-for-nothing literary specialists were in agreement with this position. Others, to please vulgar sociology, dealt with the epic literally - here is Manas, the main hero of the epic; here is his father Yakib - a Khan. All implying, Manas belongs to a privileged class. Hence, this epic praises an ideology quite alien to real Soviet citizens! On such a wave of pseudo-criticism arose the quirky attitude that "Manas" was a species of apology for the Bey-feudal system of those days. In itself, a reply to the succeeding paranoidal ideas of "The Master of the Kremlin". On newspaper and journal pages both, articles exposed and unmasked the folk-epic. Evidence, of course, that dark clouds were gathering above the great "Manas". Overall, things started to smell of disaster and imminent misfortune.

Simultaneously, honest voices rang out in defence of this epic. All the same, nobody listened to them, nor wanted to hear.

When our society divides so, and remained undecided, we took it for granted the Kirghizian branch of our USSR Academy of Sciences would organize a conference devoted to these issues, wherein the fate of this folk-legend would be settled. Anticipation arose! When this congress was finally called, we could barely waiting for the end of our lectures. In a mass, we young Kirghizians dashed off to get places at this gathering. If I am not mistaken, it was in the autumn of 1952. Unsurprisingly, in the Kirghizian Academy building, it was hardly possible to move. Packed to the brim, people hung from the door-handles, even standing in the street hoping to hear something. You should have seen them, how excited they were about the fate of their "Manas" - silently holding their breath to hear the verdict. Somehow I managed, step by step, to worm my way into the hall, standing just inside the door. I stuck out my neck, and saw the presidium of ten, or fifteen, people at the table. In the centre, sat the first secretary of the Central Committee of the Kirghizian Communist Party, Iskhak Razzakov. To his right - Mukhtar Auezov, who at that stage I had never met personally, though I often saw his name bandied about as the author of many books. I looked at him, and couldn't take my eyes away from this fellow. He seemed to shed an invisible radiance round himself.

One after another the members of the Presidium went up on the tribune, and spoke against the epic, tearing its pages to pieces. Auezov, sitting with an impenetrable face, listened attentively to each of them, and from time to time dotted down notes on his paper.

"The epic "Manas" is a work foreign in its nature to the Modernist line of the Party ... It appears to be, in fact, propaganda for the ideas of Pan-Turkism" announced one of the main speakers, a Party "literary worker", A. Borovkov. Having no real facts to go on, in his attacks he affirmed these thrusts, and blackened the whole epic. The hall began to buzz, as if it were a disturbed beehive. Lacking bravery, nobody denied such slanderous allegations, or made any protest against them.

Outside the doors could be heard a hub-bub of voices. To all, it seemed that at any moment we were going to lose our beloved epic. Then, at this tensest of moments, Auezov made his way to the tribune.

"It is possible in the "Manas" epic there are elements of approval regarding the rich and other elite personages", he began, "but all the same this is, beyond all doubt, a priceless treasure involving the history of a whole people, with its heroics, its traditions, its spirituality, and its immense cultural power: handed down from one generation to another, from mouth to mouth, in the pure poetic tongue. Therefore, to take this epic away from the life of its people is like cutting out the tongue of our whole folk. Will our society be cured of superfluous energy and speed, if along with the forelock we hew off the head?" Concluding his speech, he then turned to Borovkov who cowered, while drawing back his head to his shoulders like a Turkey.

The width of Auezov's circle of vision, his deep knowledge of world literature, his ability to express his thoughts and make his decisions in philosophically, his unusual delight, and his bowing before the spiritual riches of the Kirghiz people, set up an unusual atmosphere in the hall. What a bold and brilliant orator he was! Speaking only the truth, this historic speech saved "Manas" from becoming numbered on the black-lists of anti-Soviet literary productions. Thanks to Aiezov's wise and touching speech, Iskhak Razzakov listened with specially concentrated attention: here and there nodding his head in agreement. Understanding the priceless nature of the Kirghizian epic, he was, however, obliged to take account of the bitter political struggle of that time, and to control his emotions. That was obvious. As a prior warning, the imprisonment of Tashin Baizhiyev, for his repeated speeches in defence of "Manas" (despite forewarnings), operated as an ongoing threat.

Be that as it may, as the conference ended, happy cries from outside resounded: "Bravo, bravo!" "Manas" is saved! Where is Mukhtar? May the mother who bore him be blessed again, and all Kirghizians!"

Hundreds of excited, joyful people (many with tears in their eyes), happily embraced and congratulated each other. It was reminiscent of a bubbling sea, as folk washed up against the walls of the Academy of Sciences.

SHAKHANOV. At that same time, the majority of the finest works of folk-lore and literature among the Kazakhs were also entered on a black-list, including tales, legends, and poems - the best examples of oral folk art. Auezov himself being destined to know what it was like in prison, although innocent. He was given two years in gaol. Even after his release, he was still under suspicion and hunted down.

They say the Republic Committee of State Security once phoned Auezov, an unknown woman warning him: "Try to conceal yourself, whatever the price, or else it will be too late. Sanctions are being prepared for your arrest!"

The same evening he secretly left for Moscow. Trusted friends helping Auezov to escape without being followed. Later he became a professor at Moscow State University.

Yet, the fact Auezov stepped forward to save "Manas" was certainly evidence of his great civic courage. Do you not think so?

AITMATOV.   I do, indeed! I have already said how his soul suffered for the threatened epic he saved at the conference. If I had known then, I would become the chief editor of his first complete edition of "Manas" thirty years later. Equally, I may have found the courage to speak with him at other world conferences!

My first meeting with Mukhtar Auezov was especially interesting, and I afterwards counted myself as his pupil. In those days, I was studying at the Moscow Gorky institute of Literature. If I recall correctly, back then, in the capital's literary circles there began a fierce discussion about Vladimir Dudintsev's novel "Not by bread alone". Here one would praise it delightedly, there another would reduce it to dust and ashes. Finally, it was decided to arrange a general gathering in the Central House of Literature. I came early and took a seat. The presidium was crowded, one may say, with many important names and officials. People came crowding in, till there was no room to move. Some sat on window-sills, others spread newspapers on the gangways and sat there, on the floor.

There was no end to the clashes of opinions. After a while, I looked towards the door and saw Auezov, caught in the throng. He was slightly late, and could not make his way to the Presidium, where no one seemed to notice his difficulties. There was no going forward nor back - he just had to stand stuck in the doorway.

At last an interval was announced. People with flushed faces then tried to make their way from the stuffy hall. I hurriedly pushed forwards toward Mukhtar, greeted him with both hands outstretched, saying:

"Mukhtar aga* there is a place for you. Come with me, I will show you the way. I offered him my stool in the row. He sat down to rest, following which he asked, a bit surprised:

"Who are you? From where do you come from?"

"I am from Kirghizstan", I replied, "I am studying here in the Moscow Gorky Institute of Literature!"

"Ah, I see!" he exclaimed, "Now everything is clear! Thank you very much my dear fellow" he said, to me with a warm smile on his face. I was rooted to the spot.

There could not have been better words of gratitude for me! So, our first introduction was made, an occurrence I shall remember all life.

And did you succeed in meeting him personally? You were still quite young when he passed away, I believe?

SHAKHANOV. I can say that I was just about lucky! A little while before he passed away, in the Palace of Culture of the Shimkent Lead Factory, there was a two-day readers' conference, devoted to the epic "The path of Abai". In this Mukhtar took part, having come from Alma-ata. At that time there was a well-known young poet named Mamitbek Kaldibayev, who gave me an invitation ticket to the conference. There I saw the world- famous Auezov for the first time.

---

*aga -that is the way of addressing a person who is older and respected.

It was interesting for us as youngsters to observe how he spoke, how he moved, how in moments of pleasant satisfaction he scratched the tip of his nose. He was wearing a grey suit. In contrast with the photos on his books, he looked somewhat lean and haggard. Maybe it was his new book - "Young Tribe", which tool such a toll? Anyway, after he started "The path of Abai" new thoughts and agitations appeared to tire him.

Furthermore, the conference had barely ended, when we stood in a queue to get the old writer's autograph. People crowded round, here and there, all inquisitive and holding copies of his books in their hands. The queue moved slowly, and at last I stood before him. I knew some parts of his book "The path of Abai" by heart, and wanted to recite them before him, but did not have the daring to do so. However, the queue pushed me forward, and there I stood, looking akward ...

"What is your name, my lad?" Auezov asked, opening my copy of his book.

"Mukhtar! My father named me in honour of you, having read your books!" The words came from my tongue nervously and quietly.

The writer looked at me very kindly, and wrote on the fly-leaf:

"To young Mukhtar, from grandad Mukhtar - with best wishes!" His handwriting was uneven, but boldly cursive.

That was my first and last meeting with the great writer. I remember, when I was studying extra-murally at the Shimkent Teachers' Institute, there was a lecturer named Adil Yermekov, He was remarkable - knowing the whole of Auezov's book "The path of Abai" by heart! With his phenomenal memory he reminded me of the well-known Kirghizian reciter-Manaschi, Sayakbai Karalayev. Often Adil would recite passages from your book "Motherland Field", Chingiz! He equally knew many of my early poems, but read them in his own way. Once he even informed me of an interesting occurrence in his life:

During his latter years Auezov, working on an ordinary novel, frequantly coming to the southern region of Kazakhstan. On one of these trips Adil Yermekov sat in the same compartment with him on the train. They spoke about this and that, and then Auezov recalled an event from his student days: when he was studying with Kanish

Satpayev, in Leningrad, and both of them had their fortune told by a gypsy woman. Looking over Satpayev's palm she said:

Many difficulties will trouble you in your life, but you will overcome them and very soon become a famous scientist. Then she took a look at Auezov's hand, and thought for a moment before sayingi:

"You will also become a great man!" Curiously continuing. "Your fame will fly all over the earth. But your way will be hard and uneven. Your fate will be to escape death several times. Many torments you will suffer, before you achieve great honour. Three times you will be married, and will meet your death under the knife!"

"Yes, she was right. My life-road was long, thorny, and uneven" said Auezov, turning to his listener. In troubled times I could have fallen - shot down as "An enemy of the people". Fickle chance saved me. My good name, to a certain extent, also saved me. The gypsy woman was right. I was married three times. Now the threat of the knife she mentioned troubles me. I try to go about in company, not alone on dark nights, and get home reasonably early.

My dear Chingiz -Auezov died during an operation in the Kremlin Hospital. In which case, the fortune-teller was again right.

AITMATOV. I saw Auezov for the last time in 1961, in the Hotel Moscow, before he went into hospital. He was in very good spirits, even spreading on the table some mare's meat sausages brought from home. We made tea together while, like father and son, kept up a slow but very sincere conversation. In this manner, we sat talking till well past midnight.

"I have come to be cured in "Kuntsevka", he told me. By the way, my physicians have said the polypuses are non-malignant, presenting no kind of danger to my life. Of course, I must have them removed, all the same, while I still have strength, and am not too old nor worn-out!"

If I had only known then that I was seeing Auezov and hearing his kind wishes for the last time! The next day, not suspecting anything, I flew off to Frunze.

SHAKHANOV. But did you know that Mukhtar once organized a feast in honour of the French writer Louis Aragon, in Moscow?

AITMATOV.   No, I didn't know that, but I did know of their close and friendly relationship.

SHAKHANOV.   Well, so it was. Everyone knew that Auezov was a big hearted personality. Additionally, they invited Dinmukhamed Kunayev and Kanish Satpayev to tea. Both being distinguished in stature and manner. Along with them another tall young writer took his place. Pleased with these four superb fellows, and enjoying intellectual conversation with them, Louis Aragon could not help asking:
"Are all Kazakhs as tall as you are?"
"Yes, our whole people are like us, shorter ones you will rarely find!" answered Mukhtar jokingly.
It appears that Louis Aragon took this reply literally and did not stop wondering at them. At which point, the door opened and a short stout man entered the room: the chief ideologist of the Republic in this period, and by the way, doing it more harm than good ...
"Oh, he is an exception!" Auezov instantly quipped, reacting to this uninvited and most unwelcome guest.
Dear Chingiz, another idea has suddenly entered my head: I think that Louis Aragon, on translating the famous "Path of Abai" into French, had an extra motive when referring to your works. This thought of mine, by the way, is confirmed by your Kirghizian folk writer Zhunai Mavlyanov, who wrote: "At a spacious dacha, on the banks of Issyk- Kul, during the meeting of these writers, speeches focused upon literary works. Being an honoured guest, Mukhtar immediately began with Aitmatov: "Today, neither in Central Asia, nor in Kazakhstan, nor in the whole Union, can one find anyone of a similar standing to Chingiz. You know I am a member of the Committee dealing with the award of Lenin and Republic prizes. I have read many and various articles by a number of highly praised authors. Yet, none of them can equal the work "Dzhamilya". Regarding which, I have frequently spoken. Indeed, few praise Chingiz as strongly as my French friend Louis Aragon. Surely then, from times immemorial Kirghizians and Kazakhs have ruled over the whole vast steppeland, from Alatau to Issyk-Kul: holding joint pasture-lands and speaking languages close to each other! So here, I think, one can name Chingiz as the son of the two peoples, both

elevated by his talent, and leaving no place for any kind of jealousy. Tfu-tfu! Touch wood! May they never look on him with an evil eye!" Auezov concluded joking.

AITMATOV. I remember a small, but unusually kind article written by Auezov in the "Literary Gazette", when "Dzhamilya" had just seen the light of day: an interjection by a great prose writer. As for me, I felt an enormous responsibility before my teacher. So, when my story "The camel's eye" was printed in the Union press, I was anxious at receiving a telegram from Auezov in Alma-ata:

"Dear Chingiz", I read, "Your publication I liked very much! I am very glad for you. Continue in this spirit". Obviously, I have preserved that telegram in my archives to this day!

In the early sixties, Mukhtar Auezov came to Frunze, and I invited him to my home. Having heard that a great writer was visiting us, my mother, Nagima, became befuddled. She put everything in order in the house, and placed the softest cushions in a place of honour. Moreover, she herself prepared the table, and set out special dishes for our guest. My first-born Sanzhar, however, on seeing some beautiful red apples on our table, began to stealthily sneak them away, one by one. He took them out on the street, eating what he could and giving the others to our neighbours' children. Eventually, he was caught by his grandmother at the "scene of the crime":

"My goodness! He has taken all the apples! What shall we say to our guest now? She exhaled a series of "Ah's" and "Oh's" and led her grandson by the ear to the door. At that moment it opened, and in came Mukhtar. He laughed heartily on hearing what had happened, and said to my mother:

"Don't be angry with the little one - he's merely a child!" Then, he took Granny by the arm and led her aside, thereby saving the little rogue from further punishment. In those days, we lived as neighbours, door to door, with the Manas reciter, Sayakbai Karalayev. He was an old and close friend of Mukhtar. The meeting of these two masters of the word was followed by a long and wise conversation, which I listened to with great interest the whole evening through.

At midnight our guests decided to take a breath of fresh air. Going towards the door, Mukhtar noticed that my mother had taken the hand of her young grandson Askar, and leading him to the spot where Auezov had sat, bundled him down.

"What are you doing with him?" he asked, surprised somewhat.

"That, my man, is a good sign. I wish him, the thoughtless one, to become a respected person, like you".

Smiling, Mukhtar nodded his head in agreement.

SHAKHANOV.   They say that once Auezov, having seated Sayakbai Karalayev in his car, took him to Alma-ata, to a specially arranged meeting with students of the Kazakh State University.

"Just look and listen to the last of these Kirghizian and Kazakh Mohicans" said Auezov to the students - presenting Sayakbai Karalayev, the great Manas specialist, and reciter.

Few people know that in the last years of his life the writer often visited his Issik-Kul country house, where he had collected material for a great epic novel. In it appeared Manas, Sayakbai, and strong-man Boltirik. How can one not complain of fate, when it threw a lasso round his dream, and forged fetters for it? That novel, so long dreamed of, was never to be written ...

When I was the chief-editor of the Journal "Dzhalin" the adopted son of Louis Aragon, Jean Rist, visited us. We roamed in picturesque places near Alma-ata for a long time. He clealry took a fancy to them as we chattered away. Jean, more than once, said how Louis Aragon, to his last days, considered you the bright light of the twentieth century: always remembering you with great respect. Your loyal readers, however, remain your final testament. Following the death of Louis Aragon, you wrote a remarkable article about him, and specially went to Paris, in order to bow your head in respect before his grave. It is really only thanks to your efforts, and your authority, that during the days of totalitarian authority, you succeeded in publishing Auezov's story "Wild Times" in "The New World". Strangely, it was considered thoroughly depraved, which is why you let the people themselves judge its worth. An action bringing you even greater love and respect generally.

Dear Chingiz, there are but a few today who live and thrive, having reached success in their lives, mindful of those to whom they are obliged for this success. I am glad to say such arrogance is alien to you.

I like to remember your words: "Every time I travel to other lands I always have two treasures with me: "Manas" and Mukhtar Auezov's work. When people ask: "What are you, Kazakh or Kirghiz?" I mention those two national literary achievements. "They, both of them. Are symbols of my people". A revelation, to my way of thinking, which provides the best proof of what I have already said.

AITMATOV. I believe we should return good for good. In reality, I do cannot repay a hundredth part of that which l have to from my people.

SHAKHANOV. Stepping on the sacred ground of Kirghizia as an ambassador, from the Kazakhstan Republic, I, curiously, felt bitter regret ...

AITMATOV. What did you regret?"

SHAKHANOV. The fact I had never succeeded in meeting with your Sayakbai Karalayev. Many a time I enjoyed his recitation of "Manas" in the documentary films of T. Okeyev, B. Shamshiyev, and M. Ubukeyev. Hearing how, in wonderful accord with the flow of events, his voice changed its tones, how accurately his intonation corresponded with passing action, following each movement. I experienced, at times, such a powerful stirring, it brought tears to my eyes. With a trembling soul, therefore, I visited the grave of this great "Manas" reciter: along with Mendi, the wife of my poet friend Zholon Mamitov, who quit this life way before his time. Additionally, I was with his children Aigerim and Azamat. Saying a short prayer, I laid a bouquet of flowers on his gravestone, in respectful memory of this great artist of the word.

What remains in your memory of this phenomena of the tewntith century?

AITMATOV. I remember that long ago I met Karalayev by chance in one of the offices of the Chu Region. News about his arrival flew round quickly. Soon from distant farms and pastures, coming down to the foothills, some in cars, some on tractors, a crowd of people began to form. Those who dreamed of hearing a professional "Manas" reciter gathered in such numbers, the Kolkhoz Club-house could only hold half of them, and the others squatted around outside. Seeing this, Karalayev decided to recite "Manas" in the open air, among the crowds.

Sayakbai found a place on the steps into the Club, while his numerous listeners just crossed their legs, or squatted on the ground. Some sat on the roofs of cars, others remained in their seats on their steeds. Young boys climbed trees, and perched on branches. All held their breath, and attended quietly to the "Manas" reciter.

At that same time, clouds began to gather above the nearby crags. Suddenly, as if turned on by a magic hand, down came the pouring rain-storm. However, as if competing with the rain, the Manas reciter carried on with his performance. Not wanting to get soaked, because I had put on my new suit specially to meet Karalayev, I went to one side, and took shelter under the eaves of the Club-house. Amazingly, as I looked around, none but I had moved. I felt rather awkward, and returned to my place. The rain continued, yet not one person moved - they sat and listened till the "Manas" reciter had finished his act.

Before this, another interesting occurrence had taken place, which I remember all my life. It was in 1959, when I finished my studies in Moscow, and returned to my native land. One day a Party School invited to their meeting several famous Kirghizian "Manas" reciters and elders: among them Sayakbai Karalayev and Karamoldo Orozov. Amid the audience were not only Kirghizians, but Russians too, and Germans and representatives of other countries. By the will of Fate, I also went. I recall waiting for Sayakbai's turn to recite.

"How old were you when you first began to recite "Manas"? Who was your first teacher?" Questions came flying from everywhere.

"Once, many years ago, when I was a boy, feeding the sheep, I dozed off and began to dream under a shady tree!" So Karalayev began his tale. "At about five o'clock in the afternoon, the loud beating of horse-hooves awoke me. I opened my eyes and saw a handsome horse with a grown-up rider in the saddle, carrying a spear in one hand - with its tip gleaming in the sunlight. The steed's eyes were flashing like lightning, and from its nostrils poured gusts of steam. Having halted his mount right beside me, the rider unhurriedly dismounted:

"Hey, laddie, what are you doing here?" he asked me.

"Well, I'll tell you what - I fell asleep for a little while! ..."

"Great good luck has come to you! From this day you will start to recite "Manas", and will win great fame. Now, then, open your mouth!" I had barely done so, when the stranger let out a stream of urine into it. White foam, as it were, full of tiny pearls filling my mouth and almost choking me ... I had hardly come to my senses, when the rider disappeared, just as if he had never been there. Most likely it was the prophet of good luck, Kidir. Whoever it was, from that day I began to recite the epic poem "Manas" ...

Karalayev told his story, and I translated it, although when I came to the piquant place about making water, I didn't know what to do. I could not translate it literally, because there were women in the audience, and some men of other nationalities - who might not know about Kidir, the prophet, and his "water of life".

Hesitating, I finally translated that part of the story by saying: "The stranger then spit into my mouth". An innocent translation still causing great animation in the hall. Nevertheless, time has passed by, and not just a few years. But, in all of these seasons I have never told a single person more about this episode. It was only recently, in Belgium, in one of my meetings, I spoke about this event a little ...

"Why did you remain silent about it, up till now? It is a remarkable story, and these are occasions for story-telling" said one of the listeners, clearly interested.

SHAKHANOV. In the folk-lore of various peoples there are many wonderful epics, lyrical tales, and historical legends. One must say, however, that not one of them comes anywhere near the colossal scope of the epic "Manas". If you put the "Iliad" and "Odysseus" together, their scale is twenty times less than "Manas". The pride of the Indian people - their "*Mahabharata* " is about two-and-a-half times shorter than the Kirghizian epic "Manas".

In olden days, great Kirghizian story-tellers, not knowing the art of writing, would tell their story chapter by chapter, over a period of six months - and still not be finished! It is simply a wonder, how much a man, when he wills, can hold in human memory, and then repeat the material!

History, one regrets to say, has not preserved the names of all those great ancient reciters of "Manas". Maybe, because the epic was seen as an unshakeable tradition, and each of the reciters counting it as his sacred duty to deliver its entirety, passing these verses on from lips to ears: from generation to generation, as a spiritual testament.

Strikingly, the last century saw more than forty of the best "Manaschi"-named epic-reciters, who knew this glorious text by heart. The most gifted of them being Sagimbai Orazbakov. He died, sadly, in 1930, when he was sixty three years old. Thankfully, those who value oral folk traditions succeeded in writing down one hundred and eighty thousand lines of the epic, as he recited it, making several good thick volumes!

In those past days there were neither magnetophones, nor tape-recorders, and one had to write it all by hand (completely swallowed up in the episodes of this great epic), as the professional reciter chanted them. What pains these reciters took with their task! Just imagine, to yourself, some fiery steed, flying over the steppeland, stopping now and again to get his breath back: following which, he swiftly returns to the beloved excitement of the chase!

They say that Sagimbai, at times, grew full of fury. That he was quite exhausted from the steaming vexations of his performance.

Begging the question, no doubt, how can we repay our debt, our gratitude? And our obligation to such special sons of the Kirghiz folk as Balik, Keldibek, Togolok Moldo, Moldobasan, Dzhusip Mamai and Seiden? To all of those who preserved for us this time-woven cultural thread? For example, Togolok Moldo (1860-1942) not only recited the epic, but wrote it all down on paper! Reminding some, he earned the epithet Moldo for his early learning, even though by birth, he was called Bayimbet. Incidentally, due to his short stature, the villagers named him Togolok, before he became a famous reciter.

Memorably, a young woman once came to me at my work-place. She was called Bermet Zhusupzhanova. Visiting me, from the Kurtke Aktalinsk region, in the Narinsk province of Kirghizia, to give me a copy of Togolok Moldo's manuscript. Written by that wise man in Arabic. Taking this priceless edition of our epic in my hands, I let my eyes run over the manuscript made by the old reciter.

"Why didn't you give this manuscript to the National Academy of Sciences?" I asked the woman, surprised.

"In their time Chokan Valikhanov and Mukhtar Auezov did much for the development of the scientific side of "Manas" studies, and made priceless contributions to the treasures therein" she replied, then adding: "Take this gift as an expression of my great respect for all those, for whom our "Manas" has become a part of their lives, and also for you personally. What you do with this manuscript is your own affair. I have passed it into trustworthy hands, and in so doing have fulfilled my duty".

Now, I am preparing to hand over that wonderful work to the Academy of Sciences of the Kirghizian Republic.

AITMATOV. I think what you have just said is evidence of the trust placed you have amid Kirghizian folk. Even though, I regret to say till this day a complete copy of "Manas", as written down by the reciters, has not been gathered together.

SHAKHANOV. We have already spoken of this, and how Sayakbai Karalayev was the most distinguished reciter of his times. Another remarkable man of culture, whom our President, Askar Akayev, named "a real Kirghizian Michaelangelo", and whom we know as Turgunbai Sadikov, equally earned solid social standing in these matters. Not so long ago, in the name of our Kazakh President, Nursultan Nazarbayev, I awarded him with the Order of Honour "Parasat".

As an aside, Turgunbai himself shared his reminiscences with me, about how they made a sculptured statue of Sayakbai:

"In the seventies, having decided to erect a sculptural ensemble in honour of "Manas", with his figure in the centre, and the reciters of the epic on both sides, I met Sayakbai Karalayev. Wishing to render his figure in marble, I spoke to him for some time, both in his home and in his garden, about this project. Time passed, and I could not get the impression I needed for this statue - to show his real self, the secret spark of his song. I almost lapsed into despair. A simple statue of him would have been of little use.

"Sayakbai, let me hear you recite a passage from "Manas!" I asked him, when I could stand the strain no longer.

A wonder then occurred! He began his recital, and immediately he started to change before my eyes. Of this quiet and humble old man, not a single trace remained. The deeper he went into the legend, the more sparks gleamed in his eyes, his shoulders shook and his hands flew like wings as he waved them in the sky ...

Reciting the episode of Manas' duel with Kongurbai, he grew so disturbed, that he seemed to raise a storm around himself. A tempest which at any moment might blow me down! Holding my breath, I gazed at the old reciter, who had lost all contact with the present world, and dived ever deeper into the past, into the image of old Bakai in the epic, or else Sirghak and Almambet, or maybe Shuak, as tears of inspiration shone within his eyes.

This was just what I needed. Taking the moment in hand, I quickly made a sketch of him.

That sculptured statue of Sayakbai showed the reciter at the height of his emotional art: with his face turned towards the sun, and his arms stretched towards the steppeland of Kirghizia. It was erected in Bishkek, in front of the State Philharmonic Theatre, named after Toktogul.

Dear Chingiz, the Kazakhs and the Kirghizes can boast of not a few great men. One of them was a giant of oral tradition, Zhambyl Zhabayev. He was widely known among Kirghizians and Kazakhs. Undoubtedly reaching the heights of fame during the last nine years of his life. All prompting the title of a modern day Homer.

AITMATOV.   I agree, Zhambyl was a rarity, not only in everyday life, but even in the epicentre of cultural life.

SHAKHANOV.   You are right. I will tell you of another interesting occurrence. In 1938 we celebrated the seven hindred and fiftieth anniversary of the Georgian poet Shota Rustaveli, and his "Knight in the panther's skin". A number of Kirghizians and Kazakhs took part in the festival - all men of literature, and of the spoken word, with Zhambyl at their head. Now see, during this visit the sharp eye of ninety year old Zhambyl saw one young Georgian beauty, slim and slender as a reed, with burning eyes, and arched brows, and she conquered the poet-singer: quite inflaming his heart ...

AJTMATOV.   Good man!

SHAKHANOV.   In memory of that story, I wrote the following poem;

Though here with years his soul did not spend all its flame,
Though there did the frantic squall of Beauty not fade –
Invited as guest to Georgia, what wonders there came!
The hundred-year-old Zhambil fell in love with a maid!
Here's a knight of our day, an old man with aging not full,
By no hurricanes bound, nor by thunder of rumbling years.
The power of Beauty is boundless, they said to Zhambyl,
With envy, or joy? Of a Russian poet one hears?
Yes, we have old people, who are not the victims of Time.
The years mean nought, when you straddle your steed in a dream.
I see, young man, you no more understand Beauty's line!
That means your soul's grown tired - you've grown old, I deem!
Are there tracks on earth which have no place in the sun?
Are there any who could not last out a century alive?
Are there women who're old when they've thirty become?
Are there bold riders who're old when just thirty-five?
Be glad, then, if Beauty your feelings have now set free.
But how old you are - we'll let the whole land decide.
Old age means the dying of fire, but the young, you see –
Those with servile souls - are a danger which spreads far and wide.
An old man is glad if his eyes can drink in new days
From the spring of Beauty, so of the years don't complain.
Don't try to be sly, for your age even children can say.
They know what years are - like mountains they soar away.
Not with them you'll measure your age - do not try in vain!

AITMATOV.   Without a doubt, Zhambyl was one of those few wise old men who was able to grow old gracefully. That is a rare talent, and a great art - to preserve the spirit of youth. Of course this romantic episode must be taken mythically, with a legendary key - here imagination played a large part. In that mere improvisation is also included.

It is no secret the word "wise" was applied for their own ends by communist propagandists. Particularly in recent totalitarian times, when trying to influence the best popular talents and minds. In the same way one might relate oneself to Zhambyl. Knowing of his illiteracy, Party secretaries got especially close to him, and then suggested themes for future works, chosen in response to the advice of art specialists in the civil service. Was this not so?

SHAKHANOV.   Possibly ... Although to this day various stories of dubious legitimacy are doing the rounds. Some speak of the absence of any really great poetry in his texts, others are of the opinion his position in literature has been too puffed up. To be fair, nearly all the "Wise Men" of those days competed with one another in praising Lenin and Stalin. Such were the times. Yes, and old people, without hesitation, and young ones too, adored their leaders. If we blame someone for specific acts from those days, judging by standards of our contemporary age, we make a great mistake, and do them a great injustice.

AITMATOV.   Your words are true, my friend.

SHAKHANOV.   Over the course of many years, Zhambyl was not only a close friend to the most talented and artistic men, singers, Improv dramaturges and reciters, becoming their professional brother, he personally brought delight to people. Undoubtedly, this contested, great talent often shows obstinacy of character, which caused some suffering. But our two peoples, in hard times, always helped each other out.

AITMATOV.   As an example of this, you will remember how a famous Kirghizian wise man, Toktogul, escaping from his Siberian exile, did not return to his people. Going, instead, to his friend Zhambyl.

SHAKHANOV.   A clear affirmation of this truth. By the way, Zhambyl more than once recited "Manas" all day long. Did you hear about his competition with the famous reciter Muratali? In that duel, Zhambyl excellently performed thirteen Kirghizian folk legends, while

Muratali enacted fifteen Kazakh ones. Until today, elderly people speak of this great event with admiration.

At one time, Masimkhan Beisebayev worked as President of the Council of Ministers in Kazakhstan. I have just remembered one of his absorbing tales about Zhambyl, which raised a great deal of comment.

"When I was First Secretary of the Almati Regional Party, Zhambyl was already quite famous, and praises for him rang everywhere. I jokingly added that even Stalin honoured him, along with the whole Soviet Union. However, once I had heard Zhambyl was approaching his hundredth anniversary, and was intending to get married again, I was astonished. Indeed, he had already chosen a bride for himself, and named the wedding day. It seems she, in turn, had agreed to this. Thus, the First Secretary of the Central Committee of the Kazakhstan Communist Party, Zhumabai Shayakhmetov, went into a panic, and called me to his cabinet. Standing with his hands behind his back, he strode nervously from one side of the room to the other. The situation was clearly an unusual one. Firstly, this unexpected whim of the highly respected wise old man, whose name was the pride and glory of the Republic, was bewildering, while secondly, it openly contradicted the Communist moral code of those totalitarian days.

"We must see nobody knows of this disgraceful behaviour!" said Zhumabai Shayakmetov. "We must cut all of this away as soon as possible!" Say, has the woman some responsible relation or other?"

"They say she has a son, who works on the Kolkhoz!"

"Then get in touch with the Chairman of the Kolkhoz, and tell him about it. Let her son persuade his mother to break off this ridiculous wedding. Only make sure Zhambyl does not suspect anything or anyone, especially her son. What kind of mad devil would he be if he didn't take steps to save his own mother from shame? I'll tell you what - if he doesn't fulfill my instructions, you can say goodbye to your position" With that, he banged his fist on his desk.

I quickly fulfilled the task for which he made me responsible. After going through a series of improbable scenarios, the woman who was to have wed Zhambyl changed her mind. We hastened with this glad news to inform Shayakhmetov, and then we all paid Zhambyl a visit, and a quite unexpected one at that.

"Peace be with you, Zhambyl, our wise friend" we all echoed, when Shayakhmetov had greeted him. Zhambyl was lying on his bed, with his face to the wall, giving answer only with a wave of his hand. Oddly, his daughter-in-law came in, pulled out the night-pot from under his bed (in front of us) and took it outside. All generating a natural pause, allowing Zhambyl to slowly turn over, and say:

"Hey, you women, wearing the trousers!"

Sneering at us angrily and added:

"Do you think it was from some mad passion that I wanted to get married again? Our folk have a proverb: "It is a great misfortune to lose your horse half-way on your journey!" Since my last wife died, I have been completely in the hands of my daughter-in-law. You saw how shamelessly she came in and took the night-pot from under my bed in front of your very noses! If I had another wife, things here would be easier for me, don't you see? Can't you understand me? How long have you been at the head of things here in Kazakhstan, but have as little a brain as a bird!" Thus, both angry and offended, he turned again to face the wall.

AITMATOV.   Not in vain they pronounce: "Paint wears off, but the wood remains!" It simply is remarkable, but in Zhambyl, skylarking and wisdom were closely combined. On the whole, close relationships existed between Suyunbai and Katagan, Zhambyl and Toktogul. Togolok Moldo and Umbetali, Keken and Alimkul endured, keeping a genuine unity between the peoples of Kirghizia and Kazakhstan. As for Zhambyl and Shabdan, they remained great friends to the end of their days. But that is another story ...

SHAKHANOV.   Yes, the warrior Batir Shabdan, an aristocrat as I recall, attained a high rank in the Russian Army. Using these privileges for the good of his own people. Even though he was an official, and belonged to the ranks of the feudal upper class, he enjoyed widespread fame, honour and influence: being considered a respectable, open-hearted, and generous fellow.

In relation to this, I remember a tale told to me by the Kirghizian President, Askar Akayev personally.

"Known for his obstinacy, Zhambyl, it appears, was offended by a hot-headed village Bey. Sitting on his horse, therefore, he turned his head towards the southern spur of Ala-Tau, and said he was going to see his Kirghizian brother Shabdan. Yet, simultaneously, it came about that Shabdan, living on the banks of the Chon-Kemin, received a summons from the governor-general Kolpakovsky, asking him to come and visit. For his part, Shabdan ordered a cart to be harnessed, and was preparing to set out, when he saw Zhambyl hitching up his horse in the yard.

"Stop a moment, or two" was Zhambly's reaction to this decree. "Well, even if Kolpakovsky had been the Tsar, he was no higher authority than Zhambyl!" Thusly, Shabdan replied: "Okay, I'll set off in a couple of days, after making sure all is as it should be! Explaining these new circumstances to his people, Shabdan then ordered a special six-section white yurta to house Zhambyl: calling his tribesmen to greet him appropriately and to listen to his words. Following which, Zhambyl recited "Manas" and "The Saranch Knight", long into the morning: enchanting Shabdan and the other listeners.

"My little foal, from his earliest years showed generosity in his nature!" said Shabdan's mother, Baali-baibishe. "At three years old, when I had still not taken my breast from his hand, he called his playmates together, and came to me to give them my breast!"

Without contradiction, one of Shabdan's photographs shows a young officer - with two medals on his chest. In another one, much later, he appears as an elderly man, with a single medal only. The reason for this is hidden in another story, which runs like this:

Once, when Shabdan was at home, a poor beggar appeared at his door. Shabdan invited him inside, asking him about local news. It seemed the beggar was an orphan from early childhood, and all his relations were lost. Explaining, of course, why he had to get a living by begging from passers-by. Hearing this, Shabdan looked around his poor dwelling for something suitable to give him, but found nothing. His earlier prosperity (when serving as an officer in the Army) had vanished. He had nothing left to live on, except one old gray Ox. So, he unfastened one of the medals he had received from the Russian

Government, which adorned his shredded uniform and put it into the beggar's hand, adding:

"Take this to the Pishpek market bazaar, and sell it there, or exchange it for some cows, and try to change your pitiful way of life for the better. Anyway, I wish you the best of fortune"

Here is another story. There was one rich man named Baiake, who had a woman farm-worker and servant called Sedep. From morning till night, she worked about the house with no rest, and no amusement. She was squint-eyed, and she stuttered and lisped. She had no relations whatsoever, nobody, and nothing dear to her, not even a dog. All she had was a small pitiful tent, made of branches and two or three poles - standing like an Indian wigwam.

"Why does nobody kill me, and let the earth take me?" she cried, and with all her heart, cursing her unhappy fate...

Yet, time waits for no man and Baiake needed to leave his autumn pasture for the winter one. Meaning Sedep was left alone. Unsurprisingly, she could not sleep at night, being shaken with fear by wolves howling outside her tent. The next day, on leaving her modest dwelling, Sedep saw Shabdan and Baiake on their horses, while a small group of riders trotted behind them. She was so delighted that she shouted out:

"Shabdan, my friend, come in and taste a glass of maksim!"*

Shabdan straightway turned his horse towards her humble home, refusing to acknowledge the fuss and displeasure of officials and regional chiefs in his group...

Having poured out some maksim in an old chipped glass, she held it out to him but, still seated on his steed, he stretched out his hand and covered the drink, saying mournfully:

"Eh, wretched one, take away your poor brew: this is not fit for a knight!" Slowly, he shook his head.

"According to our custom, nothing can be better than food".

"All right" Shabdan responded and, stretching down his hand, took the glass and drained it. "M-m, m-m, how tasty! You were right, by the way. It quenched my thirst nicely!"

---

* Maksim - Kirghizian national drink, make from millet-seed.

Having praised her drink, he promised on the morrow he would send some young horsemen from the village to take her tent down, and move her to join the others in the winter pasture.

"Be patient a little longer, and all will be well!"

Wending their way, the riders withdrew. However, after a few moment Shabdan angrily turned to Baiake and exploded:

"Baiake, what is your power worth if it cannot assist one poor, unfortunate, woman?"

Shortly afterwards, Sedep was re-settled. Shabdan also ordered his men to construct a small four-sided tent for her, besides providing six sheep and a mare to help Sedep out of her misery.

Yet another story comes to my mind:

On one occasion, a Russian General, Skobelev, arrested an Alai Queen, Kurmandzhan for taking a stand against the Tsar's colonial policy.

"Where are your children?" enquired the General. However, the valorous woman replied scornfully and mockingly: "I see a tree, but where do its branches hide?" Not being able to break down the Queen's stubbornness, the enraged General set thirty guards to keep watch over her every movement: not letting her out of their sight.

It goes without saying, Shabdan stood up for her straightway:

"If Queen Kurmandzhan disappears somewhere, you can shoot me instead!"

So, taking the part of the arrested Queen, he won her release.

In 1909-1911, Shabdan opened a Mussulman school named "Shadmania". Therein, children were taught to read and write, while Kirghizian, Kazakh, and Uzbekistan youngsters, along with Russian ones, got a good grounding in knowledge. Later, he even found them places in the gymnasia of Verny, and other educational institutions.

Having finally reached a venerable old age, the knight who had been made wise by life experience, gave this testament to his children:

"I am the last of the Manaps. I hope you will not gape at such a title. The riches, the glory it brings, are transient things. Believe me, there is nothing better than cultivating your soil, growing your grain, and living by honest labour".

AITMATOV. History, as a rule, confirms documented facts. Although, in the everyday life of our peoples, facts often take on a legendary form. On these data, however, are unlocked the relations and attitudes of our contemporaries and successors become clear. Hence, legends and traditions trickle down to us, expressing a reality, as well as our folkish assessment of events. Here is another illustration from a legend about Shabdan. Old people remember 1912, in Shabdan's native parts, as a great feast arranged in memory of this famous warrior. Thusly, a huge crowd of guests came from the southern and northern spurs of Ala-Tau. The best representatives of the Kazakh and Kirghizian peoples flowing into the village. Enshrouding the entire area in clouds of dust raised by hundreds of riders on their horses.

Zhambyl, who had deeply respected Shabdan when alive, came to the feast with his two brothers, Kenen and Umbetali. Everyone celebrating, until the feast closed with a noisy supper and a singing contest. From the crowd emerged one reciter from each of the peoples, each showing his mastery in the competition. All to the accompaniment of fat Beys, and boastful Manaps swallowing down sausages of horsemeat, and juicy entrails of sheep, washed down with fragrant mare's milk. Then the Kazakh singer, Umbetali Karibayev, took his hand-worn dombra* and started to drub it with his fingers: singing songs of friendship and brotherhood between Kirghiz and Kazakhs, while praising anew the arts of Toktogul. No sooner had he mentioned this name, however, than one of the Manap lords sitting nearby showed his teeth:

"Be silent!" he bellowed at Umbetali, while to Toktogul himself, who was sitting with Zhambyl, he stated:

"Hey, you shameless deserter, get out of this yurta" - intending to deliberately shame the great reciter, since he had only just escaped from exile in far Siberia.

But here, they say, Zhambyl grew furious, and that was no joke:

"Listen, my dear fellow", he pulled him up at once, "Shabdan was not only the son of Kirghizian folk, but of the Kazakhs as well - to whom he brought no few blessings. Alongside us, Toktogul, sitting

---

*dornbra -a two-stringed national musical instrument

here, is equally one who serves other folk and his own. How can one be praised, but the other trampled on? Have we so many great souls amongst us? Bards and wise men, like Toktogul, neither Kazakhs nor Kirghizians give birth to more than once in a hundred years. If you say another word against him, I shall be forced to leave this memorial feast".

These righteous words of Zhambyl subdued Shabdan's successors, so they threw round his shoulders an embroidered dressing gown, bringing before him a splendid white horse to boot. To this action he replied:

"For this honour and respect I say an enormous thank-you. But I wish to hand these gifts over to Toktogul, who has returned from Siberia with nothing". This action raised him yet higher in the eyes of the surrounding tribesmen.

SHAKHANOV. Not very long before his end, having seen and tasted all which fate laid open to him, Zhambyl (early one morning) called to his bedside villagers, relations, grandsons and great-grandsons, addressing them all with a farewell speech: "My inevitable parting from you has come. I know that soon I shall travel the road from which there is no return. At night I had a dream, wherein I saw a red tiger, left to me by candidate Saribai, which abandoned my threshold and went off in the direction of Kirghiz: towards the southern slopes of Ala-Tau. Three times I called him back, but he did not return ... When I leave you, bury me in the garden I cultivated myself".

They say such dreams are seen in the last hours - not by every famous warrior or wise man, but by those chosen and set aside by fate. In the form of a beast, or some other being, appears the guardian-angel of mankind. Disguised, this angel comes in a dream and gives a sign, trying to help us with forewarnings. For instance, the guardian-angel of ringing-voices Kazibek, once appeared to him in the form of two wolves. Furthermore, to the wise man Kempirbai he appeared as a coloured duck.

The successor to Zhambyl, the writer Nagashibek Kapalbekov, told me years back that he had witnesseed how you came with your son Askar to the wise man's village, and following good signs, set your son down on the sacred spot in the garden where Zhambyl was buried, and where his dust lies at peace in the mausoleum there ...

AITMATOV.   I will tell you a story, heard in my youth, from one wise old man when Zhambyl died. The news did not reach Kirghizia at quickly. Most probably because some high government official forgot to inform the neighbouring Republics. Anyway, at a memorial feast the following week, when the majority of people gathered to pay tribute to the memory of the deceased, three Kirghizian wise men come galloping along on their sweating steeds, led by old Alimkul: neither trying to hide their sorrow nor their tears ...

"O, our dear brothers", they cried, raising their hands, "Do you think that Zhambyl belongs to the Kazakhs alone? How could you bury him in the earth without Kirghizians present? You have struck our hearts an unforeseen blow - show us his grave! In the name of the Kirghiz folk, we want to cast a few handfuls of soil on it! Then the wise old men, one after another, took the dombra in hand, and began to sing their praises of the deceased.

Local people burned with shame, understanding the justice behind such bitter reproaches. They stood with bowed heads and downcast eyes. Until, from out of the crowd, came Umbetali Karibayev with a dombra in his hand. Starting to sing, he evoked the long-standing unity between Kazakhs and Kirghizians, reminding them of Zhambyl's words: "My bones are Kazakh, my flesh is Kirghiz!" Indeed, he sang in such a spirited style, it was not possible for cracks, or splits, to separate folk. Having finished his song, the wise old man asked the assembled Kirghizians, as brothers, to forgive them. Additionally, in the name of the Kazakh people, he threw his hat at the feet of their visitors, along with his long gown and his belt. Humbly, he knelt before them with his head bowed low.

Real brothers, of course, should remain brothers in times of sorrow or joy. Therefore, these three honoured Kirghizians, seeing sincere regret and confusion among the Kazakhs, speedily dismounted and began to sing in return. They eulogized the terrible loss which both folk had suffered, as well as Kirghizian sympathy for their Kazakh brothers.

What can be at a greater than real, true, brotherhood?

Our national inclination towards epic styles, and romantic stories, are in their own way quite excellent. Indigenous legends being sweet and attractive, yet unspoiled by fancy. Among skilled native singers preserving these genres, I discovered Raikhan Shukurbekov and Midin Alibayev - while you have Bauirzhan Momishuli!

SHAKHANOV.   Who else, and what more? He is a phenomenon amid Kazakh folk I think that in the former Soviet Union one could but rarely meet with such a person: with such a tragic and yet so happy a fate! Speaking of himself, Momishuli declared: "In military life, and in the ranks of writers', I remained among the Colonels!"

Concerning Bauirzhan, it was Azilkhan Nurshaikhov who wrote a remarkable book called "Truth and Legends". Therein lies extremely interesting information about how Momishuli (having shown rare bravery and heroism in the Great Patriotic War), become a legend during his lifetime. Even being called a "Hero of the Soviet Union", three times, although he was not awarded with the title. So, aware of officialdoms double-standards, he quickly finished with the Military Academy: never rising above a colonel's rank.

One of your friends, the writer Takhaui Akhtanov, who accompanied Bauirdzhan on his last journey, pronounced over his grave: "He lived in ordinary times, in an unordinary style!" These words becoming, as it were, a winged aphorism among the folk.

Yes, Bauirzhan could not countenance strict Soviet rule, and lived according to his own nature. He was a firm, rigid, uncompromising character, who always spoke the truth and looked a man straight in the eye. All depriving him of a well-earned titles and ranks.

It is well known, how injustices plagued him, not only in times of peace, but also during the war years. However, his achievements, as a man who two hundred and seventy two times roused his troops to battle, became one of the bright pages in this Patriotic War. Can one really ignore the fact overseas Military Institutes teach Momishuli's war experiences in class?

AITMATOV.   During my studies in the Dzhambil Animal Veterinary Technical School, I read a book by A.Bek, named "Volokolamsk Highway". I already had a great sympathy towards Bauirzhan, due to his firm will and stubbornness, so didn't need to be won over.

I am always amazed that such a famous hero dwelt among us, and lived like some noble knight from previous centuries in our times.

Could I know that, having received the Lenin Award, I should get a touching telegram from Bauirzhan in Alma-ata, expressing his sincere and warm congratulations: or that we should later meet and converse together in Moscow as well as Alma-ata? Meeting him on the Arbat, in Moscow, he said to me:

"Listen, Chingiz, there are one hundred and twenty waggon-loads of gossip running around about me. In one of those waggons lies the truth. In the other hundred and nineteen all is rubbish and falsehood. Said so, I will tell you one thing that happened in reality. Once, when I went to Cuba (by personal invitation of Fidel Castro), a beautiful young girl ran up to me, and cried:

"Colonel! I have heard and read so much about you that I have been in love with you since childhood! If you wish it, I am ready to become your wife and go back with you to your native land". Not embarrassed in any way, she stood there gazing at me.

"Young lady", I answered, looking into her eyes, "we Kazakhs have a saying - when young, everybody looks lovely, so where do men get ugly wives from?' You don't know my character, but if you did, you would not make such a sublime offer".

If I had married such a girl, who made a proposal herself, and brought her back home, then there would not be merely one hundred and twenty waggons of gossip going round, but two hundred or more!" We both laughed very heartily over that, I must say.

SHAKHANOV.   I remember the visit Momishuli paid to Shimkent. At the time, I worked as a correspondent on the Republic newspaper "Lenin's Hour" in the southern district of our city. I was twenty two or twenty three years old, dashing after every bit of news: thereafter bombarding the journal with my articles. One day, the editor was phoned by a writer you know, Sherkhan Murtaza. Thanks to an excellent translation he had made in the Kazakh language of one of your works: you seemed to speak Kazakh well... He told the editor:

"Bauirzhan is travelling to rest in the health-resort of Sari-Agash. Tomorrow morning he will arrive in Shimkent by train. Inform the local governor, so that he is met by someone - as he should be. Also, you should go in person to meet him ... at once, I contacted the secretary of the District Party Committee, Suleiman Zadin, and told him news about Momishuli's visit. For a while he was silent, then he exclaimed:

"Mukhtar, listen", he paused and sighed deeply, "Last year our Knight reprimanded me in front of other people, and offended me. Please don't ask this of me as it would not be a worthwhile meeting. Say I am absent on important business. Call the School Director, Sipatev, under whom Bauirzhan once studied, and let him go to meet him - and take his Pioneers, with their flowers to greet him. I will leave it with you".

Now, it was my turn to tremble! I had heard a great deal about the sharp nature of the old warrior, and still needed to go and meet him: expecting little pity along the way! He would attack anybody, if so inclined, irrespective of rank or position. He even threatened Aleksander Bek, the famous writer, saying he would cut his fingers off, if he found the least falsehood in his book "Volokolamsk Highway"- giving the latter real reasons to be scared.

I myself was a witness to similar scenarios, when, on the approaching Day of Victory, one journalist, having been ordered to interview Momishuli, begged for pity: "Better send me to the zoo, to stroke a hungry lion - than send me to Bauirzhan!"

There was another occurrence, which is often gossiped about by the general populace. In those days writers lived little better than others, as you know. Even a moderately good writer, having worked a year or so to make a book for publication, might only receive a car as an honorarium. Government officials placed their hopes on the fact most writers were unpractical by nature, and would resell this car cheaply, when they (having resprayed it), needed some extra money.

Well, one summer these profiteers began buzzing around again. All provoking one writer to play a trick on these "big business men", by confidentially whispering to them he had heard of Bauirhan's intention to sell his "wheelbarrow". Go and try to get in contact with him. If agreeable, he may sell his car for next to nothing - he's a wonderfully generous fellow!" A story giving them the hope of a significant financial kill. Practically floating, therefore, they went straight to Momishuli's house.

By the time they arrived, he had just finished drinking his morning cup of tea, thrown his dressing-gown over his shoulders, and was reading a newspaper. Indeed, not expecting the door-bell to sound, he nonetheless opened it and let in his unknowns guests. Looking at them suspiciously, he still kept up Kazakh custom.

"Hey, wife, put the kettle on" he cried, running toward the door of the kitchen. Rather confused, the two shuffled from one foot to the other, then, proceeding forward, began to speak about the purpose of their visit. Bauirzhanm however, cut them short:

"Wait a moment" he said, waving his hand, "according to Kazakh customs, guests must first taste the food prepared for them, speaking afterwards about their business. To my recollection, you have not yet eaten!"

Thus, they all sat at table and drank a cup of tea together, while his wife brought in some tasty vermicelli. Having eaten, they all arose, washed their hands in a bowl and settled down to business.

"Let's hear what you came for" said Bauirzhan, calmly placing a cigarette between his lips.

One of the guests took it upon himself to speak, and began to explain;

"We have heard you wish to sell your car. They say you do not use it any longer. We could buy it from you ...

Momishuli's noble nature was quite foreign to trading, or to bargaining. Hardly ever had he felt at ease with such lowly things. Jumping up quickly, he took a pistol from the table drawer.

"Stand!" he roared at the two young traders. They jumped up immediately, but could barely stand on their feet for fright. "Lie down here!" he commanded them sternly. The muzzle of the pistol brazenly pointed at them. Full of fear, they did as he ordered. In a fury still, he repeated: "Stand", causing them to jump up again, scared out of their wits. This went on some thirty or forty times, till, at last, they could barely move - laying trembling on the floor, covered in sweat.

"Now walk away" he cried, "I would sooner burn my machine than sell it to such scoundrels as you!"

Many such stories I heard about Bauirzhan, and truly, I too was very nervous about meeting him at the station, with only Pioneers as my guardsmen, and young ones at that.

At that time, towards the south, there lived a wise man called Narbai: a gentleman of quarrelsome and prickly mind. More than once he had boastfully appeared before me, saying Bauirzhan was a close relation of his, almost a blood-brother, who until that day had done little more than annoy him.

Not seeing a better way out, I phoned Narbai.

"Hello - you know Bauirzhan Momishuli, I believe?" I said by way of introduction, and we exchanged greetings:

"What, simpleton? How could I not know him, he is my blood-brother".

"Excellent!" I replied, cheerfully. "Tomorrow morning Momishuli will arrive by express train from Moscow, in Alma-Ata. Let us go to meet him together. I could call for you by car, agreed?" He agreed … I laid down the receiver, and gave a sigh of relief. Apparently the threat I feared was now at an end. Firstly, I knew that Momishuli showed great respect for elderly people, and secondly, it was very likely that he and Narbai were indeed of the same tribe. Only his account of Momishuli's unquestioning submission to his wishes aroused doubts in my mind.

Be that as it may, the next morning I picked Narbai up by car, and we travelled together to the station. Three Pioneers were already there with flowers in hand. Beside them, the Headmaster of their school, Zhumagul Sarsenov stood proud. On schedule, the Moscow express slid into the station. Upon stopping, Momishuli climbed down the steps from the carriage in holiday mood. Two soldiers bringing a pair of huge suit-cases behind him.

According to custom, the eldest should be the first to welcome him, so up went Narbai. It seemed that they were, indeed, well acquainted. Afterwards, Bauirzhan was welcomed by Sarsenov, who prodded the three young Pioneers forward with their flowers. I then made a respectful bow, and went forward to pick up the suit-cases.

Bauirzhan, smiling, kissed the Pioneers, and hugged them when they presented their flowers to him. Following this, he moved towards the car, compelling Narbai to conversationally ask: "Bauirzhan, why didn't bring our daughter-in-law with you?" The old warrior pretended not to hear, so Narbai repeated the question, still getting no answer. As we got near the car, Narbai, at his heels, like a worn-out record repeated the question. Instantly, Momishuli stopped, his eyebrows raised, his whiskers too:

"What do you want to see my daughter-in-law for old timer? He hissed through his teeth. Narbai trembled, and went white:

"No, nothing, I simply ... I mean relatives ought to meet more often!"

I was also a bit scared, thinking there might be a quarrel, or some sudden scandal. Fortunately, we speedily arrived at the hotel "Sunrise". We had already booked a room for him, so I merely had to show his passport to the girl on duty, in order for her to fill in the documents. Bauirzhan gave me his passport. I should say the passport surprised the girl as well as myself. It was tattered and torn: scarcely holding itself together. Where the photo should have been there was just a blank space.

A little while later, I glanced into the room we had reserved, while Momishuli and Narbai were having a quiet conversation together. I wanted to creep off, if I could, but there was no excuse to leave. Finally I decided to wish them goodbye, but had only just opened my mouth, when the old warrior cried:

"Hey, young lad, downstairs on the first floor there is a restaurant, isn't there?"

"Yes, there is, I can guess what you mean".

"Very well, go there and order something for us to eat. Put it on my account. The old fellow and I will come down presently".

I went to the restaurant, sat at one of the central tables, called the waitress and explained that Momishuli was coming down to dine.

"Ah, that capricious old man!" muttered the waitress, and set about her business, hurrying to the kitchen to fulfill the order.

Soon those two came down, both seeming contented and happy. In a short while Zhumagul Sarsenov joined us.

The table was set with all kinds of dishes. While dinning, Momishuli told us he had spent his holiday the previous year at Issik-Kul. Just then, a fat old man who, as I knew, worked as Director of a collective farm in the Sozak region, came to our table. Not slowing his steps, nor glancing at the others and went straight up to Narbai: taking him by the arm:

---

*aga -that's the form of addressing a person who is older and influential.

"Welcome, Narbai-aga*, I heard you had come to our farm not long ago. I regret I was absent", he went chattering on. "Come to us again, we shall wait for you!" he piped up, looking only at Narbai, and ignoring everyone else completely.

"Very well" said Narbai, nodding his head and hoping to avoid arousing anger in the old warrior, while trying to rid himself of his persistent admirer.

"Keep well" said Narbai at last, as his very persistent visitor turned towards the hotel exit.

"Eh, young rider" sharply Bauirzhan called the newcomer:

The farm Director turned, and again stepped up to the table.

"They call me Bauirzhan Momishuli. Say, what forebears of yours taught you to say farewell to one person at table, and to ignore the others?"

"Oh, excuse me, please" said the "young rider", confused, not knowing where to put himself, "Is that really you, Bauirzhan?"

"This is the Director of one of our collective farms", said Narbai, trying to clarify the situation, but Momishuli broke in:

"First of all, he must learn to observe his own culture. Then he can start ordering people about. "March away" he commanded, threateningly bristling his whiskers.

When we had finally finished our meal, I was almost ready to pay for it myself, although I didn't have enough money to do so. With an inspiration like Solomon's, however, I decided to leave my passport, and pay for the meal afterwards. Yet, the moment I put my hand into my inner pocket Momishuli stopped me and said:

"Youngster, leave your pocket at peace and sit back. I have never visited a place where it was necessary for someone else to pay my bills when entertaining guests".

He called the waitress, and asked for the bill. Half embarrassed, and being in the presence of a famous man, she playfully concealed it: starting to blink her eyes, and wiggle her buttocks before mentioning the amount to be paid. Unimpressed, Bauirzhan felt inside his pocket, took out the needed sum, and sternly pronounced:

"I am no cavalier of yours, and there's no need to wiggle-waggle before me, so off you go now" he commanded the confused waitress.

AITMATOV. Of course, ignoring the uneven traits in his character, and the complexity of his nature, Momishuli was, without a doubt, the great favourite of the vast majority of the people, He always honoured the aged, and respected the young.

SHAKHANOV. Sooner or later truth will triumph. Nearly a century after the ending of the Great Patriotic War, thanks to the manifold appeals of Nursultan Nazarbayev, Moscow at last awarded Bauirzhan the title "Hero of the Soviet Union". A happy event all Kazakhs understood as a popular festival day! Clearly, in answer to my request, one famous Kazakh artist painted a picture showing Momishuli astride a white horse, with a spear in his hand. Beneath the picture were a few lines of verse which I, myself, composed. This humble present I gifted to Oralzhan Masatbayev, hoping he would hand it on to the son and daughter-in-law of the warrior Bakhitzhan and Zeinep, who take care of Momishuli's grave. Overall, I wanted to express my great respect for his irrepressible character.

AITMATOV. Do you remember, when we travelled to Talas valley for the thousandth Anniversary of the Jubilee of "Manas", our route took us through the town of Zhambyl? There we saw enormous posters, nearly two storeys high, with beautifully inscribed words by Momishuli- hung through the instigation of the leader of this region, Omirbek Baigeldi. I don't know why those posters seemed to stand out more than all the others we had seen? Perhaps, it was their brilliance.

SHAKHANOV. Once in the Kazakh Embassy in Bishkek, there came a young American scientist Dan Prior. We started up an interesting and pleasant conversation, during which he commented:

"This year is the one hundred and fourtieth anniversary of the book "The Festival of Khan Koketei" from the epic poem "Manas", written down by your great scholar Chokan Ualikanov, at the time of his visit to Kirghizia. Without a doubt, that event is of great significance. How are you going to set about celebrating it?

I honestly confess this question confused me. Here comes an American, living beyond the seas, attracted by the scientific researches of Chokan. Moreover, by pondering on his admiration for Chokan (who drew his own sketches to illustrate his point), he seemed to be walking along the shores of Issik-Kul in Chokan's tracks. He even mounted the hill known by the name of Manas, and photographed the Tyup ravine.

AITMATOV. As a young man, Chokan fulfilled a task worthy of a hero. Although "Manas" is considered the common heritage of all Turkish-speaking tribes, the real composers of this legend were Kirghizians. Chokan was the first to make this known in Europe. At that period, it was as good as the discovery of a new pyramid - don't you think?

SHAKHANOV. Truly I do! Not everyone knows that during his travels to Issik-Kul, Chokan visited the Kirghizian singer, up in the mountains, on a slope where people gathered to listen to his recitals. It was near the Tyup ravine, where he wrote on one page of his diary these words: "Today, I met a Kirghizian songster. From his own lips I wrote down one episode of "Manas" which he named "The Funeral Feast of Koketei". Obviously, these was the first recording of words recited by the Kirghizian on paper. Presently, I am translating the epic into Russian to help facilitate scientific research in the East. After all, not knowing the languages or dialects of the locals, I am preparing a dictionary, which gives a short list expressions".

This book, The Funeral Feast of Koketei by Chokan, was translated into Russian in 1861. It was then presented to members of the Russian Imperial Geographical Society, where it was judged by Russian scientists: headed by the famous Academician P.P. Semenyov, from Tyan-Shan.

Later a renowned scientist, N.I. Veselovsky recalled that meeting: "How boldly and correctly Chokan used the Russian language! Evoking through a few words the deepest of meanings, thereby achieving a brilliantly artistic and beautiful translation of the Kirghizian epic!"

A little later in 1861, that chapter of "Manas", accompanied by a comprehensive research article under the heading "Notes on Dzhungaria", came out in German: then in English and French. In this way the great epic "Manas" was brought to the attention of Europeans.

AITMATOV. No matter what you say, the short life of Chokan was full of secrets and hidden guesses. In the recollections of Dostoyevsky's wife, Anna Grigoryevna, I discovered one fact. A year after Chokan's death, F.M. Dostoyevsky, the great Russian writer, who was already a friend of Ualikhanov, had an early morning dream in which he saw Chokan, strolling along the banks of the Irtish, gazing lovingly at its flowing waters – seemingly even conversing with them. At that time Dostoevsky was still a bachelor - the fates apparently having turned their faces away from him. Yet, interpreting his dream of Chokan as a good sign, Dostoyevsky, on that very same day, proposed to Anna Grigoryevna: with whom he had long been in love.

They say that Dostoyevsky often recalling his dream, said he was much obliged to Chokan for acquiring such a wonderful wife.

SHAKHANOV.   Investigators write that after the death of Chokan, his friend, G.N. Potanin, who went to school with him, travelled to Kushmurun, to Chokan's father Chingiz, in order to express his condolences at the loss of his dear friend. That same Potanin, later searching through Chokan's records in Omsk and Petesburg, found some of Chokan's manuscripts, allowing him to publish his first book of scientific research.

Here another anecdote comes to mind. One ignoramus did a barbarous thing - he sawed off part of the memorial statue of Chokan Ualikhanov to serve as a grindstone for his handmill. This was in 1917. Relatedly, I'd like to quote from a ballad of mine about Chokan and his great friendship with Dostoyevsky:

> *"My dear friend Fyodor, a last wire I'm sending –*
> *My looks, and sighs.*
> *The fossilized gossip's unending,*
> *Where black and white in shades of grey unite,*
> *Confusion hides true colours from the light.*
> *And, torn to pieces by my end, folk*
> *Now bear me off to a dark, graveyard, yoke.*
>
> *So let my strength and energy, splashed out vainly*
> *Harrow my folk: to the grave, quite plainly,*
> *With common hopes before The Judge I go.*
> *There still remain those who'll bring me back, I know!*

Well, when these lines of mine you start a-reading,
The grave upon my life -juice will be feeding.. .

So large is my account with laws swift-flying,
And slippery as the ice on cliff-slopes lying.
You were the source of my first love, exciting.
To you, the last, go my spirit, and my hand-writing!
There are rivers on earth which flow from land to land,
And bear great riches, reflecting the heavens grand.
To break their freedom of will is beyond man's power,
And thousands of cunning Khans no longer flower.
Let life, capricious, resist, and shake its head,
And show off, with proud put-on manner instead:
The greatest of us still onward like streams go fleeing.
Who jokes straight out with a noble human being?
O river, so great!
Say, who can match your forces?
Within your waves all thoughts are borne off their courses.
We, mortal ones, can we then understand
Your depths? Against which waves a-foam so grand?
Bright friend! Nobody can hold you back at the border,
And only envy everywhere fashions disorder.
Your ponderings form a cradle for all the world;
You are my shield, and also my good unfurled.
How I should like it, if all Kazakhs as one people
Should love like I, with brotherly love, not feeble!

With a smile I rose,
The light in my closed fist holding,
I wished along with you to start blooming, unfolding,
But short was my path, and not too serious seeming,..
And many thoughts I borrowed from you, and dreaming.. .

The moon grows red behind that mountain Matay.
The morn grows crystal, with one single star yet higher
Although trembling, as if some Evil it now perceives.
Chokan is no more. This letter must immediately cease.

Was it not he who struck at the named century,
Or was it the century fighting with him eventually?
At the height of his might, all power to everyone giving,
At twenty-nine, he began a second time living ...
In the naive heavens there trembles a lonely star,
And from itself, in the darkness, it runs afar. ..

How the century faded away, we can't say at once –
But Dostoyevsky was then a prisoner in Omsk.
But talent by Time can't be changed in the century's story –
Just the opposite - Time's the companion of lasting glory.
So the funeral mound was witness to many a meeting,
The Altinemel mound, where deep in eternal dark
In glory Chokan lay quietly, peacefully sleeping.
So with that we finish - the last exclamation mark!
If there are no sudden actions we do not expect,
Whose burden above time comes heavily sagging,
Then sense, through the passing years grow more correct.
But take a swift glance - your understanding is lagging.
Chokan's warm spirit seemed worthy of some monument,
And Russian friends then agreed upon a memorial,
And they were able to find this in Tashkent,
The needed stone block, and soon sent sparks in an aureole.

But human pettiness, found among thieving clobber
Which hides in corners until the time comes to appear,
Then showed itself in the heart of a rough-handed robber,
Who wanted to split that stone in half, it was clear,
To chip it in halves, to make two stones for grinding
Some grain he had, not letting its owners see,
The great profit from this he'd soon be a-finding –
He thought everyone around was blind as could be!

But he had only begun his secret stone-chipping,
When up flew a splinter, and stuck itself straight in his eye,
And he fell backwards from pain which his head was gripping,

And grew and grew, and flew from the floor to the sky.
He lay there half-blinded, cursing his fate, and swearing,
His mouth full of sand, and the carpet to shreds he tore,
And conscience looked down on him, and what he was bearing,
As though he came from strange worlds and times, what's more ...
And then that spring, above the cone-shaped Matay,
There swept a crane-flock, and tighter their circle became,
So friendship ubiquitous, sacred, flew higher and higher,
And passed on the news to Petesburgh, where they came.
Tears rolled down the face of his dear brother,
And he then grieved, but thought: "It served him right!"
There is a punishment, legally paid to the other,
And there is friendship which puts all evil to flight!

AITMATOV.   *Yes, any good or evil intentions, or for that matter actions, never leave anyone without responsibility for their enterprises. You have recited a wise poem, which explains that our existence has a much deeper meaning than we imagine, and deeper still than we currently understand.*

SHAKHANOV.   *Chingiz. I remember that when the great modern musical composer Dmitri Shostakovich died, they published in the journal named "Musical Life" your memorial article in his honour.*

AITMATOV.   Yes, I first met Shostakovich in Moscow, in the offices of the Committee for Lenin and State Prizes of the USSR. Along the wide corridor, deep in conversation, moving very slowly towards me, came Shostakovich and Tvardovsky. Having caught sight of me, Tvardovsky turned to Shostakovich and said:

"Dmitri Dmitryevich - let me introduce you to Aitmatov, about whom I have so often spoken".

Shostakovich glanced at me, gave me a kindly smile, and gently pressed my outstretched hand in greeting. Since then, we have always sat together at the meetings of the Committee.

Each time, when it was his turn to speak, he always tried to put on one side works which were permeated with political ideology, and to vote for those which were artistically creative. Our opinions on those matters, and our points of view always coincided.

Once we started a serious discussion of Shakespeare:
"Shakespeare is immortal. Therefore among us live Hamlet and King Lear!" said Shostakovich, leading the discussion on to modernity: "Do you believe in the possible birth of a new Shakespeare?"

"No, another like him there will never be. Yet, a genius on such a grand scale may arise, if the conditions are right!"

"I am not sure of that!"

"But I am" he retorted, setting out to prove his point of view with conviction".

"For the appearance of a new Shakespeare in our present era, there are many grounds and possibilities. In earlier days people did not undergo such many-sided developments, particularly in the spiritual life as we do today. Sooner or later another outstanding genius will arise, and will make the world bow its head before his all-powerful artistic capabilities". Listening to him, I involuntarily agreed with what he had stated.

"Chingis", he addressed himself to me, "I have one or two requests. Firstly, as far as possible, try to step out on the road of philosophical comprehension as seen through the eyes of the heroes in your novels, and secondly, treasure every minute of your life on earth. It flies so quickly for real creatively. Resist social work and public affairs! You know, I suffer too in that same sense - no time!

Whether I can, in single combat with life's collisions, follow the advice of my friend - life itself will show!

SHAKHANOV. Yevgeny Yevtushenko speaks of his first acquaintance with Dmitri Shostakovich in this way: "In spring 1963 he phoned me at home. My wife went to answer:

"Excuse me for troubling you - we don't know each other. I am Shostakovich. Is Yevgeny Aleksandrovich at home?"

"Yes, he's working. Just a moment, I'll call him for you!"

"No, not if he's working - I shan't interfere with his creative labours. I can phone later, at any time". Shostakovich was already saying goodbye, when I took the receiver and quickly spoke to him. I then heard that he wanted to write music for some of my poems, and had called to ask permission. I well remember that call, along with the soft and slightly agitated voice he had!"

That little episode very clearly illustrated his great humanity, his surprising humility, and his love of work as a great musician.

Nowadays, one meets young people, who have succeeded in writing a few lines, and persistently hang around one's home, not thinking, of course, whether one is occupied or not. They do this in order to get a poet's opinion of their verses, or the possibility of getting a collection published. Meeting such young people, one remembers at once the bright image of Shostakovich, and his kindly, confused, smile.

AITMATOV. Once Shostakovich invited me to his flat on Gorky Street. There I also met the distinguished composer Kara Karayev. In the centre of this spacious chamber sat a quartette of musicians who played the "Fourteenth Quartette", written by Shostakovich. It was a quiet, calm piece, rousing kindly feelings and a gentle softness of soul. In himself, Dmitri Shostakovich was severe and concentrated. He sat beside me, not saying a word, but from time to time shook his head, negatively.

Karayev, on the other hand sat with gleaming eyes, excited, elevated, nodding to keep time, and drinking in the music like wine. I asked what the music was about, and Shostakovich briefly replied that it was hard to say precisely, although it was necessary to feel it, to sense it.

The musicians ceased playing, and Kara Karayev straightway exclaimed;

"That is a wonderful piece! What wonderful feelings it awakens and sustains!" Indeed, he heartily complimented Dmitri Shostakovich for his great success, and expressing appreciation, said he was simply shaken ...

The composer, in reply to these warm congratulations, only bowed his head politely, then stepped up to the musicians, and began with a stern look to make critical remarks about their renderings.

"The performance was not taken far enough, and did not attain the necessary level. Too much was played superficially, without the necessary thought and feeling!"

Karayev, feeling the rising awkwardness, stepped up to the musicians and using more restrained words, and expressing himself more softly, tried to cheer them up.

Following this, we all went back to our seats, and the quartette was again rehearsed. Watching Shostakovich, I was surprised to observe the difference between his usually delicate manner, and the agitated and severe way he behaved during a rehearsal of his musical composition. This great musician demanded an extremely high quality in the playing of his music.

In the beginning of spring that year, his wife Irina Antonovna, phoned me at home. She informed me Dmitri Shostakovich's sickness was getting serious, and asked me to help them find a curative herb, known as the "Issik-Kul root", which grew in the mountains of Kirghizia. I at once gave friends and relatives living in Talas, the necessary instructions, and they were set to find the needed herb on the mountain slopes. Less than a week later I had a collection to hand, and sent them immediately to Moscow.

A short time later, we met Shostakovich again at his summer dacha, and spent an interesting evening with him. The dacha was a two storey one, of singular construction. I stayed there with my son, Askar, and Shostakovich, for a while - knowing it would interest my lad. We even explored the simple in-house lift, taking it up and down repeatedly. However, our happy evening with childish laughter, fun, and games, led on to interesting adult discussions. As it happened, this was my last meeting with that great composer - a farewell festival, but who could have guessed it?

With hindsight, Dmitri Shostakovich, a man who could attain wonderful harmonies in life, as well as in his compositions, wrote me two letters. One of which I keep to this day among my personal archives as a valued relic. After the composer had read my novels "Farewell, Gulsari!" and "The White Steamer" (the latter written when he was in hospital in Ilizarovsk, in the Kurgan region), he expressed his delight in my work. If only these letters had continued .....

At times, loaded down with troubles, and various heavy thoughts, I remained alone, in isolation from others. I notice, however, if I hear one of Shostakovich's compositions, my heart grows warm and beats faster - in waves, after which I felt relieved again.

An untiring passion for life, and a wonderful spiritual purity and clarity - these were the fundamental elements on which the world of Shostakovich was built. He was one of the best representatives of the Russian people, possessing boundless spiritual riches, and the most unusual kindness and generosity, a readiness to help others, near and far, ever attentive to their needs. Though a man of complex character, how clear and simple was his world!

SHAKHANOV. Maybe the main worthiness of real creative work lies in its availability to the understanding of peoples from various nationalities, no matter where they may live, or what tongue they may speak.

AITMATOV. You often reminded me, by quoting your Kazakh saying, that the unity of a people lies in the friendship of individual persons. How then can I fail to remember the excellent mutual relations in our recent past, between the bright stars of our literatures? It is impossible not to be delighted by how they long to be with one another, and how they enjoy every opportunity for meeting and conversing together. Some are lean, tall, and swarthy, like Gafur Gulyam. Others, have a reserved sensitively capable of intuiting the inner world of another person, like Aibek. Also, always smiling and throwing open his arms in welcome, stands Sabit Mukanov.

Of course, living is such contradictory times, everyone has his own days of success, or of failure, or of shortcomings - even of dependence on certain conditions, or other people's actions. To cast some into the darkness of forgetfulness, or to underline the names of others, who have enjoyed and enriched the spiritual treasures of our nations would be an injury to our history, causing it to suffer unforgiveable losses. As far as friendship between peoples is concerned - that is carried on among their successors and heirs everywhere.

Many years ago I met Gafur Gulyam in the Moscow at the Writers Union.

"Chingiz, my brother, how many woes this earthquake has brought!" He cried, not holding back his tears. In that year such catastrophes had carried away many human lives, especially in the Tashkent area ... There colossal damage was done, and people remained inconsolable in their sorrow. Yes, at all times, for great peoples great sorrows wait.

SHAKHANOV. Every meeting of great peoples becomes a festival, and friendship between them then becomes legendary. The famous Uzbek Nasir Fazilov, once wrote a memoirs about Sabit Mukanov under the title "Kindness". In these memoirs this amusing event occurs:

Having come from Tashkent as a guest of Sabit Mukanov, young Aibek seated his friend in his car, and drove off to an area drowning in green grass and lovely gardens, He wanted them both to enjoy the region of Ala-Tau, and its picturesque beauties. Curiously, as they travelled past smooth reddish blocks of granite, he braked the machine, got out, went round one of the huge blocks - its surface carefully polished by nature itself - and then stood shaking his head saying "Beautiful! Wonderful!"

Sabit respectfully walked up to Aibek, and, sensing his friend's intent, gazed at the stone saying:

"I see why you like it so much"

"That's wonderful"

"I'll make you a present of it! Not from me personally, but from all the Kazakh folk. You may regard it as though you have received the traditional present of a fine horse".

So decided, this stone was given by Sabit, and accepted by Aibek in the wilds of Ala-Tau. Soon afterwards, Aibek travelled back to Tashkent, while Sabit brought a stonecutter to inscribe a permanent inscription on this stone, which said, "This smooth stone was presented to Musa Aibek by Sabit Mukanov 3. 6th. 1962".

On that day Sabit, as a man known to keep promises, returned home in an elevated mood. Happily muttering under his nose. When Aibek heard of all these things, he murmured to himself:

"I have seen a number of generous people in my life, but none can compare with Sabit!" Spontaneously adding: "He presented me with a huge boulder of red granite!" Indeed, he repeatedly recalled this unusual occasion.

AITMATOV. Yes, it is hard to forget a good thing - when humour and kindness accompany one another on life's road!

SHAKHANOV. You have no doubt heard about the wrestler Kazhimukan Munaitpasov, who contested with his opponents in famous sports, and won victorious medals?

AITMATOV. How could one fail to hear of him? That is the world famous Kazhimukan, a pupil of the well-known wrestler Ivan Poddubny?

SHAKHANOV. It would be interesting to know how many millions of sons were born to Kazakhs in this last half-century, not saying a word about today! Well, then, among them until now not one has been found who could have conquered Kazhimukan! Such a man will not soon be found again! Though I am a child of the steppe where Kazhimukan was born, and though I have heard, since childhood, many stories connected with his life-history (which would amaze you more than ever), I am not impressed to the same degree by these modern wrestling men. Moreover, contests between lightweights, small in stature, who just wriggle about on the mat leave me indifferent, I would rather listen to a competition between famous singers, such as our Uzbek brothers love to organize.

Anyway, our unforgettable Kazhimukan is a rare phenomenon. An assertion partly demonstrated by the house-museum in his village of Temirlan (towards southern Kazakhstan), which has a photograph of Kazhimukan pulling a cartload of twenty people by a cable gripped with his teeth. No mean feat, but ultimately nothing compared to stopping a moving tractor by lifting it up from behind with his two bare hands! They say, he could even let a car drive over planks placed across his chest. Innumerable seem the fantastic episodes of that mighty giant.

AITMATOV. Once I read in a journal, that Kazhimukan would have gained victor if there had been a contest with Poddubny.

SHAKHANOV. Notwithstanding the fact that in Kazhimukan's passport his place of birth was given as the Akmolinsk region - his real birthplace was located in the village of Aktobe, in the Atyrau region. Evidence of this was gathered from local wise old men, and was written down by a well-known southern Kazakh historian and composer Mukhamedzhan Rustemov.

"Hardly had Kazhimukan appeared in the world, when his father then quarreled with relatives, collected his things together, and left his native village. Knowing the stubborn, silent nature of Munaitpas, the elders sat on their steeds, and set off after him. By that time, however, the wanderer had reached Sozak. The elders halted, calling to Munaitpas:

"Come back! Don't break off the ties which bind us, and don't leave us"

"Forget the offence. Don't hold on to spite!" cried another.

Then Munaitpas stopped, turned to the elders, holding little Kazhimukan on his knees, and shouted his reply in angry tones:

"Leave us alone! If you come nearer I shall hurl this child at you, instead of a stone. I've had enough!"

It was transparent that Munaitpas had not changed his decision to leave, so the elders with a sigh of regret, said goodbye to the stubborn one:

"Well, if that's how it is, then go your own way - and may it be a good one! Allah protect you wherever you go, and keep the child safe!"

Munaitpas chose a distant road and eventually reached Akmolinsk territories. Once settled, documents located the birth of Kazhimukan in this region. Such was his interesting beginning!

As the years unfolded, Kazhimukan proved generous by nature, and sensitive as well. He especially loved reading literature. Developing, later in life, close relationships with writers like our Mukhtar Auezov, Sabit Mukanov, and Isa Baizakov. He was, so they say, very quick witted, a passionate story-teller, and a composer of verse. I have a copy of the "Memories on Kazhimukan", written about this most unusual man. Here is a small extract:

> "Kazhimukan, a giant of a man,
> Unconquered wrestler of the Kazakh plain,
> Weighed over one hundred and sixty kilogram,
> And ate at each sitting a whole roasted ram.
> He was at that same time tender of soul.
> In love till tears with poetry, they say.
> From time to time expressing himself in verse.
> And after he fought, victorious, proud and strong,
> With the champion of the world, and earned his curse,
> His countrymen made for him a festival grand,
> And praised him, since a champion he'd hurled:

"You're not alone the strongest in your own land,
But also the strongest wrestler in the world!"
"Just wait!" replied Kazhimukan, "Just wait!
There's something magical to be found in sport,
At times more exciting than the blind ways of fate,
And therefore sport needs rules of the strictest sort.
And bodily power is beautiful only as long
As it is strengthened by spiritual powers too.
Look, here is someone stronger then I in this song –
And clapping a hand on his shoulder, he led him through.
A shy and modest, curly-headed chap,
With nothing about him special at first glance...
A long and doubtful silence followed that...
This was young Mukhtar Auezov, and not by chance.
The words of Kazhimukan were prophetic then,
For thirty-six years later it occurred –
One of Japan's great champions, strongest of men,
Had read a book of Auezov's - was deeply stirred:
"What strength he shows, for when I read his book
I was conscious of my spiritual weakness, look!"

AITMATOV. Did you ever meet Kazhimukan personally?

SHAKHANOV. In the year of the Great Patriotic War, despite his old age, he went round most of the villages, reciting, singing, and playing his dombra. Any money he received he gave to an aircraft factory, which made fighting machines for the front. He received a telegram from Stalin, thanking him for his contribution to the war effort.

When I was about five years old, Kazhimukan came to our collective farm with his recitations. People didn't have a moment's rest from toil. Neither morning nor evening. So, they could hardly believe their eyes or ears on seeing the giant and hearing his folk songs. In those days, we lived in Kaskasu village – presently in the Tolebi region. Maybe because my father and that old wrestler belonged to the same clan (and thus were bonded), or maybe because of a similarity in spirit, they felt an instant empathy, like brothers. I don't know. Either way, following Kazhimukan's recital he came with a gang of exited youngsters to our home. Out of respect for such an honoured guest, my father killed our one and only goat - which supplied us with milk - and calling in our neighbours, made a small feast. Taking up half the cushions, Kazhimukan lay half-erect on them, and for a long while drank cup after cup of tea. As sweat began to flow from his brow, he wiped it off with a huge handkerchief. Later, my mother told me how I had stuck to him like a magnet, after climbing on to his shoulders and then sliding down his colossal chest on to his knees. From there, apparently, I worked my way down his shins to the floor, like a goat-kid down a cliff-side. Kazhimukan, laughing at all this, went on drinking his tea. Taking no more notice of me than if I were a fly. ... Chingiz, they say Kazhimukan once met the Kirghizian strong-man Kozhamkul - is this right?

AITMATOV. Yes, that's true. Having grown up in poverty and want, Kozhamkul, when he was mature, became the best Kirghizian wrestler. According to the word of witnesses, he was so tall that his head almost came up to the shoulders of a man sitting astride a two-humped camel. With stern shaggy eyebrows, and a beak-like curving nose, he just scared all who saw him. At the beginning of the century, in Pishpek, they organized a great sports meeting where wrestlers and strong-men met together. There the Chinese brought with them one of their own champions, a man nicknamed "The Bull". Unarguable, it was the custom to name such gigantic men bulls, and camels, and mountain rams, to encourage their aggressive spirit? In any case, the Chinese set their "Bull" in a kind of bridle, down on all fours, with a blanket over his back, leading him into the centre of the ring. There he pawed the earth, and kicked up dust with his feet, and roared thrice. Withstanding such a psychological attack, however, the broad-chested Kirghizian wrestlers (though giants themselves), got a bit confused and gave way to the furious braggart "Bull". Men who had not seen such things before also lost their heads and didn't know what to do. Yet, to hand the main prize to an outsider, especially one who had not even fought any contests, was out of the question. Hence, the Kirghizians started to call aloud their tribal names as, one by one, they formed a phalanx behind the towering Kozhamkul.

Seeing him, the Chinese "Bull" threw off his bridle and blanket, reared up, and went into the attack - with another mighty roar. Trying, with various tricks, to get Kozhamkul down. Retaliating, this stubborn and mighty Kirghizian cried wildly, "Up with you", seizing the Chinaman in a fast grip, and heaved him through the air above his head. Then, he hurled his opponent him down on the ground. The Kirghizians who had been watching apprehensively till now, raised their voices and cried: "There you are". What a hulabaloo they made when they saw the "Bull" go down!

The elders still speak excitedly of this bout between Kazhimukan and Kozhamkul. It being equally pertinent to remember Kazhimukan used to perform in the circus. He became very famous. On one of his tours, he came to the cattle market of Pishpek. All prompting people to encircle this famous athlete and look with inquisitive eyes at his mighty muscles. In a mere moment they had set up a yurta, killed a mare, and whipped up kumis to start a feast. Indeed, with open mouths they listened to the breath-taking stories of his contests with African wrestlers, along with his victory over the Japanese champion Sar-ki-ki. Getting a taste for further victorious contests, his audience decided to arrange a match between Kozhamkul and Kazhimukan. Ground rules were plucked from the ether, and they all agreed rewards for the victor following a contest of three parts, with nine bouts in each. Inspired so, they sent a rider to fetch Kozhamkul. Soon he appeared on the scene, and at once went to the eldest among the wrestlers to pay them his respects.

The news about this grand contest flew around the region, and people began to congregate. Splitting in two halves, they all waited for a series of battles - the like of which had never been seen before.

"Kazheke" said the Kirghizian strong-man, turning towards Kazhimukan, while all the people looked on, "We both are sons of two brotherly peoples, who are near and indivisible as two eyes on one face. You are to me an elder brother, and I am to you a younger one. It would not be befitting for one of us to start boasting of victory over the other, while he lies in the dust. Apart from that, you are our guest. The spirits of our forefathers, therefore, will not forgive me if I go and start wrestling against you. Let the prize be awarded to you, in any case" and so Kozhamkul conceded the reward to him.

"I was waiting myself to see what you would do! Now I know you have seen and understood much in this world. You Kirghizians can be proud of your son – a man of such delicate feelings. May you be happy in life". With that he embraced his Kirghizian brother, and saluted him warmly. Furthermore, having received his prize, he distributed it among the poor beggars and orphan children.

SHAKHANOV. What to do think - can one place Kazhimukan and your Kozhamkul on a level with the widely-known wrestling "stars" of today? You see, our strong-men were not only full of bodily strength, but had spiritual powers as well. Wonderful characters, excellent social habits and communal social actions - such as are rarely seen today anywhere.

AITMATOV. Yes, there are many such "stars" a-shining today. Many are spurred on by big-business-men. Today they can count on thousands of dollars for a single match, appearing well advertised on the stage in the light of the arc-lamps. Speaking with them one feels their superior attitude to all others, as if they are the very centre of the world, nay, of the whole universe, but you will be amazed at their spiritual poverty! Will such strong men realize where real strength lies, and pay some attention to spiritual riches, and cultural wealth?

SHAKHANOV. Wherever man is found, that problem is found too my dear Chingiz! When we spoke about Mukhtar Auezov, I remembered the name of Issik-Kul's strong-man whom they call Boltirik.

AITMATOV. I remember the first time I met Boltirik was at Auezov's funeral. He was a hefty, earthy, strong and handsome chap with sparkling eyes. All the same, I could not see why they named him the "son of Abai", for the life of me.

SHAKHANOV. Having been called up for service at the front in 1916, this strong-man was found in various Russian scraps, and by the vagary of fate, at the end, landed in the city of Semipalatinsk. Having heard about the strong-man's famous name, the successors of

Abai specially sought him out, and finally found him. They told him the following:

"When the war is over, and things quieted down, you can return to your native Issik-Kul. Meanwhile let your home be here, in Zhidebai!" They made this proposal to Boltirik, brought him to their tribesmen, and there they set up a yurta for him, and gave him some cattle. So, finding a refuge there, the wrestler soon became one of the sons of Abai. There he also married a girl by the name of Fatima, and started up a family. In those years Auezov studied in Leningrad University, and coming home on vacation, got to know Boltirik very closely. It is said Auezov himself gave him the name "Son of Abai". Certainly, their meetings grew into a deep friendship, so when Boltirik and his family returned to Issik-Kul, this close contact was maintained. We know now that Auezov even thought about writing a novel on Issik-Kul and Kirghiz people, including those he had met and admired, like Sayakbai and Boltirik.

AITMATOV. When Mukhtar Auezov passed away so suddenly, I, at once, flew to Alma-Ata. From Frunze there came a delegation with Ali Tokombayev and Suyunbai at their head. One of the delegation was Boltirik. At the funeral, he helped to carry the coffin. Nowadays, he is no longer in the land of the living.

SHAKHANOV. Chingiz, my dear fellow, what first awoke in me a great interest in Kirghizian people was your creative work. Secondly, I may name the undoubted influence of Zholon Mamitov; thanks to which I began to passionately meet with this son of "Manas". I initially got to know Zholon in Moscow, at a meeting of young writers. He had an unusually broad, open nature, but at the same time would swiftly check any lying, or two-faced people. Overall, I remained close friends with that excellent and unique Kirghizian poet until the last days of his life. I shall not likely meet such a good friend again. Every time we got together, it was simply a festival for both of us.

In 1969 Zholon and I agreed to take the higher literary course at the Moscow Gorky Institute of Literature. Back then, each Republic was allotted one place. Without any opposition, Zholon stood as the candidate for Kirghizia, since he was already living in Moscow. Every two or three days he phoned me, and hastened me on. I was then living in Shimkent, and worked at the Secretariat of the Writers' Union of the Kazakhstan Republic. There, a year before, they had recommended sending me to Moscow for advanced studies. With no further doubts, I gave up my work, collected my things, and travelled to Alma-Ata to get my air ticket for Moscow. On arrival, however, I came up against an unexpected snag. My candidature was challenged by a local editor of the Writers Union, who wished to go in my place. To boot, she was a beautiful young poetess whose verses and appearance pleased all and sundry. The injustice of the proposition roused my anger, since it blocked my way to additional study. Of course, at the same time, I did not wish to push the young poetess aside. There it was - two people for one place. So, the conflict began. Two people stood up for me -one was a classical poet from Kazakhstan, Abdilda Tazhibayev, the mentor of many young poets: the other was the Director of the "Zhazushi" Publishing House, the famous writer - llyas Yesenberlin. Defending my candidature they phoned Moscow, in addition to writing several letters to the Moscow Writers' Union.

To all appearances, our chances were equal, and gave both of us the dreary possibility of struggling until the next course began. In the end, our Writers Union of Kazakhstan gave the one place they had over to the Mongolian People's Republic, probably due to the fact this problem could not be solved in time. I was deeply disappointed.

I phoned my friend and told him everything. Knowing I could not attend. For his part, Zholon almost wept. It turned out, I was able to go to Moscow only when he had finished his second year of studies. At the hostel where he lived, I did not find him in, unfortunately, and could only leave him a note. That night, on the door of the room I occupied in the hotel "Moscow" I heard someone knocking. I opened it, and there stood Zholon, along with a bold young fellow with a moustache whom I recognized at once as Suimenkul Chokmorov. Zholon and I embraced each other, and still hugging, entered my room...

"Kirghizians have the face of Chokmorov" said Zholon introducing us at once. In that huge Hotel, in the next room, stayed llyas Yesenberlin. I informed him of guests from Kirghizia who had come to me, and he, despite the late hour, got up from his bed, and soon joined us. At that time his trilogy "Migrants" including three novels "The Conspirator's Sword", "Despair" and "Khan Kene", all gaining public appreciation everywhere in the Republic. Yesenberlin was a man of medium stature, with silvery hair. He was a great writer, well-known for his restraint, although that evening he was free and easy, telling us many interesting secrets from foreign sources completely unknown to us. Zholon and I, one in Kirghizian, and one in Kazakh, recited our poems to him in turn.

Informing us about the recent shooting of scenes in a film by the film producer Bolot Shamshiyev, entitled "The crimson poppies of Issik- Kul", where he played the part of Karabalta, Suimenkul, he suddenly asked: "Do you know the Kazakh Academician Omirzak Aitbayev?"

"How could I help knowing him?" I exclaimed, "In face and in stature he is an outstanding person, an excellent poet also - as famous as those in olden times who sang their verses to the public. I have the deepest respect for him as a man, and as a worthy son of the Kazakh people".

My reply was heartily supported by Suimenkul, delighting him greatly.

"Well, from him I learned how to perform pieces by the Kazakh composer Birzhan in public, namely "Temirtas". In our film "The crimson Poppies of Issik-Kul", Karabalta sings, accompanying himself on the dombra. Insofar as Omirzak's voice is more open and melodious than mine, it is his voice which is heard in the film, while I merely moved my lips in accord. In making films all sorts of tricks are used" he laughed, but later sang the song himself for us, in his pleasant, full sounding voice, re-echoing round and round our smallish chamber.

Point by point, our conversation discussed the achievements of Mukhtar Auezov, following which Suimenkul excitedly remarked:

"The great good that was done by this noble-hearted Kirghizian cannot be priced, in terms of gold. Nowadays the times are such that one is not allowed to build a hen-house in their own village, without permission from the Moscow government. Yet, Kirghizians must all the same erect a memorial to Mukhtar Auezov!

"I have already made him one!" replied Zholon, jokingly.

"You have! How's that, then?" we exclaimed. "I gave my daughter the name of the beloved wife of Abai - Aigerim, about whom Mukhtar Auezov wrote with such inspiration".

"Excellent! I think the time has come for at least one big toast" and with that llyas Yesenberlin stood up and raised his glass: "May the valuable qualities of nature, of those older than Aigerim, who at one time captured the heart of the great Abai, appear in the future, in our little Aigerim". "I thank you, Ilyas-aga! You are a unique person, one of those outstanding sons of the Kazakh soil! May your words come true" answered Zholon then, with heart-felt emotion. Because of our jovial conversations, we did not even notice the daybreak.

AITMATOV.   Yes, both Zholon and Suimenkul, one with his verses, and the other with his great art as an actor, left on the thorny path of Kirghizian Art their personal stamp.

In 1968, shooting Bolot Shamshiyev's film "Shot on the Karash Pass" based on Mukhtar Auezov's work, Suimenkul caught a cold in both his kidneys. Not paying much attention to this, Suimenkul, in his free time during the filming, framed a canvas or two and went off wandering in the mountains, along by the Issik-Kul lake. Melting, as he did, into the ring of Nature around him and painting exciting pictures. Just as actively as he worked on his films: giving a vivid and unforgettable portrayal of Daniyar, in "Zhamilya", of Akankul in "Kokserek", of Karabalta in "The crimson poppies of Issik-Kul", and of Chzhan-bao in "Dersu Uzala", which till this day live in our memories.

SHAKHANOV.   I heard an unfortunate accident had left its fatal mark on his health. While he was playing in Vidugris' film, in the role of Kasim, he trod on a loose part of the cliff, and unfortunately fell on a sharp boulder lying in his path. Usually, he would have at once jumped up, not paying much attention to a few light scratches, but this time he could not even move. In the fall he had struck a serious blow to his already injured kidneys. His companions quickly called in a helicopter, and took him to the hospital in Frunze. After treatment there, as soon as he was discharged from hospital, he continued his previous work on the film, and on the same spot where he fell, finally finished the film.

AITMATOV.   They say that God protects those who are patient. But to describe those torments - which he went through afterwards - is a difficult thing to do. Beginning in 1982, for the last ten years of his life, he underwent fifty-six operations. How much courage and patience it demanded from him I do not know!

SHAKHANOV.   The story goes that when Suimenkul was severely ill, even coming to Moscow for treatment, you often helped him along and took steps to obtain for him the necessary apparatus?...

AITMATOV. I did nothing out of the ordinary. If my memory does not fail me, in the spring of 1982 my wife Mariam and I visited Suimenkul in hospital. Though the light of love for living and creative work still shone in his eyes, he himself had grown perceptibly quieter and thinner.

"At first they wanted to implant an artificial kidney", he told us, "I was ready to take the risk and agreed, but somehow the doctors did not agree among themselves!"

Then, in conversation, he recalled that overseas, as he had been told, there existed a certain very expensive apparatus which might prologue his life for five or six years. To find such an enormous sum, however, was for him practically impossible. Thus, he felt he needed to be satisfied with what was is ordained by fate...

My heart trembled. Those were the sentiments of a brave man, ready to face his tragic situation head on. Apart from that, we were amazed he could speak about this matter so ironically, almost jokingly, without making any pathetic appeals for additional aid.

The next day I went to see the Central Committee of the Communist Party on the old square - was received there - and straightway phoned Apas Zhumagulov, who was then the Chairman of the Council of Ministers of Kirghizia. With his help, and with the aid of the First Secretary of the Central Committee of the Communist Party of Kirghizia, Turdakun Usubaliyev, we succeeded in obtaining State aid, to the value of three million roubles, in order to purchase this unique Swedish apparatus for treating the kidneys.

SHAKHANOV.   As far as I know, with the help of that apparatus they were not only able to help Suimenkul, but also prolong the lives of others suffering from serious infection of the kidneys - and the like...

I am especially moved with respect for Suimenkul's elder brother, Namirbek Chokmorov. Over the course of many years, when Suimenkul lay in hospital, fighting his complaint, he regularly came from Frunze to see him. He stayed each time for a week, sometimes a month, and never left his side for long, giving him his full support. Not everyone is blessed with such a considerate elder brother.

In those last ten years of his life, Suimenkul had his kidneys cleaned every two days with the aid of the "Freestool" apparatus. If a sick man, suffering from kidney trouble did not use the apparatus for two or three days successively, then there were terrible consequences. Namirbek said his brother's arms, legs, neck and head, were full of needle-pricks. Add to them the fifty six operations he survived, and it becomes astonishing that he never entirely gave up his film work, nor his painting. I never knew any other Kazakh, nor any Kirghiz man, who so persisted with his love and thirst for creative work.

On one occasion, the renowned professor Aleksey Byelorusov (head doctor of the Moscow Centre for Kidney Disease), said to him, "In this work of mine I have seen thousands of patients, yet never one so surprisingly brave and strong in spirit, or able to withstand each successful, albeit painful, operation - as though it were no more than a flea-bite!" Certainly, others speak similarly about his character in general. All agreeing he was firm and unshakeable. Can they not equally say the same about the characters he created in his films? Real heroes every one, without the slightest doubt.

Pay heed to one more story. You know already that Suimenkul was a highly generous and loving person. Moreover, the apparatus used for cleaning the blood of his kidneys had not previously been seen in the Soviet Union. It should come as no surprise, therefore, that he bought three such apparatuses with his own money. One of which he gave to Tolomush Okeyev, who took his film to the Hollywood Festival, along with the famous producer - Andrei Konchalovsky, the one-time husband of Natalia Arinbasarova. Interestingly, both Suimenkul and Arinbasarova in the film "Zhamilan- interpreted the script from motives and episodes found in your novels.

What did he do with those other apparatuses you may ask? Well, one he gave to the Centre, headed by Byelorusov, to a brother Georgian in actual fact - who lay next to him in hospital, and the third, sewn inside himself, worked awhile then went out of action ...

The death of Suimenkul was a heavy blow for those in hospital, and for those outside as well. Namirbek recalled: "Wherever it appears, humanitarianism inevitably gives birth to deep respect. Relatedly, I remember an occasion when, having gone home for a few days, I returned to that Moscow hospital and, after looking around, found the empty tables - no food - nothing. It turned out the money he earlier given for medicines, fruit, and vegetables, had been donated to a young fellow from the Altai, who lay beside him in the ward. Indeed, without the faintest chance of seeing these finances again. Often it happened that people who were sick, or up against some unsolvable problem, came to Suimenkul, and requested his aid. Then, he would ask his film-producing friends to try and help them: even on the level of Ministries of Foreign Affairs. A place where Rosa Otinbayeva, one of his film-friends worked, along with Stalbek Turginbayev.

Most likely it was this fellow-feeling of his, and his responsive nature and his kindly generosity, which was responsible for the many thousands who crowded at his graveside for the burial ceremony. Especially memorable were the words of a lad of twenty six, on crutches, who leant on his mother's shoulder eulogizing, "Since I am on the list of those destined for another world, I need to express my thanks for expensive medicine which Suimenkul found for me. They have prolonged my life. Even my own father did not do so much for me. Soon, however, I shall most likely go to that other world above and find him there. With this in mind, mother and I have collected about five thousand roubles. I personally hold about three thousand of this fund. If those worthy refuse to accept them, I shall be wounded at heart. I beg you to take them, as a sign of my deepest respect for that good man". Those words of his roused tears in the eyes of everyone present.

The main characters in the filmed versions of Auezov's novels, particularly by the director Chokmorov, are depicted with great care and understanding. In a sense, they are a monument to these outstanding works. It is no secret that before Chokmorov, no one had been able to express - through the language of cinema - such in-depth portrayals of Auezov's works. If Suimenkul had lived longer, he would undoubtedly have been made a People's Artist of the Republic. Either way, the Embassies of Kazakh and Kirghizian Republics awarded a prize named "The Golden Bridge": placing him as number one on the list of those bringing cultures and peoples together. An award given to his wife Salima Shabazova (also now deceased) in his stead. In the great hall of the Embassy, we additionally opened (with your participation), an exhibition of the paintings of Chokmorov - having set up a monument to him. We wrote to the President of the Republic, and to the Government, with a request to open up the house where he used to live when staying in his village - as a Museum to his memory.

AITMATOV. Has not his poetic line "Kirghizia has the face of Chokmorov" become a winged expression of the bonds between us? Today that stone-hard son of Kirghizia, who every other day faced a sudden end, but fought for life, has succeeded in leaving behind him a rich spiritual inheritance; a bright unfading memorial - and taken on a new life in the lines of his created works.

Yes, how many stars which once shone on earth have now reached the heavens ... Have you a poem, perhaps, which might sum up this talk?

SHAKHANOV. I have! An excerpt from a poem on "The Death of Tolstoy"

AITMATOV. You know it by heart, I expect? Then recite it, please!

SHAKHANOV.

"All's dark with sorrow in that simple chamber.
All ruffled up, exhausted by permanent pain,
Here Lev Tolstoy lies dying, in constant danger. ..
His wife comes in. She bends o'er his bed again:
"Forgive me, Lev, forgive! I'm the guilty person!"
But he kept silent. He thought: "Oh, my poor dear,
Don't cry - my sorrow's no less than yours, I'm certain,

No matter what tears you shed, my end draws near!
You know I loved you, but it ended sadly,
For by your deafness I've been torn to bits.
You could not understand ... I know, you suffer badly,
As the wife of Tolstoy, a heavy cross dulls your wits.
But a heavier one I bear - your not understanding.
You could have understood, but had no desire.
We've spent long years together, now we're disbanding.
Here I forgive you, forgive your husband's ire!. . "
He closed his eyes; with a hundred ills so spiteful,
So bitter it was to be not understood by his wife.
TOLSTOY no longer lived. O, genius, just delightful,
How unhappy you were, though one of the wisest in life!
Where's tenderness found, that will accept us with passion?
Who'll cool us in heat, and shelter us from cold?
Three measures in life - height, depth, and breadth we fashion,
Not knowing these are the core of darkness untold!
From soul to soul there lies no pathway trodden.
To be not understood - there's no crueler curse!
The way from soul to soul is a fight unforgotten.
How steep is that path to a circle of friends, what's worse!
No understanding - what's that? The fault of the faultless?
But no wish to understand - that's a heavy crime!
O, how many ways do I really know in their fullness?
O, how many springs dried up at their source in time!
No understanding - there steals the slayer and traitor,
The executioner, tearing in darkness and waste.
The fire of Dzhordano behind you blazes later.
You are Galileo's judge - that must be faced!
With your noose Birzhan-sal you captured,
Extinguished the starry light of Ulugbek.
With the curse of the Devil you always were enraptured.
For you there is no forgiveness - a noose round your neck!
Abai, straight in the face, you gave a back-hander,
Auezov also you overtook in your time.
You envious eyes could not from his work wander,
And so the whisper went round about his line:

"His novel does not touch one in any measure –
He does not reach reality in the height!"
Auezov smiled sadly at bitter words for his treasure:
"The folk will JUDGE, and will UNDERSTAND alright!"
And so they did! Accounts we, shall be keeping!
What blindness - to look, and not to recognize!
And those who don't understand' are their consciences sleeping?
Not to wish to know - what a crime, just to close one's eyes!
Not to understand - a sudden mist, where all's feeble,
It shrouds the horizon - by day the sunlight dims.
Here's youthful talent - which flies towards the people,
So, while he is young - let's understand all his whims!..

AITMATOV. I remember that I read that poem once in one of your early books. It is a wise and deeply penetrating song, and touches the heart.

Like a mountain peak, enshrouded by heavy clouds, stands every one of those whom we remember were pursued through life by the lack of understanding - about which you speak so clearly in your poem. In conflict of mind, and the flesh, lasting through the ages, people have firmly (upheld by the power of their great talent), passed into nonexistence, some earlier, some later. Leaving their successors an unfading memory - the treasure of a spiritual inheritance. What happy feelings are called to mind in remembering this, how bright and light becomes one's soul! I am convinced that to recognize and to appreciate someone's outstanding good qualities and actions, means to make one's small contribution to the development of our world and the Universe around.

First of all, to know and understand the truth ourselves is an absolute necessity. Secondly, it is our duty, a sacred one, as sons of those mighty and powerful predecessors of ours. Let this understanding be like a handful of native soil, cast with love and respect upon their holy grave, where they may then rest in quietude and peace!

CRIMES AND BARBARITIES
THROUGHOUT THE AGES
OR
THE MARQUIS DE SADE, DONENBAI, AND THE
POISON OF AN AFRICAN TWO-FANGED FISH

... One may rob people of land, of riches, and even of life, but whoever thought one might rob people of their memory? 0 God! If Thou dost indeed exist, how did you inspire those who rob folk of their memory? Is there not enough evil on Earth without such criminal activity?

> In lucid early morn, or noon-tide heated,
> When one has risen in an aircraft again,
> One flies on high, above the clouds beseated,
> And glances down, and level-level plain
> Seems then to you to be but puny gullies,
> And heaps of soil by narrow burrows of snakes.
> So many secrets then the distance sullies...
> O fate of mine, which strength within me wakes,
> Allow me to glance in the hearts of friends and foes,
> Not from afar, but from a look-out close!

SHAKHANOV. There is no doubt that you and I are not alone in thinking about how the spiritual riches of mankind, gathered during the ages, are today subject to the general devaluation of moral and essential values. How has it occurred that ever more frequently bad feeling, callousness and bitterness increase, while kindness and good-heartedness from day to day diminish - and disappear from their native harbours and highways?

When weeds are not cut down, rice cannot hope to thrive and to multiply. If one does not carry out "weeding" in good time, to neutralize primitive instincts and the cultural inclinations to sadism, hiding in the minds and consciouness of men, then one must not be surprised when transgressions against humanity go beyond a potential threat and become the legalized "norm" of behaviour.

On the screens of commercial TV, on video tapes, as well as in amusement salons, as if their strength were never-fading, we see horror films day and night in all tones and colours, extolling the taste for violation, torment and torture. The book-stalls are crammed to breaking-point under the burden of boastful, beastly books with dubious qualities, further enlarging the "fighter" and the "thriller", and having nothing in common with high-quality decent literature or art, but just the opposite, are full of choking atavism and cruelty and bestial barbarity. In this sense, the everyday growth of the assortment of "lethal" weapons is given full freedom on the bazaars, in the streets, in villages.

AITMATOV. The facts you put forth are indeed the bitter truth. Where is the success for which we awaited: and still await. From the market "economy of enlightenment", so highly advertised and propagandized, and alas, successfully implanted in the minds of many people, as a "way of life" quite foreign to their strategic ideals, and traditional, ethical, and national experience. Thus, for example, the researches of investigators indisputably show, that the psyche of the infant growing up with a toy gun in his hand, shows an especially quarrelsome turn of mind, with rampant ambitions and aggressiveness. Whether we like it or not, from early years we encourage the cult of violence and brutality.

I noticed, by the way, the same modus in Soviet literature, when it called upon to educate our youth and adolescents with a heroic-patriotic spirit: with an irreconcilable and merciless attitude towards the sworn enemies of Socialism. What is the real difference, after all? In principle, there is none, no matter with what sauce it is flavoured, we all receive either a self-slaughtering Kamikaze or a brutal and barbarous James Bond!

SHAKHANOV. In a book-dialogue with a Japanese thinker D. lkedo you say to him, warning him of the dark physiognomy of the times to come: "Each family should be ready to protect its children from all kinds of ideological aggression". But will they take any steps to do so? Unfortunately many parents, instead of this, ignore the alarm signal, make no preparations to defend their children, onstead, like a wild mustang, not looking around, take a course on some unseen orientation: go galloping, galloping forward ...

Once, in Spain, I chanced to hear an opinion expressed by a writer about the Soviet Union. He said: "The Bolsheviks came to power in the country by means of sadism and bloodshed. That aggravating factor could not fail to cast a shadow on future generations - those who saw it with their own eyes and those who read of it in books". An echo of that saying remained with me for many years.

AITMATOV.   With such statements one cannot quarrel. The crisis of humanism in the twentieth century world is an obvious fact. By the way, it began much earlier than expected, the reasons of which need a separate conversation and explanation.

I think it is worth dealing with this problem a little more fully because nobody will start to argue that before explaining how to protect Nature, to get rid of hunger, war, and the poverty of a technical materialistic civilization, it is necessary to understand how a man can remain a man: in the spiritual sense of the word; and moreover, a man not only sensible, but knowledgeable, conscious and conscientious. A certain amount of common sense is seen in all creatures, yet conscience is a peculiarity of man alone. Let me stress alone, since I completely share the point of view of outstanding thinkers and humanists of the West in these matters. To my mind, the most frightful of all catastrophies for us is not so much an atomic, thermal, or flooding, outburst - threatening the physical extinction of humanity, as is the extermination of humaneness in humanity, meaning that man remains nothing more than some wild animal.

SHAKHANOV.   Or, maybe, remains in some inhuman form?

AITMATOV.   One or the other, equally terrifying to think about! However, let us return to what stung you so deeply - the words of that Spanish writer, which penetrated, in my view, to the very core of communism. Even further - to the essence of all forms of totalitarianism, wherever it put down its poisonous roots. Now, it is sensible to concentrate our attention on the prerequisites and motives of sadism, from whence and for what reason it arises, and what kind of influence it has had on the moral conditions of society, and what results can be expected from this condition in the future?..

Maybe not everyone knows what "sadism" really means? It is tied up with the name of the Marquis de Sade (1740-1814). As a sexual perversion, in which full satisfaction is attained by inflicting on one's partner physical pain, and also by an abnormal passion for cruelty and an enjoyment of the sufferings of others, deliberately inflicted.

Along with that, we should add scientists have distinguished many kinds of sadism, connected with inherited defects of the mind, having the same results as narcomania, and alchoholism as well as with the sharp and shattering results of social life - due to perceived exploitation. One must not ignore the first two reasons, but take a special look at the third - social life. Are you not surprised that the French writer, the Marquis de Sade thought of himself as a thoroughly convinced Republican?

SHAKHANOV.   Ahem! So to speak, how otherwise?

AITMATOV.   In some book or the other I encountered one extremely interesting thought: what a unique conclusion the Marquis de Sade, came to, as a result of the French Revolution.

SHAKHANOV.   Interesting, indeed! What conclusion was that?

AITMATOV.   It was this! No criminal offences against people in the Revolutionary period could be punished or judged, because under this regime, crime itself was the usual rule.

SHAKHANOV.   Very cunning!

AITMATOV.   Yes, indeed. I'll tell you. Nonetheless, you will most likely begrudge him credit for his flexibility of mind, and mental refinement.

His books, full of scandalous intrigues, with piquant details of his intimate life, - were served as an apology for the idea of refined cruelty.

It is notable that every evil, along with the cause of his own debauchery, he viewed as the crimes of his times, all round him.

That era, certainly, passed under the sign of catastrophe, because the setting sun of the French aristocracy left concepts of nobility without their previous power and influence; forcing it into a trap. A decline, as it were, a confusion and moral putrefaction. Out of all their previous privileges only one survived - the right to fight for the preservation of an image of feudal despotism. All gifting a freedom to act in bed as they wished - according to the attractive principle: "Every man is a tyrant in bed!"

SHAKHANOV.   Having tried out his scepter as a tyrant in beds of love, the Marquis de Sade ceased to differentiate between satisfaction and suffering. Visiting a house of prostitutes, he took a whip in his hand, and then beat his partners till they are half dead. Finally, lashing himself till blood began to flow. "I am fully convinced of the boundless enjoyment this procedure provides", he more than once expressed.

One scene of extreme brutality, found in his novel "Justine", focuses on a personage by the name of Jerkand. It opens with the deliberate wounding of his wife, before proceeding into ecstatic vocabularies at the sight of blood flowing from her wounds. This occurs regularly, we are told. Shockingly, the protagonist only ceases these tortures when his wife, quite bloodless, falls to the ground unconscious. All making this an exceedingly difficult novel to digest. Even more challenging, perhaps, is the character of his kindly, submissive, wife, who can do little apart from engender sympathy in a reader's imagination. What she suffers in their home, as some kind of servant or slave, is tantamount to heroic! He violates her, crucifies her, beats her with a whip, sets dogs upon her and, with sheer delight, cuts open her veins to watch her blood flowing! ...

Her husband even throws a noose round her neck, and methodically tightens it while he shares his bed with a prostitute! The choking coughs of his victim doubles the pleasure he enjoys with the strumpet ... Only when Justine loses consciousness does this lover of extremities decide to loosen the noose a little. As far as the author of this book is concerned, these oppressive scenes of pitiless behaviour are written by him with indescribable joy.

Since not one evil remains unpunished, sooner or later, one must pay for the wickedness one does. Therefore, in Marquis de Sade's actual life a series of ordeals emerged. Frequently, he found himself put in prison after prolonged questionings by the authorities. Moreover, having roamed as a vagrant round the whole country, this maniac finally made a necessary escape to Italy. One of his contemporaries writing of him in this way: "On the 7th of September, 1778, the Italians sat him in a cage like a wild beast, while later he was taken and thrown into the river".

In Italy the sexual sickness of de Sade grew sharper. However, from the moment of his inglorious return to his homeland, he at last was able to finish with the cruelty, which had poisoned his whole life. Eventually appearing before the world as an experienced author. Soon, alone with Nature, he began to pen the story of his life.

AITMATOV. So it was that the personal muddles of his life, the brutality of his behaviour and the blood-thirsty intemperance of the Marquis de Sade found incarnation in the creative work of this onetime maniac. The bitterest thing is discovered in the horrors and terrors he had inflicted on others, All catalogued without the slightest shade of disgust, but with a certain unprecedented enthusiasm. Those, who praised the evil of this book, were unknown to him in his isolation. A place where curses were heaped on his head and where he finally gave, before his death, his own condemnation of himself - "even traces of my grave should not remain, and I cannot doubt all memories of me will be wiped from human memory!" In our own day, his life-story is translated into numerous languages and reprinted in endless new editions.

This is the dead-end we are in now.

SHAKHANOV. The pictures of boundless bestiality in de Sade's works devastates souls and deserves nothing except anathema: a man violating his own mother, a maniac-father licking the body of his own daughter - to read such horrors is sheer torment enough. Yet despite all of this, there are thousands who thirst for and delight in such beastial books.

AITMATOV. Should I, out of inquisitiveness, read in one of these beastial books about the dirty and devilish devices of Beria in those life-tormenting labour camps? I can quite honestly say I should not!

For those who thirst for such sadism, and go to every extreme to obtain it, market book-stalls are packed full of such materials. Who are the authors of this terrifying trash? The Devil only knows! One thing is certain however - they are dirty, dishonourable, dealers of trash - who have received, sad to say, the freedom to churn out their drab desires for decadent readers who share their ethical inferiority. For authors and readers of this type, there is nothing sacred left in our world! That is the dark side of democracy for you, my friend!

SHAKHANOV.   Not long ago, in "World-wide News", I read an advert of the following nature: "I am a tall, slim, attractive - and would like to make the acquaintance of women and girls who get satisfaction from beatings and prefer (as a prelude to the sexual act), physical torment with straps or whips. The switch-over of roles not excluded!" Then, I remembered an episode with one woman, whose strange behaviour completely changed my youthful world outlook.

A good-looking young woman from our village, usually of a quiet, domestic character, suddenly, for no apparent reason, began to go mad and publicly exhibit her vices. In front of her husband, and in view of the general public, she began teasing him, cursing him to the devil, and scandalized everybody. The moment finally came when her husband lost all patience and began to beat the devil out of her. Their neighbours, touched to the heart, came to see her, and said: "Young woman, you can't go on like this, there is no place here for such conduct. Give up this madness and these crazy habits of yours!"

Oddly, the woman replied:

"When he beats me, my whole spine rings with happiness -oh, it is so pleasant, just as if I had been born into another world".

"How can that be so?" they said to her, "Who gets pleasure out of being beaten by a furious husband?"

Later I learned the word "masochism". I understood it meant one of those psychological irregularities, difficult to explain. There exists some hidden connection between the motivations of de Sade and the story of this village woman, who provoked beatings (thus reversing cruel negative actions into a pleasure.) Who knows - it may be worthwhile to ease the feelings of a mental patient who wishes to crawl beyond standardized limits and give him, or her, satisfaction?

Once I was returning in my car from Merke. It was nearly midnight. I had just passed the village of Uzunagash, when I suddenly saw a militia-man from the State Auto-Inspection Service, pointing his baton at me. I stopped the car. The militia-man came up and, recognizing me, said:

"Ah, is that you, Mukhtar? Where are you going at this time of night? "He then made a request, quite unexpectedly:

For God's sake, could you take this young fellow with you to Alma-Ata?"

"Of course! Let him sit with me. I was bored alone anyway!"

The young man approached and took his seat, as I had invited him.

"We'll have a good journey and a chat on the way, if you like!"

"Well, have you heard about the young man who murdered six women" he enquired?

"Bad news flies quickly, faster than good! I have already heard!"

"I am taking part in the investigation of this case!"

"Obviously, this young fellow has got bats in the belfry?"

"Not quite so!" replied the detective, shaking his head. "He, the accused, was born and grew up here in Uzunagash and finished school very successfully. According to his own confession, he chose his victims beforehand. He remained with them, after which, with a sweep, he plunged a long dagger into their hearts and began to twist it round and round ... each poor woman's soul trembling before leaving her body. Apparently, it was the agony of his girl-friend that gave him inexpressible satisfaction. The more the victim suffers, the longer the maniac's extreme bliss lasts ... As we travelled on towards Alma-Ata's outskirts the detective said to me urgently:

"Stop here, please Mukhtar, I will show you an interesting photograph, although you had better put the brakes on first!

I put on the brakes, without a word. Opening his attache-case, he drew out a picture and handed it to me. Terrible!! On a table stood the hewn-off head of a woman, her hair all clotted with blood, the face pale, eyes closed, the lips slightly parted:

"His latest victim!" he commented, placing the photo back in his case. I was quite lost. The detective went on with his story: "A specially invited psychiatrist from Leningrad made the suggestion that the seventh forefather of the criminal used to be a well-known cut-throat.

In other words, the urge to kill and deface his victim with special cruelty was in fact inherited! This might mean he did these dark deeds, maybe, against his own will and innermost heart.

Are there only a few events in history which would make your hair stand up on end? Take, for instance, the Hungarian Countess Bathori, living in the sixteenth century. That nobly-born dame was distinguished by "good manners". She took baths full of the blood from young girls, specially slain for this purpose. At the very moment of this bloody ablution she felt herself the happiest of women ... What pleasure to immerse oneself in blood, knowing the youthful gore would have a good effect upon her personal beauty! In this way the self-centred evil-doer sacrificed the lives of six hundred and fifty slaves, all daughters of the peasantry, without the least hesitation whatsoever...

The Western mind, having ruined traditional values and treasures, and in the name of experimental science (at the dawn of this century), dissected and systemized "the three-dimensional world" and then turned their attention to the seamy side of existence: to the dark "other side" of human nature and man's world. Everything forbidden, unusual or unknown, attracted their attention, while ordinary, traditional, and down-to-earth affairs, lost all value for them.

This fundamental change in European consciousness determined the general atmosphere and cultural orientation of the West at the end of the outgoing twentieth century.

The sources of sadism are rooted in the depths of unconscious impulses. Western psycho-analytical research scientists reaching predetermined results in the exploration of these phenomenon. European culture, unto this day, hinges itself on the circles of Hell and has no power to overcome the Gorgon-like attraction of destructive temptations and ideas.

Moreover, Eastern experience in overcoming such problems is not always acceptable to Western conscience, nor to another kind of metaphysics founded on a rational mentality, even though the West stands on the threshold of discovering meta-historical realities, along with the methods required for their attainment...

AITMATOV. I am fully in agreement with those who think any road to the embittering of man goes through difficult living conditions and surroundings. I have experienced these pressures myself. In one of the most complicated periods of the Great Patriotic War, it happened that I was in a terrible state of fury and almost killed a man. Only after many years had passed did I write about it. Would it not be instructive to tell you Mukhtar, my friend, what I remember of that sad day?

Well, it was winter, the beginning of February 1943. A time when misfortune had overtaken our family. I do not speak of hunger and poverty or war itself; this is not necessary. Rather, of those things which we suffered under Stalin's regime as "Enemies of the people". Four children round one mother, who herself was suffering from inflammation in her joints - probably a result of the huge shock she experienced when, in 1937, our father was shot as a criminal. Remember, I was only fifteen years old, the eldest of her children.

The village where we lived after his death is known till this day as Jeeda.

We took refuge in a half-ruined clay-walled home. We had no shed for our one cow (I still remember her name - Zukhra), given to us by our relatives before the war. Indeed, we had to get permission from the Chairman of the Kolkhoz to keep her in their cattle shed. I repeat all of this so you can grasp how important this cow was for our daily life. Indeed we children quickly realized that without her, we would not survive. As such, we took care of her all day long, fed her, watered her, and gave her scraps of food collected from neighbours to eat. In these ways, we helped prepare her for calving. Speaking amongst ourselves about endless fresh milk, cottage-cheese, and sour cream.

I shall never forget that misty morning, when I got up very early and went out in gusty winds to the cattle-shed to look after our Zukhra. As the first one there - no cattleman was present - I could not understand why our cow was missing. The stall was empty. Her neck-strap was hanging near the exit. An oddity, even though the gates were never closed properly in this old half-tumbled-down shed. Usually Zukhra would "moo", when she saw us coming. Yet now? Maybe she had got out and wandered off somewhere? Indeed, I looked around, but found no trace of her. Confused, I went to find the night-watchman who was still sleeping in a corner of the shed. However, the old man knew nothing about our cow or, at least, made out that he didn't. To my questions he simply replied; "Perhaps she has broken loose and gone off somewhere into the field!" To be honest, this alarmed me. Therefore, I dashed off to a stream where they used to water the cattle. No - not a sign of her. Our Zukhra was officially missing! Instantly, I knew she had been stolen meaning, of course, our whole world had collapsed into darkness. Without any doubt, she had been driven off by thieves. At home everyone wept on hearing my tale. "What shall we do now" they cried? Showing solidarity, our neighbours, on hearing of our woe, raised their voices in pity and cursed the robbers, while praying to God to punish these miscreants. In my own soul a strange but decisive maturity arose. After all, I was the eldest among us children - I had to protect the younger ones. I had to act, fight, battle, with our foes and revenge our sorrow! In my consciousness one single thing stood out – I needed to kill the thief! I even went to one of our neighbours to borrow his gun. Certainly, I knew Temirbek would trust me in these matters. All the previous autumn I had served him as a water-bearer. Now, as he lay sick in bed, feverish with sweat, he would still help us. For his part, Temirbek already knew about our loss, saying: "Take the gun there on the wall. There are some cartridges in the bag nearby. If I were well, I would come to help you find the robber.

Immediately, I went out from his chamber with the loaded gun in my hand and a thirst for revenge in my breast. Looking back, this feeling of spite swallowed everything else. I could not think of anything, except a burning desire to punish the thief mercilessly. That feeling arose from an irrational conviction he could not be very far away. A cow, at the end of the day, is not a horse - it does not gallop! Moreover, the thief dared not move by day, he would be spotted at once. Also, if he decided to slaughter the cow straightway, he would have to hide the meat somewhere. One further thing I blackly mused - the thief might imagine that in our poor family there would be no-one to hunt him down, but I would prove him wrong! If necessary, gunning his entire gang down. Yes, yes, just so, just so!

I hunted round the fields and gullies, quickly, quietly, went across our neighbourhood, right up to the foothills. Not noticing, as I went, the cold, freezing, temperatures. In an almost paranormal fashion, some weird inner heat kept me warm and strong. It seemingly made me impervious to privations. My sodden soft leather shoes - which I occasionally shared with my younger brother – becoming a minor inconvenience. The nakedness of the fields in front of me driving me to despair. All around stood lifeless mountains and empty places. Nobody had left tracks.

Then I thought - most likely the thief went straight to the nearby town of Zhambyl.

From that simple guess my heart started beating hotter in my chest, and I went to the road leading into town. Nothing! Truly, this road was a long one, and I could not get there until morning - even if I walked all night without rest. However, I was ready to do so, without any hesitation. So, coming down from the mound where I had been surveying the countryside, I went onto the highway. I already imagined myself there, at the town bazaar, looking for traces of the crime: freshly-scraped skins etcetera, or finding these crooks by their guilty faces, cunning eyes, and shifty looks. Undoubtedly, he, or they, would recognize me too, but it would be too late for them to do anything. I would shoot them down in front of the meat-stall.

So I went on, clutching my gun, following the highway. Occupied with my thoughts, I did not notice an old man coming towards me on a donkey, poorly dressed, with a warn cap and a grey beard. The donkey trotted along, taking the old man past a half-seen graveyard. Our paths crossed and I would have gone on, yet he stopped:

"Listen, laddie, are you going to kill somebody?"

"Yes" I replied, for some reason not being surprised at his words. "I want to kill somebody alright!"

Our glances met. I saw a wrinkled face, with a quiet, understanding, look on it. He nodded his head:

"If that's the case, don't be in a hurry. Stop a moment. Let's talk things over. Why are you thinking of killing somebody?"

"Our only cow has been stolen. There are four of us, youngsters, dependent on her, besides our sick mother!"

"Ah, so! Bad luck! Nevertheless listen, sonny. Don't burn yourself up with spite and revenge! Don't kill anybody, even in your thoughts, even some accursed criminal cow-thief!"

I kept silent, holding myself back, so as not to shout.

"I understand you," slowly continued the old man. "I sympathize with you. But listen to an old man. Don't go and kill! Don't have this wish in your heart! Return home and think again - life punishes those who do evil to others. Have no doubt, punishment will dog their steps, awake or asleep. Life will recompense you for your loss. You will be happy and not notice it. It may seem to you I am saying empty words however, believe me, they are true. Go home, my lad ... Ultimately, you will be convinced of these truths. Eventually, you will have many cows, maybe, hundreds ... Go home and tell all I have said to your mother and I'll go on my way ..."

I still hesitated, glancing at the old man as he trotted off on his donkey. He didn't look round, as I went along the edge of an empty plain, carrying on my shoulder a gun no longer needed. I do not know what happened to me, yet I suddenly started weeping. My sobs shook my whole frame as I tramped on in my worn-out shoes...

I forgot about all this for many years, and only recently recalled it. That unknown old man on the road came to life in my memory again with his last words: "Never think of revenge, my son, whatever it was they did to you!"

So, you see, I had teachers of life-skills in my time. I bow before them now, those sacred and pure-hearted people on this earth! They are a real support for my spirit. Maybe the essence of the lesson lies not in "going back home" but never at any time in your life - in moments of great joy, in the hour of honour and glory - never forget who you are, what you are, and how you are obliged to people, who for reasons unknown, love and respect you as an individual!"

Someone my own age who had heard this story once asked me: "How many cows have you got nowadays?"

"Not one!" I replied - but afterwards I thought about what he meant. Yes, each of my books, going all over the world, in large editions, has more value than a cow! What a prophecy that old man gave to me!

Mukhtar, dear friend, I remembered all this while exploring the topic of sadism! Mindful of sad times in childhood, those freezing February days, when we literally writhed with hunger. Although, with hindsight, I am glad those thieves, whoever they were, did not fall beneath my gun-shots. Heartlessness breeds heartlessness. All meaning, one cannot exclude the thought that sparks sadism - caused by social evil and the destructive action of a small group – could even break out in me. Maybe a human soul is a casket containing a number of unsolved riddles and puzzles.

Lev Tolstoy advised us we should not count every unsuccessful action as a misfortune. For this failure might be the beginning of real fortune. Had I stumbled, being young, I would have regretted my decisions. I tremble to imagine it. Who then was that noble old man who pulled me aside from the path of evil-doing?

SHAKHANOV. If you believe specialists, then, for the last thirty millennia the human brain has not undergone any great changes. By itself, that postulate contains a good deal of information for thinking over and grounding our discussions. If one's predecessors were philosophers and aristocrats or, on the other hand, vampires and swindlers, can one expect to see the outcome every seventh generation? Does that mean the white magic of the good and the black magic of the bad will fatally predetermine the consciousness of an individual, his character, temperament, behaviour, position, customs and principles, once and for the whole of life? For instance, is it correct to suppose the person who stole your cow will father robbers and crooks?

Not so long ago, an article in a newspaper about one schoolboy, left a very dark impression on me. He was of an unsurpassably able character in class and a faultless pupil. A lad with exceptional talents for naturalism, albeit a torturer who happily killed cats and dogs for pleasure. Curiously, he was also a pyromaniac who could not pass a warehouse without unleashing the red cock of fire inside it. Once, having started a great fire, he laughed admiringly at the conflagration, while people tried to extinguish it.

At times, attracted by some unknown power, he went to graveyards and smashed tombstones. Still not satisfied, he felt compelled to open coffins and break apart the skeletons within. Unaccountably, his parents were fully unaware of the offences committed by their quiet natured son. Indeed, one evening he appeared, bespattered with dust and clay, causing them to ask him where he had been. He answered them by saying:

"I dug up a corpse out and tortured it, destroying all its bones!"

As we may hear from this narrative, one more vampire came a-knocking at our doors.

AITMATOV.   Possibly, most probably, he had no idea at all about the Marquis de Sade's life, nor about sadists generally. Least of all any inclination to write a word about his cruel transgressions. The fact that he committed them, however, is telling. What are we speaking of here? Bestiality, living in us before we are born? How and why does such deliberate bestiality appear?

SHAKHANOV. A whole mass of questions suddenly appear, scattering our thoughts on a variety of problems. Why does an educated, and not untalented youngster, from a decent family go sliding along a path to criminal actions? If he were dull-witted, we should speak in another way. Furthermore, how many such crimes remain undiscovered and what psychical barbarities are there, about which we never hear?! How can one place barriers in their way, and how effective would they be? If such people are to be counted as ordinary criminals this is one solution, yet if these sadists are beyond ordinary criminality, depriving them of their freedom could be for the best.

I think another fundamental problem appears in so-called "zombies" – people lacking brains and self-control. You speak of them in your novel "A day lasts longer than an age".

When did these many-layered and complicated subjects arise? How did you succeed in joining up zombies with cosmic "loopies" - and personal craziness with social screechers?

AITMATOV. An opinion is circulating, which I am rather inclined to agree with, that a writer writes even when he has no pen in his hand. When seeing a blank sheet of paper, I am sure you take it and start to write your theme with no inner preparation. Appearing, in the final analysis, to equal the building of a palace without materials or the instruments necessary. Needless to say, a chosen theme, successfully and full-bloodedly clothed, demands a treasure-house of memories. Recollections from childhood, your own personal experience and observations, the results of meditation, varied events and meetings which have previously occurred - all going through a thorough sifting process into a regularized system. A personal illustration comes to mind. Before I began to write "A day lasts longer than an age", I studied the theme of "zombies"- nitwits, nincompoops and simpletons, with an avid determination. Recalling, from childhood, we often heard of stupid, or outrageous actions, criticized by phrases along the lines of:

"What are you doing, you, nitwit?" Though not knowing precisely where the shaky boundary between a normal man and an idiot lay, intuition taught us using such words was deeply offensive.

Interestingly, one of the first witnesses to the idea of "idiocy" comes down to us from the epic "Manas". A fragment when, disturbed by the unlimited power and military might of the youthful Manas, local khans try to turn him into a child again, into a simpleton deprived of leadership skills.

> *"We shall take the lad prisoner then.*
> *Bind round his head a quick-shrinking skin.*
> *Take him home and torment him again.*
> *All six of the Kalmak tribes, I swear,*
> *Gathered from lowest to highest there!"*

Curiously, in the mid sixties, I became fascinated by the etymology of the words "mankurt" (nitwit) and "shiri" (camel or cow-hide), asking the Manas-reciter Sayakbai Karalayev to explain their usage. On being asked, he first became very quiet afterwards extolling:

"In olden days, during the epoch of the Kirgiz-Kalmak wars, avowed enemies stole cattle, goods, and people to be used as slaves. It goes without saying that, unlike cattle, human beings eventually tried to escape. A situation occasionally alleviated by sympathetic souls willing to send news home for them, although not in itself a final solution. So, as these captives grew older, they were submitted to the "mankurt" procedure. Firstly their heads were shaven. Secondly, their craniums were bound tight with the neck-skin of newly-slain camels. Thirdly, raw-hide straps were wrapped over their ears, brows, arms and feet. From that moment onwards, detainees could expect every hair to be forced back into the scalp like an agonizing needle. Thereby, destroying a victim's nervous system and memory. Alternatively, these permanent hostages were tied tight and left in the suns heat without water or food. Within a week or so, a prisoner had either died, or became a permanent idiot, a "mankurt". Of course, if someone died all of their sufferings ceased. If still alive, however they were changed into a mindless automaton: not knowing their own name, or relations, nor remembering anything about their past life. They had been reduced to mere machines commanded by a master.

Without irony, one could say we continue do the same type of thing. In the era of totalitarianism, for example, an ideological "shiri" bound mass society into idiocy - stifling all opposition and repressing individual interests. Everyone fell beneath this yoke.

One time, I travelled to Moscow by train. The route went through the Orda region. Over the train-radio we heard about the next launch of a cosmic craft from the cosmodrome of Baikonur. I stood at the window, lost in meditation, gazing at the eternal heat of the desert. In this blistering moment, an idea for a new novel evolved - "A day lasts longer than an age". I would base it on the notion humankind has long considered the possibility of life on another planet and personally pondered on the character of our "space brothers in reason". Contrarily, what if our planet Earth was quarantined by some unearthly brain or timespace anomaly? A thought alarming me more and more. Then the legend heard in youth, about "mankurts", received in my fantasy an entirely unexpected transformation.

In ancient times, a strong spirit and the powerful body was broken with the aid of a hoop, which made the mind muddy and killed the intellect. Analogously, what would two opposing ideological systems do to achieve supremacy? Would they go out into unending space tying each other down into an inescapable hoop? The sorrows of others do not exist for us, after all, and tragedy is always a tragedy beyond the scope, or radius, of defeat.

In this way, I was led by a desire to forewarn others of the catastrophes threatening our human race in the near future.

SHAKHANOV.   It is well-known that the term "mankurt", even in ancient times, was prevalent among Turkic peoples. What despicable secrecies they used in trying to hide the method of turning someone into a robot – to the extent this accursed word was only preserved in our dictionaries for centuries untold. You were able, having given its original middle-Ages meaning as a torture, to raise this theme to the level of a philosophical problem of humanitarian proportions. Thus, bringing the term into Global Text. Turning their attention to that subject - the means of driving a man mad - others write in various ways. All the same, that is not a fantasy, but a Jesuitical description of evil genius across the Asiatic continent.

Following your novel "A day lasts longer than an Age", the tragedy small people's face made itself known to all. They lived in a defunct Soviet Union on the brink of a cultural-historical catastrophe. Opposition to all "mankurtism" became a pressing question for them and remained a constant source of agitation. In other words, proceeding from your mouth, the bitter truth of life shook up peoples great and small.

A few years ago, one of the most obvious signs of this were some slogans I saw carried in peaceful demonstrations in the Baltic countries and Moldavia -"We are not mankurts!"

You will, naturally, be acquainted with one more crime against the mind of man and one further encroachment upon his freedom of action - going under the term "zombie". They say secret knowledge, not dissimilar to the techniques used in mankurtization (being called "the crime of the century"), was originally spread among African tribes. If you believe such events, similar to legends, then the very hairs of one's head stand on end. Generally, however, tis problem is one and the same. There are means by which human beings may be turned into implicit slaves: doing nothing apart from their master's will. Yet, with one difference -the means of deconstructing a victim into a weak-willed slave were kept in the strictest secret. So stressed, there are various stories and guesses about how it was done.

As a case in point, I have heard of an African who went onto a plantation and recognized, by chance, his elder brother – a man believed dead fifteen years earlier. Rejecting, at first, the evidence of his own eyes, he went nearer to this ghost and took a good look at him - it really was his brother. Unaccountably though, he had a strange, senseless, look about him, somehow bestial. Furthermore, he did not recognize his younger brother when he saw him and showed no kind of emotion. It was as if he was deaf; not making any kind of attempt to answer to his name. Indeed, this figure simply sniffed his nose and muttered unintelligible, sputtering, sounds. Suddenly, and against all expectations, he struck his young brother on the head with a tool he was using. Afterwards, returning to hoeing the soil. His brother, stricken by terror, looked at him again (along at those working with him) only to realize they were all living mummies! In despair he went home, told his family and neighbours what had happened, then led them off to the cemetery. Unsurprisingly, his elder brother's grave was empty when they uncovered it!

A governmental commission was formed straightway and, along with the local police, they began investigations - keeping the suspects under constant observation. Soon they found the secret process for producing "zombies" had its beginning in extremely ancient ages. A time when those looking for unpaid workers made an unbelievable "scientific" discovery. Undoubtedly, certain tribes skilled in these forbidden arts still set aside healthy young lads preselected as victims. Moreover, from those days till this, ageless alchemies would then commence, wherein rarified fish - with two fangs and sharp-edged poisonous fins – would be caught in carefully mapped reservoirs before being cooked and served with other foods. In the full knowledge this led to a full paralysis of the organs and a quick death. Afterwards, the body of their quarry was buried overnight. The next day it was exhumed and carried off to a grave in the forest. There priest-spell-binders, in special robes with painted faces, performed their obscure rituals, took up special herbs, greenery, and started to whisper neglected incantations over the corpse. Speaking briefly, by morning the spirit had returned to the spread-out body. The young man coming back to life strong, but absolutely unaware of himself, his name, or his relatives. This roughish tribe now in possession of a slave who could safely be set to work.

They say, that even day, the robbing of newly-buried corpses has not ceased in African.

AITMATOV. Mankurtism and zombism are as alike as branches growing on the same sadistic tree. Though they bear different titles, their essence is one and the same. The English writer Graham Greene, before he wrote his novel "Comedians", stayed with a tribe of natives on Haiti in order to investigate every side of this alleged "Crime of the century" - the phenomenon of "zombism". Later he wrote in his diary, "The main body of the secret police under dictator Duval, is known as "Tonton Macoute" ("mankurti") and is made up of these same "zombies". Under those circumstances, the ordinary citizens live in an atmosphere of constant alarm."

Crimes of a similar nature, as the newspapers write, are not limited to Africa at the present time. The making of zombies cannot be wiped out among the aborigines of Australia. According to ethnographers, in Australia, among the native tribes, the choice of the victims rests with the priest-magicians. Being tied hand and foot, the victim lies on his side, temporarily unconscious by pricking the heart with a long fish-bone, or a needle-bladed spear-head. The heart then stops beating, and breathing ceases. Being reanimated, after ritual protocols, this man forgets all recollections of life. They say such a zombie differs little from the normal psychologically healthy person, although he may sit for lengthy periods without moving, having fixed his gaze far away.

SHAKHANOV.   Having been a witness of one such seance, the traveler, George Wright, describes what he had seen in the following words:

"Lying dead already, a man was stretched out flat, then, as the drumming and chanting of the priest-magician grew louder, the corpse began to move. Firstly, the priest raised his hands and laid them on his victim's breast, following which he sat up. Further, when the circling chorus of singers gave out their sad soul-penetrating screeches, I did not know where to disappear to. There was nothing more terrifying than to meet the glance of a resurrected zombie and to see his blank eyes".

You wrote that one can take from a man his happiness, his wealth and finally his life. However, who can say there doesn't exist the much more terrible crime of robbing him of his reason and his memory; his innermost essence?

AITMATOV.   How widely zombism is spread aceoss the American continent newspapers have long informed us. Besides the exploitation of zombies for dirty work, those unfortunates are employed in various criminal businesses. Information is available, according to which, in place of the African rituals, there exists modern computerized equipment for making modernized zombies. Either as individuals or whole groups. If a man is thereby made into a zombie (factually proving psychical enslavement), the government of the region is then liable, under the law, to pay recompense of anything up to two million dollars to a victim.

A specific case comes to mind. Having emigrated from Haiti to America, a certain Jack Ornyuv declared himself to be a zombie and demanded recompense from the government social fund. When the management of the Fund began to make serious enquiries, officials in

Haiti sent copies of documents stating he had died in 1971, at the age of fifty.

"I died but was later resurrected", confessed Ornyuv, " As for my murder so with my revival. Human hands brought about each of these conditions. How am I to blame?" Unsurprisingly, no government agency wanted to become involved in these disputes.

SHAKHANOV. It is interesting to explore the extent to which victims of sadism and zombism can demand justice. Indeed, how many tortured and crippled victims of mankurtism and zombism can exclaim, "How am I to blame?" At one time, when I was investigating the December 1937 events, there came to me two friends of comrade *"C"* – *explaining the case of* a scientific worker in his own words:

"Once, going about my work, I found the tables turned. Instead of operating highly complex and classified machines, I was myself the target of their mysterious functions. They were directed (accidentally or not) towards my own head. Since then, I have turned into a zombie. Moreover, taking every advantage of my befuddlement, operatives from the State Security Committee torment day and night. Indeed, they set me all kinds of tasks and record my reactions. As such, my only hope lies in you, and in Olzhas Suleimenov, to free me from this torment!" He begged me to help him, while pointing at a sickle-shaped scar on his temple.

In spite of persistent rumours that the Committee for State Security had special apparatus for turning men into zombies, we had no evidence to prove it, and could do nothing.

Later on, in a series of authoritative journals, there appeared a number of articles exposing secret experimental centres existing in Moscow, occupied with the provision of psycho-therapeutic equipment for investigating the mind. Apparently, it gave operators the possibility of manipulating human intellects, wiping out all opposition; mental or physical.

So stated, any rational man has the right to ask, "So were there really mankurts and zombies? Or are all these stories just a form of phobia filling people's minds with fantastic beliefs?"

In fact, there are people who want to go further and say, "If mankurts and zombies are real, then prove it by showing them to us and by defining the technological processes which produce them"

By way of answer, it can be established that in ancient times the technology for turning men into mankurts can be evidenced, while in our own age it cannot. Nonetheless, suspicions remain.

No matter what one says, human beings may rise to unthinkable glory in this world, or sink into the very depths of depravity in their undertakings. Overall, our outlook should be positive, however. The laws of evolution themselves propel Homo Sapiens to improve from generation to generation. Even though, these immutable principles must be understood within the context of terrifying increases in crime and regular ethical transgression. Especially amongst the more exalted ranks of our societies.

AITMATOV. A worrying thought. Another example jumps into my head at this juncture. In Iraq, a man was caught in the act of stealing and hence sentenced to have his hand cut off. All begging the question, of course, as to whether, having cut off this man's hand, his criminal inclinations have indeed been reduced. Can a moral wound change his social behavior? Some say in the whole world only two hundred kinds of physical punishment exist, although this must be understood as an approximation. Is it fair to argue, therefore, that behind every one of them stands a form of sadism? In the Old Testament of the Hebrews, one reads of "an eye for an eye and a tooth for a tooth", but are these axioms distant from mankurtism in Asia and African zombiism. Let us imagine a future dictator-sadist. A man having developed a taste for both scientific revolution and technological development, who, nevertheless, becomes blinded by power. Would it be so far-fetched to foresee him installing some kind of conveyor-belt system for the production of mankurts and zombies as warriors for war?

May God not lead anyone to such a catastrophe, but fearful fancies too often ground themselves in an imagination of the theoretically possible.

SHAKHANOV. From history, we sadly know of repeated cases where the spread of sadistic instincts in society eventually gained nation-wide proportions. A general moral infection, in no small part, encouraged by government institutions themselves. Take, for instance, gladiatorial battles in ancient Roman arenas, wherein the natural instincts of healthy competition were reduced to bloodthirsty entertainments in honour of the ruling classes. A sickening form of amusement which eventually spread across the whole of Italy.

In one sense, mass entertainment is nothing new. Beginning in the third century B.C., performance designed arenas and sport complexes were constructed: equipped with state of the art technologies. Cynics argued these divertissements merely distracted the public by way of spectacle. Certainly, no expense was spared! Historical sea battles, for example, were reenacted for which they constructed replicas of the original warships and employed hundreds of slaves- all in the game! Further, military scenes, involving dozens of horses, spears, and bronze shields, were used to develop the authenticity of these shows.

Thence, having won the love of his people, the Emperor, through propaganda and jingoism, turned everyone into a worshipper. However, in order to keep up such pretenses, the level of brutality needed to increase with each generation. The overall number of victims becoming almost countless.

One of the worst perpetrators, the clinically insane Emperor Caligula, nonetheless understood these spectacles as little more than theatrical scenarios with a political purpose. Hence, he drove women, slaves and even cripples onto the arena. Following him, the Emperor Claudius employed every means at his disposal to deepen the narcotization of his fellow Roman. As I recall, the Emperor Vitellius, in honour of his birthday, arranged titanic struggles involving two hundred and sixty five gladiators, while Titus, for his part, extended such amusement to a hundred days. Most disturbingly, the so-called "feast of cannibals" witnessed ten thousand gladiators fighting for one hundred and twenty three days; slashing in a fenzy at each other's bellies and cutting off hands and heads in the process.

As for the thousands of spectators, they kept pushing their ways through the crowds to see these matches from morning till night. They hailed the victors, called the defeated weak and worthless, and applauded every clash as it came. Heated disputes with neighbours were exchanged regarding each "show" - demonstrating, no doubt, their general enjoyment. But, is there anything more mindless than peaceful people being reduced to a feeling of satisfaction though bathing in someone else's blood? Alas, the slogan "bread and circuses" lives on everlastingly it seems.

The first time Romans were released from these blood-drenched nightmares falls to the honour of early Christian faith. As soon as the Emperor Constantine the Great was baptized, his lands heard the melodic chime of church bells blessing more kindly deeds and righteous pursuits. Goodwill and hope became common aims, while strict prohibitions against violence towards one's countrymen were proclaimed central to Christ's teaching. Any infringement of which met with severe punishment.

In 404 A.D. - during the last gladiatorial clashes in Rome, a monk from Asia Minor named Telemachus, ran into an arena to separate contestants. Yet, these warriors were already so blinded by fury (apart from being sworn to fight to the last), they cut the innocent monk down with their swords. Shocked, the Emperor Honorius was shaken in his soul. Afterwards giving rigid commands to forbid all future "games". All the same, Roman citizens were actually obliged to Telemachus for these mercies, rather the Emperor.

AITMATOV. From that one can draw this conclusion: "passive" sadism was exhibited by the people, who got at least some satisfaction from the pain and suffering of others. As such, their agenda remains unchanged. Perhaps the true work of humanitarian and religious propaganda is found when it curbs these appetites?

Up to the present day, Spanish bullfighting attracts millions of impassioned fans. Demonstrating the popular allure in a man contesting with death in the form of a deliberately infuriated bull. I have even heard that during these bullfights life on the streets of Madrid quietens in a grim anticipation of potential mayhem. Perhaps most shockingly, those who for some reason or other cannot get to the stadium sit at home watching this spectacle on their television screens.

SHAKHANOV. The latest researches of scientific narcologists have led to the disconcerting conclusion that an overwhelming majority of people have an inherent inclination toward alcoholism. If this is the case, then why don't they all become hopeless drunkards? It seems the answer to this question is directly connected with the physiological peculiarities of an individual and his or her ability to control himself. A discipline emerging from congenitally received customs. Hence, the tragedy of human nature (if these statistics are to be believed) is at the least alleviated traditional wisdoms. Of course, those of a weaker will may still become oppressed by foul drunkenness: having no power whatsoever to break free from these pernicious poisons. I have heard tell, in this regard, of some insipid women who became drunkards in a manner which nearly competes with their husbands.

What is a drunkard, we may ask? A pertinent inquiry following the discovery by scientists of "fire-water" among vegetable life! Out of twenty grasses, or herbal plants, ten of them were experimentally watered with ordinary tap-water, while the others with kept alive by tap-water plus alcoholic spirits. The result being an accepted norm among the first ten, although the second ten threw out more leaves and grew taller than expected. Later, when all of these test plants were given ordinary water again, those who had previously been given alcohol suddnely lost their radiance and faded.

As for pigs, geese, and ducks, who imbibe alcohol from their regular use in factory dregs, just read in papers.

Does this imply everything living on earth cannot survive without some kind of mania?

In the latter years of the Republics, youthful crime has increased some eight to ten times. A massive percentage. Should we, therefore, follow certain pundits in the West in attributing an indirect influence on video-productions, along with a constantly tainting stream of violence and brutality on our TV screens?

In my view, from our conversations today, one can come to these conclusions: every man is inclined (to one degree or another) towards sadism, masochism, and so on. A quality akin to spiritual sickness. All meaning that, like any other malady, a tiny scratch can turn into a serious swelling. In which case, humanitarian aims and compassionate actions need to be stressed as a curing balm, along with religious teaching – if we are to cure this epidemic.

AITMATOV.   In the Soviet period, genetics itself was distorted as a science. The greatest researchers selflessly working away on types pf experimentation leading to a greater common good being condemned to prison camps and their reports destroyed - all given to the flames.

"Europe ... is the mother of all devils" the psychologist Carl Jung once wrote. If we turn to Europe, or the West generally (as a socio-anthropological or pathology warning), then we may learn some valuable lessons!

In this regard, I am haunted by first half of the twentieth century, when "Mass Society" brought an end to traditionalist treasures, along with notions of an aristocratic nobility - at the very same time as "Faustian Man" challenged the entire concept of collective endeavor.

In the light of certain psychological theories, this collective "de-personalizing" received an unexpected analysis at the hands of a prophetic Carl Jung. Especially when he wrote "psychological disorders of the normal man ... find a place for themselves in the social and political spheres. Taking the form of mass psychoses, such as war and revolution ... Then, when the majority of people begin to exhibit these psychoses, the dynamic potential of the collective man is unleashed. Bursting forth and freeing all those monsters and demons (which sleep in every man), for as long as he does not become part of the mass. On joining the crowd and becoming part of it, a man unconsciously falls to a lower moral and intellectual level".

Perhaps every crowd, in its senseless, ill-defined, unconscious outbursts, manifests innumerable unthought-of bestialities? Thereby producing almost endless victims of blood-violence and destruction.

SHAKHANOV.   At present, every man - to one degree or another - has become a battlefield for clashes between abnormal conditions. Thankfully, there may exist a number of objective laws clarifying these dysfunctions. That stated, it is interesting to note such troubles usually take shape and form in times of upheavals. Needless to say, the period of sexual emancipation at the dawn of Soviet power, with its denial of family life and accepted morals influenced youth in France, "hippies" of the so-called "sexual revolution", the Beatles, "rock-n-rollers", and even the Nazi Party with their crude cult of phallic power.

All facts bearing witness to the crisis of our epoch, as well as the promised birth of a different type of humanity. Of a new order on a planetary scale. Indeed, these shake-ups appear to reflect life-reviving processes bubbling up into our world from the deepest of depths ......

AITMATOV.   It is only necessary to place a little pressure on goodness for evil to strengthen its position. What a pity we didn't recognize this earlier, or interpret its meaning! Living men are woven from a myriad of activities: both constructive and destructive, premeditated and spontaneous. What is more, the internal labyrinths of a soul are both complex and dangerous. Thus, to avert the birth of future blood-suckers by blood-suckers, and wipe away every plague of mankurtism and zombism, we need to live by our obligations to the human race as a whole.

POWER PLUS SPIRITUALITY
AND
THEIR REFLECTION IN THE ACTIVITIES
OF TSARS, KHANS, KINGS, AND
PRESIDENTS

To unite the country, to solidify its parts, to govern its home and foreign policy, to maintain and protect its culture, to nourish the power of the government, and in all of this to hold in one's hand the reins of just control - that is a complicated and responsible task. An obligation to which not every governor is capable, or a burden which not every shoulder can bear with equanimity.

... In memory one needs to keep not only righteous deeds and acts, But also human crimes, as facts.

SHAKHANOV. United for the past seventy years, two-hundred and fifty million people submitted to "Communist" ideals propagated by the Soviet Union, even though - like a gigantic colossus with clay legs – things finally started to collapse under their own weight.

AITMATOV. Truly, but a new problem stands before us today. In what direction will ties between the Central Asian Republics develop, since they have grown from the ruins of the USSR? How will power and democracy constellate, and within whose boarders.

SHAKHANOV. Previous Republics, having previously been fed from the "centre", quickly developed mutual "brotherly" relations. Yet, upon independence, they all fell into a mire of severe economic crisis. Obviously, as centralized mechanisms no longer provided resources, each new sovereign power needed to survive according to its own means. Alas, these soon withered away without the infrastructures to meet previous demands. For example, the construction of even mundane machines required for everyday service (where one component was produced in Uzbekistan, another in the Ukraine, and a third in Belorussia) became nie on impossible to build. As an aside, it is curious to recall that in the bowels of Kazakhstan we have all the elements of Mendeleev's table in abundance. But I digress. All of which meant manufacturing and distribution fell apart because our independent nations were completely unprepared.

How could this be? Very simple! From the start far-reaching political calculations had been made. So, if any Republic suddenly demanded independence, they would find such detachment impossible. Like removing one organ from the Body Politic despite its connection to all. As such, the various republics found these processes of withdrawal grossly disabling.

AITMATOV. Churchill was right when he remarked that no matter how bad democracy was, nothing better has so far had been devised. A sad paradox, to say the least. But it is also sad to see - along with changes in economic relations - our spiritual treasures beginning to equally dwindle. Who can deny that under Soviet power artistic creation itself became a weapon of Party propaganda. An irony, since culture was already being choked by the tight framework of "socialist realism". Indeed, its unsleeping censorship and highly selective budgets was legendary. Hence, personal publications, newspapers and journals were throttled at birth.

Contrariwise, our shops now have book shelves chock-full of low standard detective stories, with badly written novels about violence, rape, murder and robbery. Provoking some pundits to say there is an open instigation to carry out all kinds of criminal transgressions.

Nonetheless, it may be a question of time. In our society, after all, there are a number of democratic freedoms which are misunderstood. What of the consequences? Are they inescapable in a period of change-over? Albeit a changeover into what?

SHAKHANOV. Have you noticed that as soon as we dismantled the old national system of education, the psychology of our society was immediately changed? Previously, our youth loved to boast about some newly-read book. Now, however, it is more likely to preen about how five dollars has the market value of ten!

Yes, time dictates everything. We cannot blame youth for that. Still, the fact spiritual values are now challenged by materialism tenfold, fifteen-fold, even twenty-fold, must be viewed with suspicion and regret by the seriously-minded.

Future society, having placed money-boxes above the moral good, will fall prey to increasing inhumanities. They tell me of a young businessman (not yet twenty five years of age), who practically swam in money, ordering staff in the hotel "Kazakhstan" -- in Alma-Ata - to drag a cannon up onto the roof in the dead of night. Without the slightest consideration for others, he then asked staff to fire a salvo celebrating his birthday while the whole city slept.

AITMATOV.   The facts say we have taken democracy to be sheer dissoluteness. Everyone has become a Tsar, a god: doing just as he thinks fit. The blinkers have fallen from our eyes for sure, yet, what do we see? Licentiousness! Democracy means law and order. It has its limits and boundaries.

A simple image will elucidate. The family is a model of the State in miniature, its primary cell. What would happen if (based on false notions of democracy), a daughter in- law becomes head of the house? Or the eldest son begins to dominate his mother? Who needs that kind of democracy, bringing with it the collapse of the family? Can sheer wantonness take the place of accepted norms?

From happiness to sorrow takes but a single step! With great bitterness, Napoleon Bonaparte pronounced this truth at the end of his career! Being deprived of an Emperor's throne and sent to St. Helena to finish his days in isolation. Unarguably, History show us it is necessary to hasten slowly.

Today, we are on the road of social recovery. So, it is exceedingly important to be clear where we are going and why. As Plato writes, "Tyranny arises, of course, not from some other order but from democracy!" In other words, one may become enslaved by extreme freedoms. Allowing empty-headed and decadent people to take the reins of power. We may liken them to tinder, ready to blaze out speeches and pointless initiatives at the merest spark of provocation. Themselves never permitting somebody else to speak otherwise. In the final analysis, seeing the People no longer deceived, these slanderers (not from spite, but from ignorance), suddenly become admirers of a salvific oligarchy. Without any irony, a tyrant rises from the roots - being chosen by the People. Then, having obedient people behind him, will he abstain from shedding the blood of his fellow tribesmen? Just the opposite! If all takes its usual course, he will start to take his opponents to court on trumped-up charges, and disgrace himself with corruption, intrigue and murder. Meanwhile promising privileges and land to his cronies. Moreover, disempowering citizens through an attractive welfare system (so that they feel the real need for a leader), will then oppose free-thinking along with any opposition to his rule. This tyrant, as his authority consolidates, will then need to keep his subjects busy and exterminate so-called "undesirables". Finally reduced to abject servitude, people will know (I swear by Zeus), what kind of wretch he is …..

SHAKHANOV.   What then -from your point of view - are the similarities and differences between naked power and democracy?

AITMATOV.   Speaking figuratively, power is the blade of the axe, while democracy is the handle. However, one must never forget it is the People who hold the handle in their hands. That is why you must not think of those two concepts as distinct from each other. So pondered, I will tell you of one occurrence, which I personally witnessed ...

One evening, my daughter Shirring said to me:

"Papa, I lost my wallet when I left the bus. Don't be cross with me please, I don't know how it happened ..."

I reproached her for carelessness, not for the loss of a small sum of money, but the loss of her school notes and teaching material. Most of all for the signatures of her tutors and the marks they had given. All of these materials would have to be copied out again. Two or three days passed, and then the phone rang in my Embassy. An unexpected call from the Luxemburg police, although I had no idea what they wanted with me?

"Your daughter lost her wallet and exercise-book, I believe. The man who found it has brought it to us and handed it over. Could you come and collect it?" said a voice at the end of the line.

Unreflectingly, I sent Shirring herself to collect her lost wallet and copy-book. I took it for granted that her money would not be returned, but only the documents, teacher's notes, and so on.

"Well, all in order?" I enquired on her return, "Notes, documents and all?" Following which she cheerfully replied:

"Yes, all in order, money and documents as well, I'm so glad!"

I must confess I was very surprised to hear her money was there too. At the same time I was very pleased. Not for the few currency notes returned, but for the honesty and sincerity of the man who kept his responsibilities before society.

No one, surely, can have any reason to accuse a man of theft if he finds an exercise book with money in it, and takes the book to the local police, yet keeps the money in his pocket? In essence, this man's honesty and recognition of his responsibility demonstrates the constructive power of a democracy. In this sense it seems that in our society neither power, nor real democracy, is known. After all, most people finding money will straightway put it into their pockets and not return it to the police, or its owner. Either way, my daughter, on seeing someone show feeling for another's loss, now equally wishes to do the same: returning good for good. Nowadays, being grown up, she continues to teach her own children to do the same thing. Hence, it is necessary to understand our democracy should not blindly imitate Western art, or bring into our lives aspects of other nationalities, principles, and manners (all strange to our mentality) - not even a reckless following of various principles of Islamic fundamentalism – but rather immutable laws for the virtuous benefit if all.

SHAKHANOV.   Although people presently suffer both economic and spiritual shake-ups, they will gradually understand the necessity of strict laws for a new social relationship. It will take, in these contradictory times, a transitional period in the Republics of Central Asia. Yet, will we take as our model of progress the flourishing countries of the East, or own cultural model - preserving its distinguishing features?

Such are the obvious questions standing before us today.

AITMATOV.   Responsible democracy - that is our common task, the load we all must bear. From the President, down to the humblest member of society. We must get rid of the mistaken idea that, having chosen Democracy, we do not need to do anything more – apart from await golden rains from the skies.

We are still a long way from an ideal society. A thesis we must naturalize with our minds, and our hearts. Only when ruling power (and its possibilities) are no longer used on behalf of personal interests, will the fruits of democracy be seen. Therefore, I count the feeling of personal responsibility as more significant today than it was during totalitarism.

Conversely, at times, I think people who call themselves democrats (often inebriated with that sweet-sounding word) should stop to meditate on its fundamental meaning.

SHAKHANOV.   You are right, my dear Chingiz. We need to grow and to develop, as well as raise ourselves little by little. Nobody yet really knows what the final results will be like.

AITMATOV.   Why nobody, do you say? Pericles, living in the fifth century B.C., knew excellently well. We may turn to him, to his famous speeches, delivered before popular meetings in Athens. Here is one of them:

"Our government order does not imitate other institutions, but we rather serve as an example for others. We name our order Democracy, because it is founded not on the interests of the minority, but of the majority - that is the People as a whole. In relation to private personal interests, our law presents equal rights for everybody. As far as any political meaning is concerned, there each one receives advantage, not because he is supported by this party, or that, but in accordance with his personal prowess and character. In the same way, the insignificance of the condition of some poor person does not deprive him of the right of offering his services to the government.

We live a free political life, and in our everyday relations do not experience disbelief in one another, nor get irritated or annoyed if another acts as he sees fit. In social dealings, we do not break the laws, merely because of a feeling of great fear before them.

With yearly contests, and with sacrifices, we enable our souls to rest in peace from our labours, and equally from the strictest laws, the daily observance of which drives away all boredom.

Besides that, thanks to the wide scale of our government, to us there flows from everywhere decisively all we need, and we can with the same convenience use those riches which are produced here, and also those produced by other folk in foreign lands.

We love beauty, without capriciousness, and wide wisdom without delicacy. We utilize riches for activity, and not as something to boast about, and admit poverty is for us no shame; just the opposite - it is shameful not to get rid of poverty by toil. One and the same person may take care of his domestic affairs, and also take part in affairs of the government. We consider a man who declines from any participation in governmental activity not a humble person, but empty.

We ourselves judge our actions, and try to evaluate them, not taking into account that speech often hinders action. The greater danger, in our estimation, occurs when someone acts without a previous judgement of the matter. With others it is just the opposite, and ignorance gives birth to valour, while thinking things over leads to indecision.

I affirm that our government is the school of Greeks, and each one as a separate person, it seems to me, can show himself to be a valuable and independent personality in the most varied spheres of action."

SHAKHANOV.   That is all indisputably so, but along with it a good time has begun for those who love to "flutter" with their tongues! For them, it is enough to conceal themselves behind a democratic mask, to step out on the tribune, and curse the whole world: and the President too. And nobody stops them. Just the opposite - for some of them that is balsam for their soul. They clap their hands till they are sore, and cannot applaud such orators any more than they do.

Does democracy really consist in seeking out others mistakes and blunderings, revealing their crimes and shortcomings, one to the other?

Where will independence and originality lead us? To what results will it bring us, and what form of experience shall we find?

What kind of things, indeed, happened at the last parliamentary elections in Kirghizstan? Were there not the bitterest tribal quarrels, when having forgotten about the unity of roots, people fell one after another, into internecine battles, making mutual accusations? Has it gone so far, that one candidate standing for a deputy, could distribute boots to all his electors - but for one foot only!

"Give me your vote, and I'll defeat my opponent - then you will get your other boot!" he said to poor people, taking advantage of their poverty. Other candidates, by the way, also did not hang back - throwing money about, left and right. Vodka flowed in streams. Nor did they hold back from gifting dresses, women's underwear, and so on. They distributed meat, flour, tasty pastries, as well as money. By the way, the candidate who gave boots away did not succeed at the elections. Another paradox of choice!

Nonetheless, many like him found themselves serving in Parliament. Many of those rogues, to whom one would be ashamed to offer a hand in greeting, were ready - for the sake of momentary advantage - to even sell their father. Today have grown fabulously rich. Profits from general privatization got first of all into their hands. Now the fate of poor simple people depends upon these "benefactors". Speaking of these phenomena, we must admit that this was partly due to our first contacts with "democracy". In ancient times Kazakhs had more than two hundred general prohibitions. Here are a few of them, to give you a general idea of the customs and habits of those days.

Do not spit in the well from which people drink. Do not put anything on a loaf of bread, nor kick it. Do not tread on salt. Enter a house with a bold step. Do not stand in the way of an elder. Do not take a place before he does at table. Do not interrupt him when he is speaking. Do not swear at parents. Do not laugh at beggars. Do not stare at a man. Do not turn your back on him. Do not beat your steed about the head. Do not rock an empty cradle. Do not whistle at home. Do not throw your hat under people's feet. Having been in the home where someone was dead, do not go straightway into a home of the living. Do not destroy the nests of ants or birds ... etcetera. These and many others like them were always kept, as the apple of one's eye, as the signs of the national character of a people. They formed our national culture, literature, speech, and beliefs of a religious nature.

Primarily, they performed the function of a national ideology. Two events connected with this topic, of which I myself was a witness, have remained with me constantly, all my life!

The Georgians have a good custom, carefully kept from generation to generation, when a daughter is given away in marriage. Among the presents received, the most important is the book Shota Rustaveli

"Knight in a Tiger's skin". Such is the special place occupied by this poem, even in our present day! That great work sings of native land, and of the honour and valour of its sons. This is why it is the most precious property in every home in Georgia. The list of gifts for the bride and groom are not complete without it, and the parents of the young couple can be reproached for its absence. Or take Canada, for a second example of mine.

In that country, they compete for old trees. The oldest receives a medal, which is attached to the tree winning it. From such a careful and loving attitude towards Nature, one feels a great satisfaction and pride in humanity as well. In the Baltic Republics too, they have an annually prepared list of the oldest trees. Once in Estonia, on the isle of Mukhu, I was amazed at the number of boats upturned and laid across an old wooden bridge. I asked what they were used for. "Those boats are between a hundred and two hundred years old. In their earlier days they worked well for our great-grand-fathers, and assisted them to meet with their loved ones, and helped them to bear children, and thus served our folk: who now cannot forget them, and all they did for our forebears!"

"How delightful, that these people treasure the memory of their ancient sires, and still show their gratitude, humanity and love!"

AITMATOV. Speaking many tongues, holding various beliefs, weighing things up and selecting the best, have predetermined for themselves common principles of law and order. Is it not so? Glory to the All Highest that it is! What will happen if, fighting through at last to their full freedom, somebody becomes a prophet, and preaches a gospel of those good old customs - worthy of imitation by our modern degraded society?

In 1993, I was asked to become a member of the Berlin International Film Festival. In the jury were many specialists, masters of the cinematic arts, and literature, from all corners of the earth. From countries such as England and America, and so on. From Russia (the previous Soviet Union) I was invited as a representative ...

Certainly, the opinions and views of jury-members were various and interesting. I hoped that I could prove interesting too, taking part in the general work of the Festival. Our task was to analyze the films, and find any deficiencies. The best new films were being shown accompanied by critical comment.

The turn of one American producer came, and even before assembling, jury members were praising the film: agreeing together it was the best one to be shown so far. It was a film about Cuba. At first I thought it would show the fate of a half-depressed, and half-starving island, and so become impatient to see this film. However, it turned out otherwise. It was a film concerning the problems encountered by American homosexuals, along with their bid for freedom and legal rights. Coincidentally, a young American activist at the Festival, (a man devoted to Fidel Castro), also turned out to be a homosexual. Once the Castro-communists learned of his inclinations and beliefs, however, they did not turn him away, but tried to help him instead.

When the film was being judged, all members of the jury, except me, were delighted with it, naming it wonderful, and beautiful. I stood alone, and told them as I rose from my seat:

"I cannot agree with your verdict. Furthermore, I would call this film dangerous! Such things as the film shows are met with in real life, I do not deny. But what is not found in life? Moreover, to turn homosexuality into something heroic, poeticizing unnatural male leanings, will unduly influence millions of spectators!" Then I added: "Nobody has the authority to encroach on traditionalist rights, not even the President himself!" Thus roused a general buzz ...

"But we have real democracy here! How do you dare stand against it?"

"I do not stand against real democracy. However, you, with such a film, exert pressure on people, on their conscience, and on their honour. In fact, under no circumstances can homosexuals stand as a symbol of freedom. Undoubtedly, that said, there is a no means of standing up against your decision on this film!" I must say I was seriously angry and disturbed.

Soon after that event I thought deeply about the matter. Maybe my views are not in fashion? But what is fashion - a momentary desire, some kind of fragment in time – something quickly passing and changeable. Only the deep feelings engendered by one's morality and inner culture can save people from baseness. It will protect them like a good fairy.

I do not know if it was my persistence and conviction which finally took effect? Either way, this film was not awarded the Grand Prize, though it did get a lesser one on the prize-list.

What is more interesting - when that film was later shown at a film festival in New York, it received an "Oscar"!

Overall, I am convinced this is a typical example of the thoughtless change-over of values in moral spheres, which is the scourge of modernity.

SHAKHANOV. Once, I accompanied our elder writer Gabiden Mustafin to Gabit Musrepov's home. There, we saw in broad daylight, a young fellow kissing his girl in the porchway. Both of them Kazakhs by the way. We thought, maybe they would be disturbed on seeing us. Not on your life! They went on kissing and cuddling even tighter than before!

Here Gabiden lowered his eyes, and gloomily pronounced:

"From a pot the lid flies off, but from a dirty dog - all his shame! The great Tatar poet Musa Dzhalil - may the memory of him shine long - wrote a poem about a girl who came home late and found the gate locked. Somehow she managed to climb over it, but tore her dress at the back. Next morning, hurrying off to work, she put on the torn dress. Oddly, seeing her come like that, her village work-mates decided it must be the new fashion, and not wishing to be old-fashioned, tore their dresses too, and felt pleased with themselves, showing off...

Chingiz, it seems to me only a miserable number of people, say some eight percent or so, (God grant I am not far mistaken in this) live in accordance with their own lights. The rest thoughtlessly copy others, one here, another there: without even bothering to consider whether their example is good, or ill-befitting. Those who have no real ground beneath their feet cannot imbibe the best of their own national culture. They almost start to imitate the apes in their primitive behaviour, copying each other blindly, and rapidly declining to a lower level.

AITMATOV. Maybe this is so, Mukhtar, yet at the same time there is an additional danger in sticking exclusively to one's national ideology. One must not forget for a moment to enrich one's native culture with the treasure of all humanity. The future lies in interweaving with the general treasures of culture from all over the world, wheresoever found.

In a word, today, when various views do not blend into a wide highway, it is necessary to work out a cultural conception whereby great thinkers, moralists, and writers are drawn together.

Every culture, as you have said, has its own "taboos". But, a prohibition is not a red "Stop" light on the road. Indeed, for some it is a green "Go" signal. Regardless, these signifiers are boundaries between good and evil, between the useful and the useless. A blind switching about, or mere imitation, is simply running after glitter, gleam, and tinsel. All characteristics of this shaky change-over period. Similar times, I hear, existed in Germany, Australia, Belgium and Luxemburg. Well, let them wash their streets with shampoo - that is no sign of culture. It is not by chance those societies appear to be returning to traditional values.

As a case I point, social tendencies such as "free love", and the "sexual revolution" in those countries have gradually diminished. Contrariwise, it is swamping us nowadays. I should like to think this ethical deficiency is both avoidable and temporary, however. As such, we must endure until truth and wisdom bring harmony to humanity.

Another example: On the streets of Luxemburg I chanced to see a slogan blazing out: "We want to be as we are" - which means like our forefathers. Simple words, it would seem, even though having special significance. After all, that small European country is surrounded by France, Germany, and Holland - powerful developed countries. Thus, these slogans are a reminder to Luxemburgers: don't go thoughtlessly chasing the ways of your neighbours. Preserve, your own language, your culture, your literature, your music, your art, and do not forget where your roots lie: deep in the past.

SHAKHANOV. Will our economy crack-up? Will our culture blossom or fade away? Will our policies lead to war, or will the live in peace and quiet? Does all thus ultimately depend on governmental leaders, although only when they are supported by the People?

If the USA has, since 1789 and up until today, been governed by fourty one Presidents, then why among Americans, do Washington and Roosevelt enjoy such high authority and superiority? The first one created one government, uniting colonies of various kinds, and forming them into one nation of a new type. The second, a hundred years later, lifted the economy of USA out of a deep crisis, and showed decisiveness in the smashing of Fascism - along with their British forebears. In this way, they earned the esteem and respect of the populace: in their own country and among nations all over the world.

Among the ranks of famous people in Britain, one can find the names of Churchill and the "Iron Lady" Margaret Thatcher, renowned for their tireless activity in the interest of their own government.

Most noted of Turks, Kemal-Pasha Ataturk went down into history as an outstanding person: selflessly battling for the unity of all the Turks. Thereafter, we keep Turgut Ozal's memory. A man who decided to introduce radical reforms - and in that way saved his country from economic collapse, when agrarian Turkey was still groaning under unbearable taxation.

In China, too, the guidance of Mao Tse Dung's rule brought this country to the logical end of crime and evil-doing. Fascinatingly, during the "cultural revolution", by overcoming the cult of his own personality.

No good deeds, or bad ones, are carried away by the wind into nothingness. All remains clearly latent in the history of a country.

AITMATOV. You have touched on what is possibly the most topical and sharpest problem of all - the role of personality in history.

SHAKHANOV. Just before we began our conversation on this topic, I took a look at the book by Niccolo Machiavelli, entitled "The Prince", where he outlines his attitude to the actions of Emperors, Tsars, Kings, Sultans, and Tyrants too. We know Stalin studied Machiavelli's book with its "precepts and injunctions" very closely. Yet, all rulers make sense according to their various intellects, characteristics, traditions, and the customs of their lands.

In himself, this author affirmed that someone who rules a land did so by two means. Firstly, by the given law, and in the second place by power. The first one is befitting to a man, the second to beasts alone. That argued, if one wishes to secure law and order in a land, it is necessary to use both means. One must learn to respect and observe the law, as well as use power against transgressors. There is no other satisfactory means.

Unite inside yourself a threatening lion, and a cunning fox. The first is needed when fighting with external foes, the second, when dealing with internal ones. Hold them fast in fear, trick them and hold them in terror. Only then will you firmly keep the reins of leadership fast in your hands: when internal foes see that you see them!

AITMATOV. Yes, throughout the centuries, throughout every social formation, and in various Tsardoms and governments, a variety of rulers have passed. They all reigned differently. Tellingly, if following his death, a ruler enjoys full respect, this may mean that he, while yet alive, was just and righteous. Possibly, even being distinguished by a pure soul with humanitarian motives. If not so, they name the deceased ruler a tyrant ... Hence, it is so important to remember the words, spoken by the father of democracy - Pericles. "Remember, Pericles, that you ruled the Athenians as free people. To govern such people one must stand without fear before them, without envy, without self-love, and vaingloriousness!"

SHAKHANOV. You have counted out noble qualities in which, as in a mirror, appears the image of any ruler. At the same time, in that treatise by Machiavelli readers find five negative and unsuitable qualities for a leader, which will bring about his downfall. They are: fickleness, light-mindedness, coarseness, slow-wittedness, and indecisiveness, all leading to faulty solutions of the problems facing him. If you are subject to one of those, then all your subjects will deceive you, and cock their noses at you- so he ends.

AITMATOV. From the writings of a few eastern philosophers, I have summarised an unvarying idea: on the whole rulers of a government can be divided according to their worthiness into three types: the first are bestowed by God with all good virtues by birth. The second imitate the doings of others. They are for the most part, cunning and treacherous. Thirdly, are those who know nothing of themselves, and learn nothing from others. By the will of fate, they come to power, and soon afterwards lose it. They decide things by shouting and squabbling, and that leads to warfare, bringing the People to destruction, and wasting away the wealth of a land.

SHAKHANOV.   What an exact definition! In reality these are three types of people. Empirically they are found so. At the end of the day, power makes good characters distort and brings out deficiencies in a personality.

AITMATOV.   If between the ruler and the ruled lies unbelief and mistrust, it will be difficult to bring them into harmonious action. Take Germany, for example. How many great musicians, writers, scientists and artists has she given to the world over the centuries! But it only needs one corporal to come to power for the land to be robbed of all these spiritual treasures. Gathered together, as they were, with patient care. You know what happened to the hard-working German people under the command of Hitler, and how the country was ruined, while equally ruining many others.

SHAKHANOV.   Narshakhi, the sage, wrote about rulers: "If your people eat black bread, you also must eat the same. But if you eat soft bread with honey, and leave your people the dry crusts, you will lose their trust immediately. You will also lose your honour, and your power over folk".

AITMATOV.   I think there are two forms of power, seen most often. The first is when a ruler serves his own people and the second - when he serves solely himself and his clan. One is born of a deep consciousness of one's responsibility and honour, the other comes from an all-imbibing egoism and depravity.

There can be no quarrelling with one fact - where power exists, there is always a fight for it. No matter what happens, however, the common social good must never fall under the single overwhelming sway of an autocrat.

SHAKHANOV.   I can't quite remember now where I read this, but it was obviously one of the wise old men of the past, who wrote: "Woe to the leader who gathers round him flatterers and boot-lickers, for soon all the others will start imitating them, with their superficial words!

Soon nothing apart from honeyed speeches will be the rule of the day, and you, the leader will be deprived of caution and circumspection. You will become accustomed to this, and will want to hear praise every day.

All that ends with personal idolizing, and soon you will make a god of yourself. Raising to yourself a golden monument. Then some lickspittle will stand and hold a sunshade above it, so that it does not suffer sun-stroke. He will be awarded by you with funds from the folk's treasury for his labours, if you can call these such.

You will forget the people. You will be blind to their need and poverty. Instead of helping them, you will build marble palaces for your own wives and children, and of course, flatterers will surround them too; uttering their petty praises!"

AITMATOV.   An Eastern poet has rightfully said:

> "Woe to the land of the lickspittle slaves,
> Who all try to flatter the one on the throne.
> The heaven-sent poet, who listeners crave,
> Is left unattended there, all on his own!"

It happens, when above their heads dark clouds gather - and other leaders arise threatening to unseat them – sorrowful days appear, and none of their flatterers can then be found beside them. At this juncture, not being able to look their own folk in the face, they suffer shame, and run away from their land.

SHAKHANOV.   Let me read you one of my poems, about a Turkish Sultan, who by precisely such circumstances was forced to quit his home.

> *"In a Turkish Sultan's harem were seen*
> *About a thousand beautiful brides.*
> *Selected from many cities they'd been –*
> *Khorezm, Gerat,*

And Paris besides,
And from the Greek Pelopennesa,
And even from the town of Taraz.
Where lived the forebears, if you please,
Of poet Akim Taraz, named thus.
Such beauties, cut off from the world, and these
Behind deaf walls were locked away,
As deaf as them, with locks unfurled,
No face of another man saw them,
Except unhappy eunuch guards.
There only the Sultan's spirit held sway.
But when he walked through the harem yards,
With golden vestments on display,
With eyes half-drunk, but full of desire,
All wives grew quiet, and started to pray:
"Ah, Allah, oh Allah,
Than all gods higher,
Set his attention on me today!"
Thus all the women switched on their charms,
And fate to one of them smiled outright,
And fate to another brought only alarms.
Maybe, in four or five years comes delight?
Another - when this old Sultan has died!
Outside, in the palace yard, meanwhile,
They played
And raced
And fought
Till tears...
The Sultan's three hundred children smile.
As like to him as drops, it appears.
Then storm-clouds gathered, and overthrew
The previous Sultan from his throne.
No more of his ladies' delights he knew.
They all were scattered, to others were shown.
And roaming abroad, he had to flee.
The Sultan then from death deferred,

One woman saved, for a certainly...
"Are you not one of my harem herd?
Your face is familiar!" said he, disturbed.
"Yes I was once, to my great woe,
One of a thousand!" she replied,
"Who satisfied your vainglory so —
It's sad, but true, and can't be denied!
You easily conquered
Other Shahs,
But could not master another heart.
Not a single woman's of all those stars,
Since feelings tolerate no smart
    When they are pulverized, cast aside ...
    And if I stretch a hand to you so,
    That's not from love, a-flaming wide,
    But more from pity for your woe.
    Such is the immutable law unfurled:
    If you can love one man alone,
    Then you may love the whole wide world.
    You want to embrace them as your own.
    But if you stay with none of them
    Then with your sorrow you will remain!"
    In Stamboul we recall a Sultan then,
    For the living giving only pain.
    He was an example of frivolousness.
    Yes, but in memory we all need
    Not only deeds of righteousness,
    But also human sins, indeed!

AITMATOV. Yes, the faults of a leader are not forgotten. The memory of them is an immutable moral warning.

By the way, those verses have something in common with those of Makhmud Kashgary:

> *"If a Sultan for himself has built*
> *A palace in a foreign land,*
> *That is an evil sign of his guilt —*

He has provided himself, understand,
With a refuge, in a difficult spot.
But for the people no refuge is there,
Nowhere to run, save to their own cot;
So you should die in your castle fair!" . –

That wisdom is a lesson for anybody, however clever they may be!

SHAKHANOV. Here is one more well-aimed saying in relation to that phenomenon, one which has become a real whip-lash for many governments. A wise man, on entering the Prince's palace left this precept: "The government treasury is the property of a people, attained by them through working with sweat-soaked brows: till corns form on their hands. The ruler should choose with great care the man to whom he hands the key of that treasury. There, where gold and silver lie, you will not escape robbery. If you catch a thief - expose him at once. If you conceal a thief and his roving robbery, then you are a robber as well!"

AITMATOV. Clever and experienced leaders did not use to nominate their near and dear ones for viziers, because they understood that they would begin to mix up government affairs with those of their families and relations. With them, a leader will not be able to speak so strictly - it would be too difficult. Seeing this, other viziers will be jealous, while things hastily get out of hand.

Take the epoch of the Pharaohs in Egypt ... A place with one of the Seven Wonders of the World. In a wonderful form, driving one stone on another, they created the great grey Pyramids: challenging both clouds and eternity ... Yes, long before our era, their Pharaohs were been widely known for their boundless power. In that long distant time I find an interest, especially I must say, from the point of view of their leaders' ethics. Due to the fact, possibly, the greatness of those rulers must be defined quantitatively - by the number and condition of their millions of slaves. "All those living, in heaven and on earth dare not look at the divine Pharaoh". Such was the formula for worship. In themselves, their lords and masters were charismatic symbols – qualitatively difference from all other human beings. According to a deep - even ideological - conviction, the Pharaohs took their mastery, and their mystery, straight from the Gods above! (That parallel was in general a popular one for the ancient historical past). So when a Pharaoh died, the funeral service was all-embracing, all-absorbing. Along with them were buried wives, slaves and servants, as well as his war-chariot and military gear. He was provided with food for the journey to the other side, and eating utensils. As a leader in this life, he had firmly held all the threads of ideology, politics, economics, war and peace. Moreover, in the next life he went would take up a similar position. Instructively then, his ritual service - one common everywhere in that epoch - concealed a very touching metaphor of humanity towards mankind. Of trust and esteem towards those in power. Yet a dead lion, if we paraphrase the proverb, is still nobler than a living dog. All touching, and hopelessly sad - they were idols, just idols, and nothing more.

Near Cairo stand the majestic pyramids of Cheops, Mikrin, and Kefren. It is impossible to imagine how, with their naked hands, thousands of slaves raised gigantic slabs of stone as high as birds fly, or place them with deadly accuracy: not a centimetre out of place, and checked on all four sides exactly, with persistent precision. I stood amazed.

Without a word, and fully understanding my astonishment, an old Beduin Arab told me with a smile on his face:

"All that is known now, was known then. We only repeat the past!"

Internally I was compelled to agree with the truth of the illiterate old man's utterance. As mysterious as those monstrous erections are (appearing between earth and Heaven) - which still stand resistant to the powerful hand of Time - are the secrets of the lives of those Egyptian masters before our period.

SHAKHANOV.   According to researches made in 1974, roughly four thousand specially trained slaves worked day and night in the course of two ten-year periods (beneath the lash of overseers) to raise the gigantic pyramid of Cheops. In accordance with the witness of Herodotus, besides those four thousand, over one-hundred-thousand slave workers were periodically employed.

The well-known Arabian thinker, Al Idrisi, travelling in Central Asia, wrote: "If the wife of a ruler interfered with the manner of construction, the tongues of slave-workers also itched!"

AITMATOV.   There, where power exists, the flame of jealousy never dies. Power is a road to attain high position, and at times it appears deceptively open. However, power - is also a matter of exceptional responsibility, as well as great danger and risk.

Responsibility, in as much as it is ones duty to handle both tasks and people. Inclusive of their talents and shortcomings, joys in creating, and sorrows in failure. Yes, the danger lies there - that in proportion to the heights reached by those in power, the number of ill-wishers equally grows higher - and they follow, step by step, every word a ruler utters. Most probably therefore, as a synthesis of centuries-old social and moral experience, as the quintessence of political clashes, there remains to successors little apart from this edification: "A leader surrounds himself with honour and with esteem when he gathers round him worthy, bold and wise men from the people. If he is afraid of them, and drives them off, he thus creates for himself powerful enemies. Better keep near you one wise man, than a thousand stupid-minded idiots, as silly as can be. This is the evidence of the wise".

SHAKHANOV.   Power is like a standard of legitimacy. At any time Shahs and Beys occupy in the history of Turkish-speaking peoples a unique place. When they enforced their decisions, there could be no agreements, or negotiated conditions. Indeed, the greatest source of advice for Beys was found in the "Khanabad" - the law of Khan Tauke on Mount Kultobe. Standing nowadays in the vale of the Sirdarinsk region, in Uzbekistan. From these injunctions, Shahs and Beys derived a collection of legal codes known as "Zheti-zhargio- that is "The Law of Seven Codes".

In legislative enactments, about which the proverb still goes round, "On Mount Kultobe there is a legal meeting every day", the Beys Kazibek, Aiteke, and Tole took part, on behalf of the Kazakhs. Bey Kokum came from the Kirghizians, and Bey Sasik from the Karakalpaks, along with Bey Edige. How could they defend their lands and peoples from any attacks by external enemies? How could they preserve unity and firmness among the tribes and people's? How could they protect, and follow all the behests of their forebears? How could they evaluate the "internal policy" of those days? How could they worthily enter the future? ... Such were the problems haunting strict law-givers and wise men at that memorable meeting. From there, clearly, they took their ideas for the unification of the Kazakh people, and the conception of its governance. So appeared historical leaders and the servants of three tribal groups - thinker Bey Tole, orator Bey Kazibek, and the analyst Bey Aiteke. They were all inseparable friends, enjoying the full trust and esteem of the people. At times they resolved all legal questions for their tribes, remaining with them on festive days, and holidays, as well as on dire days of distress, disturbance and misfortune. To extinguish the light of their wisdom, would be an unfulfillable loss, for they were able to "split the hair up", as the folk saying goes.

AITMATOV.   Yes, they were great people, able through the power of the word to gather all their folk behind them. They had that rarest of gifts - they were part of the people's flesh and bone. Let us remember history. Rhetoric, in any people, and at any time, gives a special meaning to things. In Egypt, Greece and Rome, there permanently met for competition in oratory, the greatest speakers of the day. Correspondingly high traditions arose, and new schools of oratory were founded. In those days any truth (the free expression of the folk), or important decisions made, were proclaimed through the lips of the great orators. The word "orator" is itself Latin in origin, and its meaning had already become commonly known. Let the Egyptian orators be named otherwise. Be that as it may, in our modern times this word sounds quite usual and very weighty. Expressed briefly, the role of an orator was to lay the first stones in the foundation of democracy.

Part of the rich legacy of Plutarch, if you remember, was devoted to the famous orators Demosthenes and Cicero. "They were as like as two drops of water!" wrote one historian, "Not only in manner, but in their own views on life: in their independent judgement, in their style of speaking, even in their voices. It is impossible to find two other such orators who came from the folk, and attained such popular, universal, praise".

Yet remember, the inseparable leaders Tole Bey, Kazibek Bey, and Aiteke Bey, like the Greeks Demosthenes and Cicero, were devoted to establishing the truth: with all the power and beauty of sense. Thusly, they all fought against tyrants, and also against unjust governors.

By the way, Demosthenes - having devoted all his life to defend the unjustly condemned – measured (in any forthcoming legal case) the importance of strength and volume in the voice of a plaintiff.

Once there came to him an Athenian, who complained against one town-dweller who had offended him, and struck him. Demosthenes quietly gazed at the plaintiff for some time, and then remarked:

"You have not suffered any offence"

"You mean to say I was not offended?" cried the visitor aloud.

"That's it! Now I hear the voice of a man who has been hurt, and complains against fate! In any case, I will take your part, and defend you in court" exclaimed Demosthenes.

SHAKHANOV.   A famous orator (with a Russian father and a Kazakh mother) the advocate Plevako, was decisive in his manner and did not give way to opponents: albeit with exceeding kindness. Only recently, his autobiographical details became known to the general public. The following event speaking well for his eloquence, and for his boldness:

A poor, beggarly old woman stole a bucket at the market. It cost a mere fifty copecks. The owner of the bucket caught the thief, and brought her to court. Seeing that poor old woman had no money and no close relatives - and who would anyway defend such an old crone -the judiciary board, thumbing through the law-order books, decided to put her away for a few years, and to confiscate any belongings that she might have.

Having heard of this, Plevako came straight to the court-room, and stood, looking at the jury members. He also saw the wretched old woman crying in the corner. As the judge sternly lowered his brow to give the jury's verdict, however, Plevako stepped forward and made his speech:

"Our country, since olden times, has been robbed by people who were not lazy about doing it. But magnanimous Russia forgave all petty offences! In the war against Japan, for instance, we received a devastating defeat at Port Arthur - thanks to the poor work of ungifted leaders in the Fleet. Yet, the Great Russian Empire generously forgave them all! Contrarily, today they can't forgive one poor old woman, whose heinous crime was to steal a fifty-copeck bucket! For that, their benificence and nobility does not suffice!"

From these critical remarks the jury-members were ready to drop to the ground with shame. Finally, they agreed to release the poor culprit at once ... Such is the power of real oratorial genius. Many leaders have had the good fortune to be served by such oratory also, through the ages.

What is there to conceal here, when we know that under the totalitarianian Soviet regime, we lost that golden thread of art? A thread which had not been broken for centuries, passing from one generation on to another, from forebears to successors, nourishing the roots of wisdom, and old traditions among the folk, expressing their spiritual experience.

Quite recently, we have stumbled completely, and cannot go on ... In Kirghizia, in the last year or two, upon the initiative of President Akayev, new schools of study for elders, Beys and orators, have been formed, deep in the countryside. Indubitably we shall all benefit from this with hindsight. People will listen to the advice and judgement of elders, and maybe we shall initiate some special courses, in order to strengthen these old traditions.

In such stormy times as our country is presently suffering, the criminal situation is critical. Let all large-scale transgressors answer in full for their deeds. So stated, what shall we achieve if, for the slightest infringement of the law, we send the petty sinner off to prison? Did we not witness how a young fellow, sitting in prison for some petty offence, for a year or two, in the company of deeply hardened criminals (left the cell with a broken character), lost the good qualities he had? To decide what to do in such circumstances, and what form the punishment should take, it would be better for those experienced Beys, well-educated and authorized, respected not only for their knowledge, but for their characters, to take charge.

Such upbringing would rouse the conscience of the people, and a feeling of shame in those who committed some fault. Then people would say: "Where the mare kicks, the foal doesn't get hurt!" That speaks of a Mother's character-making.

Confucius spoke of this problem thus; "Leader, if you have decided to condemn someone to punishment, remember the precepts of your forefathers! Then others will believe in your justice, and will support you!"

AITMATOV. Why can man not live on earth without power? Is it sheer necessity for ascending the step-ladder, from the primitive socialized order, to a modern type of society?

Life itself was always composed of mutuality between a person and the state around him: including its leader. Complicated and sometimes oppositional relations betwixt those two factors have never left the historical scene.

SHAKHANOV. Dear Chingiz, I am, as you know, one of those people quite far away from power politics. Nevertheless, I confess, when I led the democratic movement in Kazakhstan, some others wanted to see me in the President's regalia. I remember how I gave an interview to one reporter of a big newspaper, in which I jokingly said: "If you put me in charge of a farm it is quite likely I should let it fall to pieces in a month or two!" There is only a small section of people who are really ready to take the reins of government into their hands - having enough experience to do so. The necessary knowledge, personal qualities, and finally the psychological preparedness takes its toll. But sometimes I am quite amazed, seeing how others "grieve" in their desires to become President, though they have not the necessary words, nor experience, for such a high position.

I recall a related anecdotal story. One shepherd asked another:

"If you suddenly donned the crown and became a king, what would you do?"

"If I became king, I should pasture the sheep on horseback" he replied. Speaking without any slyness. And he was right!

History never lets us forget those hundreds of millions of people who became victims of thoughtless, talentless, power-loving leaders, who became rulers only through their own will and devices. So let us return to history, Chingiz, for a while, at least.

Under Goloshchekin (1925-1933) the Kazakh steppe lived through numberless black days. Boundlessly severe, even cruel and spiritually separated from the folk, this leader, having taken the reins of power over that enormous republic made an immediate "discovery". Soviet dominion left out Kazakhstan. For those eight years during which he ruled the republic, from morn till eve, not leaving the tribunes, he didn't find time to get interested in the life of the Kazakh villages, not even to visit one of them. Yet, he counted himself an expert of "local" affairs and life. Goloshchekin even affirmed that the October revolution had left the villages untouched! It being necessary to make "small wigs", to show these disobedient Kazakhs who was ruling over them. For this purpose - to show them who was who -victims were needed. Hence, the number of people dwelling in the republic was catastrophically reduced during his domination. Clearly, a large part of our national intelligentsia were declared "deviatiationists" who would not give way to this "re-education".

The inhuman policies of Goloshchekin - guided by the pseudo-instruction of Stalin, "sharpening class warfare in accordance with the establishment of Socialism" - devolved into the most cruel persecution, repression and unheard-of deprivations.

Genocide against a whole people began with the so-called "kulaks"-literally "tight-fists" i.e. "selfish", through confiscating the personal property of feudal lords, Beys, wealthy peasants exploiting the labour of poorer ones etcetera, while everyone else was placed under heavy taxation. Counted as "wealthy" in Kazakhstan, more than seven hundred prosperous farms and fifty thousand people of the middle class were submitted to open robbery, condemned to be thrown into prison, or shot, or exiled to the towns of other republics: such as Tyumen, Kurgan, Astrakhan, or the lrkutsk region of Russia. From whence, of course, they fled to China, Iran, India, and Turkey. However, poor peasants received some cattle and agricultural gear from the so-called Soviet Deputees, even though they found they could not use that property, because of the taxes imposed on them then, and thus, they suffered terrible hunger, which was in general already "big politics".

From the Kazakhs, traditionally occupied with cattle-breeding, they then demanded a production tax, which took the form of agricultural products. Yet, for the agricultural workers, just the opposite was true. Indeed, they placed on them a payment of taxes in the form of meat! The cattle-breeders exchanged cattle for wheat, meanwhile agricultural workers gave their wheat in exchange. Each group, after such a transaction, having little to nothing of their own produce left.

The upper crust amongst leaders then had a free hand to do what they wished. An attitude reinforced by a feeling they would not be punished, so they just ran wild. The number of levies grew day by day, until it reached the limit, sad to say, of sixteen separate payable taxes!

Still more astonishing was the fact that, supporting this freedom loving spirit, Soviet ideologists thought up yet one more tax, payable as a so-called "salvage levy", which meant people were compelled to rake out all kinds rubbish, and hand over trimmed horse-manes and tails, dogs, donkey-skins, and even snake-skins, various rags, bottles and bones, along with horns and hooves! Going as far as to posit that those who could not pay such a tax in time, should make haste to do so by selling some of their already limited stock of cattle.

Even more amazingly, all the rubbish collected as a result of such an evil order was not used in any way, just burnt!

Overall, the result of this imposition was that a vast number of animals - amounting to forty million beasts in in 1929 (although in the following years this figure was reduced by ten percent), were reduced to a mere million head when counted.

In the eight years of Goloshchekin's rule, out of four million one hundred thousand Kazakhs statistics tell us two million two hundred thousand were simply removed like flies, by purposely - provoked starvation. A tactic never used before.

Being active assistants in such a bloody murder (let loose by Nikolai II), Goloshchekin, with his whole family, and even some of his servants, brought down upon the Kazakh people unimaginable losses!

Bewilderingly, this tyrant also had helpers, worthy of him. Remember the Chairman of the Kazakh Central Executive Committee, Yeltai Yernazarov?

In Orenburg, the capital of Kazakhstan at that time, a Republic Conference took place wherein they decided to elect a Chairman for the Kazakh Central Executive Committee. When the matter came to a choice, two main groups began to fight each other for power: neither side being able to defeat the other. It was then that someone made the suggestion:

"Comrades, we have formed a Soviet Government, consisting mainly of poor people. Here is Yeltai - he is a poor man too, and not even able to read and write. All meaning, he suits us down to the ground. He pointed at Yernazarov dreamily leaning in a corner. Their opponents, doing their best not to let the other side assume power, and ready to accept any other candidate, except theirs, unanimously voted for Yernazarov.

Relatedly, they say once Yernazarov travelled on the Almaty train to Kzil-Orda. Those counting Yeltai almost a Padishah - the population of the city of Shimkent, (among them his relations and friends) – tormented by hunger due to tax and other misfortunes, needing his assistance. Apparently, on hearing of this, he straightaway dashed off to the station with one aim - to ask for their comrade's help.

Yeltai at first agreed to meet the people, but on seeing a whole horde of them thronging towards him, changed his mind. Instead, he went to the end of the train-corridor, to a small platform there, and looked outwards.

"Yeltai, our Chairman! We are all suffering from hunger!" the crowd cried, raising their hands to him in greeting.

Then Yeltai, pompous as ever in his marten-fur cap, raised his hand in answer, and shouted: "Greetings, comrades!" The folk, in hope that Yernazarov would show compassion on his native town, fell quiet.

"Comrades" he shouted once again, "we must think first of the Plan, the whole Plan! The Party's Plan! Following this, he named the central problem, then went back to his compartment - closing the door behind him.

No humanitarian, he didn't have enough sympathy to help his own countrymen, his relations or friends, when deprived of even a crust of bread!?

I remember another interesting event concerning that same Yeltai. Once, when returning with you from Tashkent, we decided to call in for a cup of tea with the sister of Zhanabai Salimbayev Shekker. Now, the father of this bold young fellow was Tasbau, and his grandfather was old Salimbai - who died at the age of ninety six. Well, in those days Yeltai was still a bare-footed peasant, and that wise old man did much to help him, from a pancake where possible, to a word or two of good advice when needed. After the election of Yeltai as Chairman of the Kazakh Central Executive Committee, the Regional Party Secretary called in on Tasbau, who sent him off to see Yaltai, saying:

Give Yeltai our hearty greetings. One other thing, the neighbouring region has a tractor, yet we remain without one. We can't plough the soil as is necessary. However, we come from his native area, so let him order a spare tractor to be sent to us.

Tasbau went off right away, but found the Chairman was out. Still and all, his wife greeted her visitor warm-heartedly and they sat chatting a little, till Yeltai returned from his duties. Arriving home, he barely touched the outstretched hand of his visitor, going off gravely into a different room. His wife timidly followed him, saying: "Yeltai, but that's the son of Salimbai, our old friend, sitting waiting for you! How did you fail to recognize him? You might at least greet him, and ask him how he is nowadays, and what he has come to see you about".

Then Yeltai turned round, and very quietly muttered:

"Well, and how's your father, our old friend, how's his health?"

Adding without waiting for an answer from his visitor:

"Tomorrow I'll be up to my neck in work. I must go and rest"

Are such impolite people any better than the shepherd who said if he were king he would round up his flock on a horse, not on foot?

One more thing - on hearing they were soon going to deprive him of his post, he asked: "Can I keep the car you gave me?"

AITMATOV.   Democrates stressed: "The art of ruling in government is higher than art". At times the fate of a whole people depends on this skill.

For example, did not Peter the Great give birth to a dark and beaten-down Russia? To emphasize the role of a "critical" personality, compelling an entire nation to make a "reconstruction", let us remember well-known facts from the life and activity of Peter. Having become Tsar, he went straight to Holland, where under the name of "Peter the carpenter", he learnt how to build ships: discovering all their secret details.

Peter's greatness was commented on by Pushkin, who wrote of him thus:

> *"Here Academic, there hero whole,*
> *Here a bold sailor, there carpenter he.*
> *And with his all-embracing wide soul,*
> *Upon the Throne he worked constantly".*

When the greed of the West (having gazed voraciously over the expanses of Russia), grew into a direct threat to his Empire, Peter decided to move his capital city from Moscow to the shores of the Baltic. In this manner, the beautiful city of St. Petersburg was meant to protect the whole of his lands. Adding a final artistic touch, Peter ordered fresh soils to be spread in the curbs, so that oak, birch, and pine seedlings, could grow.

As the author of an order protecting these plants, he decreed, "He who uproots an oak will himself be uprooted, or hacked down!" Fascinatingly, with rustling leaves still on its branches, an oak personally planted by Peter the Great has stood in its place for three hundred years.

Looking back, Peter fundamentally reconstructed the principles of government across his Empire. Greatly increasing the number of factories as well as educational establishments. Also, he created a competent and mobile army, along with a powerful fleet – all making their presence felt very quickly. Unstoppable in his innovations, Peter then introduced changes to the Russian Cyrillic alphabet by adding new letters. He even set up in St. Petersburg a special printing-house: himself publishing the first newspaper in Russian history - "Information".

On reflection, Peter would not have grown "great" had he not been an ingrained citizen of his country. As such, he saw before his eyes the future of Russia and firmly knew his peasantry would soon become members of a modern nation. Hence, Peter ordered all Russians to shave off their beards and moustaches – not to mention shorten long garments. On top of this, he insisted peasants should drink less: ordering cast-iron medallions to be hung round the neck of drunkards as a punishment for their anti-social behavior.

"If someone does not respect his parents", he said, "he will be considered a criminal, and for that he will be punished severely. If anyone does not know the four arithmetical laws, then he will not be allowed to get married till he does!" Such royal commands, little by little, moved an ignorant country towards a world civilization.

SHAKHANOV. *T*he mysterious ways of history are unquestionable! Yet this powerful Russian Empire, fell into stasis again during the reign of Anna Ioannovna. For their part, Russian historians writing that the Empress Anna was a lazy and incompetent leader, more interested in merriment and carousing than affairs of State. Certainly, she idled away her time from morn till eve with amusements of all kinds: with trickery and making a mock of the lords and ladies at court. One hears that at times, when she glanced at the grimaces of those around her, she was simply swept off her feet by laughter.

In the last year of her reign, Anna Ioannovna (for the pleasure of her courtiers), thought of an "entertaining marriage" between Prince Golitsin, and one of her serving maids of Kalmik nationality, named Buzhennikova. In winter, therefore, on the river Neva - by the order of Tsarina - a palace was erected where the wedding was to take place – although, by her wish, this palace was made of ice: with ice windows and doors, ice tables and crockery, and even an ice bed for them.

Dragged out of all the corners of Russia came Tatars, Mordva, and Chuvashes, Khohols and Vyatiches in their national costumes: to sing and dance for joy. In real terms, of course, this buffoonery showed her disregard for all of those surrounding her. Despite the fact Prince Golitsin came from one of the most ancient families in Russia, and in his princely character could contend with that of the Romanovs themselves.

There is additionally one more interesting historical fact. It became known that in 1731, new diplomatic relations had been established between the Russian empire and the western part of Kazakh territory. So, elders, leaders, Beys and Batirs (from young to middle-aged Kazakh ranks) came to St. Petersburg to pay their respects to the Empress, while bearing all kinds of gifts. After consenting to meet this delegation – and having taken with them their Tatarinterpreter - the members of this respected group were consummately ignored. Day passed after day, week after week, and still the golden doors of the Empress' chambers remained closed.

When her courtiers again reminded their Tsarina -drowning in her diamonds and gold ornaments - that the Kazakhs had come to see her, this arrogant woman announced:

"An unusually important thing have happened. The female monkey given to me by the Dutch King, has given birth to babies. They are so charming and wonderful, my head veritably spins from all these pleasures. Therefore, I cannot see anyone at present, until all becomes normal again".

AITMATOV. Similar sad and curious anecdotes are common in history. See now, I remember as we continue our discussion, a widely known event.

In those days, when the scandalous Empress Ekaterina II was still reigning, the Crimea and Ukraine both entered the Russian Empire. Relatedly, perhaps, her Governor-General - the brilliant Prince Grigory Potemkin - was named as the Empress Ekaterina's favourite courtier.

Everything boding well, until 1787 – when the Empress decided to see how dwellers in "Small Russia" (Ukraine and the Crimea) lived their lives. Taking a circuitous route, to say the least, her ladyship then stopped at seventy six stations and about thirty five small villages between Petersburg and Kiev in order to gather relevant information. Accompanied, they say, by a small army of attendants. Occasionally, of course, her entourage stayed overnight, inducing Ekaterina to be "taken with unusual gladness", at the prosperity of her "small-Russian" subjects. Needless to say, these displays of wealth were sleight of hand tricks. Each uncovered when they returned to Petersburg. Once there, it came to light that the previous year Potemkin had carefully selected those people whom the Empress would meet. Offering special training in the way they should act towards her. The fact he has arranged huge herds of healthy cattle for inspection was equally uncovered. The Prince's method being to collect these animals beforehand, get "farmers" to show then to the Empress, and, while she rested overnight, drive the very same herd to the next location. In this way, she saw exactly the same well-fed animals albeit with different shepherds.

All begging questions about the abundant forage and goods she witnessed. Eventually, this too was explained by heaps of hay and fodder, piled up in barns, beneath which there was nothing but clay! After this legerdemain, the expression "Potemkin Villages" arose.

SHAKHANOV. These sorrowful stories demonstrate continuously levels of deceit amongst niched officials.

Exemplified, possibly, by the Emperor Caligula in Rome. At first things went well. The new Emperor even commented on his predecessor, Tiberius, that, "He did nothing good for himself, nor for any others. Thus, there are certain serpents which brought misfortune not only to Romans, but to the whole world!"

Maye he saw himself as a "new broom sweeping things clean"? Either way, he was very energetic and good-willed. Re-establishing a neglected Senate and proposing well-known Romans for positions of honour in his government. Indeed, the great wealth left behind by Livius and Tiberius, Caligula distributed, according to their wishes, among every Roman citizen. Even though this was done superficially, just to give a good impression.

A short time passed, and Caligula, having taken colossal treasures in hand, simply lost his balance, and went literally off his head.

"His stupidity and thoughtlessness knew no bounds!" wrote one old historian about him. "He imagined himself to be a living god!" All his close friends and supporters, day and night flattered him, and bowed down before him. Inebriated by their submissiveness, and applauding their servility, he said to them occasionally, "Let others hate me, so long as they fear me, all will be well and I have nothing to fear!"

Considering himself a born actor, and an unequalled ruler, this Emperor gave up governmental work altogether, and turned to amusements and lechery. In social circles, taking on the form of a tragic actor, he hammered away at all sorts of nonsense, and then began dancing to exhaustion.

AITMATOV.   There are writings by Joseph Flavius, where the idiocy of those activities is revealed, and the Emperor is shown up as a disaster for the Romans: "Not speaking of anything else, Caligula tried to destroy poetry written my Homer" wrote Flavius. "There was no end to his spite and envy towards people. More than once he threatened to kill all those living, and to deprive the dead of their honours. Furthermore, it is impossible to count all of the taxes and duties which Caligula imposed on Romans.

He went so far as to scare possible successors with threats and force them write their wills in his favour! Afterwards denouncing those who did this, having them hung as criminals. Yet, Romans were frightened most when he named his favourite steed as a member of the consul ..."

The nomination of an animal for governmental position had never been heard of before in history. But was nothing to what unfolded! Caligula then ordered a marble stall to be carved for his horse, and a manger made of ivory.

During the four years of his rule, Caligula reigned so senselessly and cruelly that he changed the flourishing well-developed Roman state into a hungry and beggarly monarchy. With himself as the major robber of his own state. Others who were in power then also sucked the people's blood. It was said, two hundred million sestertia* evaporated from the state treasury in just one year. All meaning, the people of Rome became impoverished, and roamed about the streets seeking food. As if this was not enough, Caligula, who then had a daughter, turned to Romans and demanded money for her upkeep, her education, and her wedding dowry. Unsurprisingly, on the first day of a certain New Year, the Emperor of the Roman people, like a beggar, stood on the threshold of his Palace, and collected coins thrown by an unending stream of people. Furthermore, he was so glad to see this growing heap of coins that he grabbed them, handful by handful, and pressed to his breast, before finally resting on top of them with outstretched hands.

Not being satisfied by these rewards and payments, however, which he received every day from newly-appointed "officials", Caligula did not disdain to use open robbery and pillage - for which he kept thieves and plunderers at the Palace, just waiting for his word.

Interestingly, it was commented that he dressed himself in unthinkable robes and garments, sewn from variegated tasteless rags. "He came out to meet his guests in strange garments, which suited neither Roman nor any sane man. Therefore, looking at the Emperor seated on his throne in a multicoloured long-skirted woman's dress, and wearing woman's shoes, some foreign guests gibingly glanced at each other, while Romans were prepared to sink through the ground in shame" So said Greek historians at any rate.

Caligula even went so far in his fearful fancies as to cover his beard in dust, and then, having stolen armour from the corpse of Alexander the Great, donned it himself, before strolling about in front of everybody. Yet, all of these pranks angered the Romans deeply.

At last, among Roman citizens who had endured many wars, and poverty and partings, all patience was exhausted. Assuredly, they could not bear such a hair-brained Emperor any longer. Further, the people understood his continuing presence in power would lead to a

---

*Sestertia - smallest Roman copper coin.

breakdown of government. When they heard of the Emperor's death, therefore, half of the Romans decided it was just another trick of his, and did not believe it. The others, openly rejoicing, demanded payment as they spread the news.

May God save future leaders of governments from such stupid glory!

SHAKHANOV. But you see, Marcus Aurelius, who governed the Roman Empire from 121-139 A.D. was the direct opposite of Caligula. His name became famous after he wrote his fundamental work "Meditations', which is known throughout the world. This inspiring book being the main reason he is classed among the most just and righteous rulers.

In this work, he tells how one should fulfill one's task as befits a Roman, with a pure spirit, and with love for the folk - not under any compulsion, but straightforwardly and freely. "He should perform each act, as though it were the last one in his life, steering clear of stupidity and avarice. Only then will a man be happy!" He went on to add: "Before beginning any kind of action, be it military or civil, the Emperor should consult with highly qualified persons in the government!" Summing up, he said, "Listen to the advice of wise and experienced friends, rather than submit the government to the will of one man". Here are testimonies which have become historic:

Instructively, when Cassius Ovidius prepared a document in Syria against his Emperor, the messenger sent by him to his fellow conspirators was intercepted. Astonishingly, as the letter this man bore was handed over to Aurelius, who immediately ordered it to be thrown on the fire – unopened! He did not wish to know anything about his enemies or develop a hatred towards them.

Nevertheless, some Romans, reproaching Marcus Aurelius for his softness in regard to this traitor asked, "What would happen if you were suddenly unable to defeat him?" To which Marcus Aurelius responded, "Did we offend the Gods, so that they should let him triumph?" However, remembering the many rulers who had fallen by his hand, Aurelius showed example after example of weighty reasons for their killing.

AITMATOV. He set up in his land relationships befitting a free government: saving people from evil, insistently educating them in righteous ways and solidifying their work, their minds, their knowledge. In a word, in everything he showed a fine example of high morality. He always aimed at making a bad man into a good one, and a good one into a perfect one. Marcus Aurelius combined in himself a great mind, given by God, and a colossal spiritual generosity. If he had not been born in that historical epoch, the whole Roman world might have disintegrated. Violently drowning in its own blood.

SHAKHANOV. By the way, it is interesting to note how many great leaders the Roman Empire was blessed with. The names of some of them were buried in oblivion. But the silvery statue of Marcus Aurelius, sitting astride his steed, still stands erect on the Capitol Square, beloved by his people, though twenty centuries have passed since then.

AITMATOV. I read one of the works of Plutarch, "Conversations of seven wise men" – finding therein common characteristics given to Greek and Roman leaders by the philosophers Thales, Solon, Periander, and several others.

SHAKHANOV. The historian Heraclid Pontius wrote the father of Solon, described by Plutarch, was a famous man in his day, known as Eksekestid, while his mother was the grand- daughter of Pisistratus. How Solon came to power was in itself extremely curious.

Inclined towards trading from his youth, he was also absorbed with science and new ideas: soon becoming known as a wise man. Although, personal enrichment bored him. Thanks to his spiritual riches, however, he felt himself above those who were inebriated by the flashing of gold pieces. Athenians, overcome by his moral purity and mental powers, asked him to take up the position of a government leader - and put an end to wars with neighbouring countries. Yet, Solon soon found out for himself that politics was the art of persuasion. So, he promised to give land allotments to poor people, after which he attracted wealthy people to his cause by promising the opposite! As a result of this, poverty-stricken folk, and rich land-owners alike, began to count him as "theirs". Later on, for this very reason, his winged expression "Equality does not give birth to wars", became widely known. All his life having written poetry, and having placed it above everything else, Solon pondered:

> *"Power I gave to poor people, as much as they needed –*
> *Did not deprive them of honour, no special rights gave.*
> *Likewise I cared for the rich, who to none their wealth ceded.*
> *Standing between these extremes, with my shield raised to save,*
> *Thus I saw to it, that plaints from the poor then were heeded,*
> *While I forbade those with power to exploit the poor slave. "*

AITMATOV.   From this sestet of his, it becomes obvious that mere chance didn't name Solon as a reformer of the Greek legal system. As a case in point, let us take his law concerning the deprivation of citizenship. At first glance the denial of citizenship means little. However, by means of such a law, Solon attained the desired result - that citizens became sensitive to political change in their country, and jointly overcame difficulties in this way.

Yet another good action - the strict prohibition of saying anything bad about a deceased person. Along with that he put an end to abusive speaking, in temples, in government offices, and criminal courts. Anyone who did not observe such prohibitions, and deliberately broke this law was considered a criminal, suffering severe punishment. These measures, falling in with religious principles, were extremely popular with the masses. Their praises for Solon simply flowed in streams.

Counting that any government which does not keep its own laws will inevitably fall, Solon ordered craftsmen to engrave the text of such laws on tablets prepared from hard wood, thereby preserving them for years.

On coming to power, Solon cancelled all laws made by his predecessor Drakont. It was known that this monstrous man favoured the death sentence for any destroyers of temples, murderers, and even petty thieves: all were equally considered criminals. Thus, people said Drakont's laws were written not with ink, but with human blood. Contrarily, Solon's new laws overturned Drakont's severe punishments.

SHAKHANOV.   During Solon's reign in Athens, an end was put to all kinds of debauchery. His order read: "For kidnapping, or the violation of women and maidens, the fine will be one hundred drachma, and for illegal relations twenty drachma. These who sell a daughter or a sister for money shall be driven from society." It put an end to all kinds of lechery, debauchery, and dissoluteness. Really, in those times, when money was precious, it would have been better to live as a slave, than to pay a fine of twenty drachma.

AITMATOV.   In the compositions of Aristotle, we meet evidence of friendship between Solon and Anacharsis. Oddly enough, Herodotus tells us Anacharsis was a relation of the Scythian ruler Idanfaris, who fought against Darius: the leader of the Persians. Moreover, we learn that Anacharsis was a scientist and a thinker, born among the Scythians. Men, as is well-known, who count themselves the progenitors of Turkic peoples. Indeed, he was widely known as a multi-talented person: a philosopher, amongst other things, whose oratorial gift was sheer artistry. Amid those Greeks conquered by his foresight and resourcefulness, there was a widespread saying inspired by him, "So say the Scythians!"

According to the witness of historians, the Scythians came from the shores of the Black Sea to Greek soil, in search of knowledge. Hence, his friendship with Solon, and other thinkers, established his reputation. The famous philosophers of ancient times, of whom we have been speaking, gave wise counsel for future leaders. Enjoying such a synergistic relationship, Anacharsis was portrayed as follows .....

Solon: To my mind, only a ruler who is able to change his power, and the power of his leaders, into the people's power, will become famous.

Biant: In that sense alone, will he show an example of law-keeping.

Thales: The happiness of a ruler lies in this - live long, die content,

Anacharsis: That means he shows himself to be wisest of all.

Cleobul: Then, he is a true ruler, not listening idly to those round him.

Pittach: Flatterers must always fear for their heads. Only then will a ruler establish peace and quiet in his government.

Chilon: Not of death should a ruler be thinking, but of eternal life.

Periander: This is what I wish to remember - he who reasonably considers all that has been said should then take power!

In Greece they raised a statue to our forebear Anacharsis, who was born on Turkestan soil and made an immeasurable contribution to the prosperity of this foreign country. On the pedestal of his statue these words were engraved: "My tongue is my enemy."

... After the death of Solon (having returned to the shores of the Black Sea, and to the ancient Turkish steppe), Anacharsis finally fell victim to hatred and envy, and died at the hand of a relative.

A tragedy which brings to mind something equally disturbing. The French King Louis XIV, was a man who held unlimited power for seventy two years! Considering himself above all of his subjects, he treated them as he thought fit: shooting them, hanging them, or beheading them at any moment he deemed desirable. "I' Etat c' est moi!" "The State - that is I!" He haughtily, ranted.

To the end of his life, flatterers and fawners crowded around him, and competed with one another to gain favour. Early in the morning, his courtiers rushed into the King's chambers, to take part in dressing him with his crown and ceremonial robes. They did their best to please the King, some bringing pantaloons, others camisoles, while engaging in arguments contesting "What should the King wear today - white or pale-blue"? Astoundingly, this "ceremony" of clothing the King occupied him, as well as his busy courtiers, every morning for at least two hours.

Meanwhile, the King dished out handfuls of new awards and medals. Thinking up new occupations for them. Truly, not a month passed by, but one or tother would be raised to in rank.

Bewildering services were performed without question each night as well. One group was on guard, not closing their eyes for a moment, others prepared fresh underwear for the King to wear next day. Still others took care of his wig and saw it was combed and powdered and perfumed afresh, while those less fortunate took care of his night-pot. If his one-year-old daughter had eighty servants to look after her, then how many personal servants had the King? Anyway, enormous sums were spent on his endless amusements, on his hunting gear, and on the maintenance of his courtiers. Taxes, recklessly levied (mainly on the poor) were used to pay for all this luxury. Those who did not pay in due time were driven out of their homes: along with wives and children. All personal belongings being confiscated. Indeed, as the peasantry suffered from poverty and depression, the King, being bored, ordered his architects, builders, and masons, to erect a new Court in Versailles. Both externally and internally, this new Court was provided with one thousand four hundred fountains. The process of building went on for forty seven years ...

Not only because of his foppery and boasting, but also due to his cowardice, the King remained in the memory of his contemporaries. Helping to explain why his Majesty secretly kept a troop of about forty magicians and fortune-tellers around him.

Better than any historical chronicle, however, the King's imbecility and cruelty are shown by details of a happening at Court. On one occasion, the King's cook prepared exceptionally fine crabs for his master's supper. To his misfortune he forgot to add the sauce. Only remembering his omission when it was too late to do anything - the dish was already on the royal table. Knowing the severe habits of his master, this desperate chef did not wait for an inevitable punishment, but straightaway committed suicide.

Driven by pitiless repression to extreme limits French folk, after the King's death, revolted, and wiped out the entire royal family.

SHAKHANOV.   More than fifty thousand people, not blinking their eyes, not shuffling their feet, but going on tip-toe, listened to the words of Sultan Aziza, in the Turkish Palace chambers - by day and by night. The duty of one of them, for instance, was, every month or-so, to clip the august Sultan's toe-nails extremely carefully.

Gazing attentively at history, a man sees throughout several centuries. Not only really wise rulers, but also severe and cruel dictators, as well as proper clowns (who with their prankish tricks and grimaces), remind one of spoiled children.

In this respect, the Babylonian King Nebuchadnezzar II, living two - and-a-half millennia ago, is illuminating. He was married to the daughter of the Midian King -the beauty Semiramida, and though she was madly in love with her husband, she did not like the dusty and noisy streets of Babylon. Longing, as she did, for her mountainous, cool, and charming country.

Not knowing how to please his wife, the unhappy King ordered several thousands of his servants and slaves, to make a gigantic hanging garden on the mountain-sides, where grew various fruit-trees. He sent messengers to far distant lands with orders to bring back singing birds. Changing the course of a lively spring, he made an artificial brook through the gardens he created: all to satisfy his beloved and beautiful wife.

Exhausted from excessive hard labour, slaves and gaol-prisoners died like flies. Trying as far as possible to make his lovely wife contented, Nebuchadnezzar himself also worked excessively. Meanwhile, his people fell into deep poverty, and he himself grew lean and old.

The life of the Sultan of Morocco, Mulei Ismail, almost falls in line with the fate of Nebuchadnezzar II. Having robbed his people down to the last thread, he ordered them to build for him a residence, the like of which had never been seen before - stretching for forty kilometres with its corridors and fifty halls. It was even said, the stable at this palace could fit about twelve thousand of the Sultan's horses.

AITMATOV.   On the pages of history also remain records of the good deeds of some rulers, done to benefit their own people, but, of course, bad rulers also remained, with their tyrannical actions.

Did not paranoic Ivan Grozny (the Terrible) destroy the city of Novgorod, and with it tens of thousands of its citizens, fearing they would revolt against him and betray him? Even in the history of Russian people such a devastating severity and barbarism were rarely seen.

Tellingly, the names of the French King Charles, and the Roman Emperor Titus were surrounded with care and respect to that same degree as the name of Ivan Grozny was surrounded by evil allure.

It appears that if a ruler places his own personal interests higher than those of the nation, he will suffer defeat and disdain, not only in his own epoch, but before people in following generations.

SHAKHANOV.   From those same ranks come the legend of the lame wild ass of Dzhuchi Khan, which runs like this:

The threatening Genghis-Khan fought shy of his eldest son Dzhuchi, whom his wife bore beneath her heart, when taken into captivity by the Kereis - always keeping some distance away from him. Yet, out of his four sons, Dzhuchi was the smartest and most competent, so he did not raise his own hand against him. Instead, he sent secret agents to slay him, taking advantage of the fact Dzhuchi had just gone on a hunting expedition. Sadly, taken up with the pursuit of a lame wild ass, he did not notice the presence of anyone else, and fell beneath the hand of the murderer sent to slay him, by his father.

Further events developed the following way: having been informed of the death of his son, Genghis-Khan, for decency's sake, dressed in mourning garments, ordered: "If anyone gives news about the manner of Dzhuchi's death, I shall fill that throat with melted lead!" Nobody dared to say a word, going in fear with paralyzed heart, thus the silence remained unbroken.

At that time, one young singer, tuning up his dombra, and entering the tent of the Khan (who was found in deep distress after what he had done) began to his song "The lame wild ass and Dzhuchi-Khan", with its melancholy melody. Genghis-Khan, whose word was as hard as flint, demanded at once:

"Oh, pour out a cup of melted lead for that ass, who dared to remind me of the unexpected death of my son Dzhuchi!"

"Wait one moment, my lord!" exclaimed the singer, "It was not me, but my dombra, with its three strings, which reminded you of him, so you should pour the melted lead into the orifice of the dombra here!"

Defeated in this verbal duel, Genghis-Khan could do nothing else, and gave orders to pour the melted lead into the musical instrument.

Till today, in the Ulitau valley in Kazakhstan, there stands the tomb of Dzhuchi-Khan, made especially for him, where he sleeps in his coffin.

Furthermore, on this earth there is no tomb for Genghis-Khan himself, nor of any of his other three sons Tole, Ugedei, and Chagatai.

AITMATOV.   As they say - a severe ruler leaves behind him terrible things, but a benevolent leader leaves traces worthy of a great man.

SHAKHANOV. If one looks across the past five centuries, it seems the peoples of Kazakhstan and Central Asia have not come down off their horses - or as they put it - their horses' blankets are rotting with sweat, not giving up the spirit of battle and fighting. The Khan epoch, we know, had a good influence on the established nations, uniting them under one language, especially so with smaller nations and groups of Turkic stock. Throughout Kazakh history, for instance, an entirely special place is occupied by Abilai-Khan, who united three regions. The fate of a people finding itself on one side under pressure from China, and Dzhungaria, on the other, from the Russian Empire. Having nothing themselves, of cotise, except bare steppeland, short spears, and curved-up sabres. Only the politics of Abilai-Khan, and his burning desire to improve the lives of his fellow-countrymen, saved this nation from great destruction. Placed, as it was, between the shores of Syr Darya, and the foothills of the Alatau. Establishing diplomatic relations with China, however, he offered his own son as a hostage. Following which, Abilai-Khan sent his ambassadors to Russia. Though he lived in agreement with both these "lions", by stroking their manes, they, for the look of things, nodded their heads, but under various pretexts, poisoned the Kalmaks against the Kazakhs, eventually spreading stife through foreign lands, leading finally to internecine warfare.

Staving aside all hesitation and wavering and uniting himself firmly with Russia, Abilai-Khan nevertheless remains in history as a great war-leader and rare diplomat of his day.

AITMATOV. Lately, a new expression has come out, "Politics is a dirty business". Well, if politics is undertaken by people with ignoble, immoral, with vicious intentions, then the land they govern will fall into these traps and the reputation of their authorities will be worthless.

However, Abilai-Khan was indeed a noble and moral leader. There have been such people at all times. For example, between 708 and 814 A. D. King Charles ruled in France. Pipin, the father of the future king, did not wish Charles to learn the art of reading and writing. It is thus interesting to note he could not read the letter "a", when he came to the throne, although later he learned both Latin and Greek, and could read them fluently.

During his reign, France certainly grew stronger, and especially in the realms of science, art, and trade, because the King made friends with the most highly educated people of his country, the wise men, bards, architects and artists. The knowledge which he had gained he used to develop, elevate, and enlighten his land.

Abilai-Khan, of whom you spoke, also closely communicated with the wise man Bukhar-zhirau, with folk heroes, eloquent orators, and drew them all near to himself. Listening to their advice in government tasks.

But I digress. King Charles, as we've already said, knew a few foreign languages, and spoke fluently with many foreigners and ambassadors, who came to visit him for an audience, or discuss political affairs. Furthermore, he remembered the names of soldiers in his huge army, which he himself founded. Even his enemies had to admit that he had an exceptional mind, and therefore bowed before him.

So, centuries later, the name of King Charles is pronounced with the greatest respect in France, Europe, and among innumerable international leaders.

SHAKHANOV. Yes, similar good examples in world history are numerous. The son of the famous Roman Emperor Vespasian, Titus, in only two years of rule on the throne, won the love of all Romans with his simplicity, humility and diligence. He even won a place of respect among nobles. They tell that once Titus, surrounded by his entourage, walked through the streets of Rome. Of a sudden, from among the festive crowd, there stepped forth one beggarly youth in rags and stretched out his hand in welcome to Titus. One of the Emperors guardsmen drew his sword, and rushed towards the stranger ...

"Stop!" exclaimed the Emperor sternly. "What is he guilty of?"

"Is it an unheard of audacity for a beggar to stretch out his hand to the Emperor of the land, Your Majesty?"

"This child of my land is showing great respect to me. If I do not shake his hand, surely I would show my ignorance and boorishness?"

Taking the poor boy's hand with kindliness, he greeted him, and caressingly patted him on the shoulder. Then he said to all:

"If I am an Emperor, and he is a beggar, then such is the will of Gods! Glistening robes are no more an indication of humane character, than rags are of stupidity, or poverty of a soul" he said sternly to his guard.

At that moment a cry rang out among the crowd: "'Long live Titus!" and re-echoed around in the heavens over the ancient city of Rome.

People in the crowd, surprised at what they had seen, how a beggar might shake hands with the Emperor, themselves then wishing to do the same, straightway started queuing up to go and greet their Emperor.

Once Titus, who valued every minute of the day spent on improving the lot of his nation, noticed that he had done nothing specific. He spoke straight out about this, and said to them, regretfully:

"My friends – up to this day I have lived in vain!"

Precisely the opposite of this, in Siam, was practiced. Royal dictate declared nobody was to approach the Queen nor touch her, even accidently, nor to try to touch her dress, nor take her hand, with the exception of a few favoured Lords, and servants. These injunctions were sternly enforced and could only end woefully - as they did.

Once, on a fine summer's day, Queen Sunanda went sailing on her private yacht on the lake. Yet, a sudden blast of wind overturned her unprepared yacht near the shore. Hearing the terrified screams of the Queen (calling for help from the waves), hundreds of courtiers collected around on the shoreline, but not one of them dared to enter the water and save her. They all remembered the strict punishment for even brushing against the Queen's robes.

What could they do? While they dashed to and fro in a frenzy, to find a favourite, she had already sunk beneath the waves - and left this world for the next with none to help her.

AITMATOV.   The Count of Luxemburg was once looked on with esteem for his high level of justice and morality. Both across his country and beyond. In general, the title "Grand Duke" among these people is, as it were, unspotted - a crystal-clear symbol of the government itself. Whoever came to power, he must first of all respect these popular demands, or remain marginalized.

In Luxemburg, where I had the honour to be an Ambassador for the USSR, there were always competing, oppositional, powers. All the same, the Grand Duke was for them the highest authority.

That was not a sign of the absence of democracy, but just the reverse, a mark of real respect for it - put into practice.

SHAKHANOV.   Most probably so, for the Duke of Luxemburg, the major device of his life was honesty and justice, which embodied the very spirit of consensus.

AITMATOV.   That is exactly right. The Duke of Luxemburg's motto was, as you say, honesty and justice for all.

They remembered his simplicity and humble attitude towards life. When a great flood beset the land round Luxemburg (and conditions were difficult for the population), the Grand Duke and his wife were found among their troubled people. Putting on rubber boots, they went round from one district to the other, visited hospitals, and got to know their people's losses and needs. In my opinion, the Duke showed personal responsibility for each citizen of Luxemburg.

SHAKHANOV.   God blesses the simplicity of those who greet beggars on the streets, and bear responsibility for their people. The kindness and concern of those who waded in rubber boots through flooded areas likewise should touch the hearts of other presidents and government official!

By the way, Chingiz, were you not honoured with one of the highest awards in Luxemburg, when you served there as Ambassador? It was a very rare thing for a foreigner, a writer, even a diplomat, to attain such a reward. It was presented to you by the Grand Duke himself, wasn't it?

AITMATOV.   Yes, it was. "The Grand Cross of Service" was handed to me by the Grand Duke himself. For me, an altogether unforgettable occasion. Erudition, culture, and a philosophic view of life considered obligatory qualities in a leader of such a country.

SHAKHANOV.   The philosophic nature of politician's minds! Bewteen the years 551-479 B. C., in China, there lived a famous philosopher - Confucius. More than one generation of leaders benefitted from his precepts and postulates. Indeed, one of the most threatening Emperors of China, showing respect for Confucius, often said: "If we make a mistake in our government of the land, he, our great teacher, will not forgive us!" The instructive sayings of Confucius about orderly government were devoted to some eighteen thousand of his wisest contemporaries, and are now translated into almost all the languages of the world.

"Everyone should carry out his duty honestly. The ruler who leads a government, the tradesman who is occupied with his buying and selling, the father who fulfils his parental duty, and similarly the son, his filial affections. If this simple rule of life is broken, the government will begin to rot from inside, the law and order in things will be lost, and mutual respect will vanish. In the country, quarrels and intrigues will arise. A great fire begins from one little spark flying from flints".

The precepts of Confucius appear useful for all mankind till today.

AITMATOV.   I think the possibility of governing a land is only open to someone who has been forged in the fires of politics: one whose reason, education, wisdom, and expansive nature are united. One whose arrow flies farther, faster, and more faultlessly than all others.

Yes, clearly things like burdens and deprivations on the narrow and slippery road to adaptation - whether one becomes the owner of a throne and a crown - are much better known by those who rule, than by you or me, Mukhtar. Not in vain do they say: "A Khan has the mind of forty men".

Turkic peoples rarely had Khans, and Beys, even more rarely women leaders: as happened in various epochs across Europe and Russia. In this sense, the wise and free-willed Kurmandzhan was unusual - like a single ear of corn in a field of oats.

Kurmandzhan and her husband (the wise-man Alimbek), lived together thirty-five years. They had five sons together - Abdildabek, Batirbek, Mamitbek, Asanbek, and Kamchibek, as well as two proud daughters.

After the death of Alimbek (who fell beneath the hand of the Kokand Khan, Khudoyar), the people of Alaya, of their own free will, choose Kurmandzhan (already fifty two years old), to be their leader. However, the time when Kurmandzhan came to power was one of double persecution for Kirghizians. Russian colonizers being a problem on one hand, and the Kokand Khanate on the other. Be that as it may, Kurmandzhan was an accomplished diplomat, a mother of seven children, and a lively boss. She did all she could to persuade the Kokand Khanate (Kashgar and Bukhara), to cease their hostilities with Kirghizia. Instead, becoming mutual partners. Unsurprisingly, in 1864, Muaszaffar (the Emir of Bukhara) gave this wise woman her title and even made her a General. Afterwards trying, with all her strength, to free her flock from the iron vices pressing them on both sides. Admiringly, Russian officers commented on her stubborn stance when attempting to subdue the Kirghizians.

Stated so, the relationship between a female ambassador - and the imperial colonizers of Russia and Kokand - remained changeable. Interestingly, therefore, the Governor-General of Turkestan, von Kaufman (who respected Kurmandzhan), continued to involve her in negotiations. An act eventually deciding the fate of her two sons, Abdildabek and Kamchibek, who were fighting as soldiers in the Russian Army. Additionally, Mamitbek, another son of hers, as well as her grandchildren Mirzapayaz and Aristanbek, were sent to a prison-camp in Siberia - while her youngest son was hung in Osh. Some say the wise old woman saw this execution with her own eyes. Other witnesses, seeing the preparation for this execution said; "Kurmandzhan has only to give the call - Have we not been fighting for centuries for our freedom? Better death in battle, than such shame falling on our heads! Rise, good people! Get on your horses! Then, all Kirghizians beyond a doubt, will bestraddle their steeds and our wise leader save her son". Yet, Kurmandzhan preferred to sacrifice him, rather than have the sons and daughters of thousands suffer as she did.

SHAKHANOV. Alexander II, who came to the throne of Russia in 1855, was a tragic figure. Like Kurmandzhan, he protected his people, whilst in the end becoming a victim of the freedom he granted them. He was also a contradictory figure, since he caused such damage to "small peoples" living on the colonial outskirts of the Empire. For a start, military service was shortened from twenty five to *six* years. A soldier, having served his time, afterwards being enlisted amid those hoards constructing Russia's first great railway. Factories and workshops began to rise in large numbers. Equally, the quantity of unemployed people fell during his reign: consequently improving life among the poorest people. On top of which, the number of schools increased to twenty thousand and with them appeared three hundred gymnasiums. In all the territories governed by Russia, the first newspapers and magazines began to appear.

Nevertheless, there were still over fifty million serfs in Russia at that time. Subjects exhausted under the oppressive and merciless yoke of their masters - people who more and more frequently began to revolt.

Does it not happen, however, that one's good deeds sometimes come to a bad end? On January 1st 1881, terrorists from a party called "The People's Will" threw a bomb at the Emperor's coach, and severely wounded him. In this way, Aleksander II showed pity on his downtrodden people, but himself became the first victim of his liberating movement.

AITMATOV. One evening I had a long discussion with my fellow villagers sitting on the square. Thoughtfully, they spoke of leaders and thinkers from innumerable times and peoples. Including Stalin. One of the old men, stroking his beard, then told a legend:

"Stalin gathered his favourites around him, and said: "As I see things, you seem to be breaking your heads over the problem of how to govern our people. Padishas in power are not gods, but they are not less than gods! So, what do you have to do to render people fully submissive? Obviously, you don't know, but I will show you". Following this outburst, he ordered one of them to bring him a hen. When the hen was brought, right away, in front of all the others, he plucked her of all her feathers while still alive. When the last feathers had been stripped, and only bare pink flesh was seen, he set the hen free. Quirkily, commenting: "Watch and see where she goes!" The hen, her torment ended, wanted to run away somewhere. Although, in the sunshine it was scorching hot, yet in the shade dank and cold. Despairingly, therefore, she went and stood at Stalin's feet - crouching close by his legs. Suddenly, Uncle Joe put his hand in his pocket and drew out a fistful of grain. Scattered it before the hen. From that moment, wherever Stalin went, the hen followed him. Half-tired and half-yawning, the feared leader of his Party went on to say, "Well, did you see? The people are just like this hen. Just pluck them naked, and let them go. Afterwards, they will be easy to govern!"

Together, these wise-men assumed it was a made-up story. Even though they were amazed at the boldness of their leader: "What ingenuity", some quipped, "See, what wisdom!" Others adding the rejoinder, "Though it is only a legend, it is basically true". One particular sage finishing off, "Yes, that plucked hen had about as much brains in her as we did! Did they not pluck us, just as this hen was plucked? At first, the Soviet Government gave us strips of land and told us to sow wheat (to feed ourselves), while superfluous grain was to be given back to the Government. Then, when our barns grew full, they took another line - look at your herds of cattle! What tight-fists you are! Who has the right to rob another of his possessions, and deprive him of a home? If we have grown personally prosperous, this is by our efforts. Now, we see that by labouring for our own daily bread, we have merely brought down trouble on our heads. So, things not considered a crime eventually led us into prison: or to Siberia. Indeed, if someone had a prosperous business, he was the first to be arrested and taken away. Sadly, the fate of hard-working people was in the hands of good-for-nothings".

Two years later, these same envious people who arrested our fathers and called them "tight-fists" were themselves condemned, facing a judge and jail sentence. Meanwhile, citizens already plundered had scattered wherever they could. The majority of them living like the plucked hen with nowhere to shelter.

They say: "words which seethe upwards under inebriating kumiss get spoken." Thus, in this discourse between village elders, long held secrets were exchanged. In some places, they said, "Committees of the Godless" were formed, to set about destroying religious life. A disingenuous undertaking which led to many good men being shot.

Still, the behavior and actions of another live on in collective memory. A thought coming to me dozens of times. Men's deeds remain after they are gone.

In Soviet days, all our people experienced a hard and dialectical fate. The withdrawal of religious influences on a man's life invariably leading to personal losses which simply could not be replaced.

By contrast, I can describe conditions wherein the uplift of religious power continues to hold sway in people's lives.

When I worked in Luxemburg, they phoned me from the Chancellery of Herr Beitsecker - the then President of Germany – to say: "In the

Catholic Academy there will be a meeting of cultural workers and the President invites you to participate as an honoured guest. He has been wanting to meet you, and get to know you." I thanked the caller, and soon after went to the Catholic Academy. The President opened this meeting with an address in which he spoke (very forcefully) of the unity of one's spiritual inheritance, the culture of a nation, and a religion. Undoubtedly, Herr Beitsecker was a real intellectual, both well-informed and fully acquainted with world literature. Interestingly, the people of Western Europe, having similar historical roots from ancient times, never looked separately at culture and religion. For them, they are of one and the same. Related fellows, I would suggest, travelling but one road in search of perfection. All making me reflect that each nation should possess an unbroken unity between these qualities of our human souls.

SHAKHANOV.   Yes, this is what they term a "cultural conductor" in the development of a nation. Thence, I shall pause, briefly, to speak of something which happened to me - and might appear in opposition to what we have previously said:

The Pushkin Day of Poetry (having become an annual tradition) is headed by the Pskov region. In their famous Forest Glade about twenty to twenty five thousand people gather to listen to poetry recitals. The lively opening of this festival notoriously celebrated by appreciative readings from various poets. Later, this Day of Poetry was transferred to Moscow: being held in the Columned Hall of Trade Union House. An event also enjoyed by well-known poets who participate one after the other, and occasionally recorded on Central TV. Once, during one of these "slams", I received an invitation from the Republics of Central Asia and Kazakhstan to join in. When my turn came, I went to the tribune and read my poem entitled "Feeling for the Word" and came to the following quatrain:

"One must be careful of people who are crass,
Who have not any feeling for the Word.
They're dangerous when leaders of the mass,
Especially if for long their voice is heard!"

There, so they tell me, I waved my hand in the direction of the First Secretary of the Pskov General Committee of the Communist Party. For my part, I have no recollection of this happening. Anyway, my listeners met the poem with warm applause, and having acknowledged their reception, I returned to my seat in the second row of the Presidium. In a very short while, however, a man came and said to me:

"Come out here". I noticed his words were uttered through clenched teeth. Moreover, as I looked at him, his face was stern and severe. So, when off stage, I wasn't surprised when he continued: "Why did you, when reading your verse, wave your hand in the direction of the First Secretary of the Pskov Communist Party Committee?" Only then did I realize I had fallen into serious trouble. Adding to the confusion, it turned out he and his comrades on the Presidium all took the same view of that verse, and attributed a single meaning to it.

"We have decided not to let you recite here in future. Your whole poem will be removed from the Union TV screen as well" grimaced the man.

In that situation, where I didn't know whether to laugh or cry, I remembered an old parable, which helped my unfortunate situation.

"In distant parts, a certain powerful Khan, thinking he would conquer our people, led his soldiers to the border, and sent a few of his scouts to find out the military situation: "Find out about the forces opposed to us!" he ordered. When his spies returned, the Khan called his Vizier in, and they both began to listen to the reports.

"We went to many places," said one of the scouts, "and just then a great feast was going on. The leader of the people was there, in his royal yurta. Just then a young guy of sixteen or so entered, with his dombra in his hand, and bowed to the Khan. He, sitting in the place of honour, moved aside slightly, and made room for the guy, who came and sat beside him. We were amazed at such behaviour, and asked:

"Why does he show such respect to an unknown guy of sixteen?"

"Oh! He is our young poet and singer!" a courtier replied.

"We think if they have such a stupid leader as that, we could just take off our hats and throw them at the people, and they'd give in!"

"Yes!" said another scout, "To horse, my Khan! Let's get moving!" Then the Khan, who listened to the scout without a word, looked at his General Commander, and said in answer to the scouts:

"No! Move our men back! We can't count on a victory over such folk as this, who so highly respect their poets, who have such spiritual worthiness!"

AITMATOV. Yes, unfortunately for humanity, in its history at all times, the number of its leaders who depended upon spiritual riches is so small one could count them on one's fingers, without much difficulty.

Having been liberated from the blood-thirsty magnetism of Stalin's personality (following the twentieth Party Meeting) we felt the beginning of the end, the coming of more spiritual freedom. However, the old farce of his false praise was more difficult to overcome.

SHAKHANOV. Brezhnev demonstrated that with the help of flattery, and hosts of idle chatterers with false praises, even a man of limited intellect and capacity for action, might bear the name of a wise leader. Truly, practically all the Party Meetings and Plenums of the Central Committees had nothing but praise for the Party General Secretary. Brezhnev, with satisfaction, listened to those sweetly-worded speeches, rustling away like the sands of the Kyzyl-Kum desert, ready to swallow up all water supplies, no matter how much they poured out. In this manner he played a farce previously unseen on the stage of history, though it was theatrical and basically quite unreal.

An eminent Kazakh man of learning, Academician Manash Kozibayev, brings out in his article "Brezhnev in Kazakhstan" the following fact:

"At a ceremonial meeting in Kiev, on the occasion of an award to the Ukrainian Republic of the Order of Friendship, the audience applauded thirty five times the speech of the General Secretary of the Party Leonid Brezhnev. A little later on, in Kazakhstan there was to be a ceremony to celebrate the twentieth anniversary of the take-over of the virgin land, (15th March, 1974) with the participation of L. Brezhnev. So Kazakhstan, the motherland of the steppe, prepared to celebrate this special occasion. The Secretary of the Central Committee of the Communist Party of the Republic, the ideologist S. lmashey organized a special meeting, at which responsible peasant workers were strictly instructed to show Brezhnev their esteem on an even higher level than that shown in the Ukraine. Having received this special order, the regional, district, and city leaders, set about their business, and organized affairs so that after his speech Brezhnev received seventy-three rounds of applause. In this way, the "plan of praise" was fulfilled twice over, when compared with the Kiev meeting. According to witnesses present, Brezhnev was deeply touched by such a reception - almost to tears - regarding this appreciation of his "genius". Hence, this event could go down in the Guiness Book of Records, as the world record for hand-claps.

AITMATOV.   In those years Rasul Gamzatov, then a member of the Supreme Council of the USSR, sent home from Moscow to Makhachkala a telegram saying: "I am sitting here in the Presidium - but I don't feel happy!"

SHAKHANOV.   All in all, a couple of jocular words, but how much sense and truth there lies concealed in them!

Was it because Brezhnev wished to conceal his own decrepitude and inertness, that he filled the Political Bureau of the Party in those days full of elderly men? Their average age was around seventy years old. A few of them even had difficulty in climbing the steps onto the stage, and even a greater torment walking down. According to one anecdote, someone in a voice like Brezhnev's pronounced: "Please lift members of the Politbureau up here with me!"

The leaders of the other Republics, copying the Kremlin manner in everything, followed closely on the heels of those old ones in Red Square.

In those years I wrote a not very lengthy poem "Twelve to thirteen – equals?" dealing with the problem of those "Kremlin Old Men", already (through age) grown to be a dangerous element in political life.

AITMATOV.   Very well! It would be a good thing to hear it right now!

SHAKHANOV.   This is how the poem goes:

> *In that land where white-shouldered eagles grew,*
> *long, long ago there lived a mighty Khan.*
> *'Twas hard to know what was the main thing in him –*
> *The fact that he was mighty,*

Or stubborn!
He was old, but "played on his horse's ears"-
That means, he was a good rider in his days.
If he set a goal,
The target he always hit,
And the worthiness and honour of his folk
He thought to raise –
But how he did not know.
But he decided,
And issued straight away
A brand new law, which he had just devised.
Then it was placed
Before the people's eyes –
That only age would gain a mind mature,
And that the mind of youth was a danger to man.
There's nought more frightful
Than an ill-thought law,
And therefore officials, and major-generals too
Must be selected from the eldest and the best!
They will be slow in all the steps they take,
For moderate pace is found in maturity,
And wise is he who shows no sign of haste!"
So, stepping with moderate pace over all their youth,
But actually killing its spirit straight away,
About the use of youth forgetting too,
And speaking everywhere of the use of age,
The leaders quite forgot young people around,
And tied them up with disbelief in themselves.
On the flame of youth they buckets of water poured,
And soon all youth grew timid, without a will.
At twenty-five they could not, without tears,
Eat up their bowl of soup, and crust of bread.
Young folk might glorify themselves in verse –
But now was nothing left to praise at all.
To all their earthly sorrows, a new one came –
The confirmation of a brand new law.
So they grew up as terrible cowards,

When they heard the clash of enemy swords,
Just hid their heads.
The warriors just died out.
From whence then came this depression in the young,
This misery and oppression which they feel,
Which makes the souls of people and flowers fade?
This disbelief in the young
Has changed us all,
And changed their souls, so it's hard to recognize them!
The Khan first seized that Satan by the tongue,
To all the folk around he then announced:
"So that our rule should be unshakeable here,
We must make progress - forward we must go!
Have we no warriors, filled with manliness here?
Why then does fortune seem so mean today?
Let's make a war, and win new glory there,
Against.. . against.. .
And there he sobered down,
And once again
Spoke slowly, and quietly too –
Against.. . well, let us say, some other land,
Which is a quarter smaller than our own.
That surely will raise our fighting spirit again!
He did not start at once,
But merely tried,
And was at once defeated, and captive made ...
With his grey hair, like feather-grass in the wind,
And with his eyes all pallid from weeping now,
 He cannot lay the blame on anyone else,
Or justify the evil which he has done.
He has no bow nor arrow
To angrily shoot.
His visiers and elders, with their goat-like beards,
All trembling, like a little isle, stand there
 Before the threatening landslide, thundering down.. .
"Where are those days of greatness in our land?
Who dealt this blow, so pitiless on us?!!!"

Then their new ruler, who had defeated them,
  Called the lost Khan with a grin, and full of spite:
"Believer in slowness, yet you made too much haste,
You went quite off your head, and lost all sense.. .
At last you've come to yourself,
  So hasten now;
  If you can guess my riddle, I'll set you free!
If not, then you can count on it - you're dead!
Well, rack your brains, and answer, if you can –
Here is the simple puzzle which I ask:
"IF YOU TAKE THREE FROM A DOZEN,
WHAT REMAINS?"
The Khan, whose face was already deathly grey,
Already feeling the noose around his neck,
Then laughed: "Well, nine, I'd say!" was his reply,
As gay as if his wife had born a son!
Again the Emir gave a mocking grin,
  With victory's sweetness, and bitterness of spite:
"In this small fray, again the truth I'll teach –
You couldn't guess –
So bare your neck for the blade!
But among the prisoners, standing condemned around,
  One youth stepped forth:
"O, mighty Emir!" said he,
  "Death comes to all, be it soon, or be it late –
Why hasten him on his way - his slowness is wise.
The spilling of blood is an easy thing, Emir:
Well, I will answer your riddle for him now!"
Emir:
"Unending is man's struggle for happiness here.
  Say, who can stop it?
No one!
Never, I say!
Let death then punish upstart elders and Khans
Who can't believe in the power of youth, not their own.
The roots of disbelief so deep are hid,
  That they will surely hinder you, my son!"

The Youth:
"Is death the most fearful punishment, then?
More fearful still, by chance, to remain alive,
And see with your own eyes your own mistakes,
And somehow come to peaceful terms with them!
If power is taken from you, then you have no means
To put your frightful error to rights again ... "
Emir:
"My son, I passed the ninety mark long ago,
But I am glad of the growth of youth on earth.
I follow their fate, to see that it does not fade,
That flame of youth in bold and beating breasts.
The day when youthful flame all dies
Will be
A day of spiritual death for me, I fear.
I do not like it,
Seeing unloving youth,
I do not like it, seeing stones thrown at babies,
And therefore no pity to your Khan can I show,
But as for you - well, there's something in you I like,
So, very well, - I'll fulfill your youthful wish,
What can you pay for the Khan's mistake, that is,
With the flame that burns within your youthful breast?"
The Youth:
"Let not one be happy on this earth,
Who throws a mocking stone against a baby!
But to throw such stones against age is also bad!
It's unbefitting to both the baby and youth.
I like this puzzle which you have set, Emir!
Forgive me though, unwittingly you have erred,
If you name your riddle an everlasting law
Of life, of time which passes, of nature too.
If people think: "From a dozen take three away –
Then nothing remains...
That's my answer, I would say!"
Emir:
"Well done, my son! Guessed right!

So, good for you!
And how do you prove point, I'd like to ask,
For that is the final weapon in any debate?"
The Youth;
"Each year consists in all of twelve whole months.
Three out of them are Spring.
Do I get you right?
But Spring, that is the boldness of Nature itself.
Who refuses Spring, by his cowardice shows I'm right.
For youth is Spring,
And who would go against that,
 Would break down Nature's own immortal law.
Life is distinguished not by beauty alone,
But by the thoughts, which Spring's great beauty brings.
And if in Spring our apple-trees do not bloom,
What fruits in autumn can we then expect?
Thus nine months of the year would sentenced be,
 If you take away three!
Then nothing should we receive.
 We cannot, then, Emir, from a dozen take three –
Whoever does that finds woe, like our one-time Khan,
Who sees that eternal law as a riddle till now!.."
"Who's this that speaks?" thought that saddened poor old man,
Who until yesterday bore the title of "Khan" –
"Why didn't I chow him, and the other young men,
 Relying only on goat-bearded elders there?.. "
The Khan glanced sadly up at the swaying skies,
 Remembered the lad as a slave - a stable-boy.
Then he recalled his own fate,
And so he groaned:
"I'm finished, a corpse,
 I shall never rise again ...
I shan't open my eyes again ...
In my stable I kept
The ones who might have been war-leaders too.
A pitiful fool, how could I have been so blind,
Not allowing others to stretch their wings and fly?..

Is there a torment worse than this madness now,
When all too late
Has one good thought come to me?.. "

AITMATOV. Yes. I remember that poem in which the bitter truth is spoken about those times of stagnancy ... Yevgeny Yevtushenko translated it into Russian. I then wrote a preface to it, and offered it for publication in the "Change" journal. Obviously the editor there himself understood there was a deep sense hidden behind that allegory, and did not allow it to be printed in his journal, fearing of the consequences.

SHAKHANOV. Two or three years later, at a meeting of writers from Asia and Africa, in Tashkent, the chief editor of one of the largest journals, "The Spark", Anatoly Safronov, said to me:

"Give me something of yours, and I'll publish it in our journal 'Ogonyok'. I handed over the long-suffering manuscript of "Twelve to thirteen - equals?" to him. Afterwards he returned it to me with a letter, explaining that he could not publish it in his journal.

Immediately after the change-over events in December 1986, in Alma-Ata, upon the request of Yevgeny Yevtushenko, they appointed Yuri Voronov as a Cultural Attache of the Central Committee of the Communist Party, and I later met him there.

In our conversation, eye to eye, he laughed, and said having instructions from a member of the Politbureau, and the Secretary of the Central Committee, Suslov, he read my poem "Twelve to thirteen-equals?" and discovered it called up various kinds of ridicule. Put succinctly, the poem was quickly "measured out" at the Kremlin. But he, Voronov, had hindered them from placing my name on any black-list of public offenders. Only then did I understand why this poem remained unpublished anywhere, and was likely to remain so.

Well, Gorbachov came along and boldly (at a critical time for totalitarianism among ossified elder-members), brought into our lives new perceptions such as "perestroika" and "democracy". To give full freedom of expression, of thought, and of development to the nation - was certainly a radical step. That much we are bound to admit.

Chingiz, my dear fellow, you were on good terms with Gorbachov, I believe. Did he deliberately take that dangerous step, or was it made necessary due to social changes?

AITMATOV. You are right about that situation. At the time, Gorbachov was becoming an active politician who personified innovation and internal contradiction. Who knows, maybe he would still be in power if he had kept to the path of his predecessors? Back then (in our country) democratic processes was gathering force. Indeed, I recall chatting with him before one Kremlin meeting wherein conversation went along the lines:

"Let's talk things over without any rush!" he said, as he invited me into his cabinet room. "The present situation in Central Asia, in Kazakhstan, is well known to you. What do you think about the political, economic and cultural position of that region in general?"

I told him all I knew, and what I thought about the matter. Finally exclaiming, I would tell him a parable concerning this complicated matter. He looked at me, and then nodded his head silently:

"Well, once upon a time there was a very proud and glorified Emperor. On one occasion (having ridden a long way), an unknown traveler appealed to him thusly:

"My Lord, when you came to the throne, you promised your slaves full liberty. After giving your people freedom, however, you need not expect a warm reception, nor even gratitude from them. They will simply censure you, and defame you, and become a danger to your reign. They will only become quiet, when they have overthrown you. Therefore, while it is not too late, think things over. You are at a turning point on your road. Give the people freedom, or don't let power go out of your hands. According to prevailing law, interference in the activities of a ruler, or expressing doubt about the justice of his actions, are an unheard of insolence. Either way, be firm. Now, having heard his speech, the Emperor's guardsmen were ready to cut off the poor man's head. Yet, after contemplating for some time, the Emperor announced: "Reward this man in my name for his good council and let him go his way!"

Gorbachov pondered on my parable. Having understood why I told it, he even grew slightly pale. Then he replied with resolve:

"Chingiz Turekulovich, I will not give up and step backwards. That is impossible! Since I have promised to give the people freedom, I shall stand by this decision to the end. I am ready to go forward, even if they kick me out, or I lose my head as a result of it!"

"In that case, I wish you every success on your chosen road!" I responded, following which we said our warm goodbyes.

Today, it seems the Almighty put these words into my mouth!

When the putsch by members of the State Committee for Emergency Situations broke out in Moscow, in August 1991, and it was put down by other politicians under the leadership of Yeltsin, the editorial board of the "Paris Match" journal phoned me and asked: "You stand close to Gorbachov, as a fellow-thinker, but he may disappear from the historical scene! What do you have to say about this?" Curiously, I found myself repeating the same parable which I had told to Gorbachov. Vociferously, the French newspaper published immediately.

Having experienced 1989 together with Gorbachov, as a member of the delegation visiting China, I returned overflowing with impressions. The main purpose of visiting being to stabilize relations between bordering nations. It was also desirable, if at all possible, to intensify trade between our two countries. All happening, of course, during the stormy processes of "perestroika" and democratization within the Soviet Union.

To this day in Europe, they don't begrudge flattering words if someone starts to mention "Gorbachov" or "perestroika". Indeed, they remain aware that for our country this was the beginning of a new history, a new epoch. No one should forget this. Undoubtedly, one cannot be entirely free of doubt as to where it will lead in the end! After all, the doctrine of free speech liberates the consciousness of people, allowing sparks to ignite a flame. But that is a separate discussion ...

Getting back to my point, it was noticeable during our visit to China that there was a mass-movement among students in Pekin. On the main public square, thousands of people had gathered to demand a series of changes in the law. Their agitation did not die down day or night, becoming increasingly dangerous. Moreover, this unrest grew when the youngsters learned of the arrival of Gorbachov in China. Tensions increased all around.

"Let Gorbachov come before us. Let him tell us in his own words about democratic changes taking place in the Soviet Union!" Such were the demands of these young people. Astonishingly, Chinese radio and Television stations broadcast these demands. Each transmission stirring foreign ambassadors in China to wonder if Gorbachov actually would speak to the demonstrators? At one point, he even had an inclination to go out on to the square and speak about the reconstruction of affairs in the USSR. Yet, in the final analysis, he thought this might increase social strains.

Gorbachov's advisors equally warned him: "You are an official guest of the Chinese Government. Your main task is to attain the aim of your visit and to conclude an agreement with Chinese leaders. Any contact with dissidents will be regarded as an interference in the internal affairs of this country!"

Besides, the impossibility of speaking about great changes in his own country, which he himself had fathered, proved unassailable. In the end, only an open letter was sent to the students who had gathered on Tyananmen Square.

It was fascinating that the windows of the Government Palace, where our delegation stayed, looked over Tyananmen Square, full of an enormous mass of people, who here and there had erected their tents - and had no intention of leaving their place of demonstration. United by a common goal, these young Chinese students flowed in from every direction: increasing the agitated crowd. No vehicles could move across the square and even militia-men could not pass through!

What a paradox! Gorbachov himself sits inside the building, while outside its walls in the square young people stood agitated by his ideas! However, each was deprived of the possibility of meeting with the other.

Two or three days later, after our delegation had left, bloodshed began in China. Nowadays, the world knows that in Peking many of these young people died for their convictions.

SHAKHANOV. I think, Gorbachov came to power as a man of democratic leanings. That is a good thing, no dount. From the other side, however, he did not want to part with the type of dictatorship which forms the basis of totalitarianism. He made great efforts "to cook two sheep-heads in one pot" as they say. But, it can never succeed, no matter who tries to unite opposing systems. Yes, he became a democrat and he wanted to get rid of dictatorship. Or maybe he did not? Perhaps, just the opposite – he tried to keep it in another form? Anyway, Gorbachov was destroyed by hesitation - when it came to the crisis, he could not say farewell to dictatorship.

AITMATOV. Yes, your attitude to Gorbachov is stricter than mine, and that is understandable. In those events of December 1986, in Alma-Ata, one either evaluated those events from the prevailing point of view, or else kept entirety silent. At that time your speech before the first meeting of the People's Deputies of the USSR made an explosive impression inside the Kremlin walls, did it not - like a bomb going off? I must confess I feared at that time misfortune would soon overtake you!

SHAKHANOV. Maybe so. As for Gorbachov himself, power has slipped from his hands. Unfortunately, the historical significance of events in 1986 is still far from completely understood. Nor is there currently any clear international evaluation, which also gives us reason for disquiet. However, the slanderous accusation of "nationalism" made against the folk was finally removed. Seeking the truth in this matter, I had several conversations with Gorbachov. On one occasion, he even threatened me - to find a way of closing my mouth! Although, by this time I already had support from Yeltsin - now the President - and from (the now deceased) Professor-democrat Andrei Sakharov - bless his soul! But that's another story!

When in Moscow they discussed your novel "Tavro Kasandra", (knowing full well you would take Gorbachov's part), I could not come to your side because of other business affairs.

AITMATOV. Several of my friends participated in the discussions about my novel "Tavro Kasandra" – amongst them, Yevtushenko, Voznesensky, Iskander, Dementyev, Gachev and his wife, as well as the literature specialist Svetlana Semyenova. Indeed, Mikhail Gorbachov also joined in this discussion, and finally said:

"All trends of artistic creation, which previously suffered persecution and suppression, are now free to express themselves. As a result of these freedoms, literary manuscripts full of violence, murder, and pornography have thrived. If this is what is known as "freedom" - using liberty to promote opposing aims, no to mention literature of a dubious direction, I am opposed to it all!

SHAKHANOV. From our mutual friend, Rustem Khairov, who took a part in those discussions, I heard that Gorbachov's attitude towards "Tavro Kasandra" was exclusively positive.

AITMATOV. It seems the novel pleased him very much indeed. However, let us now get back again to our main theme ...

Democracy must take the form of a people's vision regarding a just future. A powerful stimulus for the strengthening of that conviction lies in the formation of a Government Constitution for the whole community. From simple participants, to persons of high position (among whom stands the President himself) - all must submit to its laws. If each time, with the appointment of a new President, or a change in the Parliament, the Constitution is changed by the elite to their own advantage, then we shall lose the trust of the people. In this, the USA provides a fine example - for two-and-a-half centuries they have survived on the foundation of a single Constitution.

Relatedly, I often remember one event which took place in Luxemburg. A Criminal Court had condemned a man as guilty of an offence, depriving him of his freedom. Having been sentenced, and having wished goodbye to his family, the condemned man appeared at the prison. However, the prison chief explained for the moment his prison was full, and asked the convicted to come again in a month's time. So understood, both the convict and his wife found all cells were still occupied the following month. For three months this continued. No room! At last, having lost all patience, the condemned man wrote a letter to the papers: "With all due respect, will there ever be a place reserved for me in prison, or not? Unjust!" On the publication of this letter, a public outcry claimed: "Human rights are being ignored!" They even demanded the dismissal of this prison governor! As for other prisoners, possibly it would have been better for them to escape, enabling a circulation of inmates to flow in and out of detention.

Only where people trust the law can things go smoothly. No matter who you are - a worker, a rich businessman, or a superman - all are obliged to respect their Constitution, and keep its codes.

Confucius said: "Where a leader is just and honest, it is a simple matter to sentence the guilty. If, however, a leader is not clean, but like a dirty dog who goes around licking others, how then can he demand from his people that honesty which is not found in the highest places?" To bear the title of President for an entire land is a great honour! Equally so, for those who bear the title of King, Emperor, Padishah, or Khan! Yet, out of the handful of those who have gained such lofty positions, how many of them, after losing their prominence, still enjoy the love and gratitude of their people? Most leaders are destroyed by excessive praise, unending flattery, an irresponsibility with power, and by the absence of moral norms in their work. All explaining, maybe, why they fall victim to the influence of dark powers, and even darker ideas...

SHAKHANOV. Having attained independence, the countries of Central Asia chose for themselves their first Presidents, and began to live as they themselves saw fit. We know these leaders of our kith and kindred have a special respect for you, Chingiz, as a patriarch of world literature ... Nursultan Nazarbayev awarded you the tribute "People's Writer of Kazakhstan". Islam Karimov pinned upon your breast one of the most highly honoured medals of Uzbekistan - the "Friendship Award".

In which case, let's speak a few words about new Presidents in our young independent countries and carry on our deliberations.

AITMATOV. Each leader gets his appraisal from history. I think, therefore, it will be hard to set observational limits to our opinions about those who presently find themselves in power as Presidents in our two countries.

Kazakhstan has more than a hundred peoples and tribes. In itself, a criterion rendering extreme complication when considering national and social problems there. In part, this is compensated for by the huge territory it covers, as well as its potentialities. To head such a vast country is no light matter, even for a gifted and well-known political leader like Nursultan Nazarbayev.

I met him in Alma-Ata, Moscow, and Brussels, and more than once had conversations with him. Instantly, I could see Nursultan was a highly educated and widely-dispositioned personality. One could have no doubts about that.

SHAKHANOV.   Breaking into our talk about Nursultan Nazarbayev for a moment, I should like to tell one story, of which I was personally a witness. It concerns Orinbasar Yerkinov, who in his days worked as the First Secretary of the Balikshi Regional Party, in the Atyrau district. An outstanding man, taken up with arts. Once, he gathered together a whole group of accomplished writers and artists, (among whom was the composer Aset Beyseuov), showing them the region, and taking them to the Caspian Sea. Inspiring Aset and myself to write a song "Cranes return from the Urals" - the music was his, the words were mine. As such, this new song was heard at a meeting in the Palace of Culture. The audience gave it a warm welcome, and asked us to repeat it. Again, our song rang out and this time Orinbasar sang it along with the singers performing there.

You know very well the etiquette for Party officials of the seventies. They have no right, as Party bosses, to appear personally on stage without permission. Even to think of doing so was thought as strange behaviour.

However, this "performance" by Orinbasar came to the ears of a local regional official. All provoking question about his potential dismissed. Anyway, he survived – to everyone's surprise.

Returning to Nursultan Nazarbayev - he was a politician who had grown up and was educated in the epoch of totalitarianism, but retained an inner empathy for artistic matters.

Not considering it shameful behaviour for a President, he still sometimes picks up his dombra to sing his favourite songs, at festivals and on holiday. I have seen him, and heard him when singing duets with his wife Sarah Alpisovna, in public.

At the end of 1993, the international association "Rukhaniyat" in Kirghizia, gave this President the title of "Man of the Year". At the ceremony Nursultan arrived in the company of famous artistic celebrities in our Republic - Abish Kekilbayev, Alibek Dnishev, Altinbek Korazbayev, Doskhan Zholzhaksinov, amongst others. Afterwards, at the party, he began (along with the composer Altinbek Korazbayev), to sing one of his songs. Is there any greater honour for a songwriter to sing his own song along with the President of the Republic?

Indeed, at those celebrations Alibek Dnishev and Doskhan Zholzhaksinov performed many remarkable songs with him.

It appeared to me I did not know some of the compositions they performed: being the latest songs in the singers' repertories. So, when making merry with the President, I made it my business to find out if he was interested in the history of his folk. In response, he put this question to me:

"Have you read the historical novel-essays of Koishigara Salgarin - "Golden Roots" and "The Tree"?

Although both these books were in my personal library, it happened I had not read them, Thus, I feigned ignorance, as though I had never heard of them.

Also, I remember one very amusing story in which President Nazarbayev himself figured as the hero. Back then, the Republics head was a man whose coming to power had caused the December revolt among students - this was the First Secretary of the Kazakhstan Central Committee of the Communist Party, Kolbin. To my recollection, Kazakhs caricatured him by saying things like: "His spit falls on the ground like a lump of ice!" So, during days when people were stirred by the tragedy of the Aral Sea, we received Kolbin's consent to call a meeting about this calamity - namely the lowering of the sea's level, and the exposure of its bed – a true catastrophe!

It was agreed our meeting should take place in Kzil-Orda. At the time, the chief of the Council of Ministers of the Republic was Nursultan Nazarbayev. All of us, along with Ministers from various branches of the Republic, flew into the regional centre. Kolbin gave a long opening speech, after which followed an address by Nursultan Nazarbayev. Then came my turn, as Chairman of the Social Committee for Saving the Aral Sea. To my recollection, I brought forward this parable, illustrating how difficult it was to express an honest opinion:

A devil tempted French King Louis XIV to compose poetry. Once, invited to his Palace, the best-known French critic was asked to read and give his opinion on it. Perturbed, the critic thought to himself: If

I tell his Majesty the truth, it will be like putting my head into a lion's jaws. Yet, to praise these verses would mean betraying my own soul and violating the truth. Therefore, he replied: "Great King! I see you set yourself a very hard task - namely to write a meaningless and trifling poem. In that, I must say, you have succeeded wonderfully!"

Having told this story, I added but few rulers like to be told the truth eye the eye. Nevertheless, one meets with quite few people who find cunning ways to indirectly elucidate difficult truths. Moreover, some of them were in attendance. Following which, I spoke everything that was boiling in my heart about the Aral catastrophe and ecological problems of our Republic - then left the stage.

A lunch-break was called. Refreshments had been prepared in one of the halls of the Regional Drama Theatre, named after Nartai Bekezhanov. To our surprise, we were invited to this table. At its head sat Kolbin, with Nazarbayev, and the leader of the Central Committee of the Communist Party (whose name now slips my mind), the First Secretary of the Kzil-Orda district Party Committee Auelbekov, and I, so there were five of us. Here Nursultan, with a mischievous look in his eye, said to me intentionally in the Kazakh language:

"Well, shall I talk to our "uncle" - I have in mind Kolbin here? Or would you prefer me to keep quiet?"

"You know, our "uncle" Kolbin is not a child,"

"All right, then, let's see!" he said, smiling again, speaking Russian.

"Mukhtar, the audience took your speech very well, and gave you long applause ... But how are we to understand your words about King Louis? What does this story have to do with the Aral Sea issue? Were you getting at Gennady Kolbin with concealed criticism?"

In that very moment Kolbin's face underwent an obvious change; "Eh, really, were you getting at me, in talking about King Louis?

"No, no! What are you thinking of? I had something else in mind, entirely!" I replied. However, I could see he did not believe me. The lunch went on, but I had lost all appetite. Matters had taken a bad turn, and I did not know how to make further replies. But then, praise be to Allah, Nursultan Nazarbayev broke in:

"Gennady Vasilyevich! I was simply joking! Mukhtar has a custom of reinforcing his words, so to speak, with all kinds of historical parallels and legends ... The King Louis story has nothing to do with you, whatsoever! People will see this at once, and not think twice about it, so don't start getting in a flurry, imagining things like that!"

Overall, he put the situation which he had created right, using powerful logical thinking and finding his way into the human psyche. Nazarbayev could always redirect Kolbin.

"Ah, ah! So I should have thought!" said he, becoming calmer.

AITMATOV. I remember now how once, when I came to Kazakhstan, Kolbin gave me a special invitation to meet him personally, and I did.

Often one's first impression of a man can be deceptive. Indeed, to me, he seemed fairly rational and reasonable. That was probably how he wished to appear before me, making a good impression.

SHAKHANOV. Really, having become the Republic leader and desiring to find support among the literati and artistic community, Kolbin was always kindly disposed towards them.

But one could feel such an attitude did not come straight from his heart. Such deceit, as one knows, is possible – even though discerning people eventually see through it.

At the beginning, he intrigued a number of people by announcing: "In a year's time, I shall make all my speeches in the Kazakh language!" In fact, he went no further than "Salamatsiz ba?" or "How are you?"

AITMATOV. But sometimes luck accompanies a man who hopes for easy success – though in this case, Kolbin remained indifferent to national traditions and thought nothing of the spiritual treasures within a people he misunderstood.

SHAKHANOV. In a personal conversation with Nursultan Nazarbayev, I recall him quoting a legend to illustrate his point:

There once lived a Khan, whose power and achievements rose as high as a mountain. So, he often went hunting with his suite of followers. Together, they all travelled through the forest and passed over mountain crests. Suddenly, one day, there jumped before them a lovely antelope, running off in a fright - with shimmering eyes and copper-coloured crupper. Then, the Khan shot his arrow, piercing its hind leg. All encouraging the Khan's warriors (with shouts and voracious cries) to drive the antelope into a dead end: between the cliff and an abyss. For its part, the despairing wild creature, limping along with one sound hind leg, entered the open door of a mountaineer's yurta. The owners inside were eating their dinner, when the deer weakly leapt over the little table and fell in the place of honour by the master. Scarcely able to breathe any longer, it settled down there.

"Drive that antelope out!" shouted the Khan, riding up, while leaning down from his horse. "I have been chasing it since noon, and nobody doubts it is my prey, so drive it out from your yurta I say!"

"You speak only of your business, my Khan," replied the old man who owned the yurta, "That antelope is your prey, you say, but he is now in my yurta, and as you see, occupies the place of honour at my table. Even deadly enemies do not break such sacred customs of the table. Though you are our Khan, you too don't dare to break this custom of your land!"

The Khan could say nothing in reply, turning his steed away.

AITMATOV.   A very instructive legend. The head of the government can attain the heights of wisdom only when he shows sincere respect for ancient tradition, customs, and morals of his people. Yet, those who ignore them, scorn them, or adopt a haughty manner towards them, inevitably meet with protests and opposition from their people.

SHAKHANOV.   In Krushchyev's time, one of the ideological leaders of Kazakhstan tried to make it clear that the ancient Kazakh custom of offering an honoured guest a boiled sheep's-head was a hang-over from feudal times, a barbaric prejudice, and had even led to herd reduction. It ended up with the whole population questioning such traditions.

There was also another story going around. Once Krushchyev came to Alma-Ata to take part in some festive ceremonial. Back then, it was the custom for leaders of Republics to gather together groups of Pioneers (with big flowers in their hands) to stand in a row in front of an airport building ready to greet honoured guests. Amid city streets it was arranged in the same way - youngsters with flowers and flags, smiling and laughing, and creating the impression of a happy environment.

On this occasion, the Pioneers had been waiting a long time before the plane arrived, and when it did, out staggered Krushchyev, scarcely able to keep to his feet. Indeed, still half-inebriated, although looking with eagle's eyes on those gathered to meet him, he took off his hat and raised it in the air crying aloud:

"Greetings to the people of Uzbekistan!" forgetting, obviously, in which of the Asian Republics he now found himself.

AITMATOV. I met the President of Uzbekistan, Islam Karimov, for the first time in 1990. Do you remember the Osh tragedy? I couldn't react indifferently to this unexpected clash between two brotherly nations: to the spilling of blood on both sides. Having met with Gorbachov I asked him: "Allow me to fly to Osh. I want to be there to try to help them, and to get to the bottom of this conflict, if I can!" Gorbachov immediately called the chairman of the Committee for Government Security, Kryuchkov, and the Minister of Defence, Yazov, and told them to prepare a special plane for flight. That same day I flew with a group of other people from the Military Airport, named after Chkalov. We landed in Tashkent, and right away I phoned the First Secretary of the Union of Uzbek Writers, Adil Yakubov. We met at the airport, and had an urgent discussion. For me this tragedy soon clarified.

How could one stop such a conflict? How could one put out the fire of hostility? Rumours increased every hour, each one touching my heart: "Tens' of thousands of Uzbeks in the Fergana region, are ready to go to fight in Osh!" And then: "Since yesterday Alai Kirghizians having heard this, got on their horses!"

Instinctively, I proposed to the leaders of various public organizations in Uzbekistan: "Let us, dear brothers, cease this fight at once. Listen to me, and say am I not right - if the truth be told we are all guilty. We will not increase the existing tension!" In the end, they gave me enormous support.

Soon, at the Airport, the First Secretary of the Uzbek Communist Party, lslam Karimov, arrived, having heard that I had come. As always he was active, energetic, concentrated on specific problems. We spoke together in an atmosphere of good faith, albeit alone. I said to him: "Stop those Fergans who are ready to go to Osh to join the fight. If the masses join in this struggle, we shall never be able to calm them down, and make peace. Everything will end with slaughter. We, from our side, will do all we can to quiet down the Osh region, and not let the hostility there spread further beyond its borders.

Our intentions fell in with those of Karimov. He at once supported me completely, and after our meeting (and agreement) took me to the plane.

Having been to the trouble spot, and having become acquainted with the circumstance which started such hostilities, I returned to the people of Uzbekistan, and spoke on Republic TV. I told them openly how the conflict began, and what terrible consequences it could have if tension increased. By my side stood Adil Yakubov and Pirimkul Kalirov, in supported. I also called on the Uzbeks to return to peaceful and quiet ways again, and restore friendly relations.

Thankfully, to avoid the conflict, lslam Karimov showed healthy commonsense and wise understanding, worthy of a great leader of his Government.

An action bringing to mind that the PEN-club of Kazakhstan once held a sitting in Kostanai to which I was invited by its President, Abdizhamil Nurpeisov. Deeply grateful for this invitation, I broke my journey to Frankfurt at Tashkent. In the evening I was visited by lslam Karimov, and discussed our thoughts on the problems of postmodern culture in Central Asia.

Previously, I had taken the man for merely an experienced host and keen politician, but this time I was convinced he was a true pundit: excellently acquainted with the history of his country, with a deep knowledge of culture and art. Certainly, it was at this meeting that the idea of forming a Central Asian People's Culture Assembly came up.

SHAKHANOV.   Yes, in 1995 in Tashkent, the work of the Central Asian People's Culture Assembly began with you, Chingiz, chosen unanimously as its President. Firstly, the literati and artists of those countries which had become isolated following independence could meet again. On that authoritative basis I was able to meet with the Uzbek writers and poets - Adil Yakubov, Shkurullo, Abdulla Aripov, Aman Matzhan, Zhamal Kemel, Yakubzhan Khozhamberdiyev, Akhmadzhon Melibayev, and cinema-dramatist Khairulla Zhurayev. From them, I heard nothing but praise for Islam Karimov. Moreover, all my friends spoke of the high intelligence of this President of

Uzbekistan. Evidenced by his efforts on behalf of writers and poets to build fifty new flats a year for them. This may be taken, undoubtedly, as an attempt to create conditions wherein the spiritual treasures of his people blossom. Although, I will not try to hide that earlier on (having heard various speeches and conversations), I was already pleased with Karimov as a politician. Nonetheless, I returned from those meetings with a feeling of respect for the President.

AITMATOV. From back in my childhood days I remember a legend related to Emir Temur*.

This great ruler, beside other things, in many ways developed the art of architecture in Buchara and Samarkand. In his day, many newly built mosques, mausoleums, and minarets - which seemed to support the very sky - were constructed. With time, he changed his country into a centre of knowledge and science. Of the beauty and elegance of his Persian Gardens and fountains, foreign rulers themselves spoke with admiration. Hence, while this ruler was creating his two pearl-like of cities, legend says the great poet Khodzha Hafiz wrote about them:

> "When that Shiraz beauty I take into my warm embrace. For her birthmark, I'd give Samarkand and Bukhara's grace!"

Hearing this verse, the Emir seemed to grow very angry:

> "Bring her to me! I want to see for what feminine birthmark a poet is ready to give away two of my beautiful cities!"

But the wandering poet could not be found. Yet, as Temur stood in the sunshine on the terrace of his Palace, Hafiz passed by. .. The guardsmen immediately arrested him, and brought him to the Emir:

> "So, it was you who wanted to trade Samarkand and Bukhara for some beauty's birthmark?" The Emir questioned threateningly.

> "Oh, great Emir! All my possessions stand before you - just as I am, and nothing more! But a poor man can be generous. That is

---

*Timurlane (Tr)..

why I offered your two cities for a beauty's birthmark!" Hafiz then added: "I did this merely to praise and magnify her!"

Temur looked at him, standing silently before him. In fact, the poet had a worn-out old gown and worn-out shoes - nothing more.

"Well, that was a noble and manly statement!" he laughed heartily. "If I am a great Emperor, you are a great Poet, you require on a place of honour at my court. Stay here for the rest of your days, no further cares and worries feel and freely write down you beautiful verses!"

Slowly looking around, he threw a telling glance at his guard: "Happy are the people where Padishahs seek their poet, but unhappy are the people where the poet seeks out his Padishah, so remember that!"

SHAKHANOV.   Let's speak of today. In the spring of 1995, the Kirghiz press raised a hulabaloo - "Maybe Aitmatov will put himself up for President!" Those who knew your gravitas in Kirghizia said: "What of it? Chingiz would make a good President!"

These rumours increased day by day, so when you phoned me from Belgium, I told you what was afoot. In reply, you exclaimed: "Please, as we are close friends and you know Kirghizians well, give an interview to the press - and try to make it clear these are empty rumours set about by those who benefit from political tensions".

I arranged an interview immediately, telling reporters that these false rumours should not be spread in Kirghizia. Later, I was told by Nursultan Nazarbayev about your meeting with him in France and about your exchange of opinions on this matter. He remarked:

"Why would a great writer need the Presidency? Literature has other problems. Praised be God, the authority of Chingiz is in no way less than that of President. These words are the chattering of idiots!"

My dear Chingiz, everyone will remember that, right from the start, when members of Parliament in the Republic proposed your name for the role of President, you refused the offer - yourself proposing Askar Akayev instead. In connection with this story, one friend and comrade-of-the-pen (also a leader of the Democratic Movement of Kirghizia), Kazat Akmatov, said:

"The Democratic Movement of Kirghizia, headed by me since 1990, suggested while in Parliamentary session to appoint the post of the President. Even though at first not a single deputee supported the idea, later on it began to gain momentum. However, our proposal was opposed by the Central Committee of the Communist Party of Kirghizia. Most likely because many people could not imagine Kirghizia becoming an independent State. Anyway, not wishing to part with their power, they announced in the Soviet Union there is only one President. That is enough. There is no need for each Republic to have its own President.

In that year, as a result of internal tensions at one of the November sessions, supporters for the introduction of a Presidency in Kirghizia received a positive vote. Their opponents, at least temporarily, were outnumbered, and silenced.

Not one candidate, however, received a decisive victory. Parliamentary processes seemed to be at a dead end. Having discussed the matter, it was decided to form a commission of twenty five delegates, and I was one of them. Our task being to find a sustainable solution.

Our concluding session was scheduled for the third day, and confessedly, we were excited. Yet, members of the Commission slowly divided into two groups. Twelve members stood out for a national referendum (trying to give the post to the previous head of the Republic), while the other twelve (one abstainee) proposed a new election with fresh candidates. Obviously, discussions got heated. The Democratic Movement of Kirghizia then organized a twenty four hour picket by youth (with banners and slogans - "Aitmatov for President!" ..... near the "White House"), at the same time as one hundred and forty people declared a hunger strike. In those difficult days, members of the Commission finally decided: "We propose Chingiz Aitmatov as President of Kirghizia. Just then, however, you were away on other business in Moscow.

"Well, get him on the phone, and call him to come home" they insisted unanimously. So, along with Tulemush Okeyev and Barpa Rispayev I got on the phone. Listened attentively to what we had to tell you, a judgement of Solomon followed:

"I am not prepared, and have no wish, to be President. I thank you all for your trust in me by proposing such a responsible position. Nevertheless, you need somebody in the line of economics, or a lawyer, say, or a specialist in agricultural matters. I have no desire to change my position as a writer for that of President. I have many creative aims and ideas which I hope to be able to put into practice soon."

Clearly, I was in a difficult position. Especially because everyone said you only needed to nod your head, and the President's post would be yours for sure.

"But whom, then, do you yourself propose as a candidate?" we asked, when we saw that you would not accept our proposal.

"Now you are speaking, bravo!" you replied. "I, for example, would have no doubts whatsoever in proposing Askar Akayev. He is highly-educated, honest, intelligent man - and would become a real leader!"

Askar was also in Moscow, at a session of the Supreme Council of the USSR, meaning they could easily get in touch with him there.

"Would you allow us to put forward your suggestion to the Parliament?" they asked. "Yes, of course I would, and please give my greetings to all deputies there. If they choose Askar, this will be a beneficial step for all the people of Kirghizia and for themselves personally!"

One hundred and fourteen deputees agreed to his suggestion, and sighed with relief!

In this way, having gained the majority of votes at the second session of the elections, Askar Akayev became President of Kirghizia.

My dear Chingiz, as it is clear from the words of Kazat, your rejection of Parliamentary position was due on one side to inborn modesty, and on the other to your devotion to literature. Is that not so?"

AITMATOV.   Every man, according to his own measure of merits and inclinations, has his own high place in society. Fate decreed for me a long-prepared writer's pen. If I can use this sensibly, then the strength of my given word may become a priceless instrument of insight.

SHAKHANOV.   I met Askar Akayev for the first time, as a member of the Supreme Council of the USSR. In the course of the session, I experienced a special satisfaction from his worthiness as a Kirghizian citizen.

At that time he devoted his energies to the question of the December events in Alma-Ata, and to getting these issues put into the order of the day. You were abroad then. In those difficult days Andrei Sakharov came to me, and advised me: "If in support of discussions around this problem one quarter of the members of one's chamber (that's sixty eight persons) sign some petition, that question will go on the agenda, without a doubt!" For a few days I went crawling around, exhausted, running after each delegate or deputy, giving him two or three pages of material to read, which I carried with me, and for four to five minutes waiting at each one's back. Three or four days I spent like this. Then out of the twenty four deputies from Kirghizstan were found only two people who were ready to sign this declaration! One of them was Askar Akayev, and the second was a driver, a chosen deputy from the Talas region, named Teldibek Kemirbekov.

You know a driver may not fear to be deprived of the steering wheel, but Askar Akayev (under a totalitarian regime) was President of the Academy of Science in the Republic. In spite of that, without the least hesitation, he supported the actions of Democratic youth in Kazakhstan, which had arisen against that regime. For even one such action he could have been dismissed from his position.

AITMATOV. At present, the republics are being tested on every side. Such burdens are the lot of any society in two conditions - one, in time of war, and secondly - in time of deep social changes.

The courage of Akayev amazes me, when he places himself right between the mallet and the head of the chisel – undergoing inescapable pressure from percussion, from heavy blows, but nevertheless continuing on the road to freedom.

What the political course of any country which appears to be throttling democratic processes, or which has dipped its hand in governmental treasuries, is not simply the will of fate. To avoid serious problems, citizens must demand every scrap of information to be made available without any concealment. Errors too must be open to sharp criticism.

SHAKHANOV. In general, Askar Akayev seems to be a large-scale figure, in which are united the talents and the qualities of a learned man, a politician, and a regular citizen. It is true, when he started serving as President, some accused him of too much softness and excessive delicacy. Later, however, he was able to show it was quite possible to rule a country without offending worthy people, without taking them by the shoulders and shaking them, and making them "Eat dust".

Anyone who has had the opportunity of speaking with him cannot help noticing what a polite smile he has and what welcome attention he shows to friends as well as rivals.

At an evening devoted to my literary work, which took place in the government Philharmonic Hall, in Bishkek, a young Kirghizian poet, Omurbek Tilebayev, read out some very good verses of his own. Sitting in the hall, the President remarked: "A great poet will manifest in that young man" and wrote his name down in a notebook. Not to turn away from talent, but to support any brilliant new ideas, to fill the government treasury-box full of national achievements, are some of the qualities needed by the leader of a country.

Akayev, out of his own resources (bonuses received from his own publications) set up a memorial to Alikul Osmonov, a great young poet, whose short life faded away due to tuberculosis. One must admit that in better years, a general interest in art and theatre, was stronger. Undoubtedly, the difficult economic situation limited our possibilities.

Bishkek Theatre, directed by People's Artist of Kirghisia, Arsen Omiraliyev, prepared for the audience a play by the Japanese dramatist Modzaemon Tikamatsa, named "Amudzima". Obviously, prominent social and Government officials were invited to the premiere of this fascinating Japanese play.

It was, of course, first presented in the Kirghizian language, although the artists taking part in the play remembered to keep as close to their Japanese characters as they could: providing an insight into oriental worldviews.

After the premiere, naturally, opinions about the performance were exchanged. Indeed, a lively debate ensued which included the ex-Chief Counsel of Kirghizia in Japan (now the Government Secretary of the Kirghisian Republic), lshanbai Abdurazakov, the Russian ambassador, Mikhail Romanov, the ambassador from India, Ram Svarup Mukidzha, the ambassador from Pakistan, Nazar Abbas, and I, and at the conclusion of our talks, Akayev took his turn.

He alone seemed to reflect the deep meaning of the play. Comparing the text with a literal word-for-word translation, and noting the particularly successful scenes. Going further, he even asked for additional pieces by Modzaemo Tikamatsa - wanting to know the other languages this author had been published in.

I don't know about the others, but I felt rather ashamed that I had myself come to the plan not really prepared to get the best out of it.

AITMATOV. It is, a joyful thing for me to know I have such a brother as Akayev.

Well, our conversation which began with Egyptian pyramids quite naturally led us to remarkable contemporaries like the President of Kirghizia, and to the Presidents of two other fraternal bordering countries. Yet, leaders who serves one and all, I had not ever met before - and did not believe in. So, it now seems justifiable for people across society to speak in a variety of ways about Nazarbayev, Karimov, and Akayev. In the long run, this is the democratic way.

We examined their first steps in taking power and their spiritual wealth. Neither of us, that said, should hide the alarm we feel for the future.

SHAKHANOV. That disquiet clearly lies in the present regime of Saparmurad Niazov, leader of the Turkmens. Knowing what misfortune the cult of personality brings, he still went along this dangerous path. Rumour has it he raised some two hundred statues to himself? Others adding, he gave his personal name to a canal and has printed his own portrait on the back of Turkmenistan banknotes!

AITMATOV. In one Korean journal published in Russian, I read a story connected with Kim Sen -leader of North Korea for almost half-a-century, and someone who has made himself into a god during his lifetime.

Once a river overflowed its banks, and flooded a riverside village. The stormy current carrying off a young mother and her child. However, on seeing a portrait of Kim Sen floating on the water, she cast aside her child and rescued the portrait of her leader, bringing it back to the shore.

The newspapers named that an action of the highest patriotism ... Of course, this was nothing more than idol-worship, and political imbecility.

It is deeply regrettable such boundless power may lead people to loose both self- respect, along with their recognition of human worth.

Presidential power, the great gift of fate, may be only the start of a man's fall. One goes up on that political Olympus, thanks to his own political talent, his sharp mind, and extraordinary qualities, and another receives the reins of government quite by chance, which often happens at a time of historical turn-over. It may even turn out those reins of government change into fetters around the feet of a people.

Many historical facts bear witness to this, as we have already said.

SHAKHANOV.   For a ruler there are only three weights on the scales of history: past, present, and future people. His mind must be the judge in these matters, otherwise he risks losing the people's trust in him.

When Akhmetzhan Yesimov, whom I respect very much, was chosen as the head of the Alma-Ata administrative region, I said to him jokingly:

"For a real knight, great duty is also a great testing. Not only nowadays, but in earlier times too, there were only a few people who proved indifferent to glory. We hope you are one of them."

As someone born in a poor tent, who has attained the heights of honour, Ayaz would hang on the door of his bedroom the rags he used to wear - as a reminder of his past days of poverty and misery.

AITMATOV.   For example, when I knew that lslam Karimov removed from their posts two leaders in the Zhizak region, who, during the President's visit hung up huge portraits of him, I was very glad to hear of it. For this self-effacement I respected him all the more.

SHAKHANOV.   That is a praiseworthy. Here, of course, lslam Karimov follows the example of his great predecessor, so I should like to read my new poem "The Last Testament of Timur*" – a work dealing with a man whose name was known across the world, but who, nonetheless, could not bear false flattery and boot-licking.

---

*Tamerlaine-Timur Leng-timur the Lame (Translator' **s** note).

The Last Testament of Timur

The warrior-men of Timur, at hand,
Came back from their campaign afar,
And they've returned to Samarkand,
Neath the shining dome of Kuk Sarai.
Timur at eve collected them
Who'd helped him gain his victory.
Above the joy of fighting men,
Quietly music floated free.
Like a white swan flew over the sky
Hodzha Hafiz then quietly stood
And read his gazelles with peaceful eye.
His verses were amazingly good.
Timur grew very excited soon,
And he began to nod his head –
What beauty there, like that full moon,
"What generous feeling!" then he said ...
Then someone stood up, from the floor,
And several times he gave a bow,
And slavishly he whined to Timur:
"O, greatest of the great, I vow,
O, wisest one of all the wise,
O, boldest one of all the bold,
You too are a lover of excellent lines,
So finely feel these words of gold.
We are so happy, and so glad
That we have such a Padishah!"
"Enough!" cried Timur, "You drive me mad –
A flattering, nattering liar you are!
Indeed, true wisdom to admire,
And thus to value beauty too –
That is the duty of every sire –
To praise me for that is ignorance true!"
Then with stern eyes he asked: "Who are you?"
"I'm Khorasan, the chieftain!" he said,
"I congratulate you with victory too,

That's what I came for!" He bowed his head.
"You are no longer a chieftain!" cried he,
"I now deprive you of such a right!"
"Of what am I guilty, your Excellency?"
A-trembling asked the chief in a fright.
"You're as cunning as a steppe-fox grand,
And knew that under flattery's wing
Nobody, hardly, can safely stand,
And not be touched by such a thing!
False praise destroys true feeling so,
Within the heart of a leader true,
And that is reflected later by woe
In the sorry fate of subjects too!
I'll have no such toads, where I am chief!
All flatterers will be punished by me,
For their deceptive, fawning Odes,
For their excessive servility.
Then in my lands good order you'll find –
So off you go, and get out of my way!"
Having spoken, Timur left the feast behind...
Yes, centuries pass, and seem like a day!
And we who now live in his land,
Hold memorial feasts for his Jubilee.
We sit with a new young chief at hand,
In the hall of modern democracy.
I wish, I wish that he would think
About Timur's last testament.
Although time flies, and our eyes we blink,
After more than six-and-half centuries spent.

AITMATOV.   Yes, we should all start to think, after such a poem! I receive many letters from all over Kirghizstan. The lowering of living standards, ecological misfortunes, the failing of morals. That is for me, and many others, a long, sad song! One letter I received especially touched me:

"We need in our Constitution a word or two about blessings and curses" writes the author. For a ruler who has done much for his people, moved social standards forward, and in difficult times has pulled us out of the rut, there should be a blessing. Even an honoured title - a Blessed man. But for a leader who heats up opposition, and occupies himself with dirty deeds, and commercialized government dealings, and places his own avarice and personal gain above the people's general interests, there should equally be an official curse – a Greedy Man - which he should be compelled to bear!.

Thusly, do simple villagers look at these problems! Let them slink away, after being exposed, and not look people in the eye, since cursed by the people, who hold these matters close to heart.

SHAKHANOV. You, my dear Chingiz, not only know the leaders of the Asian Republics, but also those from more distant lands. What would you say of them, and what alarms might sound in the future among our folk?

AITMATOV. I should say there are four alarming features Firstly, some Presidents frequently use the pronoun "I". This needs watching carefully, so tomorrow they do not say: "The State - that is I!" Secondly, it occasionally happens that outstanding rulers and are not subject to open criticism, but hide their faults from a people. Yet, in countries taking a democratic line of development, governmental structures strictly keep a check on the President's actions and decisions, which must stay in line with public support. The third of these dangers is found in a President trying to limit the power of a government through Parliament: bringing deputies under his influence, and making them submit to his will.

For instance, in one of the Western countries, the President was forced by Parliament to pay a fine, for keeping an air-liner waiting for two hours, although it was considered to be the President's plane.

Fourthly, the danger which I have heard often, and of which you have just spoken - excessively high praises, idolization, flattery, obsequiousness, and sheer servility. There are few leaders who can withstand such persistent undermining, or remain indifferent to it. Very few indeed, and one meets them only occasionally. As such, it is necessary to keep a check on oneself in the presence of high authority, and to stand in opposition to all signs of weakness on the President's part. This is important for government as a whole, and equally for every individual citizen.

We seem to have reached the conclusion of our remarks on people in power. From times immemorial up until today, spiritual leaders, religious officials, government chiefs and subordinates, all the way to judges and officers of the law, people (being people) have spoken either honestly, or in falsehood. If, therefore, our discussion enables somebody think of authorities on an individual level, then we have fulfilled the task we set ourselves at the beginning.

This may be why I would like to close this chapter with a few judgements made by wise people, living in various epochs relating to power and spirituality.

Pythagoras: "It is the same danger - to give a stupid man a sword, and to trust a completely dishonest man with full power".

Montesquieu: "There is no enemy more frightful than a tyrant, who acts in accordance with an oath, within the framework of the law, and under the shade of the banner of righteousness".

Didero: "Power, founded on violence, becomes the victim of violence.

La Bruyere: "The honorary place of an esteemed man grows higher, but of a shallow man - it melts away completely".

In conclusion, let me say: "Save us, Fate, from those rulers avoiding spiritual life and the moral values of the People".

Shymkent Famous sculptor, member of the Union of Kazakhstani Artists, AkhmetovAbdikarim devoted his work "Friendship is not subject to the death" to a friendship of the two like-minded writers - ChingizAitmatov and M.Shakhanov.

In the last years of Soviet power confrontation between M. Gorbachev and V. Yeltsin was gaining strength day by day…

IfM. Shakhanov has not attracted Yeltsin in the struggle to establish the truth about the events of December 1986 inAlmaty, who openly stood Gorbachev'spolicy, outcome of the struggle would have taken a different turn. The commission, established after M. Shakhanov's speech at Congress of People's Deputies of the Soviet Union I, headed by QadirMyrzaliev, included some of the perpetrators of the bloodshed, would started to perform a secret mission, according to which: "There are would be groups of hooligans, alcoholics and drug addicts, organized by Kunayev at the square instead of democrats". Only because of the fact that Yeltsin interfered in the matter, Gorbachev had to include in this commission eight of People's Deputies, elected from Kazakhstan, and approve Shakhanov as a co-chair. Therefore, revealing the truth about the December uprising, in some respects, owe Yeltsin.

Awarding C. Aytmatov with the title "Prominent writer Turkic world", 2007.

M. Shakhanov meets English writers Robin Thomson and David Parry

From left to right: C. Aitmatov, F. Hitzer, Nobel laureate H. Duerr,
M. Shakhanov. Paris, 1999

The opening of the Aitmatovpark. Turkey, Elazyk, 2007

Assigning the title of "The best Writer of the world" and "The best Poet of the world" among the Turkic peoples to M.Shakhanov. The diploma to M. Shakhanov is presented by the President of the Turkish Republic of Northern Cyprus, Rauf Denktash. Gebze ,Turkey

C. Aitmatov and B. Beishenalieva. Leningrad, 1959

Autographs in Otrar city

The presentation of the novel M. Shakhanov "Delusion of civilization" by UNESCO. At the podium from left to right: Russia's representative to UNESCO E. Sidorov, Director of UNESCO, Doudou Diene, C. Aitmatov, M. Shakhanov. Paris, 1990

C. Aitmatov among the staff and readers of the "Zhalyn" magazine, 2007.

The presentation of the "Hunter's crying over the abyss" by C. Aitmatov and M. Shakhanov in the conference hall of "Literary newspaper" in Moscow. From left to right: Ministry for Culture of Russia E. Sidorov, E. Bogoslovskaya, C. Aitmatov, M. Shakhanov, 1997

Aitmatov and M. Shakhanov at the VII USSR Writers' Congress. Moscow, Kremlin, 1981.

Secretary of the Communist Party of the USSR on ideological issues A. Kamshalov, writer Y. Shestalov, C. Aitmatov, M. Shakhanov and J. Mamytov at USSR Union of Young Writers, Moscow, 1969.

Near the TorekulAitmatov monument in Sheker. M. Akaev R. Aitmatov,
C. Aitmatov with his wife Maryam and M.Shakhanov, 1998

M. Shakhanov was awarded with the title of the People's Poet by
Ex- President of the Kyrgyz Republic, A. Akaev. The luminary of the world
literature, C. Aitmatov, hosted a poetic evening , devoted to this event.

Presidium of the International I Issyk Kul Forum, organized by C. Aitmatov. From right to left: Director-General of UNESCO F. Mayor, C. Aitmatov, Ex-Prime Minister of The Kyrgyz Republic

After staging a drama by Aitmatov and M. Shakhanov "Night memories of Socrates" in Kyrgyz State Academic Drama Theatre. The President of the Kyrgyz Republic AskarAkaev, C. Aitmatov, M. Shakhanov and the director of the play A. Sarlykbaev are on the stage, 1997.

After awarding of ChingizAitmatov and M. Shakhanov with the titles of honorary citizens of Aris city in South Kazakhstan region.

C. Aitmatov (first from the left) with his father Torekul, mother Nagima and younger brother Ilgiz, 1932.

C. Aitmatov and the French writer Louis Aragon, who appraised the novel "Jamila" as "the most beautiful legend of the world."

C. Aitmatov, 5th year student of Skryabin Agricultural Institute, 1957

The arrival of former USSR President Mikhail Gorbachev in Kazakhstan, when he, on behalf of the Central Committee of the Communist Party of the Soviet Union apologized on Kazakh television to the nation for the violent suppression of the December events participants in 1986 in Almaty. From left to right: C. Aitmatov, akim of Almaty V.Hrapunov, Minister of Culture and Information M. Kul-Muhammed, Vice Prime Minister I. Tasmagambetov, Mikhail Gorbachev, M. Shakhanov. Turgen, 2001.

C. Aitmatov with his wife Maryam, daughter Shirin and son Eldar.

Meeting with George Soros. Bishkek, 2001

Despite the fact that M. Shakhanov had to speak one of the first on the list at Congress of People's Deputies of the Soviet Union I, the authorities made every effort to not to allow him to the tribune, fearing the poet will touch on December events of 1986. Caught in a bind, he had to go to the trick - to prepare a letter signed by 19 deputies of Kazakhstan: "We ask to call on M. Shakhanov on the Aral Sea for 3-5 minutes". Thus, with the help of this letter Gorbachev gave permission to Shakhanov for statement. So, on June 6 of 1989 he mounted the rostrum in the Kremlin Palace of Congresses to speak about the tragic December events along with the requirement to cancel the decision of the "Kazakh nationalism". His speech had an effect of an exploding bomb. In the photo: Mikhail Gorbachev, A. Lukyanov; the leader of the meeting A. Gorbunov tries in vain to interrupt Shakhanov.

Mukhtar Shakhanov - tractor driver at Zhuldyz kolkhoz,
Sairam district, Chimkent region, 1960

From left to right: Ex-President of Kyrgyz Republic A. Akayev, President of the Republic of Kazakhstan N. Nazarbayev, President of Republic of Uzbekistan I. Karimov and M. Shakhanov. Bishkek, 1996

Work of art by Kyrgyz artist B. Abdyldaev, "Soulful Talk of friends'

THE GROANS OF LOST SWANS
OR
MEDUSA'S SECRET

For long days there resounded above the mountains the weeping of Kozhazhash, full of despair and feelings of doom: having cursed his own boundless cruelty, and pitiless injustice, which had led him to that fated cliff, and condemned him to unavoidable death. Then everyone, be they a man, or a beast, hearing this bitter cry, trembled with terror and fear. But what is the use of bitterest despair, if it comes to a man too late?

Since ancient ages, men has been used to songs. Each one, his whole life through, hums his own tune. Yet, sing it in the mountains - and wonderer's hear it long. A passionless echo returns to you so soon. The world is just, wherein does goodness keep. If one sows evil, sorrow one soon will reap.

Salvation's there, and deaths destructive lot. Then all the good which you in life may do, And all the evil things, which you forgot - Their time will pass, and life will compensate you.

AITMATOV.   Once the Almighty said to Man: "I will give everything on earth into your dominion. Here are the boundless plains, the highest mountains, the lucid lakes, the dreaming forests - all! Be the master and lord of all living things, the birds and the beasts. After Me, you will be second, you will be responsible for all. Whether life on earth becomes beautiful, or fades into dust and ashes depends on you. You will answer for all to Me!" So man received a great honour, and power over all things on this earth.

Thinking of that, how many things still live on earth, and how many have been destroyed by human hands - since one cannot remain calm and untouched by these sad thoughts.

Kirghizians have a wonderful legend about a great hunter, Kozhazhash, who met a tragic fate. Once I related this story to the famous Japanese philosopher Daisaka Ikedye. Later I rewrote this fine old tale, adding new ecstatic events:

"Many, many years ago on ancestral Kirghizian soil, with its wide, boundless steppelands, and its lofty mountains, there lived a young and eager hunter, named Kozhazhash. He was a sharp-sighted shooter, and easily shot his pellets into the eye of frightened wild goats. Indeed, he flew forward, like a bird, when he hunted down a wolf. He became bold and brave when conquering mountain peaks. His prey feeding not only those near and dear to him, but the whole village as well. Kozhazhash, whose only desire was to shoot the wild, free, creatures he saw, felt himself to be master of the earth. Hence, he lived a self-satisfied life.

Once, having prepared a present consisting of fine snow-leopard skins, with soft and silky fur, he went to court a beautiful maiden and set their wedding-date. It was quite clear that the wedding would be an expensive one, and require lavish entertainments. But, everything Kozhazhash had resulted from his hunting. Thus, he saw it would be necessary to go hunting even more, and kill creatures with good fur. He wanted nothing else now, than that the wedding day be settled with his beauty. Kozhazhash thought of nothing else, day or night; except good hunting - be it a bird or a beast of any kind which crossed his path, nothing escaped his sharp eye, or his accurately aimed musket-ball.

One day, he came across a nest of water-voles, where it seemed a wedding was also being celebrated - and they were waiting for the bride to be brought in from another nearby nest. Late at night, in the moonlight, they were playing at the wedding party, like human beings. With dances and songs they took the bride to her fiancee. Carried away with their merriment, however, the water voles forgot their customary careful habits. Openly then, the bride-groom, accompanied by his best men, went forth from their nest to meet the lovely bride. Meeting together, both sides continued their party.

Silently observing all these happenings, Kozhazhash recalled his own bride-to-be and their coming wedding. The water-voles skins represented a good treasure. It would be hard to find anything more expensive for his own waiting bride. If he could catch all these water-voles, would this not be a valuable contribution to their wedding?

So, Kozhazhash quietly took off his sheep-skin coat, and cast it over the whole family of unsuspecting water-voles, and wrapping them up in his coat very tight, began to suffocate them all, one after another ...

Afterwards, he went off and just as pitilessly shot down a great many mountain goats: driving them into corners and crevices in the cliffs where they perished from his musket-balls, accurately aimed. At last one grey old Nanny Goat who survived, drew near the hunter and cried: "Such a good, skillful, hunter who is able to shoot straight into a goat's eye, one would not find anywhere else in the world, most likely. Yet, there is a limit to everything, and you seem to have forgotten these truths. I beg you, show some pity on us, and don't touch us anymore. Out of all our herd only my mate and I have survived! Give us the chance to carry on our tribe, to bear more kids, and to renew our numbers!"

Kozhazhash's reply was short and unexpected. He simply shot the remaining grey goat in the eye, and killed him. Then, in a fury, the Grey Nanny screamed: "You have slain the progenitor of our tribe, our dear father Grey Goat, and have left us now no hope of any further successors. Be you cursed Kozhazhash!" From now your shots will not kill even one single living creature". If you doubt me in this, well just try - take aim and shoot at me!"

The obstinate and self-reliant hunter laughed scornfully at the Grey Nanny. From such laughter, stones began to tumble from the cliffs. But the words of the Grey Nanny, nonetheless, were weighty. The shots from his hand, which never shook before, one after another went astray.

"Well then, I shall pursue you, and cut you down with my hunter's knife!" cried Kozhazhash, in a temper, and ran towards the Grey Nanny. However, she quickly took to a higher stony path, jumping from rock to rock, from crag to crag. Curiously, Kozhazhash raced after her so hastily, that he failed notice he had been led to the summit of a peak where no human being had trod before. Remembering himself, he took a sudden look around, and found only naked cliffs and crags. Then, the Nanny-Goat standing beyond his reach, said scornfully: "Now it is time for you to pay for all the numberless beasts you have destroyed. How many tears have we poor creatures shed, how many loved ones we have lost, but now it is your turn to weep - for the first time and the last!"

For a long time the despairing cries of Kozhazhash re-echoed over the mountain abyss, as he cursed himself, and his own boundless cruelty, and his merciless persecution of his prey. Aspects of his soul which had brought him to this fateful cliff, with no way forward, and no way back: condemning him to an inescapable death. But what was the use of bitter repentance and regret, if they came when it was already far too late?

Waiting, and then seeking for her bride-groom, his beloved beauty went farther and farther when searching for him. She looked for the Grey Goat to ask for mercy on him, but never found this beast. She got very old. And once she saw water-voles celebrating a wedding. Seeing this, the hunter's bride said: "Oh, why did fate not grant me just a little happiness, such as these wild creatures have?"

SHAKHANOV. That legend about Kozhazhash portrays the highest stage of human suffering. A man may evaluate the situation from many points of view and understand it in various ways, but only when tragedy comes to him will he fully understand its bitterness.

AITMATOV. Once in Luxemburg, a German cinematographer came to me and asked my permission to make a short film about me.

"Where do you wish to make it?" I questioned him. "In your office please, where we shall converse awhile" he explained. "But that would be a repetition of the last film! There is one spot where I would rather go, which I find more attractive! Let us go there" I said hoping to persuade him.

We went off together to a highway, stretching from Brussels, through Luxemburg, Trier and Kovpets to Frankfurt. On this magisterial highway swished six rows of cars of every description - both night and day, in both directions - at enormous speed. Furthermore, on either sides of this highway (for a hundred kilometres), stretches a firm metal fence: enforcing velocity. In itself, this miracle of a concrete highway ran through nearby mountains, forests, fields, and even lakes. Wild creatures standing on one side, or the other, had no way of crossing that racing stream of traffic. The unity of Nature was divided. How did humans solve this problem? Well, every ten kilometres or so, above the wide highway, were constructed special bridges, for reindeers, bears, hares, beetles in pairs, snakes, and even scorpions! Just think, in our entire fatherland there are no such bridges for people to pass over, let alone wild creatures! It seems there is no problem too great for us humans to solve!

Arriving at one of these bridges, I said to the producer: Here is an example of human victory over egoism, and of a kindly, unique way with of working with Nature. With that, I climbed up on a bridge, and began my story for the film-makers. Later, more shots were added in Kirghizia, and in Talas. But this was not the main point. The issue at hand was the responsibility of every human being regarding ecological preservation.

As such, we called on people not to kill wolves, foxes, bears and little squirrels. Confessedly, our results were limited. Yet, the main aim of this project was to teach a sensitivity towards LIFE in all of its forms.

Those bridges, which I saw in Luxemburg, seem to say to live beasts: "Forgive us for intruding into your quiet lives, and breaking your peace, and spoiling your natural habitats. These bridges are meant for you to use, so do not hesitate, please. We want to see you feel contented again!" Positive sentiments, although mostly leading nowhere!

SHAKHANOV. In your novel "A day lasts longer than a century" Edigei's masculine camel bursts out of its bonds when spring comes, gallops off to the steppeland and, having quenched its thirst and hunger for freedom, returns to its own master albeit thin and exhausted. Edigei himself, knowing the habits of his camel, waiting for its return. Yet, if one thinks about it "Karanar" (his camel) had his own purposes, his own individual "I". After all, even in the grip of instinct, this beast was able to break down any barrier placed in his way.

Once I happened to see an absorbing film about the life of a wild deer. It was extremely interesting to discover how these usually timid and quiet creatures - generally seeking pastureland and water together, while defending each other from attackers - suddenly gathered on the open plain to begin measuring their strength. In the mating season, female deer collected too, trembling about, as males lowered their horns for battle. Sometimes these horns could not withstand the strain and broke into pieces, leaving their owner in a sorry state.

There was one handsome animal among the fighting males (of fine form and stature), who the previous year had defeated all his opponents to become master over twenty females. This time too, he swiftly distinguished himself among eight others. Indeed, it seemed as if sparks went flying from the clash of their antlers, In any case, the defeated males went to one side, as the previous year's victor stood sniffing at one obstinate buck who remained to challenge him. The struggle between them lasted longer than usual. Neither of the rivals thought for a moment of giving way, or admitting defeat. With pride, showing off his superiority, the young male gathered together his strength, and gave his opponent such a divesting blow with his antlers, that he drove him off the field. The females, all a-tremble having seen what occurred, then gathered in a submissive group round the hero, ready to serve his will ...

That's what it means to gain a place for yourself under the sun!

AITMATOV.   The instinct to continue their breed is very strong in wild animals. Yet, isn't conformity to natural law lodged here? Stern necessity drives them to select the best partners during a mating season, so that the health and strength of their successors are both preserved and improved. Not in vain do they say: "What Allah gave to the father, he gave to the son!" This proverb affirming how, in Nature, an uncompromising natural selection endures. Clearly, weak deer will give birth to inferior offspring, who simply cannot survive the stern conditions of mountainsides.

SHAKHANOV.   Judging by the results of recent scientific investigations, not only animals, but also vegetation, blossoming in spring and fading away in autumn, is equally governed by "selective" habits. With the aid of an ultra-sound instrument, biologists carried out the following experiment on the leaves of a plant:

Having lodged an especially sensitive apparatus on the stem of a plant, a scientist stretched out his hand as if to pluck off a leaf. Astonishingly, the screen at once displayed evidence of a reaction by the plant. Additionally, researchers noticed further signs on his screen, as if saying: "Be careful! Danger? Live or die? They will touch me! I am dying!"

As soon as the leaf was in fact plucked, all vibration ceased on the screen. A sign, evidently, of dislocated existence. How wonderful then, is Nature, which gives even seemingly inanimate things a sense of feeling, along with responses to danger. All making me mindful we destroy whole forests!

AITMATOV. Once I read some interesting observations about carnations growing in a garden. If a lovely young girl leaned over them to breathe their fragrance, they seemed to enjoy her attention. However, if some unpleasant men did likewise, they shuddered and shrank. Moreover, if some idle smoker, with a cigarette in his hand, or some drunkard breathing the smell of beer leaned over them, their petals at once closed together. Simply amazing! Yes, everything on this earth has its "I". As far as animals are concerned, they are not deprived of such feelings as real sympathy and antipathy. Their consciousness is formed on a predetermined level. Besides this, one may sometimes see signs of noble feelings and actions which they may learn from contact with people, or other beasts.

Take swans, for example, which are counted as noble creatures by men. While still young, they unite in pairs, and then continue all their lives to be close partners. Many people observing that if one of the pair dies unexpectedly, the other will then soar high in the sky, and afterwards plunge like a falling stone to the ground: not being able to bear separation from their loving mate. What is more, swans deprived of their partner will cease eating altogether and die of hunger, so strong is their bond.

I think the majority of living creatures on earth, and in the sea, or the air, know feelings of sympathy, antipathy, anger, and hatred.

Certain tribes of Taitsi, living in the Himalayas, tell young people getting married: "We wish you the love of whales, and the faithfulness of dogs!" No higher blessing than this, they say, exists among these mountain folk. Every dog-owner knows the faithful trust of his doggy friend, but of the love of whales I knew nothing, until recently. However, an article I read about an event which took place in California proved highly instructive.

A whaling-ship named "Attorante" was out on its business of catching whales. Having found a pair, they mortally wounded the female Cachelot, bound a cable round her tail, and took her in tow behind them. Her mate, seeing this, followed his spouse for a long time, doing all he could to release her. Eventually realizing, however, she had died due to her motionless behaviour. Ferociously angry, the male suddenly used all his massive weight and strength to lash surrounding waters into foam before launching a head-on attack on the small ship. Indeed, he succeeded in turning it over and sinking it. By this time, the crew could no longer pride themselves on catching a whale, but instead needed to think about rescuing themselves, and fortunately, they were able to do so.

The main mistake of mankind, I think, lies in his ignoring the feeling and sensitivity of other creatures, about which he seems to care very little.

SHAKHANOV. The great writer Tsiolkovsky, said man's interference with Nature brought sorrow upon his own head and made the world age more quickly. A very deep and penetrating thought making me recall a foreign newspaper article about an eerie event. One young fisherman, twenty six-year old Frank Charney, who was a keen lover of all kinds of fish, once caught a young catfish, took it home, and put it in his aquarium. He kept it there for some time, until it grew so large it had no room to move in the fish-tank. Neither could it swim freely, nor could it turn itself around. However, its master fed it well, and at times they even watched television together, so it seemed.

One day, Frank's young sweetheart quarreled with him and, desiring to get even, made a complaint on behalf of the catfish to a well-known defender of animal rights, Edvig Krenk. As a result, Frank Charney was forced to admit he was guilty of not providing his catfish with sufficient space to swim in. For this misdemeanor, he was sent to prison for five hours, and asked to pay a heavy fine.

Speaking to him about his offense, the animal rights activist told him indignantly:

"This is the first time I have met with such an open cruelty, confining a poor fish in a tank far too small for its needs. How would you like to be wrapped up tight in your fur-coat, and belted up so that you could not breathe, move a hand or a foot? Who can say that your fish has no feeling? No, you simply had no right to take a free creature from a flowing river, and confine it in a narrow tank! You deserve an even stricter sentence than the one you received!"

AITMATOV.   One of the native dwellers on the Altai told me a story along similar lines. As soon as raspberries, apples, pears, and blackcurrants ripened in the foothills, local people flocked there to pick fruit. And all would have been well, if they had gone quietly and carefully about their business. Yet, this was not so. They went like barbarians, tore down bushes, broke branches off trees, damaged plants, and stripped everything naked. On top of which they made fires at night, frightened wild birds, drank vodka, roared rude songs, and destroyed the general peace. Unsurprisingly, forest bears set upon them and they barely escaped with their lives: some even getting mauled. Moreover, the big beasts started to run wild, - entering villages to turn over carts and wagons as if in revenge. Afterwards, those people who had raised these storm went mute.

SHAKHANOV.   Abroad, people regard the broken branches of trees as analogous to their own fractured limbs. Such was the view here, once.

My friend, people say: "One doesn't value the gold one wears". Relatedly, you told me some people in other countries offer their guests wild goat meat as a delicacy. All reminding me of the Torgai region, in 1988, when one million wild goats were killed. Maybe this took place as the result of scientific experiments (made in the Semipalatinsk polygon), or as a consequence of secret weaponized bacteriological experiments - known under the title of "Resurrection" - which were being carried out in the Aral Sea area. Nobody, you recall, admitted responsibility for the waters lowering. No matter what alarms were raised, no matter how many letters were sent, everything was in vain. However, I was President of the International Committee "Aral-Asia-Kazakhstan", and also as a People's Deputy of the Supreme Council the of USSR, so I had the chance to personally meet President Gorbachov, along with the Minister of Defence for the USSR, Yazov, and the Minister of Healthcare, Chazov. As such, I handed them letters demanding an investigation of the Aral Sea tragedy. Astonishingly, I was informed these wild goats had caught a severe infection and died off, while their explanation about the diminishing of water-levels in the Aral Sea was an obvious falsehood. Shortly afterwards, the USSR fell to pieces and outstanding questions were never really answered.

AITMATOV. In these days, Kozhazhashes had grown more complicated, had they not?

SHAKHANOV. On TV, they interviewed a young man named Zhuma Zhumayev, who in childhood had been stolen by wolf-cubs (amongst whom he had grown up as a baby) and fed by a she-wolf for several years. He became a wild man, moving on all fours, before being discovered by some passing hunters.

At first, they had to chase him and catch him. Following which, they made a cage for him. He told how his "mother" had tried to save him from the hunters, and even attacked the iron cage to free him.

What a pity that while she was gnawing at the bars, the hunters shot her! "I saw nothing bad when living with the wolves!" he said. They act very justly and fairly. Such good relations I rarely see among people. By the way, in your novel "Plakha" wolves were given a special place.

AITMATOV. Before I begin to write about Akbar and Taschainar I studied the character, behaviour, and living conditions of wolves: reading a number of books about them. In general, the life of a wolf is strictly controlled and very disciplined, as I see it.

For instance, wolves never attack cattle found on their native territory, unless winter is so fierce that they have no other food, and are dying of hunger. Just the opposite. They do not let others from neighbouring areas (who may come hunting on their territory) remain unchallenged, but drive them off. In so doing they protect their own area. They have a system, where one wolf remains on guard at night, while all the others are sleeping. This system is reinforced when female wolves are giving birth to cubs. Thus, they protect their own borders, their mates, and the cattle on their native land - knowing that outsiders will attack them if they possibly can. Ironically, local wolves suffer at the hands of the cattle-owners, who, when their cattle are killed, hunt down nearby wolves, instead of the real culprits.

SHAKHANOV.   Till today I remember a story told to me in my childhood:

Not very far from the courtyard of a shepherd's dwelling-place, a she-wolf settled, and gave birth to cubs. The shepherd, knowing wolves' customs, took no special notice, nor precautions, since they were unnecessary. Indeed, they left the she-wolf and her cubs quietly alone. So, they existed side by side, for a long time. When local lads came and tried to carry off the cubs, they were prevented from doing so by the local shepherd, who protected them. After all, there is no creature on earth more spiteful and dangerous than a she wolf robbed of her cubs. The male wolves protect their families as well, of course. If they do get stolen, local cattle usually suffer their spite. But, something unexpected happened! Coming out of their lair, two cubs began playing and chasing each other in the sunshine, then playfully chased a little lamb - which they killed - by accident. The shepherd saw this, yet was uncertain what to do ... The next day, going to see if anything could be saved from the carcass, he saw with amazement a new baby lamb standing there, with a broken cord still tied round its neck.

It seemed as if the wolves were ashamed of their cubs' behaviour and had stolen another lamb, from outsiders, to gift the shepherd with a "repayment".

AITMATOV.   In real life, there are many interesting stories about wild creatures, which very few people know of. The reason is that we look on beasts as beasts alone, and do not credit them with humanities feelings: neither common sense, nor conscience.

SHAKHANOV.   When looking on Nature, some say: "All this around us is ours, and we shall do with it as we wish!" Strict statistical observations show that in the last ninety years, in the Alma-Ata region alone, the quantity of grown crops has diminished by fifty seven percent! Also, consider the fact that a seven or eight year old tree gives out enough oxygen in twenty four hours to keep two people alive. In which case, we often cut off the bough on which we are sitting, thus shortening our own life, as well as the duration of eco-systems around us!

We forget water, air, and soil, are our invaluable wealth. If we ruin the biological ties between them, then our life grows poorer - for water has not only single-celled organisms, practically invisible, but equally whales of mammoth size, while our earth grows all kinds of plants, from reeds and rushes, to huge forests, and all this we may consider as a pure gift of Nature.

AITMATOV.   Many years have passed, but I still remember two events which roused storms in the newspapers and periodicals of those times.

One country woman, a dweller in the Krasnoyarsk region, gathered a few mushrooms in a forest one summer, salted them, put them in jars, and left them throughout the winter. Early in spring she got a whiff of them from the cellar where she kept them. She climbed into the cellar, and oh! Horror! She saw before her some puffed-up monster, which entangled itself round her leg - making her shriek in terror. When she gave her leg a terrible tug, she was able to free herself from the "lasso" round her, yet when she looked at her fingers afterwards, she saw that the flesh was stripped off her bones.

Scientists investigated this previously unknown formless growth, and decided it was a mutant emerging from radio-active rays of some kind. Now, we have to face the problem of dealing with such mutants, which are growing rapidly in number, and can eat their way through anything, including steel and concrete!

Another monster of the twentieth century arose from the bowels of the Bermuda Triangle. Some kind of puzzling power, acting on the small harmless Medusa's, or jelly-fish - which usually grew to some forty centimetres in length - was changing them into dangerous monsters: sowing death and destruction around them. Having thought with care about this, I recalled the Bermuda Triangle was just that location where a Soviet submarine (with atomic weapons on board), had previously sunk after an accident. Indeed, dangerous substances had been released, and flooded that whole area with perilous radio-active particles. Under their influence, it seems, those harmless jelly-fish, not half a metre long, now grew into monsters measuring more than sixty metres from tip to tail ...

These monsters, scorning small fish, and even dolphins, have developed the habit of attacking boats and small vessels passing by, including sports yachts - overthrowing them by sheer weight, and feeding on their victims. In a short while, known casualties numbered about fifty, although in recent times they have increased to over two hundred. Such is the power of these radio-active mutants.

In this way, a harmless mushroom and a peaceful jelly-fish have become - through contact with radio-active rays, or some other atomic substances - a deadly threat. What will happen if such rays come in contact with huge creatures like elephants, crocodiles, whales, and lions and such? Can you imagine what monsters such creatures would then become, and what they might do?

I think every educated man must consider those words spoken by Tsiolkovsky in his day: "Man has violated Nature, and now must wait to see what it will do with him in return!"

In connection with this, we have the unexpected assertion made by some sages, that this world has seen life on it four times before. If we believe their hypotheses, then the world's first living things came to an end during a global earthquake on a massive scale. Secondly, things finished due to a world-shatteringly murderous war. Thirdly, because of high-powered weapons of destruction. Lastly, at the time of an overwhelming world-wide flood. The cause of each catastrophe being the lowering of humanities spiritual life, along with greed and godlessness.

We are representatives of the fifth civilization on Earth, and our duty is simply this - can we guard our globe against another catastrophe, or not? We are told that if people do not change their attitude towards each other, and to Nature around them, and develop more feeling and spirituality, men will be wiped out by the fiery blast of great volcanic eruptions. At which point, nobody will be able to do anything to save themselves and will need to trust in God to save him. Pundits tell us God has said: "I gave Man everything, except fulfilled desires which I kept for myself." Truly this is so. All our problems are connected with our desires and aspirations. If we do not attain higher consciousness, we shall never be able to secure a prosperous and peaceful life for everyone.

Some state the development of civilization is hostile towards Nature. However, this is a mistaken conclusion. Real guilt lies in the fact humans are not able to wisely and rationally make use of the blessings which such civilization brings. How many are willing to plant one tree in the spring time? Far too few! Demonstrating, of course, the lack of truly spiritual attitudes towards life in general, and towards Nature in particular.

SHAKHANOV.   If each man, for his child, or for his beloved one, would take and plant a young tree, this would make an excellent ethical statement. It is a pity we do not encourage such things, nor support them.

Once in spring, in Bishkek, a voluntary "working-Saturday" was organized. We, as ambassadors of various countries, took part; Metin Foker, from Turkey, Ram Svarap Mukidzha from India, Yao Pei-Shen from China, Alan Maloy from the USA, Mikhail Romanov from Russia, Nazar Abbas from Pakistan, Morteza Tavasolli from Iran, Aleksander Tumor from Belorussia, Boris Silayev the Mayor of Bishkek, and I myself, from Kazakhstan. Each of us planted a tree on a very small, but beautiful, square in the city. In the future this will become a fine memorial to those who worked, served, and lived here. On that working Saturday I planted a tree in memory of my daughter, Aichurek.

Obviously, one or two such plantings will not complete our duties, as sons of our countries, but from these actions will not a feeling of local gratitude grow up with the trees themselves, and encourage real friendship between us all?

It is no secret that the atmosphere of our Earth is now poisoned by various gases, dust, and radiation, which constitute a great danger for our planet. It is also widely known that in cities with a population of a million or more, the atmosphere is spoiled by a special kind of corruption. The World Healthcare Organization came to the conclusion that in such an atmosphere one should not raise children under the age of eight years, because it is dangerous. Among such cities we must count Almaty.

AITMATOV.   I recall how about ten years ago Tokyo (with a population of over thirteen million), came up against a serious pollution problem. Innumerable fully heated apartments, multitudes of factory chimneys spouting forth their smoke, as well as the undying exhaust gases from thousands and thousands of cars, trucks, and motor-buses, had taken its toll on this great centre of culture and technology. Indeed, it was on the verge of a catastrophe. Pollution was so bad that thousands of citizens had to wear gas-masks to protect themselves from the smog.

How do you think working people survived? At first, they announced a competition for the position of Mayor. It was decided anyone who could suggest speedy and efficient means to cleanse the city's atmosphere should become the Mayor straightway. As a result of this announcement, thousands of applications were made, and one worker who suggested a swift way of cleansing the atmosphere (and gave particulars for much needed united action), was made Mayor of Tokyo. He managed wonderfully well, in his initial six months, to rebuild Tokyo as the cleanest of modern cities. I think leaders of this type, given a free hand, and with the necessary knowledge, and technological background, would be of great use anywhere.

SHAKHANOV.   In recent days, our scientists are speaking of the urgent need to control the loss of ozone from Earth's atmosphere. This is brought about by pollution, especially by soot, and the exhaust fumes from factories, cars, and planes. Any changes in the atmosphere, brought about by human activities means - sooner or later - a breakdown in the biological ties between all living creatures on the earth, as well as living and non-living matter.

Most likely you will remember Aleksander Belaya's work, "Salesmen of Fresh Air", where he speaks about pollution in the oxygen layer of our atmosphere, and how one speculator made a fortune by selling fresh air? The monopolists, however, bought up his stock of fresh air, held it, and sold it at such a high price that poor people could no longer live in towns. Going, instead, to the woods in order to breathe oxygen.

Fantastic as these stories may sound, they may not be so far from the truth. Has not our Earth already become an enormous arena for competing technologies? Along with that, since the Middle Ages, the number of earthquakes everywhere has been steadily increasing, killing off thousands and becoming more severe over the centuries. Is this Nature's protest against man's exploitation: his pitiless and unquenchable greed, and his careless attitude?

The ceaseless sucking of oil and gas from earth's interior, and the excavation of millions of tons of coal, along with other valuable minerals from the earth's crust, is reducing her upper layers to an empty shell. Is this one of the main causes for earthquakes, though exploiters will never admit it? In Nature, there is nothing extraneous. It has an innate balancing factor, and if Man destroys this balance completely, he himself will also be destroyed.

Of course, this does not mean the complete cessation of digging for minerals, but it does mean a more careful attitude toward the way in which mining is carried out. If not, then extreme excogitations will end in a collapse. We must think, and act in time.

AITMATOV.   A few years ago I heard how in late autumn, a flock of swans - leaving kzakhsran and Kirghizia, to fly to a warmer climate - were in some way driven off their course, and finished up in the icy wastes of Yakutia. Specialists affirming that fledglings had lost their sense of orientation. Sometimes they flew as far as India, Africa, or Arabia, even though they all come safely back at the appointed time: aided by air-currents. Yet, how did those swans go astray?

Scientists proposed pollution and radiation in the atmosphere, from air-liners and such, as the problem. With their sensitivities lowered, delicate creatures like swans quickly lost contact with surrounding conditions and went astray. Hence, we must ask: "can two-legged creatures on this planet, also suffer adverse effects from pollution, radiation, and poor oxygen levels?"

SHAKHANOV.   In your novel "Tavro Kassandra", you frequently describe whales - who in defiance of all normal logic, or for some unqualified reason, suddenly gather together and swim ashore. Thus, condemning themselves to death. Yet, within this strange suicide pact, the largest creatures on our planet explain their own secrets. As a protest against human aggression towards nature, they remind us we hunt them, while polluting the ocean they swim within, and the air which they breathe as well.

I remember, Chingiz, you wrote how the breaking of even small ecological ties bears in its wake the destruction of the whole unified system of humanity, the Sun, and the Universe. It is not necessary to set off an atomic bomb in order to destroy our world, nor to await a flood that will wipe out all of man's mistakes.

We have already learned this from swans on their migratory flights, and from the suicide of whales. It is becoming ever more obvious that humanity is destroying himself too.

AITMATOV. In Nature nothing is superfluous. From the most reasonable creature on Earth - as we suppose man to be (though this is highly questionable) to the lowest worm, or the smallest insect, everything appears to have the same right to exist. Including man, of course, are a part of Nature. Since unity and interdependence are biological facts, however, it only needs one part of that system to break down for the entire process to fall apart. Break one link - the chain is useless, no matter how strong or long it was previously.

For instance, in one sea-side locality, people said sea-gulls were eating too many fish. So, it was decided to reduce the number of gulls. Yet, researchers quickly found the gulls had been feeding on the flesh of weak and sick fish, thus acting as a means of disinfecting local waters. They, in fact, has been carrying out a sanitary role in their flight, in their feeding, and in their selection of food. If left to themselves, therefore, the gulls would have protected the produce of local fishermen, not threatened it.

SHAKHANOV. In China, during the Cultural Revolution, it was decided to wipe out all flies, mosquitoes, mice, and sparrows. On this matter, I had an interesting talk with the Chinese Ambassador Yao Pei-Shen, who told me what happened:

"In January 1958, a governmental order announced to the Chinese people that destroying these four dangerous kinds of creature was essential for the betterment of people's material lives.

Every day, students was asked to quote the number of mice, flies, and mosquitoes which they had killed in the previous twenty four hours. Some of the more boastful pupils even bringing carcasses to display. Those who brought the most cadavers were counted as the best pupils of the day for having worthily carried out orders. Following this, came a check-up on sparrows. All meaning, students jumped out of bed early in the morning, took buckets, cans, and sticks in their hands, and even kettle-drums to beat, and gathered at school, before lesson time. The teacher then sent them off in small groups to nearby thickets, flat roofs of dwellings, local courtyards and so on. Curiously, other people joined in here and there - until the whole town was in a state of noisy agitation. Collective thinking naively assuming that if the birds kept on flying, they would soon tire, and fall at the people's feet. Little, however, did they know sparrows! Off they flew, once the kettle-drums started their drubbing, and school-children screamed and shouted at them, raising a terrifying uproar everywhere they could, to drive sparrows away.

Yet, they did not fall at anyone's feet! Instead, tired of the noise and agitation, they flew off to the nearby woods to find peace. Some pupils tried to follow them there, but soon gave up and returned, exhausted, to their school lessons.

Well, what about the people of big cities, like Peking and Shanghai? They were no more successful than the villagers – though, in their millions, they chased after sparrows in the streets, courtyards, and parks. Still, the newspapers made a big fuss and named their pursuers, young and old, as government heroes - giving details of various groups, and their actions. And, what was the result of all this? Very soon we were beset by hordes of tiny flies and mosquitoes, some of them dangerous, which earlier would have been food for the sparrows. Furthermore, in the absence of sparrows, the crops clearly suffered, and did not flourish as usual. Another lesson, of course, for those leaders who thought they could teach old Mother Nature her business, and to become obedient to man."

AITMATOV. Sometimes somebody's personal egoism begins to encourage governmental egoism too.

I'll tell you a curious story! A man from another planet who had flown down to Earth was asked: "How does our Earth look to you from above?" He paused for a while, thinking, and then replied:

"Well, it looks like a crystal palace, while those people living nearby act like careless horned bulls!" Very precisely put, I think!

The alphabet of ecological education we must be taught in kindergartens, and afterwards in schools. Children need to know from their earliest days, that a heartless and shallow-minded approach to Nature will birth all kinds of misfortune.

They say the Sun is bound, in the end, to cease giving its blessed warmth to this earth of ours. Not only Man is mortal. The Earth too will have its own end - and it may not be so far away as some think.

But we must help her, and this can only be done by someone with great love towards her: being able to save both her and us from a possible catastrophe.

In our present era of governmental egoism, about which we have all heard already, self-centeredness is widespread. Egoists openly show themselves by adhering to the principle "On my Earth I am still the master. What I wish to do, I shall do. I shall dry up lakes and seas, I shall change fields into deserts, I shall cut forests down and leave a wasteland behind, and nobody shall stop me!"

Such is the attitude of a few with wealth and power, and it has already damaged our surrounding ecology and the atmosphere.

One should never forget that if a huge lake dries up, then it will most inevitably effect the climate of some other area, and this in turn will have its consequences. Therefore, one of the greatest biological and ecological obligations standing before human society today is the creation of a global defence of Nature.

Otherwise our crystal palace may crumble away into ruins about our heads, and all humanity will then begin to act like Kozhazhash, and curse its own thoughtlessness, cruelty, injustice, and self-assertion.

THE SKULL HIDDEN IN A JUG
OR
A LOOK AT THE HISTORY OF THE TURKS

Every nation has its history, the story of the past whether good or bad. Therefore it would be unpardonable of the nations, to hide the bad, and to show only the good, and to put a cosmetic colouring on everything, or to glue together broken pieces to form a pretty and attractive picture. All the same, each new generation will compare its life with that of the previous ones, whether in its flourishing or falling before other countries.

Then, finding out reasons for these past events, they will set the goal of avoiding them, and making the right decisions.

What kind of secret can the black stone reveal to a poet's eye?
'Neath the great weight of sand-dunes strewn with signs of past
days - now before us.
Eyes can see, and ears can hear our forefathers, through shifting
sand,
Every sigh, and smile, and fear: every breath in their motherland.

SHAKHANOV. Not to know your history means to have no roots. No matter who existed on this earth, whether it was a great or a small people, since the time dry land appeared, and water formed into rivers, lakes and seas, each has its ancient history - going back into the depths of millennia. Whether it was set down on parchment, or whether it was trampled under the dead feet of Time, and disappeared, drying up like water in a desert - this history still has its secrets, its deep roots, its essential inner core.

The history of Western countries has been written down best, but we are not speaking of them. Rather, the chronicles of our neighbours, China and Japan - the land of the Rising Sun - which exist on parchment or paper (perused by readers of these ancient documents), can only cause a great regret to rise in the hearrs of those whose history is not so well preserved. They look at the history of other Eastern lands with interest, and with great envy.

AITMATOV.   Although we have begun speaking of our history, we must admit that neither of us is a professional historian. We have not delved into ancient archives, nor swallowed the dust off historical chronicles, and therefore all we know and understand of these questions will be easily absorbed by the average reader. Nonetheless, every man thinks about the historical fate of "the society in which he was bred and born", about the paths of its development, about the past and future days of his folk. He must know the history of his own country, the land of his forefathers. In relation to this, I think it would not be superfluous to look with the eyes of a writer on the history of his country: the more so because in comparison with the many-layered history of developed countries in the West, our historical books are not thicker than two fingers placed together.

There is no need to hide the fact that histories of the Turkic people's have been, in the main, preserved in the USSR. A story characterized by Batirs, Khans, Knights, and Sheiks, wise Judges and Beys. All heading anti-feudal and anti-imperialistic risings, before being considered unjust and blood-thirsty "Enemies of the people", by the Soviets. Indeed, up to the fifties numerous historians underwent persecutions, while many died in work-camps, or were exiled. We know very well what lay behind such action - depriving people of knowledge regarding their own history, and leading them to think it was unimportant to record who their father was, their grand-father, and so on.

SHAKHANOV.   In those days a joke by the Kazakh poet Tair Zharokov went round, which simply said: "You see, I am so cunning, that I don't dip into our history further than the beginning of the October Revolution!" Bitter sarcasm, of course, lies behind those words. After all, the poet had witnessed the injustice experienced by those historians of his fatherland who had looked into its ancient past.

My dear Chingiz, in other sections of the book we are writing, we shared with each other everything we had experienced in life, what we had seen with our own eyes, and opened up our deepest inner thoughts and secrets. Indeed, we gave our personal opinions on many questions. But such a complicated subject as national history demands from us a thorough-going penetration, along with a fundamental conscientiousness.

Here we cannot lightly, or easily, jot down things that have been said from a magnetophone tape onto paper. In this matter we have to consult various books, old manuscripts, archives from other lands, monumental inscriptions, genealogical tables and so on ... Furthermore we must study the things written down in our various diaries and note-books. We now have to work as analysts. These are the demands of this section of our book.

Certain scientists investigating history (each called to add his brick to the foundation), firmly establishing the ancient inheritance of our folk: going beyond boundaries, knowing no restraint, and interpreting every given fact to suit approved aims and purposes. Many of those "light-minded" historical articles and essays were published, and, sadly, their number is increasing. More than that, other works, based on contradictory conclusions, are now sprouting up like mushrooms after the rain. Also, sheer plagiarism is seen in many places. All provoking other historians to go even further in their praises of historic personalities, - who through their mistaken ideas - brought sorrow upon the heads of their peoples: causing events which led to conflicts and bloodshed. Perversely, presenting them as protectors and heroes. Take Yermak and his robbers, as an example. These men destroyed the Siberian Khanate in their blood-thirsty attacks on Western Siberia. Although some regard them as heroes to this day. Similarly, we ourselves glorify the bloody acts of Genghis-Khan, as if we are afraid to offend the Mongolians (who nowadays are our friends), even though by doing so we accomplish the very opposite, namely reveling the dirt and dust and dreadful barbarities.

Perhaps this warrior horde had its own way and understanding of things, and believed it was serving its people? Moreover, their commanders ordered beautiful palaces, mosques and mausoleums to be erected. But what about the lovely palaces, mosques, mausoleums, and temples which were destroyed, along with millions of men, women and children murdered? How can one justify such savagery? In other words, if we desire to look truthfully at the history of our people, we must surely strive to be objective, not just one-sided supporters of a lop-sided analysis, nor of pretentious researches that sow prejudice between peoples. Indeed, we must approach every fact with accuracy and directness, and with the necessary scientific preparation.

If we fail to do this, then we remain guilty in the sight of our forebears, as well as before future generations.

AITMATOV.   I agree. I see you and I are prepared to speak frankly about the history of Turkic peoples. Hoping possible readers will not be offended if they are of another race, or speak another language, but think as we do ... The fact is that Turkish-tongued nomadic peoples did not write their histories in due time, or in any fixed manner. All was "trampled neath horses' hooves", during those terrible wars of the Middle Ages, or records were burned in furious conflagrations - and wiped out in ashes. A few factual accounts were preserved in books, and on the memorial stones of other lands, who at various times neighboured Turkic countries.

Furthermore, what has been recorded is not always an unbroken or full account of those times. It does not precisely describe the life of Turkic peoples. Therefore, if we can give an accurate unbroken record of the development of the Kazakh and Kirghizian folk (checking in historical documents in chronological order, in various languages and sources across the centuries), it will be our small service to our readers. Also, I think we two, having decided to embark on this work, will not be subject to criticism from the peoples of other lands, our blood-brothers in fact, since we have our own quiet way of probing into our historical affairs, while not touching their historical heritage.

Neither of us wishing to separate or isolate, but just the opposite, to throw light on events which have faded in human memory, or have been wiped out by time.

"Just as a father is responsible for his son's actions, so is each nation responsible before its history" so wrote our great forbear father Abu Nasr al-Farabi.

I do not know how truthful is the assertion made by some scientists and archaeologists that Humankind spread across the earth from Africa, and I do not intend to argue about it. What we do know is that more than four billion people on our planet are divided into hundreds of nations, and smaller peoples. Equally, we know this evolutionary extension of human groups and types can be divided into three main periods - ancient history, the middle ages, and the history of latter centuries, In other words, our modern period. Behind this conditional division of humanities development, lies the complicated history of our human species, more than two million year old.

The life of our forebears in ancient times was closely tied to Nature itself. An environment slowly developing around them. Interestingly, it still remains a puzzle to determine which of the ice-ages (or ensuing period of floods as the ice melted, or maybe even in a later period), divided humanity into four major races. Each evolving, according to its place of dwelling, into four colours of flesh - white or black, or yellow, or red. The facts tell us mysteries surrounding human origination still need to be clarified.

Nonetheless, we may say the human races began to develop on this globe, actively and productively only over the last ten to twelve thousand years, when natural conditions on earth grew more pleasant.

Every people lived through its "childhood" - a period of formation and stabilization. The Germans and the English, the Spaniards and the French, the Japanese and the Koreans, the Persians and the Arabians, the Indians and the Chinese - each of them was concerned with peace and prosperity, as well as the deepening and widening of knowledge. Additionally, peoples living in Central Asia reached a high standard of development. Now it is hard to say which of these peoples first founded cities, raised tumuli, developed knowledge and art, invented methods of writing, and which, having tied up their horses' tails, set forth on military campaigns.

When today in Kazakh soil (among the most ancient burial places), they find weapons, or more intriguingly, objects from everyday life, and art, sadly one cannot say these are the remains of our forebears. To affirm that would be untrustworthy. On those great wastes in the eight and ninth centuries B. C. how many wandering tribes made their way, or settled there? Occasionally, we can say a few words about some of these objects. We can comment on the number of vagrant shepherds who settled there, set their fires and raised families. Giving one or two parallels - the forebears of modern Finns trace their origin to Kazakhstan lands! Moreover, a bronze helmet found in a Roman burial mound, decorated with the typical Kazakh steppeland wavy patterns, clearly didn't belong to any of the Huns attacking Rome. However, apart from these vagaries, who can be sure of anything?

SHAKHANOV. It seems quite possible that at the moment a new tribe was created, when man found himself in this world and began to consider himself a sensible being, he realized he was unique. In time, however, tribes needed to grow and divide. Eventually taking over new lands. Alternatively, natural catastrophes on a world-wide scale may have driven people's further and further away from each other. How else can one explain the amazing and shattering differences between African people, say, and Native Americans? Or why, as another instance, are Japanese and Indians so different, living near to each other, but as far removed in life as Heaven is from Earth?

This does not mean one people has a higher culture than another. Especially when it has been divided by natural circumstances, or chance.

Before America was "discovered", native Indians had their own national cultures, their own forms of art, and even their own ways of trading. Although during the last three hundred years they have lost many of their cultural treasures, expending their energies on preserving themselves and living separately from the colonialists.

AITMATOV. The reason for this was, and still remains, the cold colonial psychology of the American Government. Accompanied by the widespread opinion of many scientists that the "backward" countries of, say, Africa and Central Asia, or the aborigines left in Australia, lay so far behind Europe in economics, politics, and culture. Something they explained by saying that in their everyday lives and work, these indigenous folk were not as skilled as European people. It was additionally claimed "indigenous" forms of intelligence were certainly lower than well-developed Europeans. Outrageously, this point of view still lurks amid scientists' with prejudicial theories. However, the reason for this so-called "backwardness" is the strategic policy of colonial countries. A fact Europeans themselves do not want to admit. Their theory of insufficient mental ability, or "backwardness" is now a subconscious attitude. Spreading like a canker, it has become the cause of wars, division, and disempowerment amongst colonially subject peoples.

In truth, many European countries themselves lagged behind Central Asian standards of culture, and social life. Only forging ahead of us in the last four centuries.

Moreover, some areas, accounted backward (such as Korea, Taiwan, Singapore) today play a big part in the world economy.

SHAKHANOV.   Yes, there is still a great difference between desired freedom, and factual dependence. Though many peoples have attained their liberty, real freedom and full independence still lie ahead.

In themselves, slavery and subordination bring enfeeblement. When a man is not free, his soul suffers and becomes weary. The consequence of colonial policy, physical and spiritual enslavement, as well as political subjection, are felt in the national culture. In its customs and traditions. In the outlook of a people. Undoubtedly, they become indifferent, and take a cool attitude towards their native history and ethnography. Indeed, during the past century, Russian nobility turned away from their native tongue, and spoke French instead. A fine example of slavish psychology! So said, how may one explain the fact that not so long ago they praised Tsarist colonial policy as one bringing high culture and education to the peoples of Central Asia, rescuing them from wildness and a lack of culture?

In general, the history of humanity offers a number of such cases, wherein a people related by language, religion, and culture, nonetheless places pressure on another nationality by cynically naming them "foreigners".

The most unbearable consequence of racial theory was its distortion of historical truth. As one nation arose, it did all it could to push aside and humiliate other nations. Criticizing their foreign customs and so on. Such was the "modernist tendency" - a period of falsification in history, a period of artificial historical development.

Now we may consider the days of imperial oppression, by inquiring into the number of generations destroyed, spiritually robbed, and impoverished!

AITMATOV.   "History of Empires. Genealogy of the Western lands" describes the Saks tribes, which settled in Central Asia, with their boldness and bravery. Enumerating further characteristics: "They make dishes out of enemy skulls for drinking purposes, from which they imbibe wine, and they make straps out of enemy skins". (Such cruelty and barbarianism in past centuries can be traced to customs among ancient peoples, although unwelcomed by modern ones. Therefore, if we go on speaking of it now, as it was in reality, I think nobody will blame us).

When the Saks leaders died, the peoples who were under their domination nevertheless mourned them deeply: pricking and stabbing at themselves with sharp weapons. Furthermore, they buried the Khans in huge tumuli, with their wives and servants, horses and weapons, precious metals, gold and silver dishes, and prepared foods. This was their custom.

SHAKHANOV.   Is it any use to tell about the evils which one nation causes another in periods of warfare? The pain of the deceased, of the innocent captives, and of those beaten as slaves? Such things simply trouble our hearts, giving unrest. I recall a poem by the famous Kazakh poet Ziyabek Rustemov, which goes like this:

"The Arabs came to us, like a wave which spumes,
Their horses carrying dusty skulls in their tails, and on hooves raised fast.
They hacked away ancient inscriptions, engraved on tombs,
So that the folk forgot their historical past ...
Instead of early cuneiform, on the stones
They wove their serpentine letters above dead bones."

It seems to me it is necessary to read these instructive lines over again, and meditate awhile on their deeper meanings. After all, they were written to teach people to value their ancient traditions and customs.

AITMATOV.   The more so, since they speak of ancient cuneiform inscriptions. Any of which (among the hundreds deliberately destroyed), could have told us the story of a whole epoch. Yet, time had no pity on the writings of the Huns. A terrible loss when one recalls Chinese manuscripts assert ancient Turkic languages came from the Huns' culture. A claim given credence through symbols - all modern Turkic peoples share one totem: the wolf. An image that in earlier centuries was displayed on banners as a wolf's head. So, if we recall old legends of the Turkish Khan who said he was the son of a wolf, all becomes clear. As the story goes, following a bloodthirsty battle, a warlord and his elder sons were slain. Only his adolescent son remaining alive. Regardless, enemy warriors wanted to cut off his hands, his feet, and then throw his mutilated corpse into a marsh. But, a she-wolf found him and rescued him. Indeed, she fed him, licked his wounds, healed him, and later became his mate. From this union, ten sons were born. The youngest of them received the name Ashin - who later became the pro-genitor of dynastic Turkish Khans. Other sons were named Kipchak, Kirghiz, Tatar - all being the names of Turkic peoples.

I remember many legends and tales of early peoples, where a she-wolf helps a human being, or becomes one of the progenitors of his sons. For instance, take the legend of the she-wolf with eight nipples, who saved and suckled the founders of the ancient city of Rome - Romulus and Remus. Thusly, the ancient city of Rome got its name.

Their story starts with the destruction of Troy. Its surviving defenders hastily escaping on board a ship. Thanks to wise Eneus - who took them through many hazards along the way – these refugees eventually landed on the shores of Italy. Several decades later, the successor of Eneus, a man named Numitor (who proved open, kind-hearted, and generous) became the ruler of that region. However, his younger brother, the envious and spiteful Amulius, could not tolerate Numitor as a ruler. So, he rose against him, murdered him, and seized the throne. Then he tried to annihilate Numitor's offspring - among them Romulus and Remus. Yet, the man ordered to slay them couldn't kill two innocent babes. Hence, when he came across the den of a she-wolf, he left them there. The she-wolf adopted them, fed them with her milk, and brought them up. When they grew up into young men, they passed through many adventures before finally seizing power. These two brothers became the legendary founders of the city of Rome.

SHAKHANOV. Indeed, old legends, tales, myths, even proverbs found among different peoples are often similar in content - and this is another topic for discussion.

Since we have spoken of Romulus and Remus, the founders of the city of Rome, we should go on and say that in no other country are such stories so scrupulously and fully investigated. Certainly, the Romans, long before others, turned to science and knowledge, as well as recording their own history accurately, this fact does them great honour.

If we follow ancient history, we see that before the fifth century A.D. Romans had conquered nearly all of Western Europe. Holding many other nations beneath in fear. But is not imperial war, in which thousands of innocent people die, a sign of barbarism in itself? What sense is there in this?

AITMATOV. In general, whatever epoch one examines, one sees that those who seize power are socially elite: casting blame on their victims for being poor. Neither peasants or farmers, nor shepherds and herdsmen get rich on the spoil of those conquered. If historians call these victims of aggression "barbarians", then most likely it is in order to justify the violence of conquerors. How else can one justify such aggressors destroying and annihilating everything around them?

In connection with this, I recall notes by the great Roman poet Publius Ovidius Nazon:

"Around me the militant Sarmati live. In summer we are protected by the clear waters of the Danube, but when winter comes, and that river is covered by ice, the Sarmatians organize their attacks. On their swift- footed steeds they carry off the possessions of local inhabitants, and drive off their cattle, taking prisoners with them. Even in the streets of the city the poisoned Sarmatian arrows go flying!"

That record is invaluable, insofar as it consists of important and truthful historical information.

SHAKHANOV. Yes, to that poet (who at the age of twenty four was already world famous), fate itself became very cruel and bitter.

The inflammatory nature of Ovid, his stubbornness and directness, his uncompromising attitude, as we should say today, led to his disfavour with the Emperor, and he was sent into exile to the distant Black Sea shores, where he then settled down.

Just by chance, he came to that region where the Sarmatians dwelt - those hostile to the Roman legionaries. Ovid learned the local language well, the traditions and customs of these people of the steppeland, and even wrote several poems about them. For his books "Mournful Elegies" and "Letters from the Bridge" the Sarmatian leader gave him a gift, and crowned him with a laurel-leaf garland. However, no matter how long he lived with the Sarmatians, or how friendly his attitude towards them became, his heart yearned for his own land. As such, his letters to the Roman Emperor (in which he asks for forgiveness as well as permission to go back to his motherland), still survive. Unfortunately he was not destined to see his home again. The disgraced, aging poet died there, before the racing spumy waves of the Black Sea.

AITMATOV.   Let us continue with our main theme. We can find a few memorial stones from the epoch of the Saks - wall drawings in caves, and matriarchal statuettes. Indeed, even ancient Sumerian culture, its inscriptions and literature, are not alien to us.

So, turning our attention to an inscription from the Orkhon-Yenesei area, found in the land of Mongolia, in a locality known as Sudzhin-davan, we may read:

"I am Yaglakharkhan-ata, an old man who has come to a village on Uigur soil. I am a Kirghiz. I am a holder of a high postition with wide power. I am the one who fulfils the orders of Ogya, the happy Bahbah Tarkhan". We can also read the stone superscription, found near the river Talasi, "Thirty guards, if I tell the truth, were his friends, and were all very young. In the year of the Monkey, I reached the age of sixteen years, and my name is Kara Chur". In the exit to Airtash-Oi the following is engraved: "His name is Chur. He has thirty good warriors. On the road to peace and understanding they separated from us. They led the men. The warrior Chur went behind them, in their foot-tracks. Their wives all became widows." Such was the inscription, like a letter, or maybe more like a table.

These runic inscriptions, which we have cited, were engraved on stones. Yet, in many cases even these scribbles were obliterated by time. Only one tenth, or even one hundredth part of the information which we need, was preserved. Maybe we have to be satisfied with thus.

SHAKHANOV.   The memorial monuments of ancient Turkic writings devoted to the lives and activities of Kyultegin and Tonyukuk, equally tell us of lives and actions, when Turkic peoples went wandering over long distances.

Overall, this question arises: what was Tonyukuk for his people, and what did he do for them? For the people who saddled up their horses according to his orders, and loaded up their goods on camels, ready to take to the road?

AITMATOV. I hope you will excuse me, but hearing the name of Tonyukuk, I want to express a spontaneous thought which came to my mind. I think his name is really "Tunkukuk", and this may mean -"Tun" (night), and "kukuk" (cuckoo or an owl), which is where we get the expression "night-owl".

SHAKHANOV. Well, it is quite possible. That would be fine! However, the linguists say it means "knowing", so let's leave it as it is!

Tonyukuk was born in 646 A. D. or thereabouts, and died in 731 A. D., he was a leader of all the united Turks. Also, he was a teacher and commander of all the Khans (or Kagans as they call them) Elteres-kagan, Bilge-kagan, Kapagan-kagan, and the instructor of the war-chief Kyultegin. Such a defender of the people - who today would be named a patriot, and who engraved on stones many long inscriptions about his people's history, its sorrows and its joys - is rarely met. "I am Bilge Tonyukuk (Tonyukuk. I was educated in the land of the Tabgachi. The Turks at that time were found in subjection to the Tabgachi," so he wrote in his autobiography. "Tabgachi" was the name given in those days to the Chinese. According to several documents his predecessors lived on the banks of the Black Irtish river, and they came from the tribe of Karluks. Let us go back again to the inscription of historical facts engraved on the stones; "I - Bilge Tonyukuk, crossed over the Altai pass, and crossed the river Irtish ... This man who came is a hero. He does not know us. Our mother was Umai, and our sacred land and water preserved us. Why must we run from those who are great in numbers? If we are few, what have we to fear? Why should we obey? I gave the order to attack. We fell upon them. We drove them out. We took the survivors captive. We slew their war-chief-commander. The Turgeshi Khan was of Turkish blood, of our own people. Because he knew little of us, and was hostile, their Khans died". That inscription tells he didn't believed in the deceptive policy of the Chinese. Tellingly, it boasts of Turkic people slaying the Chinese leader, without mercy.

AITMATOV. For how many centuries did such an inscription of vital historical importance await to be discovered?

"Tengri our God, supported me! I did not allow armed forces to attack our great Turkish people. I did not let any armed rider draw near. The people then raised its head, and became proud and great.

As for me, I became a great leader. A great spirit. I dedicate this inscription to our Turkish people, to the people of Bilge-kagan, and order it to be chiselled on stone!" With that he gave his last word, and this inscription became a new page in Turkic peoples' history.

SHAKHANOV. We may really read heroic poems about Kyultegin. Even during his lifetime he became known as "the Blue Sabre", and "the protector of the Turks' land. His death was not only mourned by his friends, but also by his foes. Bilge-khan, describing the heroic achievements of Kyultegin writes: "My younger brother Kyultegin died. I mourned and wept for him. My eyes could no longer see, my clear mind went hazy. I wept aloud. Man's fate is decided by God Tengri, all children are born and die on their predestined day. Bitter tears fell from my eyes, my soul was encircled by sorrows, by bitter, heavy woes. Ten of my deputies from the Turkish Khanate, from the keeper of the inscriptions Makresh, and the war-commander of the Oguz, all attended the burial ceremonies. In order to plan and erect his burial mausoleum, and inscribe my words, the jewellery-master Chan Senun came from the land of the Tabgachi. Kyultegin died in the year of the Sheep, in the seventeenth year, in the ninth month, on the seventh day we buried him." Such was the inscription chiseled on his tombstone.

AITMATOV. Between the inscriptions about Kyultegin, and the runic inscriptions found near Talas, there lies much in common, even the story-telling in some parts runs on the same lines.

SHAKHANOV. My dear Chingiz, before starting this long talk with you, I had taken a careful look at the history of ancient and medieval times. My aim was both simple, and complicated: to establish at what time the Turkic speaking peoples - the Uzbeks and the Uigurs, the Kirghizians and the Kazakhs, the Turkmens and the Karakalpaks, the Tatars and the Bashkirs, the Nogais and the Chuvashi, the Khakasi and the Yakuts, the Azerbaijans and the Turks, the Karachayevs and the Bulgars, and all other peoples coming from the same root stock (and equal in origin to each other), began to split up, separate, move off in various directions, and formed their own countries.

Like branches of one big poplar tree, these peoples, the children of one forefather, entered into the historical arena by different roads and at different times and under different names. In the books of ancient authors, in ancient Greek historical documents - the Greeks themselves divide the Saks into the Massagets, the Yaksarts, the Dayevs, the Dakhs, the Farats, the Komars, the Askagets, the Issedons, the Assiyevs, the Arimaspi, the Sarmatians, the Kaspiyevs, and so on – we are shown a fairly accurate disposition of their wanderings, their pastures, and their dwelling-spots.

AITMATOV. I fully agree with your remarks about these manifold divisions into variously-named peoples, and that they are the successors of even more ancient tribes inhabiting these lands. As you say, their existence is testified by many historical documents. Thus the Huns, the Scythians, and the Saks are tribes who have entered world history. Speaking of their historical achievements, dating back through the centuries, by those Huns, Batirs and so on, it would seem we are boasting about ourselves and minimizing others. For example, in the fifth Century B.C., as we well know, the Saks-Massagets had an Empress, named Tomiris, a real feminine hero.

Certain facts are known of her, and of the times when she reigned. Indeed, she united the Saks tribal units in one country. Additionally, they had close contacts with their border-countries - Assyria and Midia. The famous Persian King, Kir 11, was a friend to the Saks, and even assisted them on some military campaigns. Later, however, King Kir grew rich and powerful: breaking off those relations. Unexpectedly, he gathered a huge army and tried to conquer the territory of modern Central Asia and Kazakhstan, where the Saks-Massagets were living, in a series of bloody battles. Yet, the Persians suffered a devastating defeat, and King Kir was slain. Concerning that conflict, the Greek historian Herodotus wrote:

"The woman Tomiris, Empress of the Massagets, after her victory over the Persians, hewed off Kir's head, and put in a bag, full or blood, uttering these words: "You thirsted for blood all your life, now drink it all!" Then she threw the bag into the river".

The Saks, through the centuries, believed in the spirit of their forebears, and also worshipped the planets, the Sun, and the Moon, and the stars. Those who eventually settled from their wanderings to engage in farming worshipped the Heavens and their protector- God Tengri - who they regarded as their defender in warfare. As a ritual, they took a sword and plunged its point into the earth, and poured drops of blood, or sometimes milk, on the haft. Interestingly, they buried the dead with great honour: especially their Empress, along with those who fell in battle; placing everything needed for the next world about their deceased bodies. Above the grave they heaped an enormous mound of earth, and boulders forming a cairn.

SHAKHANOV.   The archaeological expeditions which were led by K. Akishev, to such cairns in Issik, discovered a buried Emperor, one of the Saks - "a man of gold". That unearthing became famous in the world of archaeology. Indeed, a seventeen to eighteen year old Saks warrior, lying on his back, facing to the West broke new historical grounds. On his head there was a hat sixty five to seventy centimetres high. It was sewn and embroidered with gold thread, with patterns of animals, trees, and mountain peaks. The brow part of the hat was decorated with a pair of gold-horned horses, with golden wings, and four gold arrows stuck out of their spines. Round his neck there hung a gold chain, ornamented with three panthers' heads. This "golden man" was dressed in a long leather kaftan, reddish in colour, with almost three thousand golden button-ornaments. He wore a leather belt on which gold buckles were gleaming, on the right his sword lay, and on his left, his dagger, both with gold hafts. Alongside him in the grave there were more than thirty vessels, among them a decorated silver bowl, with a runic inscription in two lines on the bottom. None of the investigators could decipher the runic signs, but dated them at three - five hundred years before our era. They are known as 'the lssik inscription', and still remain a mystery.

Now, this "golden man" - as the most brilliant witness of the Saks epoch – has taken his place in many exhibitions, and delighted various archaeologists and ethnographists across the whole world. He explains what we failed of explain and he went where we could never go.

Every people has its memorials of past centuries, and they are simply invaluable. We are compelled to preserve them with the greatest care, as dumb witnesses of legendary days long past - beginning with the Seven Wonders of the World, and finishing with crude iron needles held in the hand of ancient craftswomen. It is impossible to live by the day or ignore our futures. Both today and yesterday need to be taken care of. Thus, we must place historical research on a higher level. Old archives too, containing the evidence of ancient times, are a priceless boon, an honoured blessing from ancient times: the inheritance of our folk. When we see how other governments carefully preserve historic relics from the past, worrying about even the smallest details, we can't help feeling ashamed of our attitude to our own history.

Such ancient times were those wherein the history of our peoples began. Indeed, tribes and peoples, nations and nationalities were unique and difficult to differentiate. In the mediaeval period, for instance, the epoch of the "great discoveries", an active extension of culture, art, and science, took place. Both the medieval ages and the Renaissance were a "golden age". It was in these ancient times when great cities were built, money appeared in circulation, alphabets of signs and letters were formed, music was heard (beginning with simple flutes), and art flourished. All beauties that will save the world from ruin and catastrophe, saved the world in premodern times.

In the Middle Ages, cultural innovators began changing what had been created before. Old traditions began to be overlooked, and boundaries began to break down. Those who for hundreds of years had lived a quiet, settled, life began to be restless. The oak club, and the short spear gave way to weapons and artillery, shooting bullets and cannon-balls, and that all led to blood-shed on a colossal scale, and to bitter experiences, lasting for centuries.

AITMATOV. Countries, which in years of relative peace and a quiet, bordered one another - for instance Russia, the Ukraine, and Belorussia - in times of warfare remained as one, helping each other. Exactly as

Turkic peoples did long before our era. Therefore, from the beginning of the present era were named historical names like the Usuns, there as the Dulats, the Khanate of Kangli, the Turkish Khanate, the lands of Deshts and Kipchaks, the Oguz state, and so on. All striving towards a unity of tribes, and not towards "these" and "those", or "theirs" and "ours".

SHAKHANOV.   That is quite true. In the Middle Ages there were more than forty such Turkish-tongued tribes, but only the Tatars and the Karakalpaks, the Yakuts and the Turkmeni, the Bashkirs and the Uigurs, the Chuvashi and the Khakasi and the Tuvintsi could establish their own individual states of an autonomous kind, while the others entered the ranks of the Uzbeks, the Kirghizians, and the Kazakh peoples.

After the attack made on them by the Persians, who destroyed the Oguz state, these numerous peoples split up in accord with the place where they settled, either by custom, or by blood relationship, into nine parts. If we name them individually we get the following: the Augan-Afghan set up their own Khanate. Twelve small groups of the Saks separated themselves. Nineteen small groups of the Konirats and twelve groups of the Taishiks, the Manguts, the Katagans, and the Kitais (as their group was called - meaning Chinese) formed their own Khanate. The Kipchaks and the Zhadigeris, along with the Kalshamis, then began to migrate to Sariarka. The Kazakhs and the Kirghiz, the Kurami and the Mangiti and the Karakalpaki - all remained isolated, and built their own hearths. Ten small groups of the Nogais made the town of Saraichik their capital, on the Volga river, and wandered along its shores, and also along the Ural (Zhaiyk). The Seldzhuki and the Uigurs also founded their Khanates. The Naimans went off to the Altai, and made their dynasty there, with their own state.

AITMATOV.   If we do not break the thread, we can go on to say that from the known Karakhans the Oguzkhans came. We are an off-shoot of one of the branches of the Oguz Turks. From the son of Khan Oguz, Taginkhan, the Kazakhs, the Kirghiz, the Turkmeni, the Kurami and the Mangiti emerged.

SHAKHANOV. If we still do not break the thread, but stretch it further, we find the names of the folk already given divide into Khanates: the Nogai Ulus, the Mangut ' Tatar Khanate, the Kazakh Khanate, and the UzbeMk aUnlugsu, t c Uonlussis, tithing at ninety-two knots.

As an example, the folk who settled in Middle Asia, and gathered round their Uzbek Khan, have centuries of oral history. They named themselves the Uzbeks, and reached a higher level of development by taking a difficult road. That territory on which, in the Middle Ages, the Shaibanidi placed their stakes, passed through many attacks, and they made many military campaigns themselves. Yet, that land knew the joy of victory, and the sorrow of defeat, and became the birthplace of many peoples.

The Uzbeks, who were known to the world as kindly, industrious, Dekhans, enriched their society with cultural sons, such as the great poet Alisher Navoi, and the scientist Ulugbek.

Neighbouring peoples, such as the Kazakhs and the Kirghiz, respect their deep historical roots and their culture. Curiously, the Uzbek folk kept old manuscripts and archives, showing the genealogy of their cultural giants, and decided to open a special Institute of ancient Inscriptions. Inside this great library the most ancient manuscripts of all the Turkic speaking peoples are preserved, as well as scientific works, and other valuable documents. In their great respect for the past, they show their pledge for to future generations.

During our conversation, we have quoted many names which have rarely been heard of before - the names of Shahs, Khans and Beys, as well as great military and social leaders - who protected their country and peoples since the time of the Huns. Furthermore, if their souls live on, up in Heaven as true believers say, they must be happy to see how people today value their great contribution to regional culture. They tried to contribute to the history of their nation, and to preserve records of their past, as they were able, and to give a just and true picture, and restore faithfulness to history.

Our historians often miss facts which stand before their eyes, and say the Kazakhs appeared in 1456, as if they descended from the Moon! They do not go back in history to see ancient periods of development, wherein various smaller groups united their forces to form greater nations: or separated due to objective reasons - until the two big unions were formed that we see around us today. Clearly, one of the most difficult things is to get historians to see with the eyes of the past, and not to look at them with the eyes of today. But, if we fail to do so, we shan't get very far I fear!

AITMATOV.   In an old French Encyclopedia I read: "The Hunnish horde consists of many nomadic peoples. Its greatest flourishing was under the leadership of Attila. Back then, they possessed a half of the inhabited world". Attila was their commander in the fifth century of our era, and his real name was Yedil, the knight Mundzukuli. This so-called "Hun horde" was formed on the northern shores of the Caspian Sea. It included many peoples living in Central Asia and Kazakhstan: nomadic tribes of cattle-breeders - Uisuni, Kangli, Dai, and Alani. The following account was written by A. N. Bernshtam: "The Hunnish tribal union of all Central Asia played a decisive part in the formation of unified tribes across Central Asia, such as the Kirghiz, the Kazakhs, and to a certain extent, the Turkmeni." As you see, he arrived at quite definite conclusions! But the French historian O. Tierri, in his works about that period writes: "The name of Attila the Hun stands on the same level in human history as the names of Aleksander of Macedonia, and Julius Caesar." Yedil the Knight, with his courage, and his military talent became famous throughout the whole of Europe, and, during his lifetime, many songs and verses were composed about him, and the horde he commanded."

SHAKHANOV.   Quite true! For example in Kazakhstan, apart from the research articles by Tursin Zhurtbayev, and the young scientist - Samat Uteniyazov, I regret to say I have met no other writings about Attila. The life story of Yedil the Knight, with all of his achievements, was described by the Roman diplomat Prisk Panisky, and the Gothic historian Jordan. Their information, priceless for science, has been researched by A. N. Bernshtam (as already mentioned), and by L. N. Gumilyev and M. Stasyulovich. Even in the works of Karl Marx and Friedrich Engels we are reminded of him in one of their articles, where Marx compares him with Napoleon. "According to Italian comparisons, Attila and his Huns would appear as gentle angels."

Prisk, in 448 A. D. travelled to meet the Hunnish horde, and found Attila himself. He thus describes his appearance: "Anyone who saw him would at once say that he was a real Asian. A big head, medium height, a strong body, slanting eyes, penetrating looks, and a most piercing glance. A ringing, silvery voice, pleasant to hear."

AITMATOV.   "The French researchers of ancient ages, who thoroughly studied in the history of the Hunnish horde (and gave to it their qualified evaluation), write that Attila drank a beverage called "Kamos". This, of course, is the original drink of the Turkish peoples - kumis.

SHAKHANOV. But it was not kumis that Attila drank, when on his horse named "Golden Mane", he headed his enormous horde for far-distant Rome. An enterprise with a greater reason than appears! Rome, in the fourth and fifth centuries of our era, was a vast Empire, which held all Europe in slavery, and kept compulsory order with its iron fist.

When Attila, first came to power, and led such an enormous horde, he tried to make a peaceful approach to Rome, and even established friendly relations. But the Romans did not look on this mass of Turkish-tongued warriors, hanging round their borders, with pleasure. Seeing in them a perpetual threat, and a great hindrance to their own plans. Hence, they treated the message sent by the Hunnish leader, and the envoy himself, with disrespect, and made no reply. Furthermore, the Romans at once made allies with those people who had fled from the anger of the Hunnish leader - and organized them against the encroaching horde. Prisk wrote of this fifteen centuries ago, in his manuscript: "We entered the tent of their leader, protected by a large number of guardsmen. Attila sat on a wooden chair. We stood at the entrance. Maksimin drew nearer and greeted Attila. He handed to Attila the present which the Roman Emperor had given him, and said: "The Emperor wishes you and your family good health and long life!" Attila bowed and replied: "I wish the Emperor the same!" Then he turned with a sharp cry to Vigil, a renegade, who stood by us. He said that Vigil was a conscienceless beast, who could shamelessly stand there in the ruler's tent. By agreement between the Hun and the Roman Emperor, the Romans had to return to Attila all runaway slaves, or they would have no right to send envoys to the Huns. "I would have cast your corpse for the wild beasts to eat, for such a treacherous behaviour, but I do not wish to break our diplomatic relations. Many of our slaves have made their way to Rome, I know!" Then he gave an order that his own secretary should read out a list of the runaways.

AITMATOV.   That was the first thing. The second was this: They tried to bribe the envoy, sent by Attila to the Romans in return, promising him mountains of gold, if on return to his master, he would kill him.

The Emperor Theodosius II, and the Archbishop Christaphi tried to organize this bribery and corruption.

Seeing that these two colossal Empires could not co-exist in the world, Attila bestraddled his horse, "Golden Mane" and set off. The folk living on the shores of the Danube, the Rhine, and the Nekkaro, under a Roman yoke, were liberated one after another, and sided with Attila. Things went so far, that the German tribe of Franks, in order to obey Attila, killed their own King - who obviously did not wish to surrender to the Huns. The remaining tribes of Thuringians and the Burgundians, went out by their own will to join Attila. Having never been together before in one union (always having been ready to fight each other), these people massed together under the banners of the Huns, and stood in unison against the Romans. That is a witness of the cleverness of Attila as a military leader, and also as a very observant politician.

SHAKHANOV.   In 451 A. D. Attila conquered the town of Maine, Afterwards, on the Catalaun plain near Paris a battle with the Romans began, which led to a terrible slaughter. On both sides there were great losses, amounting altogether to over one hundred and sixty five thousand men. Prisk saw that battle with his own eyes: "For a whole week there hung down a misty cloud, and one could scarcely see around. The rivers and streams were full of blood, the vales and gullies were flooded, and dripping with crimson. In the sky there were so many birds that flew to get prey, that it was terrible to raise one's eyes!" Thus he wrote about the consequences of this battle.

AITMATOV.   Two years after the Catalaun batttle, Attila decided to marry the sister of the Burgundian King Ildion. Preparations for this celebration speeding ahead. Having captured the whole inhabitable world, however, the great leader of the Huns died in mysterious circumstances on his wedding-day. Forty Turkic tribes, having fought beneath his banner, and passed with him through Asia and Europe, mourned for him in deep sorrow - but nobody was able to find out who was responsible for his death, and it remains a mystery until this very day.

Historical chronicles of the past tell of Attila's three wives, who bore him altogether seven sons - Ellak, Dengizek, Yernak, Emnazar, Ote, Yeskalma, and Uzuntur. Ellak became the master of huge territories on the banks of the Volga and Ural. Later, on these territories, the Turkhish Khanate arose, and finally the Khazar state.

SHAKHANOV.   The peoples of Europe until this day remember Attila as a great warrior and leader. There are endless legends and stories about him, as well as literary works, poems, plays, and historically based novels. "Where once the hoof of Golden Mane had trod, the grass grew no more" - these words are attributed to Attila himself. Additionally, this is legend continues - even though he lived fifteen centuries ago. However, Attila was a son of his times and of his people. Thus, in Kazakh folklore there is a poem about him with these characteristic lines;

> *"In very ancient times, in many lands,*
> *He conquered numerous peoples, tribes, and bands.*
> *The people of East and West he defeated too,*
> *And with his oaken sceptre he drove on through.*
> *He wanted that the numerous Turkish folk*
> *Should rule the world as master, not suffer the yoke.*
> *But pitiless Fate, and merciless Death came in sight,*
> *And, ere his time, bore off Yedil, the Knight,*
> *So thus Attila suffered man's common plight.*

Surely this is a subject for serious study by scientists, literary specialists and historians - as a witness to the ageless history of poetry, as a ghost out of the past. Following the defeat of Rome, Attila took off the saddle from his "Golden Mane" and said: "Now there is no more land for me to conquer, and nobody can stand up against my people. Now I give you full freedom, dear friend! Gallop off, wherever you will!" The legend goes that "Golden Mane" then flew up to Heaven, and is waiting there till another such master is born to the Turkish peoples. At which point, he will serve him faithfully, as he did Attila.

AITMATOV.   I would have interpreted this legend slightly different: "Golden Mane" would return with the Renaissance of our historical self-consciousness. Meanwhile, waiting for this mythical "Golden Mane" we have to take care of the fact that Attila should be given the right place in historical literature, and our people should know the truth of his world-wide achievements. Attila and Korkit-ata are both worthy representatives of our national inheritance.

SHAKHANOV.   Yes, truly so. The legend of Korkit-ata, his words, and his music, exist among all the Turkic peoples. One does not have to invent anything. The image of this man, his wise words and his touching melodies belong to all our peoples. I once heard how an Azerbaijani poet read out these lines from one of our folk-songs:

> *Just before Korkit on earth was born,*
> *The skies went dark with heavy clouds of rain.*
> *The earth was swept by a sand-storm at early morn,*
> *And while he was born, then terror on earth gave pain,*
> *But when he appeared the folk rejoiced again.*

- significant lines, and full of inner meaning.

"Korkit-ata first saw the day light on the banks of the Syr-Darya, in the Kzilordinsk region, on Kazakh soil" as I said to the poet who read his lines:

"You are right, my dear fellow-"Oguz-Name" is our literary memorial, just as Korkit-ata was our poet, and belonged to us all"- so replied my pen brother, in full agreement with me.

"Living in the Oguz-Kipchak epoch, Korkit-ata was a son of Karakozhi, and his mother was a daughter of a Kipchak." So writes Abilgazi Bakhadur in his note-book, and he continues: "On the day when he was due to be born, there was a heavy storm, with thunder and lightning, while everything was hidden in a heavy dark mist." Thus is evidenced by Academician Alkei Margulan: "When Korkit's mother was taken with birth-pangs, nature was suffering too. The mountain Karatau were hidden in a mist, and later the people named that day "kara aspan" which means "black sky". The surrounding folk were scared and, later, named the baby born on that storm Korkit, which means "a fright!"

B. M. Zhirmunsky writes in his researches: "Korkit-ata was a musician of genius, and there was none equal him. From other sources we learn that he was an adviser and a Grand Vizier to Inalkhan, Doilkhan, Tumankhan, and Konli Khozhi, and Kol-Yerki, and did much to encourage wise and just government. In his days he was well-known as a politician.

One more piece of evidence is found in folk songs, legends, and tales, in which Korkit-ata was the inventor of the musical instrument named "kobiz", like a three-stringed lute - made by his own hands. Many "kyui", folk-songs, have been attributed to him as well.

They include "Aristanbab", "Akku", Kilem-Zhaigan, Ayupbai, Zhelmaya, Yelim-ai, and Targiltana. They are all accompanied by the kobiz with its three strings, and have numerous variations in different localities.

AITMATOV.   Korkit tried to escape from death on his swift-footed camel Zhelmaya, but wherever he went he found only a tomb waiting. This became a folk catchword: "Everywhere Korkit's grave is waiting us!"

SHAKHANOV.   In relation to that I would like to speak of one very interesting hypothesis of the writer-historian Koishigara Salgarin, who gave us four historical books about those ancient times. In his novel-essay "Kombe" he suggests the Korkit-ata, and Tonyukuk, spoken of in Chinese chronicles, were one and the same person, and as an evidence of this he sets forth facts in a separate chapter of the work, showing these two had much in common. This is a very interesting and brave supposition, that nobody before has considered. For instance, the names of Khans whom they had served as advisers, the number of their children, certain "individual" acts, even the arguments and discussions they are known for seem to coincide. The only difference was that Korkit (supposedly) died on the shores of Syr-Darya, while Tonyukuk ended his days in Mongolia. Atop of which, the number of mausoleums where Korkit-ata is supposed to be buried is manifold, so where are his bones? In Derbent? In Turkey?? Or on the Syr-Darya? Or really in Mongolia? Nobody, meanwhile, has paid such questions serious attention, nor followed them up, in order to settle the matter factually.

The mausoleum of Korkit-ata (built in the nineteenth century), was beautifully decorated: being covered inside and out with ornaments and various inscriptions. Sadly, however, it was flooded and destroyed in the last century. Nevertheless, in 1980, in accordance with a project by an Alma-Ata architect Bek Ibrayev, a new monument was raised above Korkit-ata's grave in the form of a kobiz. This memorial was built on the initiative of the First Secretary of the local Party of Karmakshinsk, in the Kzilordinsk region, who found himself deeply moved by the researches of Yeleu Kosherbayev, now deceased.

If you remember, dear Chingiz, when we were entertained by your friend Abdizhamil Nurpeisov, we sat at his low table with a very good-looking swarthy young fellow. That was a son of the wise old Yeleu Kosherbayev, Kirimbek. Now he works in the Cabinet of Ministers of the Republic of Kazakhstan.

There is a special point about this new memorial, set up by Bek lbrayev - as soon as the wind begins to blow, over the steppeland the voice of the kobiz strings are heard as if in mourning.

So the spirit of Korkit-ata was reborn in his memorial.

Attila, our Yedil the Knight, died on the distant shores of Italy, whilst Korkit-ata is buried in his native soil. Relatedly, I now wish to speak about Sultan Beibars, one more of our great countrymen, albeit buried in Damascus - in the mausoleum known as Bab-el-Barid".

As the Soviet Encyclopaedia informs us, he came "from the Bersh tribe, living on the Mangishlak peninsular. His father's name was Dzhamak. His mother was called Aiek. In the time of the Mongolian onslaught, ten year old Beibars was taken captive and sold as a slave in the city of Damascus for eight hundred dirkhem i. e. eighty dinars, or eight piastres!"

I. Filshtinsky, in his work about Beibars writes: "The Mongolians seized the coast of the Black Sea, inhabited by the nomadic Turks-Kipchaks, whom they sold as slaves to the Italians. They, in turn sent them to the Egyptian Sultans. These young slaves were forcibly converted to the Mussulman faith, and given new names. They taught them the military art, and wrestling, and made them members of the Court guardsmen."

One of them, sold into Egypt (bound in chains) was Beibars. Back then, there was a split in religious ranks, between Sunni and Shia Muslims. A struggle finally won by the son-in-law of the Prophet Mahomet - Gali-Aristan. So said, he feared his own folk's anger enough to purchase servants and slaves from foreign countries. Teaching them to serve as fighting guardsmen and making them his personal protectors. Indeed, he named them Mamlyuks, which simply means "government guards". This was how Beibars found himself in the service of Mahomet's son-in-law.

AITMATOV. The secretary of Beibars, Mukhi-ad-din ibn Abu Azzakir, who lived from 1223-1292, wrote in his book, "The book of the life of Sultan Beibars" that he was "a wise government official, and thoughtful. When disruption went on among the people (while he was in charge in Egypt and in Svria) there was nonetheless law and order. Because he took a deep interest in agricultural matters, and especially in free trading, the situation of simple people improved noticeably. Also, his military activities were crowned with success. He put a stop to the Great Cross campaigns, and defeated the Cross-carriers. He also held off the attacks of the Mongols, not permitting them to defeat and rob Egypt, as they had done already in Baghdad, and drove them out." So Beibar's secretary wrote, when his master held power in Egypt! How did a ten year old slave boy, sold in captivity, become the governor of an Arabian country? There's a puzzle for you!

SHAKHANOV. Even having become the ruler of the country, Beibars did not know the Arabian tongue. In the Soviet Kazakh Encyclopaedia it is said: "Beibars, until the last days of his life, spoke his native tongue. With the Arabs of Egypt and other Arabian countries, or those coming to him as envoys, he always communicated through a translator."

From the first time he showed himself in battle (against the French King), and stepped out of surrounding dark-skinned warriors, he knew little but victory. Later, he became the commander-in-chief of the Guardsmen. Having established law and order, he then rooted out all spies: even gaining the upper hand against traitors. Equally, he survived the flames of Court intrigues to finally become the Commander-in-Chief of all military Forces. Throwing off the last traces of slavery, Beibars eventually married a girl by the name of Tazhbakit, from the Kipchaks - fathering twins: Said and Akhmet. Now raised to the position of a ruler, Beibars ordered them to prepare his own stamp. His first letter being sent to the Khan of the Golden Horde. A letter, apparently, permeated with longing for his own country. Such nostalgia never left the Sultan until the end of his days. So says the chronicle.

AITMATOV.   Beibars, having become the leader of the Arabs, later conquered Asia Minor, Armenia, and Berberia - destroying a few Frankish castles which were a danger to him. That was the time of a rising among Arab peoples, who previously had suffered considerable humiliation from their foes.

SHAKHANOV.   Truly, that first letter of Beibars reached Khan Berke in 1261 A.D ... The next year, this Sultan of the "Mamlyuks" sent his envoys, through Byzantium, to the Golden Horde. Having become a legend in his own life-time, Sultan Beibars was killed by his Vizier Kalauin, who tipped poison on a water-melon he was eating. That took place in the year 1277 A. D.

AITMATOV.   Clearly, in the last moments of life, when he was convinced of the uselessness of all human aspirations, he pronounced some words which later became a folk saying: "Why should one be a Sultan in a foreign land? Better to be a sultan at home!"

SHAKHANOV.   Dear Chingiz! Many people in their time repeated Beibar's fate, and escaping from foes, ran to foreign lands, to Africa, and Arabia, to Asia Minor and Europe. Those sons of Turkic peoples were called the Kipchaks, or Mamlyuks. Those Mamlyuks who guarded the great Egyptian Sultan in 1250 A.D. united, revolted, and placed Ubak from Central Asia on the Egyptian throne.

AITMATOV.   Those Mamlyuks continued to rule in Egypt for a long while, and their dynasty lasted right up to the beginning of the nineteenth century, when Napoleon Bonaparte came to Egypt. Loaded down with luxuries and riches, the Mamlyuk Beys could not raise sufficient opposition to him, and he conquered their country. Although he was formally obliged to nominate Murat-Bey as Sultan, in fact the real ruler was his henchman, General Kleber.

Having fought with each other, the Mamlyuk Sultan and the French General destroyed each other. Nonetheless, Napoleon was delighted to see the way these well-trained Mamlyuk soldiers fought, and afterwards made a group of them his own bodyguards. So, in his army, a squadron of Mamlyuk cavalry appeared.

SHAKHANOV.   The outstanding poet Olzhas Suleimenov, in his book "Az i Yaw - which caused such a resonance - refers to this interesting event: "I myself saw the last tormenting signs of their existence and their end under the Golden Eagles of the Corsican conqueror ...

... I return now to the apple-orchards of the area around Moscow, to the place where dusty Kuntsevo and Fili lie, on the high ridge of the Setun camp. One slow, sunny day, Setun camp was the spot where a fairy-tale took place. Workers, digging into the earth not far from the ridge-road (along which Napoleon rode to Moscow), brought to light three blackened graves. When they raised the time-rotted coffin-lids, each saw three corpses - like logs, dressed in bright uniforms.

The dry sand, in some magical way had preserved their bodies and in their dark mouths white teeth shone. Equally, their heels were together, with legs stretched out straight and their spurs curled so as not to stick into the coffin-lids. Surprisingly, on their legs high Wellington boots shone.

Overall, their blackened faces preserved a wide, peaceful smile - only their eye-lashes and brows had been nibbled by creeping insects. They had slanting eyes, and wide, rounded cheek-bones.

They were, judging by their uniforms, soldiers of a Mamlyuk squadron. Warriors who attacked Napoleon when he rode along the Poklon hills. Sadly, they seem to have ended their lives on the slopes of hills surrounding Moscow.

In that hour, when warm winds fluttered the flaps of their uniforms, like leaves, the diggers, some pilots, as well as some car and lorry drivers, all stopped to look at those mummies. Later, a scholar from the local museum directed my attention to one of the corpses – a man who appeared taller, bolder, and more majestic than the others. We could see the blue-stoned ring of his forebears on his bent dark finger (made by some frowning jewelry-master in the ancient Kipchak city of Otrar), who had engraved on it the stamp of its owner. Nowadays, only a heap of rubble, and a fine unbroken legend, remaining of that great city.

How many healthy, yellow fingers had that ring been on, as it travelled from this far distant country, over the Hungarian steppelands, by Genoa's stronghold, and the Pyramids of Egypt, across the wet stones of Venice, and finally over the dark soil of Setun Camp?

AITMATOV.   Olzhas, who already in the days of our totalitarian regime was occupied with historical research, wrote how he had witnessed the discovery of his buried forebears, and is, no doubt, worthy of continuing praise. Are not our contemporaries, such as Babur and Ulugbek also worthy of our attention?

The poet-historian and philosopher, Babur-Shah, was a founder of the Empire of Mogols in India, and a ruler of Osh and Andizhan. Like Tamerlaine, Babur carried out a number of victorious campaigns in Afghanistan. By the way, he was orphaned at the age of eleven, and more or less had to educate himself, which says much for his talents and abilities.

Yes, historians and writers, speaking of the Middle Ages, have had much to say about the heroism of Babur. The book which he wrote himself - "Babur-name", is now translated into many languages, and stands out as a history of his times.

SHAKHANOV.   Until today in the Osh region, on the Suleiman hills, Babur's house still stands. Anyone aspiring to knowledge and holy thoughts, to purity and goodness, is welcome at his house - where they read the Koran, and listen to stories about the life of Shah Babur.

The Prime-Minister of Pakistan, Benazir Bkhutto, known in the Islamic world as a politician and social activist, is a successor to Babur. Indeed, she came to Kirghizia on a diplomatic mission, and visited these places where her great-grand-father ruled, Bowing to the spirit of her forebear and fulfilling her duties as his great grand-daughter's.

As far as Amir Temur (Tamerlaine) is concerned, he is known all over the world as a great commander. His grand-son-Ulugbek, is additionally famous for his interest in science and culture. He ruled those lands (where Samarkand, Bukhara, and Maverannakhr are found), for thirty-seven years and never lost any of their territories: even increasing them without bloodshed. When in neighbouring countries people's blood was flowing, and tribes were fighting one another, Ulugbek opened up an observatory in Samarkand to trace the orbits of planets and stars.

AITMATOV.   Ulugbek gathered together scientists from across the whole world: from China to Byzantium, from Iran to the Osman Empire, so that they might share their knowledge of mathematics, geometry, and nature. He also supported art and literature, which flourished in his reign. Sadly, only one astronomical work of his, "Ziydzhin" has been preserved through the centuries. All meaning, it was a real pity when Ulugbek, standing at the foundation of the Turkic science, was prematurely killed at the age of fifty-five.

If we go back to our original conversation, we must say in earlier periods people opened up new horizons, while in the Middle Ages, they bitterly fought one another for the right to rule. Afterwards, returning to their native countries, to their own soil, to dwell within their own boundaries. What is most surprising is that the English, the French, the Spanish, the Arabs, the Mongolians and the Mussulmen tribes at the time of the Arabian Caliphate and the Osman Empire, finally felt obliged to return to their own old historical territories. To the birthplace of their forebears. With this move, territorial repartition is finished. It is as if life itself had taught them a lesson - that to conquer another people's country and live there permanently was impossible, no matter how much blood had been shed, nor how many murderous wars had been won.

However, in history there are also examples of another order, quite the opposite to this. For example, when Columbus discovered America, the native population consisted of about twelve million Indians, living in the North, while today they have almost completely disappeared. The Kazakhs and the Kirgizians equally suffered in these last centuries. Moreover, in the last few decades, our sufferings have increased due to various struggles with Russia and China. There is something here to seriously think about, insofar as behind these facts a great secret is concealed, or some great reason remains undiscovered. Thence, in speaking of Indians, we must be mindful that their misfortunes only began when they forgot about their unity as peoples, and split up into small tribes. Since then, they have not been able to solve their internal problems, remained divided, and fall victim to the merciless invaders. Indeed, the conservatism of their outlook and the ambitions of a few petty leaders, who did not wish to think in terms of their situation (but spoke only with arrows, and later with musket-balls), led to their collapse, and eventual defeat.

SHAKHANOV.   We have touched on some remarkable points in the history of the Turkic peoples and have thrown light upon the questions of their origin. Now I would like to say a few words about other questions concerning the direct history of the Kazakhs and the Kirghizians. Both peoples, after all, are blood-brothers. Take for example the chronicles of I. Bichurin, where we read Balasaguni fathered Belek, Belek, who fathered the Kultek Kagan, Kultek who fathered Khakas, Khakas, who fathered two sons, Alashkhan, and Talaskhan. Alash who ruled the Kazakhs. Talas ruled the Kirghizians.

AITMATOV.   The history of the Kazakh and Kirghizian peoples shows much in common between them, although only written down at a later date. Not always written on paper, of course, but inscribed on stones. The Orkhon-Yenisei inscriptions about Kyultegin and Tonyukuk were direct witness to the antiquity of these peoples. Unfortunately many of these stone inscriptions have disappeared. Some were taken away by foreigners, who excused themselves by saying they wished to study them intensively. Either way, these inscriptions on stones are in St. Petersburg, England, and Germany.

SHAKHANOV.   When I was in the Hermitage Museum in St Petersburg, I saw the stone image of a fat old woman (Balbal) brought from the Semipalatinsk region, and an inscribed stone from the Mangishlak steppeland.

AITMATOV. A prophecy of Amir Temur engraved on one large stone is also in the Hermitage Museum.

SHAKHANOV. The time has come for us to seek out these lost records, and to collect those documents scattered with the passing of years. History - is the passing of time, and a sequence of bygone events. The host of history - is the people. Therefore we must not judge past historical events by today's standards, but look at them in context.

The first thing I would like to say is a well-known to you, an axiomatic expression: the "Kirghiz and the Kazakhs became blood brothers." This is not invented by us. No matter how hard things were, no matter how difficult for the people, neither the Kazakhs nor the Kirghiz ever stepped back from that relationship. A union bequeathed by our forebears, which helped our peoples to survive, and overcome all obstacles. But in every people one will find those "know-alls" who are ready to raise doubts in the minds of others. Questioning them so: "when were the Kirghiz and the Kazakhs born of one mother, in what century, eh? Who saw the cut of their umbilical cold? Some lived on the Yenisei, others on the Syr-Darya, from the Altai to Atyrau droving their cattle to and fro! What does ancient history say? What evidence, or proof, have they got"? With such remarks they wish to draw a line between us.

AITMATOV. Yes, you also meet some who do not wish to see friendly relations between our two peoples. Our distant Kirghizian forebears already lived in Central Asia by the third century - the time of the Huns. Only later they did migrate to the Yenisei area.

SHAKHANOV. In your novel "The White Steamer" there is a story of a Kirghizian youth and maiden, who, escaping from enemy pursuit by riding on a deer, come to the shore of the Yenesei, and the Alatau mountains. Behind that legend there is a great historical truth. Yet, for what reason did the Kirghiz migrate to Siberia?

AITMATOV. Everyone who considers himself a son of his own people is obliged to know his history. So it is necessary to learn the true history of the Kirghizians, now having their own state, and preserving their own language. It is important to know and remember who ones father was, and ones grand-father and great grand- father too, and to know the history of the steppe land, and its mountains. Every time we hear the beat of horses' hooves, we shall be carried back through dust-clouds, to ancient times, and we shall be attracted by those yellow-paged parchments leading a reader through century after century. In accordance with the chronicles of the Chinese and the Arabs, the Persians and the Russians, the English and the Germans, among many other peoples, one meets the name "KirghizU- a folk who lost a great deal in the past, and maybe only by the will of God remained safe and sound. We were known in history as those who wore hats with white crowns!

SHAKHANOV.   The Greeks named you "kherkis" or "khergis", the Arabs and the Persians called you "kergiz". "khirgis", and "khirkhir". The Chinese named you "guan-gun", "gegun" and "kiguVall these names belonged to one nation.

AITMATOV.   With our neighbours, the Chinese, we at one time made friends, and at another regarded them as enemies, but in their writings we first meet the ethnonym "Kirghiz". In these writings we get to know "on the territory of the Eastern Ala-Too, and the crest Boro-khoro there lived people named "Kirghiz", already settled and forming a unity. In the year of 2001, Ogiz- Khan moved his horde to the West, and came into contact with the Kirghiz, whom he destroyed" so says the archive. Judging by this evidence the ethnonym "Kirghiz" was the first among Turkic peoples and had a defined meaning. For us this shows the Kirghiz ethnicities existed during the second millennium in Central Asia.

But if one comes to this conclusion, another opposing question raises itself. For a thousand years the Kirghiz lived on the Yenisei, nearby Minusinsk. However, from where did they come before? Were these, Minusinsk Kirghiz the descendants of those Kirghiz who dwelt in Central Asia? Or was it another nation? A problem remaining unsolved for hundreds of years, and putting researchers into deadlock.

The Persian scientist Gardizi thus writes about the Yenisei Kirghiz: "These Kirghiz cremate their dead as the Hindus do. According to their belief, fire is a bright and purifying element. Devils and evil cannot approach the flames. If one cremates a dead person, he is thus purified of all evils!" Yet, Chinese historians write that the Yenisei Kirghiz are fair-haired and blue-eyed. These are their inherited characteristics.

Evidently the Kirghiz formed as a nation in Central Asia, and were one of the branches of the Huns. Afterwards intermixing with people of European descent, known as Din-lin. These Din-lins were experts in the production of iron, and the Kirghiz too were masters of the art of forging and forming iron weapons: introducing decorative jewelry within metal.

"Those Kirghiz who had relations with the Slavic peoples until now have auburn hair and pale-blue eyes, and they are many among the modern Kirghizians" so wrote an Arabian traveller Al-ldrisi, in the Middle Ages. There are also similar lines in Tonyukuk's inscriptions. "First we beat the people of Chik and Az. We attacked the Kirghiz at night and smashed them. We opened our road with spears ..." In ancient times Chik and Az peoples lived there, whereas today the Tuvintsi dwell in this region. The war-commander Bilgekhan Kyultegin conquered these two peoples, and later, crossing over the Sayansk peak, came to the Minusinsk valley, where he attacked the Kirghiz.

Whatever is said about it, that historic facts stands. It seems to me that to explain why those Central Asian Kirghiz had to migrate to the Yenisei, and who fought with them, or drove them out, and later allowed them to return - they themselves must have chosen this route. Eventually returning to their homeland on the Alatau mountains. After all, migration was common in those days.

Didn't it occur in this period of great migrations that the Saks and the Huns (who lived in the Carpathian Mountains) 'were found in front of Rome's walls and in Byzantium? And on the shores of the Sea of Azov"? The Kipchaks, subject to Kotankhan battled with the Mongols - and when pushed out by them - were found in the region of modern Hungary. Ten centuries ago the Turks, until that time found in the Turansk area, migrated to the Sea of Mramor, and on its shores founded the Osman Empire. One branche of the Turks - the Gagauzi - live and prosper on the territory of modern Moldavia: far distant from the homeland of their forefathers. Furthermore, why should we forget that Ugro-Finnish tribes lived on the steppeland of Deshti Kipchaks? Manas's father, Jakib, ten centuries ago migrated from Ala-Tau to the Altai Mountains: only returning to the home of his forebears much later. Additionally, the topic of geographical-migration in "Manas" centres round precisely this - the return of the Kirghiz from Siberia to the bosom of their native Ala-Tau. Or take, for instance, in the Soviet era, the fact that great tribes of Turkmeni were re-settled on the river Amur, where they remained and survived.

Do we need to start arguing, that, because of the circumstances, one people was compelled to leave its native country - and when it came back after several centuries to its homeland, do we need to raise the question - if it is the same people, or another one? At some time in the future, of course, scholars will equally question why the Kirghiz appeared on the shores of the Yenisei, what the cause of that was, and in what century they returned to their native mountains of Ala-Tau? For now, it remains clear to us the Kirghiz in the sixth to seventh centuries lived in Central Asia, and went as far as the Turfansk oases. Later living in Tuva, and beyond the Sayansk mountains on the shores of the Yenisei, having migrated to the East. They were participants in those events taking place on the Great Silk Road, which connected China and the countries of South-East Asia with Western lands. Hence, "Kirghizians name their leader "Azho". He wears a crown on his head, and sits on a throne. Their city is well-defended." So wrote Al-ldrisi in his notes.

SHAKHANOV.   The Kazakhs say: "It's better to shout Azhi and stop Koshi"! The word "Azha" is taken from the Kirghizian tongue.

AITMATOV.   Concerning the Central Asian Kirghiz of the seventh century, there is interesting even though contradictory evidence. Judging, however, by the fact their leaders, both in Central Asia and on the Yenisei, were called by the same name (all be they separated by thousands of kilometres) such hints suggest these were one and the same people, undivided. Speaking openly, they spread out here and there, at their own behest, as any migratory cattle breeders would do, seeking new pastures.

In the ninth to tenth centuries, a large tribe of Khakas stopped at the river Abakan, in the Minusinsk hollow. Thus, the Yenisei Kirghizians moved from Baikal to the Irtish, and from the taiga they roamed to Turkestan. A few clans went on through the forest, and came out upon the Altai, while others settled on the lands of Dzhungaria.

Having united, the Kimaks and Kipchaks, mixed with the Turko-Mongolian tribes. The Kirghizian people, after the Mongolian onslaught, settling on the sacred slopes of Ala-Tau, which had been their home long centuries before. Clearly, having appeared as a people on Central Asian soil, having migrated to Siberia, and having left their Khakas relations in the forests, these Kirghiz wanderers returned to the Ala-tau Mountains. "The prickles tore their clothes, but their leather tunics remained whole. Beys disappeared, but the folk remained whole". Yet memories of their adventures remained. So this is a short history of the Kir hizian folk, as an independent, sovereign nation.

SHAKHANOV.   But where did the Kirghiz people get that name?

AITMATOV.   The son of Oguz was Taginkhan. He had five sons, and one of them was named Kirghiz. He is our ancient ancestor. There is also another version: this is the one I believe myself. "Kir" means "mountains, a crest" and "oguz", meaning "a bull" - one of the iliain divisions of our Turkish ethnos. Therefore the Kir hiz i. e. "Kir-Oguz" is simply "mountain bulls!"

SHAKHANOV.   Quite possible! A people, a nation, consists of three essential parts - the land, the language, and the culture. Three values eternal and unforgettable, passing from one generation to another. To the glory of God, the Kirghiz and the Kazakhs received their names, and their dwelling places, on the geographical map of our world. Nowadays we are relearning our languages and customs. If, therefore, a nation belonging to universal society does not lay a "golden bridge" between the past and the present, if they do not set up a relationship with the spiritual inheritance of the past, and an historical acceptance of the present, and the future, then they will stand in shame before our successors. You, when asked about the history of the Kirghizian people, gave really scientific replies, showing great personal understanding. This is a good sign.

A few years ago, in Scotland, at my work in Glasgow University, someone put a question to me:

"The Russians name themselves so, because they once used to live on the banks of the river Rus. What is the etymology of the word "Kazakh"? What does it mean? In which century were you so named?"

That question was not only put to me, but to all our historians: learned men and literary specialists. Until today, no precise answer has been given. The problem has yet to be solved.

AITMATOV. In many cases, among vagrant tribes, any historical event may serve as the basis of a legend or a myth, which then changes and transforms. Thusly, it is difficult to arrive at a real beginning. Can you say what legends or myths speak of the origin of the name "Kazakh"?

SHAKHANOV. There is a widely-spread legend about the knight Kalsha Kadir. In very ancient days, in one of his bloody battles defending the freedom of his people, he was seriously wounded, and left unconscious on the steppe: as one dead, alone, and without his horse. Indeed, there were no others near him, who might lift his head and give him some water. As he prepared to die, a white swan - "ak kaz"- suddenly flew down from Heaven and saved him from thirst and death. Afterwards carrying him to the shores of a lake. Once there, she plucked various kinds of herbs with her beak, brought them to the suffering knight, and placed them on his wounds to heal them. When the injured warrior awoke next morning at dawn, there stood beside him a white-skinned maiden "ak kaz". This was witchcraft, since she had first appeared as a white swan. His fate was, therefore, sealed.

Swiftly recovering, he united with the maiden who had saved him. In time, they became husband and wife. When their first son was born, they decided to give him the name of White Swan -"Kazak", in honour of his mother. Growing up and eventually marrying, he had three sons - Akaris, Bekaris, and Dzhanaris. They themselves fathering three related tribes: the oldest Akaris, the mid-aged one Bekaris, and the youngest Dzhanaris. So goes the folk-tale.

A legend is only a legend - but among the Kazakh tribes till this day there is a group called "Kaz". Not so long ago, Lake Balkash used to be called "Kaz Koli"- that is Swan Lake. Furthermore, in this locality there was a small town "Kaz kalasi", which means Swan Town.

Obviously, the Kazakhs, like many other folks, consider the swan to be a sacred bird, and bow before it in respect, and will not permit anyone whatsoever, to hunt it. Also, the "baksi"- famous folk-doctors and folk-magicians - decorated their headgear with white swan feathers, while our mothers have a habit of sewing white swan plumes on children's dresses, not merely as a decoration, but for their protection.

AITMATOV.   Not long ago I read a work by the great Abai, wherein I found valuable assessments on the origins of the Kazakhs and the Kirghizians. This genius-poet gives a most memorable interpretation of the issue, which goes as follows:

In the period of their victorious wars, Arabian forces got as far as Central Asia: eventually appearing on Kazakh soil. As a point of information, the Arabs call migrants "khibai" and "khuzagu". Having seem migratory Kazakhs, the Arabs decided they were also "khuzagu"-wanderers, roaming from place to place on the unlimited steppeland, just like wandering flocks of birds, geese and swans, "ak kaz". Hence, they named indigenous peoples Kaz-ak.

SHAKHANOV.   One can't help wondering how Abai, who scarcely ever left the borders of his native land, and for a long period lived in the Chingiz Mountains, could have had such a deep knowledge of science. Individually, he makes an analysis of where the Kazakhs and the Kirghiz came from, and illuminates Chinese history too: giving information about the migratory travels of various tribes and where they lived before. I can give you an example here: "In Eastern Siberia there are a few Kazakh tribes who have not adopted the Muslim religion, even though they are related to us by their language, by customs, and physical form. Also, in the Yenisei province, amid the Minusinsk region, there lives a people called "Yasashinaisk Tatars". They take the Kazakhs to be their blood brothers, and those who see them side by side, would not disagree.

Here it becomes clear, Abai (speaking of a people living on the Yenesei, but believing in another religion) says they are our blood-brothers. As such, he has an almost postmodern approach to facticity. Furthermore, he develops his thoughts by claiming, "Neither a Kazakh nor a Kirghiz has ever argued against these facts. As such, when examining Chinese names for these Kirghiz as "Buruts", he additionally asks why do they call them the Buruts? Then, Abai proceeds by taking up the question of how the Kazakhs and the Kirghiz came to the mountains and foothills of Ala-Tau.

From all this one sees the great poet was acquainted with the history of Chinese peoples, as well as knowing the Kirghizian epic poem "Manas" - having heard it from reciters. Thereby joining a number of dots to arrive at useful conclusions. Indeed, the fact is that in "Manas" it is said the Chinese and the Dzhungars called the Kirghiz Buruts (hoping to humiliate them as ignoramuses), is highly instructive.

Abai equally writes the Kirghiz and the Kazakhs, since time immemorial, went together, never divided, and were, in essence, one people. He wishes to emphasize this fact, and thus writes about it. Adding that in the Minusink hollow there live people related to us: reminding his contemporaries too.

Even closer to the truth goes one legend. According to it, "Kazakh", "Alash", and "Three tribes" means they are close to each other. An attempt, of course, to explain their origin in the distant past.

In ancient times, on the shores of the Darya, there lived a numerous people ruled over by a Khan named "Kizil Aristan", which means "Red Lion". That Khan sometimes warred with his neighbours, and sometimes lived peacefully. Once, however, he attacked two foes, and seized great booty from them. Including captives, among them being a beautiful maiden, whom be made his wife. After the passing of predestined days and months, a child was born. An infant strangely covered with multi-coloured spots. The Khan and his people were scared, and he decided to get rid of it. Yet, his oldest wife (his "baibishe"), ordered the guards to throw the baby into the river Darya. This baby, who from birth, had scared a whole people, did not drown in the waves but was carried by them to a bankside. Where lived an old beggarly, childless, fisherman. For his part, the old man - who was delighted with the child God had sent him - took the infant home. There, both he and his wife brought the baby boy up, and seeing he was covered in various-coloured spots, "ala", called him affectionately "Alash". This is how his name emerged. In time, the lad showed himself very clever, bold and strong: a fighter, who with his achievements attracted people's attention.

His actual father - Kizil Aristan - recognizing in him his own son, became filled with regret for what he had done, and wanted to become closer with him. Yet, on the advice of Maiki, the Bey, his boy was sent (along with three hundred companions), to the distant steppe. When there, they campaigned until this warband had gone further than anyone else onto the steppe - thereby extending territory and building a new Kingdom. In which case, the people proclaimed him a Khan. It was said, those whom he had left behind began to envy him, and named him and his people "Kazakhs" that is "independent". Predictably, the three hundred warriors who had accompanied him, formed three "zhuzes", "Zhuz" – which means a hundred, and a country, where the Kazakhs live. Our wise old men, until today still say: "Our grandfather was Alash, and we are called the Kazakhs". Moreover, the name Alash is often met in the works of well-known historians, such as Kadirgali Zhalairi, Rashid-ad-Din, and Abilgaz-bakhadur.

If we rely on the works of the last two, we learn from them the summer home of Khan Alash was meadowland between the Ulitau and Kishitau mountains, while his winter settlements were found in Karakum and Borsikkum. Curiously, ruins have been found in the Ulitau Mountains of a palace named "Khan Alash Horde", whereas the nearby river Karakengir is where Khan Alash's mausoleum can be seen.

AITMATOV. That is a very interesting information. The Nogais who live in the Caucasus, give the name "Kazakh" to those who carry themselves independently, freely, boldly. You don't have to go far to remember those who bear this name -the Russian muzhiks (who escaped from their lords, from slavery, or exile to Siberia, and went to the Don, or to the Urals), were named "Kazakhs" meaning free. Judging by many proverbs and sayings of neighbouring peoples, the word "Kazak" or "Kazakh" has not only external morphologies, but internal morphologies of meaning as well.

What is more, Ch. Valikhanov places the word "Kazak" among military terms - used in the sense of "bold" or "brave". All agreeing with the well-known scholar V. V. Radlov, who understood this word as meaning "independent" or "bold" ..... an interpretation upheld by the Turkic language specialist A. N. Samoilovich.

SHAKHANOV. In historical chronicles Zhungo (the name of China) in the second century, is said to be the region (Aral and Caspian Seas, the deserts), where wanders a people called "Khasa", or "Kasa", whilst the Central Asian historian Ruzbikhan informs us the "Kazakhi - with their carefree heroism, strength and bravery - became familiar to peoples almost everywhere. Their fearless character is often described in works in the Arabic tongue.

In this way, the fact these people are named "Kazakhs" has in itself every justification.

For all this, one more piece of evidence emerges: in the south of Kazakhstan there is a mountain pass which is named "The summit from which Yeskender turned back". This is a lofty mountain crossing- as I recall. Yeskender Zulkarnai - is Aleksander of Macedonia who, in the fourth century, smashed the army of the Persian King Darius Ill to pieces in Asia, before going to Central Asia. Once there, the great Greek Commander subjugated Samarkand, although, when preparing to ford the Sirdarya, he was met with such fierce opposition from the vagrant tribes on Ala-Tau, he had to turn back. Since then our people sing:

> *"Before all those who follow you,*
> *Hurl down all barriers in the way,*
> *And grind all boulders to powder too,*
> *Draw near to folk, sing your old lay:*
> *'That peak from which Yeskender turned aside,*
> *Let it be blown by blasts whirling wide."*

People's memories well fixed the circumstances forcing Aleksander of Macedonia to retreat. Some say the song was composed later. But the words: "mountain peak from which Aleksander turned back" after twenty-four centuries remain as they were in those ancient times.

The historian A. N. Bernshtam, researching the economics and trading practices of those days (in Midia, Assyria, and Persia in the fourth and seventh centuries, came to the conclusion that having associated with the countries of Asia Minor, the ancient Saks tribes appeared as the forefathers of modern Kazakhs. This opinion is shared by ethnographers, archaeologists, and anthropologists of those ancient times.

After the Saks, the Turks set up shop (sixth and seventh centuries A. D.), while after them the Karluki (ninth and tenth centuries A. D.) did likewise. Following them, the Kimaki (ninth and tenth centuries A. D.) then the Kipchaks: a Khanate which lasted till the twelfth century - when the Kazakhs were a part of the White Horde - taking part in all battles and attacks under the command of the Mongols. The state of the White Horde was situated precisely on the present territory of Kazakhstan. "Six sections of Alash were settled on territory from the Altai to the Caspian Sea, from the Tobol to the Syr-Darya in the Seven Rivers area. In the second half of the twelfth century, they separated from the Golden Horde, and founded their own state - the White Horde - "Ak Orda".

When the the White Horde had fallen, the Khans Zhanibek and Kerei founded their own Khanates, independently from the successors - the Shaibani Khanate. Before that, separation from the Horde, among some groups and tribes which made up the Kazakh people, according to the information given by Mukhammed Khaidar Dulati, the author of the books "Shaibani-name" and "Tarikhi-i-Rashidi", were as follows; in the fourteenth and fifteenth centuries, the Naimans moved from Ulitau to Ishim; the Konrati and the Kipchaki lived in between Turkestan and Karatau; the Argini - on the shores of the Irtish, and in Central Kazakhstan, on the Syr-Darya; the Kerei on the Tarbagatai, the Irtish - by lake Zaisan and the river Tobol; the Dulati on the rivers Ili, Chu, and Talas; the Kangli and Uisun in Zhetisu; the Alshin on the Yedil, Zhaik, and the shores of the Caspian Sea. You will most probably say, Chingiz, in place of the Saks tribes and those with whom they joined, the Kazakh tribes and groups came, because they lived on that same territory where earlier the Saks were to be found. From all this comes the conclusion, that with time the names of those tribes and clans and groups changed, but the peoples themselves remained what they had been during the course of many centuries. They lived on their native land, where they were born, all being the very same people. Or as the famous Kazakh poet Zhuban Moldagaliyev said: "A thousand times they died, and a thousand times were reborn!" Yes, we on many occasions belittled and destroyed ourselves ... "The foes of the Kazakhs are the Kazakhs!" said one thinker. The Kirghiz folk too. In totalitarian days, when looking into the eyes of the Central Committee, we ourselves often repeated the peoples of Kazakhstan and Kirghizia (before 1913), had barely two or three per cent literates. We also said that under Soviet rule, our peoples became fully educated, one-hundred per cent - being able to read and write. We went on the stage to the microphone, and ourselves narrated such things, solemnly and seriously. We looked upon our folks as being ignorant, without history, and of little importance. We ourselves place this slavish psychology on our heads. Sadly, ordinary people at meetings just clapped, and applauded our speeches unanimously, and found nothing strange in that!

AITMATOV. Yes, having studied in Cairo and Damascus, in Morocco, and in Kazan, Tashkent or Bukhara, and knowing the Koran, the sacred book of the Prophet, entirely by heart, even well-prepared and quite disciplined people shared these perceptions. Curiously, having taught children, not only in towns, but in villages too, and not only about Islam, but also about the world as a whole, the East and West, the mullahs were not included within the two to three percent of these educated people. One must bear in mind that most educated folk were taught in Russian, whereas, other people were taught in Arabic.

In ancient times we had an alphabet, and a written language, but unfortunately we cannot prove anything except this fact.

An inscription on a silver cup from an Issik burial mound relates to the fifth century. In Mongolia an inscription was found on an amulet – mentioning the word Sengir, which shows is a reminder that the Hun epoch belongs to the Turkic peoples, since the word "Sengir" in Turkish means "mountain range, or chain".

Amid the Chinese chronicle of 192 B. C. "Memorial book of History" it is stated; "When the blessed epoch of Mete Tengri came, the Huns grew stronger, and started out on the road of written and engraved inscriptions, and as a result of this left a great inheritance to others"

SHAKHANOV. That is one more witness to the fact Turkish writing arose earlier than many other kinds of written characters from Western Europe. It is equally an indication that this writing, spreading far and wide, from the Siberian forests to the steppe of Desht-i Kipchak, and from there to Central Asia - served the requirements of the Saks and Huns. It was due to the use of runic inscriptions (as a means of communication between the officials in an enormous government, or between several such governments, under which the Turkic peoples lived), that these characters survived from generation to generation. Indeed, it was precisely those runic inscriptions on Orkhon and Yenisei stone memorials which gave the possibility of filling in blank spots in the history of Kazakhstan and Kirghizia.

AITMATOV. One-hundred-and-twenty memorials of the art of writing have been found between the Yenisei and the Tuva, also related to the Kirghizian folk and its tongue. For every ancient rune engraved on stone memorials, whole epochs may be rediscovered.

SHAKHANOV. Once, Gabit Musrepov, inspired me to ask: "Why did the Turkish Khanate, existing from the fourth to the sixth centuries, fall to pieces?" **I** replied:

"Their enemy proved to be stronger. Their land was large, people were few, and still worse, there was no real unity among them."

But Gabit was not satisfied with my reply. Shaking his head he said: "In general you are right, yet you have not mentioned the main reason" and then he explained his own question like this: "They fell because although they might stand up to their foe as warriors, they could not stand up against themselves."

Yes, in this world there is nothing more oppressive than spiritual slavery. Aren't there peoples on this planet, who having mastered the language and culture of those more powerful than they are nonetheless lost their own native culture, and history?

To finally and completely conquer the earth, and spiritually to enslave other peoples, the colonizers use three main means, three ways to attain their aims; they seize their land, change indigenous religion, and force "natives" to forget their past history - and even their mother tongue. They do so, in order to make people forget their culture.

One has only to remember how many hindrances there are on the road to rebuilding the national character. We suffered, because of the efforts made to compel us to use the letters of the Latin alphabet.

How could it happen, that our alphabet of runic signs, became utterly lost?

AITMATOV. I don't quite agree with you here! The Latin language could have brought unification to Turkic writings. In general, not only the Kirghizian and Kazakh writings and culture, but also that of all the Turkic peoples for the past twelve to thirteen centuries.

We may count them up so: in the period from 634 to 710 A.D. masses of warriors from the Arabian Caliphate captured Syria and Iran, Jerusalem and Afghanistan, Central Asia and Byzantium, Armenia,

Egypt, and parts of Western Europe – as well as those territories where they began to introduce the Muslim religion, along with Arabian writing. In 715 A.D. the Turkestan region also came under the Arabian domination. The historian Narkhashi, in his book "The history of Bukhara", writes of the severe nature of the Arabian War-Commander Kutaiba: "He killed all who were unfit for military service. The rest he took as prisoners. Kutaiba built many mosques, burned the books of unbelievers, and those who worshipped fire".

The great Biruni with regret, anger and bitterness, reminds us the Arabs wiped out over three hundred cities, towns and villages which stood in their way, additionally destroying unique historical treasures, and whole peoples with their language, their religion, and their writing.

SHAKHANOV. In order to enslave people spiritually the Arabs found a direct and simple way - destroying first of all their foe's religious life: replacing it with their own. Then they wiped out their writing, burned their philosophical and historical books, archives, as well as manuscripts connected with their history, and erased runic inscriptions engraved on memorials and tombstones.

AITMATOV. After the victorious Arabs had destroyed Hunnish, Turkish, and Khorezmish inscriptions, they turned to the destruction of the people's treasure - their culture and their literature, their customs and their traditions. They even changed place-names, and the names of people. Thusly, we began to lose our historical memories. Arabic writing, with its twenty eight letters, which we were compelled to use until 1924, came to us in that compulsory fashion.

It seems that just as there are laws of Nature, there are also laws which govern social development in history. If war breaks out between two ethnic groups or between two religions, sooner or later, nature, time, and history will level things out. I speak of this because before the onslaught of the Mongols, with Genghis-Khan at their head, from the East to the West and from the West to the East, there were frequent attempts to conquer people by the power of arms, which were called "Cross Campaigns" - that is Crusades. They lasted for two centuries, and held people in fear and tension for three. In the Middle Ages I think there were no bloodier events than two centuries of constant attacks.

The West and the East - enormous territorial regions found at significant distances from each other - developed quite differently. By the tenth and eleventh centuries Eastern lands, curiously, had become richer - their cultural and economic lives flourished, as did their science and literature. This Eastern Renaissance began, as the name implies, a rebirth. However, this strengthening of Eastern powers did not give European feudal lords a peaceful night's sleep! Instead of plague-ridden Western cities, these Kings and Dukes wanted to water their horses at the Nile, Tigris and Euphrates. Yet, in order to campaign so far away it was necessary to give Europeans a reason fight.

An excuse quickly discerned, since Christian holy things, sacred places, the sanctified city of Jerusalem where the grave of Christ lies, the Holy Temple of the Jews etcetera, all lay under the heels of the Mussulmen! "Let us save Christ's grave, good people" - this call, resounding throughout countries of Western history, struck home. So started a war which lasted over two hundred years, and brought sorrow and suffering to people who stood on-route. The first of these crusades was headed by Pope Urban II, who came from France, in 1095 A.D. He gathered round himself neighbouring Kings, knights, and simple warriors, making a huge army, and flooded Asia Minor and Syria with blood.

The second and third crusades, led by the French King Louis VII, and the German ruler Conrad Ill, achieved nothing. They simply failed. The fourth crusade was instigated by Pope Innocent Ill, who equally gathered soldiers and peasants round him, while the fifth crusade (lasting from 1217 to 1221 A.D.) included German, Hungarian, English and Dutch knights who participated in many frays. They could not, however, hold the conquered territory for long, and were compelled to leave.

The sixth crusade was initiated by the German Emperor, Frederick II himself. He set out for the East, accompanied by a huge army. He defeated Jerusalem, and entered Damascus, but he could not maintain his power in these cities when the Mussulmen made their counterattack, and he was obliged to turn his horse's head again towards the setting sun.

The seventh, and the eighth, crusades were prepared and set in motion by the French King Louis IXth, who himself was the Commander-in-Chief of the forces which he gathered, but he died in Tunis from the plague of cholera, and his huge army was scattered without a leader.

I have mentioned all this for one simple reason. In striving to win flourishing and developing countries, the attackers made use of religious ideas and ideals as a mask, to conceal their real purpose, but the instigators of those unrighteous wars, and those who took part in them, came to an inglorious end. In addition to that, in Nature all is harmonious, and seeks for balance, and so these crusades of the West provoked the answering onslaught of Genghis-Khan from the East. That was one more affirmation of the fact, that in history too, there are laws which level out the relations between peoples with the passing of time.

SHAKHANOV.   The second attack on our historical memory, and our culture, was made by Genghis-Khan with his numberless hordes. But the difference between the Mongols and the Arabs was simply that the Mongols seized the land and the people, and extended their power over them (as their main aim), and they didn't involve religious ideas, and paid no attention to that side of their conquest. For three hundred years they were masters in Rus, and no writings, no language, no religion problems did they touch. Therefore Russian culture remained unchanged.

AITMATOV.   Genghis-Khan began his aggressive campaigns, with his undefeatable army in 1207-1208 A.D., by seizing the lands of the Buryats and the Yakuts living in Siberia. His aim being "to reach the edge of the Earth". As such, they pushed on westwards, conquering more than a hundred lands and their peoples, thus gaining an enormous territory: stretching as far as the Adriatic Sea, and only then turned back. The leader of the Yenisei Kirghizians, seeing opposition would only bring his people misery, and that they could not stop this dark hurricane sweeping everything aside, decided to yield quietly. Hence, it is written on the "Sacred stories of the Mongols", Zhoshi was presented with a white hawk, a white steed, and a black sable coat". The Kirghiz leader at that time was Aris Ainal Aldiyaruli.

Around 1218 A.D. Genghis-Khan had subdued the Tangut Khanate, the towns of Turpand, Zhungo and Khambalik (Beijin, modern Pekin), his next goal surfacing as the Seven River region.

Already having reached the level of tribal unions, Turkic folks, as "The sacred stories of the Mongols" also tells, for more than twenty years fought for their freedom against the enormous army of the bloodthirsty sons of Genghis-Khan - Zhoshi, Shagatay, Udegey, and Tole. At that period of internecine warfare and internal contradictions, which tore the leadership of the Kazakh people to pieces, they brought poverty and suffering to the Kazakh people. Clearly, they didn't have the strength necessary to oppose these invaders. By 1220 A.D. the invaders had seized the Seven River region, and Ulitau, Karatau, and the Kipchak steppeland, wiping out the towns of Otrar, Sauran, Siganak, Zhent, Taraz and Uzkent from the face of the earth, and with fire and sword levelling all around in their path. Interestingly, for six months Kayir-Khan with his warriors heroically defended their town of Otrar, and another Shah Mukhammed in Khorezm equally fought against the invaders, until he saw no further hope. Historians record him as saying: "Before I see Khorezm turned into dust and ashes, I would rather leave and die somewhere as a vagrant!" Nevertheless, he retreated as far as the Caspian Sea still not giving in to his overwhelming foe. His words proved to be of a prophetic, however, since in the end he died on a desert island from hunger, sickness and sheer despair.

At that same time Zhebe the Noyan, and Subedei, the Bakhadur, with thirty-thousand cavalrymen, passed through Central Asia: taking Iran, Azerbaijan, and then riding into Georgia. Following this, they turned towards the Volga, and came very near to the Russian steppeland.

SHAKHANOV. A learned man from the Hungarian people, close to us in origin, professor Konir lshtvan Mandoki, said to me at one of our meetings: "Mukhtar, the land you are coming to is the Balkan mountain area, wherein we wandered a long ago ... We have a song about it which you may have heard? You remained among your people, on that land where you were born, but our distant forbears under Kotan-Khan, wandered to the Balkans. In other words, we are blood-brothers, and have a common ancient motherland. We became strangers later. That was how it really was!" Then he added with a sad smile, "I was belted with a wide strap. Oh, life, why did we leave those places!?"- Those words form a part of the song I mentioned, also they bear witness to those ancient times".

"Do not be sad, my friend. A people lost by us is drawing near to us again, thanks to your activities" I told him.

Sometimes fate is very hostile to people, to our great sorrow, and so shortly after, Konir Mandoki died very suddenly in Daghestan, but in accordance with his last wishes, he was buried in the land of his forefathers - in the foothills of Ala-Tau, in the Kensai cemetery.

Yes, Kotan-Khan should take a worthy place in our history, because he was a leader who differed from others. It was he who said to Prince Mstislav Romanovich, of Kiev, these historical words:

"If you do not help us today, we shall die, but tomorrow you will be destroyed!" Those words were written in the Lavrentev manuscript.

With hindsight, he was one of the few bold and desperate leaders who tried to oppose the invasion of the great horde of Genghis-Khan, sometimes succeeding here and there. He defended the freedom of his folk, and till his last breath fought against the Mongols, not bowing his head before the foe. Such was the last Khan of the Desht-i-Kipchak steppe, its great defender.

It is well known, from the story of Zhoshi-Khan, Genghis-Khan's son that he received into his keeping the settlement of the Kipchaks, but he died in 1227 A.D., and his younger son Batu, took his place. He was not very satisfied with the small region left to him by his father, and at the head of a large army he crossed the Ural River, in 1236 A.D., beating down the Bulgars on its shores, and falling upon the Vladimirsk, Ryazansk, and Moscow principalities. In the course of seven years he won Kiev, Poland, Hungary, Moldavia and Czechoslovakia.

AITMATOV. Afterwards, due to victorious campaigns Batu-Khan moved the capital of the Golden Horde from Sarai-Batu, to the banks of the Volga, to Sarai Berke. He gave the territory to the east and north of the Aral Sea into the charge of his elder brother - Orde- Yezhen, and named it Ak-Orda (the White Horde) and the land to the south of the Aral he gave to his younger brother, Shaibani-Khan, and named it Azure Horde (the Blue Horde).

SHAKHANOV. Yes, historical facts speak clearly about this. I want to add at that time, when Batu-Khan already owned the Kipchak land settlement, Kotan-Khan was still fighting against the Mongolians, winning here, losing there in smaller battles - finally meeting his enemies on Russian soil. These words from the Lavrentian manuscript were written when Kotan-Khan saw (with his own eyes) how merciless and blood-thirsty the invaders really were. Although he acted together with his son-in-law Mstislav Udaloi, and fought by his side. With other princes, however, he was not so successful in forming such a friendship. Indeed, when the foe drew nearer, the treachery of the Kiev Prince Mstislav Romanovich led to a conflagration in Russian lands. Multitudinous, like black ants, the Mongolian warriors swarmed in and destroyed princedom after princedom, burning and laying waste everything around. Corpses lay in heaps, blood flowed in crimson streams. The outstanding scholar L.N. Gumilyev wrote about it: "In that conflict ninety per cent of the Russian warriors were slain".

Not having died in the fighting, Kotan-Khan and Mstislav Udaloi - all the time retreating from their foe - crossed the Dnieper. In order for the enemy not pursue them too easily, they burned all boats on the near-side of this river. Yet, the Mongolians relentlessly followed. Kotan-Khan only escaping their grasp because he rode off from Novgorod towards Kiev. Having destroyed the Russian princes, one after another, Batu-Khan in 1238 A.D. again met Kotan-Khan near Kozelsk - where the Kipchak leader waited for him with reinforcements - and, thus strengthened, they renewed battle. However, retreat followed retreat. By then, the Mongols, had beaten the united armies of the Poles and the Germans, the Hungarians and the Khorvats: entering into the territory of Hungary. The latter life of Kotan-Khan is described by L. Gumilyev in his book "Ancient Rus and the Great Steppe". As he states therein, "Bela IV took to himself the Polovetski horde of Khan Kotan. The Polovetskis, in accordance with a signed treaty, were then baptized into the Catholic faith - forming a powerful force under the King's direct orders. Be that as it may, the Hungarian magnates, disturbed by the growing power of the crown, treacherously killed Kotan-Khan in Peshta, along with other new converts to Catholicism. On hearing of this, the Polovetski troops mutinied, and went off to the Balkans".

The Balkan Mountains, about which Konir Ishtvan Mandoki spoke, were the very same ranges of mountains.

Now the successors of our forefathers, who seven centuries ago were driven away from their land by enemy attacks, and had to seek refuge in foreign lands, are found today in distant Hungary.

Fascinatingly, they remembered their Kipchak language until the middle of the eighteenth century, kept up their old customs and traditions, and lived as they had done on the steppe. But can Time be stopped? Truly, till this day they name themselves Magyars, and remember they are from the Kipchaks, and that their ancient motherland was our ancient steppe. For instance, they kept counting from one to ten in the Kipchak tongue, naming the figures, in this way:

1. bileu, i.e. bireu. 2. yegeu, we say yekeu and so on.

10. - oimak; I1 - carali zhumbak; we say - on bir.

Undoubtedly, they still use this vocabulary when teaching their children to count. Additionally, they call their land Ulken Kipchak -or "Great Kipchak", and Kishi Kipchak - means "Young Kipchak", and so on. They also have a town bearing the name of their heroic Khan (that is Kotan). Such was the life and struggle of Khan Kotan, who swore he would never lose his freedom.

AITMATOV. The weakening of the Golden Horde was brought about, to a considerable extent, by their defeat in the battle of Kulikovo Field, in 1380 A.D. Yet, its final disappearance from the historical scene was due to Tamerlane's opposition. Building support, he both respected people and gathered around him masters of Science and Art - taking them under his personal protection. Finally, however, having bided his time, he went on two campaigns against his relation Tokhtamish of the White Horde in 1391 and 1395 A.D. This caused the fall of his neighbouring state - as historians know very well.

SHAKHANOV. And those two campaigns ensured that finally the Russian Princes attained their freedom from the Mongolian yoke - which had lasted for three centuries. Indeed, not only were they free, but Russian folk generally were emancipated from the oppression of their Mongolian masters.

If we look at this from another point of view, we may say that after the Iron Gates had been thrown open, the Turkic peoples of Kazan, Astrakhan and the Crimea freed themselves from the hands of the Mongols.

In the final analysis, whatever one may say, the Golden Horde was the most multitudinous and powerful government of Europe and Asia during the Middle Ages. Tied, as it was, to East and West alike. One more indisputable truth was that this enormously powerful government was finally overthrown by Taragai Bay's son Temur. Coming from the tribe Barlas, this future ruler grew up in an atmosphere full of intrigues and clashes between the Mogolistan and Shagatay hordes, as well as the settlement of Khulaga in Iran.

He attacked neighbouring Urgench five times, and reduced Khorezm and Turkmenistan to ashes, along with Desht-i Kipchak, and the Seven Rivers area, the Turkish Sultanate, India, Iran, and the Golden Horde.

Be that as it may, in his days were built the most beautiful mausoleums, palaces, and temples. In Turkestan the Mausoleum of Khodzhi Akhmed Yasavi was erected, and in Samarkand a complex composed of wonderful architectural edifices was constructed.

Only when Turkic peoples were gathered into one great throng - as the owners of the widest territories, and the largest armies in all Eurasia - would the Golden Horde began to weaken and fall to pieces. Of future expansion, division, and falling away, the famous Kazakh writer Mukhtar Magauin had to say:

"On the shores of the river Yedil, where the Bulgars used to reign,
Newly rose the Kazan Khanate, powerful in its majestic strain.
On lower reaches of the Yedil, rose the Khanate of Khadzhi Tarkhan.
The Crimean Khanafe by a Black Sea rose, and upon its shore began.
Twixt the Yedil and Zhaiyk there rose the banner of the Nogai Horde.
In Siberia there arose a Khanate with a Siberian lord.
Where once lived the Azure Horde, the Kazakh Khanate was newly formed.
Twixt the Yedil and the river Don, there arose the Mighty Horde".

"In this way, previous strongholds were broken and the centre of our Turkish people was divided into seven parts, before it disappeared from the historical scene".

The Kazakh Khanate, taking the place of the Azure Horde grew much stronger after these events. Hence, in the time of Khan Tauekel an independent government developed. Unfortunately, Oraz

Mukhammed fell into the hands of the Russians around then. He was a son of Ondan Sultan, a grandson of Shigai Khan, who was an elder brother of Khan Tauekel. Certainly, that same Oraz Mukhammed later became famous (despite the pressure of long imprisonment), as one of the most respected people in this Moscow Princedom: even heading Russian soldiers as Commander-in-Chief when they attacked the Kasimov kingdom. Occurrences M. Magauin wrote about within his novel "Troubled Times, - "Alasapiran" in two volumes. Thus, in the history of Russia, there appeared a noteworthy son of the Kazakh people.

The town Berke, was mercilessly robbed and ruined, of course, and given to the flames. In that way - towards the west of the Kipchak steppe - this most beautiful and rich town was destroyed: literally wiped from the face of the earth; the rubble left to crumble into dust, or to be covered with sand from the dunes. White stones from the town were, one and-a-half centuries later, brought by Russian merchants to Khadzhi Tarkhan and they formed a part of the small Kremlin; Looking back, this city was once was the centre of three governments - the White, Azure and Golden Horde, even though it now lies entirely without attention. Indeed, does anybody take the initiative to think of the city of Berke, where undiscovered treasures might be brought to light? When are the governments of Central Asia and Kazakhstan going to do anything about it?

Unfortunately, while we are discussing what should be done here, the ones who seek quick returns are digging, uncontrolled, into various parts of the city site - and whatever they find they will appropriate for their own use.

On a related note, about ten years ago, I had a chance conversation with one lad who took part in unorganized expeditions in the city of Berke who told me:

"Each spring, or autumn, we take our spades in hand, and some wide-headed picks, and shovels, in order to go digging in the old part of the city. Around the sites we found fragments of old vessels, horseshoes, reins, bridles and bits, broken arrows and spear-heads, wherever we trod. One year in particular we found a spot which we thought to be the old centre, and started to dig ... Soon we came upon a huge pitcher, with a large, long carved spout, and lid. We were very happy with this, and thought it a real success. This pitcher was as large around its waist as a man, and we at once thought it might contain gold coins, so we started to open it. We looked carefully at the exterior, and on its upper part, on one side, we found some inscriptions in Arabic. The master who made this metal pitcher, had obviously engraved them himself. We banged the pitcher to loosen the lid, inverted it, and a yellowed human skull out rolled! We didn't know whose head was it. We were looking for gold, and felt deeply disappointed. So, we threw the skull into a ditch, and went off digging in a further spot. A week later we came upon a silver cup, and a golden stamp, with an inscription engraved on it. Both these things were found beside the skeleton of a man, gone white with age. Usually, we sold our findings at the Astrakhan bazaar. One old Kalmik, coming from the Caucasus, read the inscription on the stamp, and said with a joyful cry: "Yes, this is the stamp of Batu-Khan himself!" He began to kiss it, pressed it to his brow, paid what we asked for it, even gave a little more, and took it and the cup as well, very satisfied indeed!"

I think (as you will understand) such a shameful lack of governmental interest and control will result in the loss of such treasures! As for me, I simply hated that young robber. No words, nothing! I could not bear to sit with him any longer. I just could not breathe!

The great Russian poet, A.S. Pushkin strolling with Anna Kern in the park, picked up a stone upon which she had stumbled, and placed it on his writing table in his cabinet. Now that stone has become a great treasure, valued as a historic memorial ... And we?.. What do we do?..

Whose head was in that pitcher? Who decided to put it in there, and why? If we had only read the inscription what secrets might have been revealed, what puzzles might have been solved then?

AITMATOV.   In the fate of our people, in its history, much remains unclear. There are many unknown pages, and judging by what you have just said, how many black spots remain undiscovered, out of sheer ignorance and avid greed? Golden pages from our past are lost, through the avarice, and unthinking greed of such "archaeologists".

During the attack of Genghis-Khan, people suffered much grief. Many Turkic tribes and clans, living in Central Asia, had to quit their homes. They went as far as Asia Minor, where they were taken under the protection of the Seldzhuk Sultan. As the leader of these Turks was called Osman, they were named the Osman Turks. Moreover, it was these Osman Turks who became the founders of modern Turkey. In 1299 A.D. these tribes established their independence, separated from the Seldzhuk Sultanate, and became a self-standing government. Osman, for his campaigns and achievements, and his constant care of the people, was then named Bey.

SHAKHANOV. If we trace the history of that epoch, and those people who previously left Turkestan soil, up until the time when Kemal Ataturk became the head of their government, we see that they had to fight many foes and bloody battles. We must frankly admit that the Osman Turks took part in many attacks, were the cause of many serious wars, and always showed a militant character. For instance, in 1326 A.D. they seized the Byzantine city of Bruss, and made it the capital of their government. Furthermore, as they expanded their territory to the Sea of Marmora, they subdued everyone there. Later they crossed the Black Sea, and their horses' hooves resounded on the soil of the Balkans. They subdued the Serbs and the Bulgarians, and then reached the borders of Hungary.

AITMATOV. I think you know too that on June 15, 1389 AD, - on the Kosov field of battle - the Turkish Sultan Murad conquered the Serbs: making their country a part of the Osman Empire. Why do I repeat this? Because, in the folklore of the Balkan Peninsular, there remains a historical song "Murad on the Kosov battlefield", which they sing till this day. It has a wonderful melody, and though it is not on the same grand scale as "The plaint of Prince Igor's warriors", nonetheless, there are many historical facts preserved with artistic worthiness.

SHAKHANOV. The leader of the Turks, Sultan Murad, strove to widen the borders of his government, and went with his warriors to the Danube - in one campaign, near Varna, coming up against the united opposition of the Czechs and the Hungarians. However, this bold and capable commander destroyed that large army and, in 1475 A.D., the Turks became masters of the Crimean Peninsular.

When the Osman Turks came to Europe, it was mainly the Serbs and the Balkan tribes who suffered. Tired of those constant attacks, and alarmed by their consequences, the Serbian King Stefan Dushan, in 1349 A.D. composed and distributed among his people a code of laws, similar to the code of laws delivered by Tauke Khan "Zheti Zhargi" and consisting of two hundred and one statutes. The twenty first Statute read: "He who changes his Christian faith, and goes over to another faith, shall be punished for his treachery, and shall have his hands and his tongue cut off". That law was a protective measure, making it possible to strengthen the defence of his lands from attacks, while leaving no place for compromises.

AITMATOV.   Because Stefan Duman was an honest and just ruler, the clashes between petty leaders finished, and an agreement was reached. The people began to trust one another, and a new order was established.

The King wrote with his own hand another Statute: "He who dares to deliberately kill his father or his mother, his brother or his sister, or any children, shall be burned on the fire". Those words only illustrate what has been said already.

SHAKHANOV.   "News of me shall pass through all Great Russia" - so wrote Pushkin in his day. In 1833 he left Petersburgh to go to Orenburgh, to follow up the Pugachev mutiny, and came to the Orenburgh Boundary Commission. He was accompanied by his friend on this journey, who was a connoisseur of literature, and an official of the Commission - Vladimir Dahl. They drove through the Kazakh territory in a coach, drawn by a pair of horses, and got as far as Yaitsk township by the Ural river. The great poet stopped on the shore of the Ural for three days, studying the spot where the mutiny started, visited the smithy where the mutineers forged their weapons, visited the home of Pugachev's young wife Ustinya - and spoke with many older residents of that region, from whom he learned much.

AITMATOV.   After that trip Aleksander Pushkin wrote his novel "The Captain's Daughter". What is interesting here is that - Captain Mironov spent his childhood on the banks of the Ural, and his prototype was the father of the Great Russian fable-writer Ivan Krilov, as Pushkin specialists informed us later!

SHAKHANOV. Yes, Pushkin met the outstanding Kazakh bard, Makhambet Utemisov, who later headed the anti-colonial rebellion in the Bukeyev Horde, from 1833 to 1838. Makhambet came to Orenburgh to change the documents of his son Nursultan, wishing that he should remain in the Orenburgh military corps, and stayed in Uralsk. Along with him there was a singer called Zhankisi. Vladimir Dahl introduced Pushkin to Makhambet, and two letters to Dahl are to be found in the archives. At the time of this meeting with Pushkin, according to the bard's word, the lyrical-epic poem "Kozi-Korpesh - Bayan Slu" was written.

One-hundred-and-fifty years later, in the journal "Russian Herald", our colleague in the Embassy, a talented young fellow, Rakhimzhan Otarbayev, whom you know well, found out that fact, and decided to share quite an important piece of work, "The earth where the stars fell". During his stay in Kirghizstan, two of his plays were staged -"Abutalip Apendi" and "Abai - the Judge", which received warm approval from the audience. Having seen "Abai -the Judge" you also expressed a favourable opinion. Personally I await great things from such a talent!

In the Pushkin Museum in Moscow, eight pages from the text of the poem "Kozi Korpesh - Bayan Slu" appear as one of the valued exhibits. The poet prepared to write an epic novel on the motif of that Kazakh epos, but he did not succeed in realizing his plans.

AITMATOV. Still, it is an episode worthy of mentioning, I think.

SHAKHANOV. Regarding the name change of the river Yaik (Zhaik) into Ural, I should like to say a few words. On the shores of that very river, Emilyan Pugachev collected his forces together - as head of the greatest eighteenth century rebellion against the Tsar. A revolt which literally shook the Russian Empire. Indeed, this mutiny deeply frightened the Tsarina because Russian peasants, as well as Yaitsk Kazakhs, Bashkirs, and Kazakhs took part in it. After Pugachev had been betrayed and captured, therefore (and the people cruelly punished), the Russian Imperial Administration decided to wipe out all memory of this affair.

Hence, he made a special law, in accordance with which its name was changed to Ural. In ancient times this river had witnessed one of the prophets, blessed Zaratustra, but, nevertheless, the river needed to change its name. Perhaps I should add, those who speak Kazakh still use its true title.

In the totalitarian period, many tribes and peoples were almost permanently deprived of their historical past and its memories. All resulting in half-truths and open lies becoming common coinage. However, standing against any corruption of sources were the works of scholars like A. Levshin's "Descriptions of Kirghiz-Kazakh or Kirghiz-Kaisatsk horde: of the nineteenth century", A. Gumilyev's "The Great Turkish Khanate" and "Azure Turks and the Uigur Khanate"; N. Bichurin's "Yenisei Kirghiz" and "History of Central Asia and Kazakhstan"; V. Radlov's "Ancient Mongol-Uigurs" and "Orkhon-Yenisei inscriptions"; S. Malov's "Ancient Turkish writing"; N. Aristov's "Turkish peoples and tribes"; V. Bartold's "History of Central Asia and Turkestan".

In this field, for many years without a break, there also worked one of the leading Kazakh scholars, Academician Alkei Margulan, who considerably enriched national historical science. Furthermore, great works in the development of history were added by the researchers K. Akishev, M. Kozibayev, M. Kadirbayev, S. Akinzhanov, L. Erzakovich, A. Amanzholov, M. Magauin, A. Derbisaliyev, K. Salgarin - the author of the historic trilogy "Kazakhs" T. Zhurtbayev, (who wrote two volumes about our joint heroes and leaders, from the earliest times till today). Equally, the scientists Uakhap Shalekenov, Karl Baipakov and Bulat Kumekov made considerable additions to our knowledge in the field of archeology and history.

Similarly, filling in the blank spots in our knowledge of the Kirghizian people, a task of demanding manliness and persistence, A. Tinibekov, O. Sidikuli, K. Kharasayev, K. Yudakhin, B. Zhamgerinov, K. Usenbayev, A. Batmanov, 0. Karayev, V. Ploskikh, V. Mokrinin, Ch. Omiraliyev, A. Omiraliyev, K. Esenuli, K. Beishenaliyev and other researchers, have put forward new ideas in their works, widening our historical horizons.

AITMATOV.   I know that in Japan, for example, all pupils in their schools are able to answer any historical question about their people, their culture, literature, music, creative art, and so on, because they learn these things along with their other studies. Moreover, they do so because they want to know more, and understand more. A pupil who knows the history of his native land, his grandfathers and forefathers can better understand the history of other peoples as well. But with us, all falls otherwise. Our pupils can answer questions about Ludwig and Wilhelm, but when questioned about their own people remain silent, lowering their regretful eyes, because they have only a faint idea of their history. Thank God, there are signs in recent years that we are curing this sad disease: our lack of knowledge and understanding ...

SHAKHANOV.   The Mongolian invasion, and their mastery over us broke the economic basis for the development of the Seven-river Region, and Southern Kazakhstan. Genghis-Khans warriors destroyed agricultural areas, ruined cities and towns which showed any opposition, and reduced them to dust. But with time, those wrecked places and peoples came back to life again, since they became a part of the Golden Horde, indivisible from their masters. More than that, in the thirteenth and fourteenth centuries, the Golden Horde began to develop trade with the well-ordered countries of both East and West: with India and with Egypt, and opened up a caravan route from Asia Minor to Western Europe. So, though the Golden Horde had once been a destructive force, now it had changed into a constructive one. Each passing century it assimilated more and more the ways of European peoples, took up the Mussulman faith, taught the people the need for agricultural labour, and raised the cultural and economic levels of life. At that time the cities of the Golden Horde - Sarai Batu, Sarai Berke, Kerish, Urgench, Siganak and Khorezm became firm trading and cultural centres - and there trade was developed along with science and art, literature and folk-lore.

AITMATOV.   That period, in truth, one might call "The golden age of the Golden Horde". In this epoch the literature of people speaking our Turkic tongue was enriched by many significant works. In particular, in 1233 A.D. the poet Ali wrote a lengthy poem about Zhusup (the Biblical Joseph), and in 1303 his famous "Codex Kumanicus" while in 1310 Zabgizi he came out with his "Hissasul anbia". In 1341-42 the Kipchak poet Kutb's book "Khosrov and Shirin" first saw the light, and in 1357 Makhmut Kerderi wrote his prosaic work "Nakhzhi Ulfaradic". Additionally, in 1359 Saif Sarai finished his long poem "Gyulstan bit-turki". In 1409, Durbek wrote his variant of the "Poem about Joseph", calling it "Joseph and Zuleika", which came out as a separate book, and soon spread widely among the Turkic peoples. All these compositions, often published later, showed significant scientific and artistic thoughts, and until this day have not lost their meaning as compositions enriching the treasury of folk-wisdom and expression.

While the people of Central Asia and Desht-i-Kipchak could not raise their heads as a result of the Mongol invasion, in the fifteenth and sixteenth centuries, Italy was passing through its Renaissance period. All meaning an age of travelling had commenced. Masters began to work producing goods. Caravans bringing satins and silks from the Far East, from China mainly, returned home with Italian products. So an enlivened trade followed. Slowly the standard of living of simple folk improved, and life became a little easier. More attention was directed towards art and learning, to cultural matters, and to literature. The architecture of those times bears witness to the high level Renaissance art - the internal and external decoration of palaces, halls and museums, even the paintings on cupolas and walls. The inimitable forms of production showed the genius of skilled human hands, and also indicated that in the government of Italy there was peace, joy, and harmony. This art began to spread to other lands as well, and so peace reigned generally, not the sword and the spear.

In that period keen research into the language and style of antique Latin writers, into Latin and Greek literature (which again began to be of service to people, thanks to the efforts of the specialists) reignited. They collected the compositions of Cicero and Titus Livius, and made good use of them among a wide circle of readers.

The Italian humanist, Leonardo Bruni (1374-1444) headed the campaign for the restoration, translation, and publication of the works of the ancient Greek writers and philosophers, such as Aristotle, Plutarch, Plato, and many others.

The well-known Italian poet Francesco Petrarcha (1304-1374) not only conducted research and analyses into the works of the antique writers, but also praised in sonnets his beloved mistress Laura, and expressed his feelings towards her. Later his contemporaries wrote: "That what Petrarcha saw and reflected in his verses, what his divine eyes captured, nobody can any longer see". Wars in Europe and Asia destroyed not only cities and people, but art as well.

SHAKHANOV.   One must suppose that our ancient forefathers were wise enough, and well-educated, not just simple, wild people, as several of the Eastern specialists have tried to portray them. They did not immediately after birth, seize the pick or a spade, nor grab the handle of a hoe, or the haft of a sword, or the shaft of a spear. Through the passage of many centuries the knowledge and culture of Turkic peoples developed, competing with each other. The fact they later began to lag behind others, (and that the dust of the years lay upon them), may be blamed on certain difficult circumstances. Such as the attacks of enemies, and colonization. Surely we all know that in the Middle Ages Central Asia and Kazakhstan were among the foremost in the number of scientific discoveries, and literary innovations - proceeding ahead of many other nations? It was as if in olden times under the pens of Central Asian writers and scholars there poured out literary works and scientific treatises one after another, significantly enriching the world's treasury of thoughts. Now these works appear as the pride of many libraries across the globe, in book conservatories, and among archives. If one believes the evidence of the erudite scholar Abu Reikhan al-Biruni, on the territory of modern Turkish governments there have blossomed out architecture, and sculpture, arts, keeping in step with science - and developing in their own original way. That great doctor and healer of the East, Ibn Sina (Avicenna) thus speaks in his remembrances of the period of his study in the Islamic school in Bukhara: "One day I asked my tutor's permission to go into the library, and take some books on medicine, which after study I would return. The tutor agreed, and I entered the library, which consisted of several rooms. In each one there were large trunks containing piles of books ... I saw there volumes of which people had never heard - books about which the learned men of the world never guessed, rarities unknown, unread. But I read some of them, and learned all I could that was useful ... I carefully saw what each author knew, in this or that book and thus I precisely absorbed those new facts which would be useful for science.

In those writings placed on paper about ten centuries ago, there lie great secrets and great sense ... Otherwise is there any sense in wondering why the great poet Omar Khayyam in his day wrote a learned work "Difficult problems of Arithmetic", in which (five centuries earlier than Newton), he put forth a theorem solved by a decimal fraction? Ulugbek, long before Galileo, revealed that the Earth turned around its axis. Biruni knew Sanskrit, Persian, Arabic, Hebrew, Greek, along with other languages well, and he was the first to compile a geographic map of the whole planet. Al-Farabi, during his lifetime was named "The Second Teacher" (i.e. next to Aristotle) and the great German poet Goethe admitted: "In the East there are seven great poets, the weakest of whom stands higher than I!" For him that was something to wonder at, and to be proud of. All this shows that every epoch had its periods of great lushness and blossom, and heightened levels.

Secondly, in those times when some peoples could not raise their heads, because of persistent wars, and were unable to open their eyes and look at the world, in the lands of medieval Europe they had already gathered strength in art and in science, in the modern sense of those words. They already had spread powerful wings, and soared away.

In particular, in 1200 A.D. in France, the Paris University was founded. In the thirteenth century in England Oxford and Cambridge Universities were opened. In Spain the Saloman University, and in Italy the Neapolitan University was founded. In the fourteenth century in Czechoslovakia the Prague University, and in Poland the Cracow University were opened, and in Germany the Cologne, Heidelberg, and Erfurt Universities were working, All of these assisted in the development and strengthening of the national culture of all peoples, and then slowly changed their outlook on nature and the Earth.

All in all, in Europe in the fifteenth century there functioned sixty five centres of learning, giving students the possibility of a higher education. Those Universities and High Schools founded in that period stand today, and still bear knowledge to people across our planet, still serving their goal.

AITMATOV. There is justice in that. But do I need to point out what a great and painstaking task it is for scholars, intelligentsia and society in general to put itself into order, and in studying the works and publications of great scientists and writers, who were not given due consideration in their time, but only stand out today? Do I need to speak of the necessity of every year publishing at least one book of Firdousi, Dzhami, Saadi, Fizuli, Kliayyam, Abu Nasir al-Farabi, Mukhammed al Khorezmi, Abu Bakir al Narshakhi, Abul-Gafa al-Bozzhani, Abu Ali Ibn Sina, Abu Reikhan al Biruni, Yusuf Balasaguni, Makhmud Kashgari, Rashid-ad-Din, Abilgazi Bakhadur, Kadirgali Zhalairi, and many others, outstanding wise men of the East - historians, mathematicians, astronomers and astrologers, physicists, philosophers and geographers? We are boundlessly grateful to enlightened society abroad, that they translated and published separate collections of their major works.

Yet, in this field we have certain shortcomings which only hinder us in our work of researching the past. The fact is we have shown a tendency, sometimes changing into a rule of bad tone, when, grasping what great meaning for all of us our forebears had, we begin to draw one or another of them to a particular side, and claim them as our own. For some reason we see where a great man was born, and then determine to what tribe he may belong, looking at those places as they are today, and so try to give him our own nationality. In this way it appears that Khodzha Akhmed Yasavi is a Kazakh, Makhmud Kashgari is an Uigur, Yusuf Balasaguni is a Kirghizian, Mukhammed al Khorezmi is an Uzbek, and so each one of them receives his own measure, as if it were his birth certificate. Along with this, arguments spring up, even among learned men, and sharp clashes arise, afterwards fading away in embittered quarrels. If the history of our own peoples begins in the Saks epoch, and those people - up till a certain period - were named Turkish, then our great forbears and their scientific, artistic and creative work cannot remain our inheritance in general. Insofar as our forebears lived in a common home, spoke and wrote a common tongue, why do we today make a problem of this, where none really exists? Who needs such an old empty squabble, with no firm subject matter? Why doesn't anyone say the time has come to thoroughly study together common problems: to learn its roots, then systematize it, and not drag it out into various corners, but rather gather it into one place? Why cannot we work out canonical texts, publish them as the common inheritance of the Turkic-speaking peoples, and accept them into our history as a fundamental part? Or is that the consequence of our old imperialistic political motto: "Divide and rule!" which we cannot rid ourselves of? We need only to make up our minds to eliminate it!

Insofar as we share an inheritance common to the Turkic peoples, then we have a solution. For example Akmoldu is acknowledged as their poet by the Bashkirs, the Kazakhs, and the Tatars. Shozhe similarly belongs to the Kirghizians, and to the Kazakhs - they are his common forbears. In each people there are such examples, when writers and poets use two, or even more languages, and consequently can belong to each nation equally. From such art or literature another people will not suffer, but will only become enriched.

Moreover, Insofar as our peoples, having reached the Middle Ages, separated, and formed their own governments, whereas before their territory, language, customs and traditions had been one, we may say that now - like pieces broken off a golden object, or like coloured ribbons from one piece of fabric, the names of our great forefathers, and the inheritance the left us, now belong to us all equally.

SHAKHANOV.   Incidentally, we have an enormous epos, common to all Turkic nations: peoples or tribes, which are called "Forty Crimean Knights". In that long poem composed in a brilliant, vibrant, fashion, the story of forty great warriors and their achievements (during the period of the Golden Horde's onslaught) is written. Each knight has his own poem, which the people heard from the lips of one famous reciter, Murinzhirau Sengirbayev - a phenomenally strong personality. In reply to an invitation by the Institute of Literature and Languages (after the Great Patriotic War), he came to Alma-Ata, where, following his fine reciting of "The Forty Crimean Knights" it was decided to write the text down. From morn till eve, day after day, for six months he dictated the text of that great poem, and still didn't reach its end. Yet, with only five or six episodes of the story left to record, he said: "I'm going to see my grand-children. I've grown tired of this! I'll stay with them awhile, then I'll be back" - and off he went to Mangishlak. Sadly, having arrived home, he fell sick, and died. Thus, we cannot publish the complete story even now.

AITMATOV. You rightly say the epoch of the Golden Horde was a time when "Forty Crimean Knights" was composed, and even more correct in asserting that it is common to many Turkic peoples.

SHAKHANOV.   Yes. For example, the chief heroes of the poem "Orak-Mamai" were known as the military leaders of the Golden Horde. Mamai was a Khan of the Golden Horde from 1361 onwards, and was one of the main war-leaders taking part in the battle of Kulikov. Karasai-Kazi and Seitek, from other poems, were also historical persons. Yedige, in the poem bearing his name, lived from 1352-1419 A.D. and fought against Toktamish, being a leader of the White Horde. In the poem "Asan Kaygi" the story tells of a bard of that name - **a** legendary poet and philosopher, and a social activist. He was one of the Bey-Judges, under Khan Ormambet - a leader of the Golden Horde. His judgements as a Bey, were noted for their justice. Later, after the fall of the Golden Horde, he became one of the founders of the Kazakh Khanate.

AITMATOV.   The Dzhungar government, (Oirats) having brought great woes upon the Turkic peoples, decided to play the role which Genghis-Khan did in Mongolia, but they did not take into account that times had changed, or the great power of their opponents. Firstly they were alone against the Chinese Empire, that "Chinese dragon" which had annihilated the union of Oimauts, Torgauts and Durbuts, plus a million Kalmiks. Secondly, in the period of Genghis-Khan's attacks, the Turkic peoples were still in a period of formation, although, five centuries later, when the Dzhungars came, those peoples were already independent nations with their own legal systems.

SHAKHANOV.   The tribes of the Oirats, making up the Dzhungar government, left in the second century A.D. for the Mongolian steppes - because at that time a great massacre was going on. The Oirats wandered into the territory of the Kazakhs and the Kirghiz, in the foot-hills of Ala- Tau, where they settled for some time. In the following century, during the reign of the Mongolian Khans (under the pressure from the Kazakhs and Kirghiz), they lost their pastures. Indeed, they had no place to feed their flocks, or an opportunity to trade with other governments, because, in themselves, they had become very weak. Later, in the sixteenth century - having been defeated in one of a series of battles - the Oirats became a part of the Kazakh Khanate. There is witness of this found in diplomatic correspondence of the day.

Unmistakably, a letter written by the Kazakh ambassador in Moscow, Kulmukhamed to Sultan Oraz-Mukhammed, in 1595 A.D. reads, "Your relation, Prince Tauekel, has become a Khan of the Kazakh horde, and his younger brother, Shakhmagambet, he has been made a Khan of the Kalmiks. They wander to either, and keep close together".

AITMATOV. As we know from history, in 1635 A.D. the Oirat-Kalmik folk united, and set up a single government. Albeit placed precariously between the Chinese, the Kazakhs and the Kirghizians. Feeling restricted, the Dzhungar Khanate eventually began to think about extending its territory and moving from their mountainous pastures to richer grounds - capable of feeding much larger herds of cattle. In this they didn't waste much time, but formed an army of fifty thousand well-trained warriors to attack the Kazakhs, Uzbeks, and the Kirghiz. The first major battle taking place on the shores of the river Talas. In this initial struggle, the Uzbeks were led by a skilled war-commander Aldishukir, and their united forces were able to ward off the attack. The next foray took place in the southern regions of Kazakh territory (near the city Sairam), where these three brotherly peoples stood firm and defeated their foes.

SHAKHANOV. This well-armed, huge, Dzhungar army made seven attacks altogether on Kazakh soils, seizing the capital of Turkestan along with the city of Tashkent. Likewise, it took Sairam, and all territories from Sariarka up to the Volga and the Ural - bringing local inhabitants untold suffering. Unjustly robbed of their cattle, these people were on the verge of starvation: running wherever they could to escape their merciless enemy. It was said, these attacks were so pitilessly that people needed to run for their lives bare-foot, Hence the phrase "aktaban shubirindi" which means the "march of bare heels". This war was followed by periods of terrible hunger, wherein people were reduced to feeding on wild herbs, roots and nuts.

Sometimes, I think such misfortune befell our peoples because we could not fully unite against our foes. The Russian envoy to Bukhara, Florio Benevini, writes about this in 1725, saying: "In Central Asia now a pitiless war is raging. In it the Afghans, the Persians, the Khivintsi, the Bukhartsi, the Kazakhs, the Kirghiz, the Karakalpaks and the Kalmiks are taking part. Each time they seem to have reasons for fighting against one another".

Yes, the appearance of the Dzhungar Khanate on the historical scene affected not only the Kirghiz, the Uzbeks, and the Kazakhs, but the Chinese and Russians as well. Certainly, having armed the Kalmiks with weapons (even cannons), these two empires hurled them against the Turkic peoples, while they themselves stood quietly aside - watching the conflict, and enjoying their own cunning. The fact was - from the river Khuankhe, to the Volga, and from Siberia to Iran - there stretched a great steppeland with riches untold. In which case, jealousies raged across it. Allowing sly, Machiavellian, powers to provoke the Dzhungar Horde and the Turkish tribes into destroying one another. After all, one side was bound to lose in this fight - and could then be wiped out with minimum force. In a literal sense, one might just knock off their hats with one blow.

Thinking over such far-reaching plans, Russia suddenly became very generous. Giving lands to the Kalmik tribes of the Torgauits, the Durbits and the Khoshauits on the shores of the Volga. Also, weapons and artillery. Finally, therefore, following a century of wars with Dzhungari, Turkic peoples lost their common culture. It ended with colonial enslavement and complete dependence on Russia.

AITMATOV. In Zhetisu, it is claimed Dzhungar detachments attained victory on more than one occasion, and seized Narinkol, Bayinkol, Kastek and Kaskelen. Indeed, having crossed the Ala-Tau, they appeared on Kirghizian territory. In a battle near Issil-Kul, and in the Chuisk valley, Kirghiz folk could not resist their opponents. Thence, an expression was often heard among our people: "If a Kirghizian baby cries in the mountains, Kazakh mothers in the valley feel a pain in their breast!" Striving to defend his brothers, a noble Knight named Karasai (from the Shapirashti tribe), collected together five thousand cavalrymen and gave battle to the Kalmiks in the valley of the river Chu. Karasai himself slew the Kalmik war-commander in single combat. So uplifted, Kazakh and Kirghiz warriors – calling on the spirits of their forefathers - showed unimaginable bravery in their final battle.

Ironically, we lost our independence due to this war, even though the Dzhungar government itself disappeared from the Earth completely.

That is the essence of destruction, I suppose. A great service to Turkic solidarity had been done (particularly by Khan Yesim, who earlier than others understood the dangers), but vital powers had been drained away. Initially able to unite previously hostile groups like the Bukhara, the Turfan, and Kashgar Khanates, into a union defending Issik-Kul", it was still the case that Khan Yesim was no miracle worker. Truly, some continued to comment "If there had not been such an example of unification, then those merciless warriors of the Dzhungar invasion, who, constantly receiving reinforcements from Siberia, as well as new weapons and warriors, would have been devastating for the Turkish people, who had practically no fire-arms " – but an ever-ongoing and perpetual war proved beyond all mortal powers to solve.

If proof were needed, however, about our peoples being unified in ages past, then the epic poems demonstrate these truths. Along with proverbs and oral stories.

SHAKHANOV. At celebrations held in honour of the epic "Manas'" thousandth anniversary where the guests - officials, literary specialists, writers, translators and artists coming from many lands – were addressed by an opening speech by the President of the Kirghizian Republic, Askar Akayev, few anticipated his agitated joy. Clearly, in recent years I have not heard such a poetic speech, causing those seated to applaud vigorously. When the interval came they congratulated him, and I too approached him to say, "Your speech was no speech at all". Missing the joke, people standing nearby misunderstood my stern expression and were confused. One of them even squawked "What, didn't you like it, then?" Amused, I replied thusly: "That was no speech, as I said - it was simply poetry!" They nodded their heads in agreement.

Also, at this meeting was the Kalmik poet David Kugultinov, from Elista, who additionally made a joke, by jibbing; "You are deeply indebted to those ancient Kalmiks. If they had not been strong and aggressive, but weak and cowardly foes, you would not be celebrating the thousandth Jubilee of "Manas", and he would not be glorified as a great knight!" Obviously such words from a famous poet rang warmly, albeit weirdly, in the hearts of all those present. Especially when he spoke of the great significance "Manas" enjoyed across the globe. To his knowledge, in China, there was a city and a spring named

"Manas", while in Japan there is a city named after his son, Semetei. More than all this, there is a poem "Manyosyu" in Japanese culture, reflecting the epics themes. Unsurprisingly, Indians too respected this gigantic cultural achievement. On top of this, in Latin America, there is a modern city bearing his name and Korea boasts of a mountain called "Manas" - whereas, in the Crimea, a village bears the epithet – as does one in Hungary. Of course, this list could go on and on. "Are not the Kirghiz a great nation, having created such a hero?" Kugultinov, rounded off by stating - showing his unusual knowledge, as well as his kindness and width of intellect.

If we continue this conversation, then we must return to the fact there were four major attacks made on us. Each designed to wipe out our culture from the face of the earth, and from the people's memory. After the Arabs, and the Mongols, a third major attack was made by Russian imperialists - resulting in our loss of independence. To attract the Turkic tribal peoples into their sphere, and to deface the culture of those defeated, the colonialists used all their technical and political superiority. A move making great changes to our ethnic life.

AITMATOV.   There you have your own dialectics, Mukhtar! The Russian factor appeared everywhere, both as a loss, and as a gain. Those gains included the fruits of European and World Civilization. Without them we would not get far today, and could not have attained our independence after the Soviet period - without a certain readiness to the demands of modern life.

SHAKHANOV.   Taking the long view, I suppose it is so. Yet, how much it cost us! Assimilation, on the verge of annihilation, accompanied by the disappearance of our own national culture. The same thing has taken place in Tibet, as well as amongst the Uigurs due to Chinese invasions. Will indigenous groups be able to survive, will they be able to preserve life beneath the pressure of Imperialism? To be, or not to be - that is the question!

On Kazakh and Kirghizian soil, at the time of the Russian Empire, there were over two hundred villages named Alekseyevka, Pavlovka, Nikolayevka, Vladimirovka, Antonovka, Nadezhdinovka, and so on. In the Soviet period the "russification" of local populations went on more swiftly than under the Tsars. The fact was that Stalin, though not a satrap of the Tsars, imitated their policies. As for the Georgians, who always considered Turkey their enemy, and Turkic peoples of the empire as a threat, our "great leader", being Georgian, quickly adopted their prejudice. As such, he decided that if the Turks were not separated, they would probably take the road to Pan-Turkism. Although, even he did not immediately make them switch from an Arabic alphabet to the Kirillic - but in the middle of the twenties, ordered Turkic peoples to use the Latin alphabet. So, people who had long become accustomed to Arabic writing were compelled to change their alphabet. Moreover, books printed in Arabic were burned because of their "religious" nature, or destroyed otherwise.

Gaining momentum as an initiative, all papers, archives, and similar documents written in Arabic were slandered, as having been penned by mullahs, or as being quotations from the Koran, and, therefore, dangerous.

When all said and done, the fourth attack was made on our writing and language. Indeed, in 1940, all Soviet Union pupils were compelled to use a new revised form of the Kirillic alphabet – except Georgia, and the Baltic Republics. An exemption being made because their tongues were "timeless". Again we, like many others, found ourselves forced to learn foreign writing, spelling, and reading. Something especially offensive, because those sounds and letters (of ours) not found in the Kirillic alphabet needed to become the subject of a special commission. There were eight such letters - and they are common to various Turkic speaking peoples. Assuredly, they had nothing in common with this new alphabet and were written differently. All meaning, what had previously been clear in conversation was now unclear in writing. Our peoples couldn't recognize one another anymore, or for that matter read each other.

What about the Turkish alphabet and graphic arts? Hadn't the Arabic alphabet serve us for ten centuries? Nobody remembered our primitive cuneiform symbols, but at least these forms of communication were ours.

AITMATOV. Yes, these are depressing facts. Nonetheless we should always see what we have gained as well as what we have lost. Russian culture led us into a complicated process - an involuntary enrichment, and introduction, to the fundamentals of European civilization and twentieth century national cultures. As far as religious feelings are concerned, they survived, and were enlivened. Like politics, the spiritual life also struggles with time and location. In this, all peoples are united by evolutionary desires to know more, to better themselves, and to improve their forms of self-expression. No withering wind can change or ever shake these truths.

Religion, since the day of its birth, has played the role of collective instructor. Though there are many religions and sects on Earth, basically they only number four or five in total. Christ is the founder of Christianity, Gautama Buddha of Buddhism, Zarathustra of Zoroastrianism and Moses of the Hebrew religious line. It goes without saying that the prophet Mohammed is the founder of Islam.

If we keep to religious precepts, we acknowledge God as one. Also, all religions call humankind to honesty, justice, holiness and righteousness. However, with the passing of centuries, religion has become a weapon in the hands of priests and politicians, and an open mechanism for colonization and oppression, serving those in power.

Religion was precisely the reason why nations trampled on one another - as they did in the name of Christ during the Crusades. Today those who stick to some fundamentalist faith look down on those of a different persuasion. An attitude leading to mistrust, impatience, and opposition. But all those who use religion for their own purposes have little to do with people who sincerely believe in God, and follow humanitarian principles. So I would like to think.

SHAKHANOV. This are entirely realistic remarks. Once I wrote in my note-book remarks about sources of common inheritance - of cultural and literary memorials. I even made some copies and photocopies to this effect. Simply wanting to know where our books are now? For instance, the journal "Serke", where M. Dulatov's poems (1907) was published, is to be found in Tokyo. The book of A. Baitursinov, "Til Kurali" (1920) is to be found in New York. "Ogiz-Name" (13th-15th cent.) "Babur-Name" (15th cent.) "Tarikhi-i-Abil-Khair" and also three books in foreign languages about Kazakhstan, are found in London; "Korkitata Kitabi", (9th cent.) in the Vatican, Rome; "Codex Kumanikus", (14th cent.) in Venice; the 600-page book "Kudatgu Bilig", by Jusup Balasaguni, (11th cent.) in Gerate; "Al-kitab-el Geomini", (1734) and "Divan lugat at-Turk", (1074) by Makhmud Kashgari; "Divan-i- Khikmet", (12th cent.) by Khodzha Akhmed Yasavi, are kept in Stamboul. But this is merely a modest beginning. Along with these texts, more than four thousand books (published in the Kazakh tongue, before the October Revolution), are to be found in the libraries and archive funds of Moscow, Kazan, Ufa, Yerevan, Kiev, Minsk, Ashgabad, Namangan, and Samarkand, from which I received replies to my enquiries. Additionally, one could name books which escaped the fires of prejudice -being written in Armenian - and, as such, preserve accounts of Turkish history, as well as genealogical tables of our forefathers. Moreover, "Dana Khikar Sozi", (fifteenth to seventeenth[h] century) and other books kept in Armenian monasteries, or in the funds of Yerevan, prove both priceless and significant historical witnesses. A similar list has been written by the scholar Tatar Karimullin, to whom (for all his sins) we are obliged to say "Many thanks!"

AITMATOV. Written down with a goose-quill pen, in their time these books played a significant role in the welfare of all Turkic peoples. They did not let native culture and literature die away. Equally, they developed native interests and widened the horizons of our folk. Every book, therefore, coming to us from antiquity, has the right to be read with attention, and a careful attitude. It is a good thing that you, dear Mukhtar, show particular interest in these questions.

In general, how many languages do you think there are on the earth? Till today nobody has accurately defined this number, but altogether, as far as I can gather, there are two-and-a-half thousand up to about five thousand. After all, each nationality and tribe has its own language or dialect - with a conscious history behind it.

SHAKHANOV. In 1919, in Tashkent, in the recently organized Turkestan Republic, as a chairman of the Mussulman Bureau, they elected a well-known son of the Kazakh people: a social and revolutionary worker, Turar Riskulov. In the same Bureau there served the representatives of the Turkish folk - N. Khodzhayev, Y. Ibragimov, and A. Mukhittdinov, and Y. Aliyev. All sharing a resolution (taken in the name of ninety five percent of those dwelling in the Turkestan Republic - and in the name of all Mussulmen), that the leadership of the Central Bureau would set up an organization to serve all Mussulmen: economically, culturally and in military matters.

Understanding, furthermore, that successors to the Russian Empire would continue their colonial attitude towards Central Asia, they wished to secure for their peoples a bright future. As such, they worked out a programme for the united development of that land, taking into account linguistic and religious problems. Moscow, however, fearing independent policies from the Turkestan Republic, broke up this Bureau and retained the reigns of government over them. We know what happened, of course, to these independent Mussulmen - with Riskulov at their head, and how much blood was spilt.

AITMATOV.   What in the past we broke with our own hands, and trampled with our own feet into the soil (due to our misunderstanding), was almost extinguished. This may be why it would be so difficult to regenerate it. Confessed so, we now need to pay back our debt to religion, language, and culture. Indeed, the names and works of those innocents who died in the years of the repression, must be rehabilitated. Perhaps, we even need to bow our heads before the victims of those difficult years - before those who starved, and underwent Stalin's prohibitions, and give a memorial feast in their honour.

Though we say the true master of history is a people, actually historical processes are pushed by time and circumstance. Although, as the fates and lives of our forefathers passed between these two criteria, they created our world. Indeed, the successes and failures, the joys and sorrows, along with the victories and defeats of our ancestors, were given sounds by the dombra and the kobyz, by the ringing voices of the akyns, and zhyrau, and all of those who prepared for the future.

SHAKHANOV.   In the past, we treasured every single page and step. Nonetheless, in the records of ten independent Kazakh people four important events should be written down, one after another.

In 1456 A.D. the Kazakh people escaped from their submission to the successors of Shaibani-Khan, and founded their own government. That was five hundred and forty years ago. For the people who lived and developed on their own land, with their own tongue, and with their own culture, this was a source of great joy. All implying, however, that future generations had a great task ahead of them - to raise the names of their earliest Khans onto a pedestal - and to inscribe their names thereon forever.

In the passing of the last five centuries, having seen merciless foes, having witnessed multitudinous onslaughts and bloody frays on the road to freedom and independence, the Kazakh people, survived more than three hundred various battles and invasions in order to gain their liberty.

There lies the significance in the mutiny in 1916 A.D. After all, our one-sided relationship with those claiming to be our friends led nowhere.

Indeed, this movement against totalitarianism, against more than seventy years of oppression and humiliation, became our first taste of democratic changes. Hence, in the events of 1986, in Alma-Ata, the winds of change started to blow. Usually historical events fade with the years, take the form of legends, and only after the passing of decades does their real meaning become clear. Yet, those events were a manifestation of the people's will, concluding more than five hundred years of struggling towards liberty.

Whatever you say, those major historic events became living symbols of the folk's fight for their own future.

AITMATOV.   Tyrants try to steer history, but its flow is controlled by the general populace. Yet, in these two opposing maxims there is something of a commonality. At the end of the day, tyrants - for the sake of their career - make sacrifices. Whatever you say the crowd, and an individual, always bounce off one another.

It is said truly: "People who have no history are like a child without a father or mother, and must learn everything for themselves from the start. To drive people to that extremity, one must use every ounce of strength. People which have lost their historical memory are like a flexible vine -wherever you bend it, there it goes." So it was in totalitarian times - we knew we had fallen into dependence, closing our eyes to wounds still streaming with blood, not learning our own history carefully, but learning somebody else's as our own. This was a consequence of tendentious one-sided ideologies. In a sense, we become orphans in our own home. Moreover, our history was clearly disfigured and altered by "expert butchers". Was all of this an accident of historical narratives? Not likely!

Whether good or bad, each nation has its history, its true past. Therefore it would be unforgiveable to hide the bad side, and put forth only the good: colouring history with cosmetics and gluing together broken pieces. All the same, each new generation will compare its life with periods of enlightenment in other countries and try to find solution to their internal problems.

Let those historians (who in difficult times stepped aside from the truth) be ultimately forgiven, for like fish out of water, they need our sympathies.

Both of us, before this conversation, and during our discussions, read and re-read "World History" and "The History of the Middle Ages" along with other books on this theme. We took their contents to heart and analyzed ancient comments on these questions. Some events, and the circumstances around them (even when thoroughly researched and checked), gave birth to doubts, and sometimes led to new meditations and conclusions. Nonetheless, there was one factor common to all. Namely, some parts of those tomes describing Rome, Iran, Japan, India, China, and other countries, were written from a nationalistic point of view, not from the perspective of scientific authority. To my mind, this is dangerous, and may lead historians to dash from one extreme to the opposite - hunting after a "truth" which suits the moment.

Overall, the time has come to gather carefully prepared ruminations garnered by serious historians from every country (showing constant insight), and begin to write our own history again - beginning with the most ancient times up until today. But where is the Academy that would take upon itself such an important and responsible task, which would attract the best known historians from all over the world? Would UNESCO, maybe, take upon itself such a terrific labour, or a section of the United Nations? Whatever happens, it is time to unify our efforts, and give an objective evaluation of humanitarian issues. After all, what has humankind done in this world so far, epoch after epoch? No event, not even the smallest, no periods of enlightenment or tyrannous darkness can be left out. Bravely, we need to retrace our steps till human nature is fully revealed. This should be done without humiliating the smallest ethnic group, or over-evaluating greater nations. Otherwise we shall not be able to get rid of national egoism, and shall, as before, become stuck in the mud of our own local bog. Far too often, national egoism was the root of clashes leading to bloodshed and suffering, wherein innocent people died and the blind grey masses praised bloodthirsty, sly, tyrants, as gods and heroes.

We must not forget that the history of a country, when it is being recorded, demands every letter written down for the fate of all who come after us.

WOMEN IN OUR FATES
OR
AN EVENING OF POETRY FOR TWO

The twentieth century made humanity a witness of not only two World Wars, and thousands of local blood-lettings, nuclear explosions and destructive earthquakes, but also mastery of the cosmos, and scientific progress. Strangely, this brought an unprecedented lowering of spiritual and moral norms, crystallized out of the past millennia of our forefathers' experience.

That great inner feeling, like love - the keeper and motivator of life, is giving up its position, is being mocked by youth. In my view. For human society this is a frightful danger, even more dangerous than the perils of nuclear warfare.

> *"Days which pass with love - are life.*
> *Days which pass without -just days ..."*

SHAKHANOV.   Chingiz, what if we two, so near in spirit to one another as men, dip into a boundless and endless theme?

AITMATOV.   Judging by the fact we are secluded, you are going to speak of women and the feminine problem?

SHAKHANOV.   Yes, indeed, I am! I think the time has come for us to share our thoughts and feelings about life-giving power - namely about women.

AITMATOV.   Then, for a start, to get our conversation going, you should read your poem, devoted to them -"Women".

Let's recollect the past. Once Labryuier noted: "Among a number of different voices the most pleasant and soft is the voice of a beloved woman." Let dear images, a little bit faded out, revive in our souls. Let's settle one more thing. During our talk about women, please, read your poems, more often. Let this talk be a peculiar evening of poetry, devoted to women.

SHAKHANOV.   Agreed. I shall 'do so!

"Once, by the hospital window, it occurred,
> *That having seen me sitting, and looking sad,*
> *A girl then told my fortune, every word.*
> *Her eyes were lit up by a smile, so glad.*
> *What will the cards say, rustling quietly there?*

> *"Your sickness will be cured!*
> *On your parched lips*
> *The honey will flow. ..*
> *Why sit and stare?*
> *You will not lose that special warmth which grips.*
> *Shh! Since your childhood, from your boyish tricks*
> *All these four queens will never leave you, sure!*
> *'Love's an achievement!' - thus you always said.*
> *Alas, poor Poet, clearly that's true. What's more –*
> *No poetry and no drama lives without love.*
> *In verses thoughts of beauty are woven so*
> *That truth we know, all fortune-tellers prove –*
> *From women come your happiness, and your woe.*
> *So fly to them, but beware of women, as due!"*

> *I had to laugh! "A clever girl you are!*
> *Tell all our troubles, guessing them! First class!*
> *You put all gypsies out of face, by far;*
> *And leave them out of work, my dear young lass.*
> *You'll be their queen! Well, thank you. Let me pass!..*
> *But that amusement proved to be the key –*
> *The sacred casket of thoughts it opened wide.*
> *Of women endless tales you hear, like me.*
> *Such stories weave through the world, like veins inside.*
> *But woman is the crown of earthly gifts.*
> *The one who does not know what woman means –*

He is no man!
Just half-a-one, he seems!
The road to beauty's an icy one, which lifts,
But how we prize its slipperiness and dreams!
Your fate slips too –
Catch hold of it, my friend!
And having caught it, hold fast,
Don't let it go!
Hold fast, or you'll be lost, and that's the end ...
Yes, women can be a blessing,
Or curse, you know!
But beauty - that will burn us badly too,
And weak ones' - envy slings its lasso, once more.
I glance upon those burial mounds anew –
There young men lie - for there has been a war.
There, for a woman, tribes have been at strife,
Like Greeks in Ilion,
Fighting for their Helene!
All knights are mortal - but she has lasting life.
The poets, so well-beloved by their people then,
Were burning for one single woman again,
And for her honour died, in combat vain.
But women, those who with cold beauty shone,
The crowd forgot. They were doomed to dark anon.
To be a flame, yet with no warmth to glow,
To be a woman, and yet no beauty show –
What meaning lies in such contradictions, say?
Can they change their nature, their whole life betray?
And so become unhappy, all their way?
But in their spiritual depths real beauty lies.
External beauty is fruitless, teases one's eyes.
What lies in glitter, if shallow is the sea?
The ship will shortly, surely, come to grief
The captain will set the vessel upon the reef,
And those accursed will die, hid in mist will be ...
No, woman is not shallow, nor can be inside.
She's a fortress of honour, the aim of masculine pride.

To find such a one
You must penetrate right through time,
For such is the dream of all the masculine tribe.
And there's a law:
Make haste to gain the height,
And give one's life
For such a beauty's plight,
And bring her to the light, from out the gloom. ...
Although that does not always happen so soon.
For many, gladness lies further off than woe.
Not all are able themselves to sacrifice so.
But where is valour, when there's no soul athirst?
For thirst it is which calls forth beauty first.
I know that citizen's life is wingless therefore,
If it's quite dried out, like yellowy feather-grass,
When love has not bestowed its raindrop store.
O love, don't leave me, that I beg, don't pass!
So that my soul does not lose power once more,
But still believes: That strength will ever last –
That woman, whom so deeply I adore!

AITMATOV.   Believe me, dear Mukhtar, in your verses I hear the voice of another century, and another people! An Armenian poet, I heard there, Narekatsi, living in the tenth century. That is excellent! Wonderful, isn't it? No? Perhaps not. Such is the quality of really fine poetry - it ties the heart and times together with the knot of innermost feelings and thought. You say, for instance in your poem:

> *"To be a flame, yet with no warmth to glow,*
> *To be a woman, and yet no beauty show –*
> *What meaning lies in such contradictions, say?*
> *Can they change their nature, their whole life betray?"*

Narekatsi, with that same inexpressible yearning and sorrow wrote, (I am reciting from memory but guarantee the essence)

> *"To be a shower of rain, and not to fall,*
> *To be a flower, and put no blossom forth,*
> *And find no happiness at all? ... "*

There is only one final difference - that Narekatsi, being a monk, turned to God, calling his poem "A word to God" - coming from the depths of his heart". But you address a Woman! A woman, for a real poet, is a Goddess! Through her God created everything!

A poet is given a great assignment from above - to maintain the symphony of peace, which once born must not be interrupted for a moment, or still worse, must not become a cacophony, destroying one's soul. More than that, there are many people who are ill-intentioned, or who involuntarily want to change the harmony of Nature's universe into chaos.

Among us Kirghizians and Kazakhs, since times immemorial, there has been a healthy respect for women. If a lad was educated in such a way that he, "would not be consumed by fire, nor drowned by water", he may not share these inherited attitudes. However, we have always felt a maiden should be protected and cared for. Moreover, she must be carefully looked after, like an ingot of gold. As such, the wives of elder brothers feared the evil eye - and would decorate girls' headgear with a protective amulet made from the feathers of an eagle-owl. Additionally, it was felt necessary to preserve beauty and tenderness: meaning the same to us as protecting the good name and honour of our national identity. According to folk wisdom, setting off on a migratory journey needed to be discouraged until the time when swallows (who had woven their nests on the roof-wheel of a yurta), had trained their fledglings to fly. Thus, our forebears were sensitive to every action. For example, they would never slay a mare who had given birth to a fine race-horse. Indeed, a mother who had given life to glorious successors was really worthy of all honours.

SHAKHANOV.   In the Caucasus, a woman has only to cast her white handkerchief between two adversaries (even if they were engaged in a blood-feud), to stop the fighting at once. That was an unbreakable law. Any man who did not submit to a woman's will, or to a mother's authority, brought great shame on their own heads, as well as their entire generation.

AITMATOV.   Yet, it seems each society forms its own viewpoint, and its own policy, towards women these days. In the first years of Soviet power, hunger and repression were seen. Also, following the Great Patriotic War, reconstruction themed everything across the USSR.

Hence, women were compelled to forget their feminine nature and distort their fundamental essence. In those years unbearable burdens were laid on their shoulders. Yevgeny Yevtushenko, our mutual friend, wrote some verses on this topic:

> *"How could it happen in this world of ours,*
> *That having forgotten those who this life began,*
> *We cast out woman from her earlier powers,*
> *And lowered her down to the common level of man?"*

Sadly, critics saw little more than criticism in these words and said they were against the spirit of the times.

Today, it is even more difficult to imagine what kind of "inspiration" stimulates poets and artists – who portray woman as giants with steel muscles! Be that as it may, the greatness of women started much earlier. Remember what Nekrasov said: "They stopped their horses at full gallop, and strode into their huts on fire." It was when the seeds of a future "ideal" were sown, that feminine beauty became a matter of experiment: materialized, dare I say, in the world-famous statue "A Kolkhoz farmwoman and a worker". This statue shocked people, and caused admiration. "Let's have more like this", some critic shouted. Nowadays, it is easy to speak ironically about such works, although back then it was claimed one challenged the progress of psychology, history, and art. Absurd? Of course - from our contemporary point of view. Yet, this absurdity reflected a living reality. Isn't it a fact, women themselves tried to underline their equality with men, in the way they spoke, dressed and acted? If society had only started to think about this so-called equality beforehand, it would have been clear where it would lead to.

Yes, it is a sorry situation! On the other hand, it is currently clear we shall not construct our "brave new world" in this way. Even though, we may be forced to learn our lesson from bitter experience.

Do you remember how once, as guests of Apas Dzhumagulov, (also accompanied by Askar Akayev, a man who became our President) we carried on an interesting talk about women? A conversation attracting general comment? That evening you amazed us all with your poem about being a real man. I looked for it later in your books, but could not find it. Recite it again, please, I like it!

SHAKHANOV. That is a long poem, I'll recite an excerpt which suits the theme of our discussion:

>*"Once there lived an old man, much respected*
>*By the folk of the city Otrar.*
>*He had a steed, by himself selected,*
>*Race-horse breed - the best there are!*
>*It was so swift and independent,*
>*Bit at the bridle, till blood began.*
>*Of that race-horse, swift and splendid,*
>*News flew round in Kazakhstan.*
>*He had a stentorious voice when neighing,*
>*Echoing seven hills away.*
>*From dirty ditch-water he was staying –*
>*He would rather die, I'd say.*
>*There was no man so bold nor haughty*
>*Who would dare step up near him.*
>*With his hooves, black fetlocks sporty,*
>*All intruders - he beat them grim.*
>*He made cares for his old supporter,*
>*But he still gained mountains of praise!*
>*With this wise old man lived his daughter;*
>*Many she pleased with taking ways.*
>*She was an independent maiden.*
>*Many fellows' eyes pleased soon.*
>*Fiery-eyed, like day just breaking,*
>*Shiny-faced this maid, like the moon.*
>*For her soul, he was not despairing,*
>*Rather happy, to save her so ...*
>*And his daughter too was declaring*
>*That she'd save her sire from woe.*
>*And she suddenly started crying*
>*To her father, with tender voice:*
>*"Vainly with your steed you are vying.*
>*Give it up, make some other choice!"*
>*"What's all this?" replied her father,*
>*Who was troubled, thus put to shame.*

"Just explain, I'm worried rather –
What are you saying, all the same?"
"Wouldn't it help if you sold your racer?
You, dear Papa, are growing old.
You can't live as a stallion-chaser,
He's too obstinate and too bold!
"Daughter dear", he sighed, "I'm troubled.
Maybe there's truth in what you say
But reply: Whose soul is hobbled?
Really in vain do I pine away?
He, who is born for fullest freedom,
Who has some rags of honour and fire,
He is worthy, like wind in season,
To go galloping off, head higher!
My good steed is my dream undying,
He is the memory of my youth.
There's no wonder in worlds a-flying,
Nobler than such a steed, forsooth!
Ah!" he sighed, with visage brightening,
As he stroked his daughter's long black hair,
"How I remember, rather frightening,
When I galloped that race-course there!"
Thus he sighed, and murmured quietly:
"Do not judge my steed for his ire.
He is wrought for races rightly,
Like cast iron, hot in the fire.
From a breed of steppeland freedom –
In the contest he won't give way
Sweating blood from morn till even,
Fighting hard the live-long day!
So, for this very special glory,
His stormy moods can you not forgive?
We have to bear this bitter story,
Carry the blame, as long as we live".
There the tired old man desisted,
And he gazed, as though in a dream:
"Do we lack peaceful old jades?" he insisted,

"In this poor world of ours, I mean?
What use are they? But wait a moment –
People all praise such quiet old nags!
Maybe, that's why our racer's in ferment,
That's why he's burning, all worn to rags?
What do we know? If he were speaking
In a tongue we could understand,
He himself the word would be seeking"
Here he glanced at his daughter at hand.
"I am troubled by what you've been saying!"
Said her old father, again with a sigh:
"Daughter, I fear that joy won't be staying,
But will be leaving you, by-and-by.
Know, my dove, that to a bold stallion
People have likened man long ago.
Not in vain gave him the medallion –
Only to real men, so you must know"
Father proved right. Upon one side then
Happiness did his daughter evade:
Without women there's no real life then –
But I speak spitefully, maybe, dear maid?
I cannot stand a man who's a "sissy"!
I am for women. But at the same time,
I cannot stand a male woman! What is she?
Nothing at all - spits at reason, or rhyme!
If I see women with men's made-up features –
Tell me, what is the reason for that?
Take them away those stillborn creatures –
Slighting reality, leaving life flat.
Making up faces with daubed paint so filthy!
Is that then really a masculine maid?
Or is it merely the mode that is guilty?
Or did not Nature come to her aid?
Try to accomplish this feat? What torment!
I pity women, and also such men
Who have forgotten themselves for a moment,
Losing their honour and nobleness then!

It is still frightful for me to conceive it –
How strange 'twould be, should such parodies reign!
Those named as "men", who themselves believe it,
Having forgotten their honour again!
Those who just love to hear flattery pander –
May deepest sorrow such fools overthrow!
May God above there, in all His grandeur,
Keep up that aspect which all real men know.
That which long ages ago He predestined –
If you're a man, then show masculine power...
Physical weakness in women's invested,
But moral fibres brought out in full flower!
God grant to us in this world where we're living,
Such a real woman we may chance to meet,
One who does not cease from loving and giving,
When some misfortune throws us off our feet –
Maybe conceit, or some swaggering madness.
But if real gladness to us starts to haste,
Flashes away then like race-horse's happiness,
And like the Sun hides away in the waste,
Was there a hawk in the heavens grievous?
Then your lowering glances abate.
Do you wish to return to days previous?
But I'm afraid you're too late! Too late!

AITMATOV.   Postmodern interferences in human nature, with their insolent conviction that someone is able to make (create, stick together, assemble?) "A new man" from biological material – are actually nothing more than spiritual ignorance - bearing within themselves a violent intrusion into received wisdom. I am frozen by it. How can one entertain such nonsense? What happened in the consciousness of these "Frankenstein's" who think of turning reality into a fairy-tale? Moreover, what kind of tale? Even the Devil couldn't invent it!

But, such is the nature of the subject - a psychiatric clinic pretending to be a socialist heaven!

By the way, to realize these senseless ideals (which to their authors seem the most humane of humanities), the full equality between men and women suddenly became an urgent need. Albeit allied to an expedient -the lack of working hands. All explaining, possibly, why certain slogans started to say: "With an iron hand we shall drive mankind to happiness!" Afterwards, there resounded appeals for all women to master technology, to stand night and day behind lathes in gigantic factories and workshops, to work in the zone of eternal frost on an equal footing with men. Oddly, this call was heard, and accepted. Delighting, of course, newspapers which carried endless photos of strong women from the Komsomols, driving tractors.

Few positive things can be said about this clearly politicized "emancipation" apart from the fact it was a serious mistake! A move tantamount to being a crime against femininity. More than that - against the divine organization of our world. Indeed, when people take upon themselves the role of God monstrosities quickly arise. Maybe the most dangerous temptation being to inflict an imaginary utopia on youth - a mythological "foundation area", according to the expression used by A. Platonov, which must present itself as the form of "Heaven on earth".

SHAKHANOV.   Yes, the road to Hell is paved with good intentions! But it seems nobody at that time remembered Biblical wisdom, or took no account of it. Instead, throwing Holy Books down into the muck-heap of past history.

Should we, therefore, wonder why - at the beginning of the sixties - the Komsomols in the Shubartau District, in the Semipalatinsk Region of Kazakhstan, appealed to graduates in the Republic to work in cattle-breeding? In those days, I worked as an editor on a regional newspaper in Shimkent, and wrote an article on the graduates of one school who warmly supported this initiative.

Then, on my counter-initiative, a regional club for artistic young people was founded. This year, the famous writer Gabit Musrepov visited us. Together with the secretary of the Regional Komsomol Committee, Indeed, I went to welcome the writer, afterwards hearing Gabit was interested in local news. Delighted, the Secretary of the Regional Komsomol Committee (an energetic lad), boldly gave him his report:

"Two thousand graduates of the regional schools are ready to support our appeal for cattle-breeders. After their examinations, with their Komsomol passes, they will begin working in cattle-breeding. More than half of them, are women!"

Hearing this Gabit Musrepov frowned:

"The greatest misfortune of our society is loading onto women more than half of man's obligations!"

I was terribly surprised at such sharp criticism of a Party initiative. In those years nobody could even think of it. A brilliant victory on the part of Soviet ideology. Undoubtedly, in difficult times, it is easy to understand why women take on themselves unbearable burdens. Relatedly, I remember your story "Dzhamilya" - which Louis Aragon called the most beautiful love story in the world, wherein mention is made of women, as well as old men and young boys, working from dawn till dusk during the Great Patriotic War.

However, I digress. Why did Aragon describe it as a love poem? Because you showed it was love, above all, which ruled everything! Including death. Refusing to speak of submission to patriarchal-feudal laws "Dzhamilya" proclaims we must live according to the laws of a free and passionately-loving heart.

Unsurprisingly then, this novel evoked severe criticism from overly-jealous, dilapidated, false moralists, The type of men driving human feeling into a cage of blind orders, and thus killing them.

You, Chingiz, showed that toil alone could not make a man happy. Partially explaining why Dzhamilya awoke in millions of our contemporaries (irrespective of the nationality), a thirst for freedom in their hearts and minds. Certainly, it was not by chance that people took this statement as a protest against the power of a totalitarian society over women.

I am convinced that wherever people cease to accept and value tenderness and beauty, there begins the road to ignorance and vulgarity.

I remember, at the beginning of the fifties, one woman from our village - being already pregnant - went out seeking firewood in the field. What can be worse than sheer need in our perishable world? Anyway, having loaded a huge bundle of brushwood on her back, she began to go home. At this very moment, however, birth-pangs started. Soon afterwards, the birth itself. So, using a sharp stone, this woman cut the umbilical cord, wrapped her baby in the hem of her skirt, and returned to the village bearing the firewood. Furthermore, she did not think about resting when she got home, but began her usual domestic duties. Obviously, her husband, and some neighbours, were quite amazed when they unexpectedly heard the cry of a new-born baby in the corner. The woman thereupon calmed them down, simply saying:

"That is our baby. I gave birth to it when I went for firewood!"

AITMATOV.   Not in vain did Russian women, who hundreds of times experienced the joys of a wife's portion and the "gentlemanly" attitude of their husbands, sing sadly biting couplets like this:

> *"I am a horse, and I am a bull.*
> *I am a woman, with man's strength as full!"*

Here, alas, we strove, as "engineers of the human soul", to bring into our literature, (without feeling embarrassed and following the principle of socialist realism), additional developments in this new kind of woman. We required them to become Party directors, Party Secretaries, and so on. All showing a masculine greed for position, rough manners of acting, and insensitive ways of dealing with others. Thusly, communist "constructors" tried to level out the difference between men and women.

SHAKHANOV. Due to the present course of our conversation, I would like to read a ballad called "Night in La Vallette", from my archives; I wrote it about fifteen years ago, but it has not so far been published.

NIGHT IN LA VALLETTE

I

> *In the flash of an eye,*
> *And forgetting all sorrow,*
> *Maturity reaching,*
> *The beautiful Sandra,*
> *Whom people had named a bride for tomorrow,*
> *In her long black hair*

Wove some pink oleander.
A dish full of fruit ' neath the window
She placed.. .
The guide then answered the questions he faced:
"Oh, that's an old custom, through Malta wending,
It lives in the villages, never-ending.
The one who himself a suitor would call –
He must at a tournament conquer all.
And suitors, each against others strumming,
Must sing songs of praise for the beauty who's coming.
Whoever can praise her, and bring her delight,
To him then will Sandra belong, by right!
To him at whom her window she's smiling ...
O Hymen, rejoice! There's your wife, beguiling!
So, if you are wed, do not moan that your mate
Appears now and then to be stupid, irate!
Don't complain - what use if already married?
You're married for good. It were better you tarried.
Although one another you now come to hate,
You must go on so, to the grave, with your mate.
You must not dare of delight to dream so!
O hood-winked Hymen! O, blackest of woe!

II

We were introduced by Malta.
We were led to the sea by the Moon.
"Give me your answer, do not falter!"
But I got no answer so soon.
Little fires were blazing brightly,
La Vallette was entering night.
We were helped by that island rightly,
Overcame parting grief all right.
Sleepy shores the waves were licking,
Overcome at times by the heat ...
"Come to me, I am not tricking,
Open your heart up, sister sweet!"

"Elder brother", she answered humbly,
And meanwhile could scarcely breathe:
"I'm a sad vessel", she added numbly!"
"Very unhappy soul, please believe!"
Then I looked at her and wondered:
This is a vague, strange tale, I see.. .
"Brother, know, by black shades we're sundered.
They have plagued the life out of me!"
I stay silent - a misanthrope –
Waiting to hear what she says:
"My beloved decided to hop it –
That's why I'm in low spirits today!"
Then her look became wild and fearful,
So at her I could no more gaze.
There was no joking, she was tearful:
"Life, from now on, means vengeful ways.
Him I shall not forgive, to the finish,
He so deeply offended my love.
Cursed be all men, may their life diminish!
May they be drowned in their own blood!"
Now I am gazing in the distance –
There the round moon is a crimson shield.
Had I known, here in Malta for instance,
To what chances I'd have to yield!
Still, I must risk it. Gathering power,
I then turned out a word or two:
"Is it true that you loved for an hour
Him, whose love was dead for you?"
Then her anger again was firing,
And she fell silent ...
"It must be confessed –
She who loves cannot start desiring
Death for the one she worships best!
Here I speak, not to soften, nor harden –
Not for nought have I lived till grey?
I'm prepared for all men to beg pardon,
And forgiveness for them I'll pray.

I myself, am guilty, maybe,
But for that I'm not really to blame.
So, be patient, and tender,, lady,
Reviving his heart again!
One must not one's days start hating,
Changing light of day for night!"
But my sister, no longer waiting,
Hastened away and was lost from sight!
That was all.. No consolation
Could I bring her, in her dark hour.
Sailed over Malta, in vast formation,
Vaults of heaven, with light a-flower.
By the sea-side, until the dawning,
Bitterly then I pondered thus:
"Is it so, that Nature, fawning,
Also suffers, just like us?"

III

Night, with blossom of oleander,
Poured itself over heaven's vault.
Oh, my lovely, most beautiful Sandra,
Does misfortune her now assault ?
... In dark dreams I see that island,
With its ever-allowable waves.
Ah, it's hard, when all is silent,
To confess our guilt in our graves!
I go out on the sea-shore lonely,
Just to get a breath of fresh air.
Life is finding and losing only.
Search eternal, on roadways bare.

AITMATOV.   *Nobody ever wishes evil to the one whom he really and truly loves. Therein lies the difference between love, and capricious passion. A loving heart is self-sacrificing. It is ready itself to die, to save the chosen one. Your character is self-loving, an egoistic being, there are multitudes of them. Until recently, certain of our contemporary women held male communists* *close to them by their tricks and enticements - thus poisoned their own lives. Moreover, men who decided on a divorce in such cases, awaited a judgement from the local Party Committee: after which he had to pass the seven circles of hell, in the bureaux of the Regional Committee - and later in the Moscow Committee. Their choices were minimal: either live together until the grave leading a cat and dog's life or just put your Party card on the table and receive the label of a criminal. Saying farewell to your employment in the process.*

Such was the attitude of the Party and the State to the rights of a man in the most "humane" society.

So women should be grateful to the Party for compelling their errant husbands to live under one roof with them, silently despising or hating them.

SHAKHANOV.   The problem of masculine women and feminine men has had a bad effect on the upbringing of youth.

When I studied at school, there were mostly male teachers. Furthermore, their role in school life was hard to over-estimate. Several were a really good example for us, and an ideal to follow.

AITMATOV.   In the last fifteen to twenty years of Soviet power, higher education saw the number of women teachers increase. Even today, rising generations receive a predominantly feminized type of learning, whether in kindergarten, primary school, or University. Never feeling a masculine influence, a child, or youth, imitates the attitudes of their women instructors. The lowering of the number of men who are truly manly and ready to die - rather than not to keeping their word when given, forms a great problem for our generation.

It turns out, therefore, we have a generation growing up with a pampered understanding of both men and women.

Why are men so ashamed to become teachers? The answer is quite clear - they have low prestige and a low salary. So their self-esteem suffers. In Germany or France, or for that matter in most western lands, three careers are included amongst highly ranking professions: teachers, doctors and soldiers. In Great Britain, for example, in order to become a teacher in a kindergarten, one has to pass a strict examination. This is only right – parents, after all, do not wish their children to be taught by inferior or indifferent teachers, without sufficient training, or by someone who has taken up teaching because they cannot find any other work.

Here in the East, we used to esteem teachers as responsible and important people, but is it so today?

In this life, feminine tenderness –which is celebrated in the songs of Homer, and dramatized in tales by Shakespeare - must remain the moral and spiritual support of society. No matter what kind of changes it may undergo.

SHAKHANOV. *I*t seems it is time to carry this conversation to ourselves. Nothing human is alien to us. If, for instance, one bold lad chases after ten girls at the same time, nobody will pay any special attention. Yet, every step taken by a well-known writer, such as Chingiz Aitmatov, is open to all.

AITMATOV. Everyone meets their own fate - an endless and complex secret. On one's path through life everyone meets with men or women, predestinated for them by fate. Having met, they begin their life together in a search of happiness. I am no exception to that rule. In my life, there have been unforgettable hours - still calling forth heart stopping feelings. I have nothing to conceal. In my student days, at parties, I got to know many girls. All leading to sleepless nights, suffering and torment, forced confessions and swollen letters. Atop this, there have been innumerable scarves and autographed kerchiefs (you remember, there was a fashion for that) sent to me. Judging by your smile you also received them. But these feelings manifest quickly and fade away fast. They leave no real traces on life. Later on, unforgettable encounters with real love captivated me! We did not seek them out. Everything took place by itself. Such unexpected meetings became for me the dearest of the dear - the gift of fate, my destiny. A woman who illuminated my life in such a manner (a star of Kirghizian arts), was the famous ballerina Byubyusara Beishenaliyeva. Her dear image still appears in my dreams, disturbs and agitates my soul, and brings the past to life again.

At the end of the fifties I graduated from the Gorky Literary Institute in Moscow. My works began to be published in the central press, and people started to speak about me. Around the same time, a group formed to aid young Kirghizian lads serving in the Baltic Fleet. Hence, I was invited by the first secretary of the Frunze city Party committee, Turdakun Usubaliyev, to fly to Leningrad.

Coincidentally, as it seemed a troupe from the Kirghizian Opera was performing in Leningrad, at the studio of "Lenfilm", where they were shooting excerpts of the ballet film "Cholpon". Interweaving events bringing the female lead - Byubyusara Beishenaliyeva, into my life through an act of fate.

When I arrived with two or three sailors on a cutter to the cruiser "Aurora", there, on the deck, our delegation stood waiting. Among its members was the bright-faced, shiny-eyed, Byubyusara. Her shapely body and dark hair lightly caressed by the sea-breeze. With a smile she waved her hand to us. Earlier we had heard about each other, but had never expected to meet. Anyway, we soon got talking, and felt a wonderful mutuality. I expect you would not believe me if I tell we both blazed like a flame? Indeed, we ourselves were surprised - it seemed we had known each other since the dawn of time, although in fact we had never previously met.

Those around us, the singing of birds, the rustling of leaves, the swish of the waves, all seemed different somehow. We scarcely recognized the world. It was brighter, more lovely!

After this, we spent happy hours in endless conversation, as we wended our way along the shores of the Neva together - during the so called "Leningrad white nights". All previous existence seemed to disappear into a secondary plane. Only she and I were real. I and she ...

A few days passed, and our delegation went back again to Kirghizia. How I suffered, not wishing to leave half my heart on the Neva's shore! I went through sheer torture, not finding the strength to stand. Finally, stressing that I needed to spend a few extra days in Leningrad before travelling back to Moscow, I remained there. Eventually, when I left for Moscow, I found Byubyusara following after me: hot on my heels. One day and night we spent together in the hotel "Moscow". They were quite unforgettable hours of close spiritual communication. We often said goodbye, but simply could not part! Unsurprisingly, I finally accompanied Byubyusara all the way to Leningrad (by train) to her home. Then, when I was ready to leave again, she once more wanted to come with me. Only with great difficulty did I persuade her against this decision.

From that time, right up until her death - for the duration of fourteen years - the fire for her in my heart was extinguished.

Of course, all through those years, idle gossip and rumours went round, making life very difficult for us.

Getting her education in Leningrad, Byubyusara understood the problems of theatre, cinema, and literature. Her assessment of art was deep and original. It is hard, therefore, to say just how far this extremely talented, and devastatingly beautiful woman, influenced my life and work.

Someone may raise the question - well, why didn't those two join their fates in marriage? To my recollection, when I asked Byubyusara the very same question, she immediately turned our conversation in the opposite direction, saying I should wait awhile and not to be in a hurry. Confusingly, we later received new flats in a block on the Dzerzhinsky Boulevard. Something, however, had changed. When we met together again, Byubyusara said with a sad smile:

"Achinov" (she made up that name out of the initial letters of my personal and family names) "I understand what you want to say. Some people asserting those who really love each other should marry"- she became silent for a while - then added. "Maybe it cannot be so. Family life and everyday affairs can kill intense feelings. Why should we risk our love, and tie ourselves up like that?"

Only later did I understood Byubyusara's refusal was an attempt to protect me (not thinking of herself) from cruel reprisals by my Party "comrades", and from scandal amongst my literary "friends". Do you remember what a divorce meant in those days? Was I right to accept her sacrifice? That question will surely torment me all the days of my life!

SHAKHANOV. Yes, official attitudes to divorce was repugnant in those days! It was the same among Kazakhs too. One writer, Gabit Musrepov, as well as the famous hero-writer, Bauirzhan Momishuli, and the well-known singer Yermek Serkebayev suffered long term ostracism, had articles written about them in the papers, and found it difficult to remarry.

AITMATOV. Whatever you say, Byubyusara sacrificed her own happiness in order for my star to shine. Only a great personality could unite two fundamentally opposed things and deny a loved one for his own sake.

Once Byubyusara and I, returning from Moscow to Frunze on the express train, shared a comfortable compartment for two passengers. Nobody could bother us by telephone, or poked their noses through the doorway. For three days and nights we lived an endless fairy-tale. Time, it seemed, just disappeared. We found ourselves in another dimension. Our conversation explored everything, our most sacred thoughts: things never before shared with anyone. We discussed literature and art - making me understand that there was no higher happiness than to find a friend near to you in thought, spirit, and character.

"There is a day which one would not exchange for a century! Today is this day - the happiest one in my life!"

Could I ever forget those agitated and excited words of Byubyusara? The train ran smoothly on, like a trained race-horse. At times we cast a look outside the window, as if bewitched. - the surrounding scenery also enchanting us. Endless were the green plains of Russia. Boundless were the steppes of Kazakhstan. When the express stopped in Aral, we stepped outside for a breath of air. Back then, the waves of the Aral Sea came right up to the town. Playful spume glittered and gleamed in the sunshine. We passed Kzil-Orda, Aris, Chimkent and Tyulkubas ...

Do you remember how we two once went in your car from Tashkent to Bishkek? The red sun sank below the horizon, slowly turning every inch of sky into a canvas streaked with rosy colours. It was an exciting moment. As I recall, near Tyulkubas, the railway line makes a big curve, circling round a hill. In spring and summer, this place - wholly buried in flowers - is quite changed! I asked you to stop and got out of the car. Oh, what a miracle! Allowing me to think of twenty five year previously, when, along the hill in the direction of Almaty there moved that train. My heart trembled as I recalled how Byubyusara was delighted at these sights. I got excited too. How many memories filled and flooded my mind! How many places she and I visited! Just take Frunze! Passing some houses and crossroads, I recollected how we laughed, how glad, and sad we were!

You and I, dear Mukhtar, were, not so long ago, at the Kirghizian State Opera and Ballet - do you remember? I did not listen to what was going on around me, but was occupied with my own thoughts. The inimitable talent of Byubyusara bloomed upon the stage there. Before my meditative eyes these pictures were projected. I blinked, and saw her again as the White Swan. This is the role I always see her playing: like a memorial statue to her eternally young soul!

From one of her tours she returned unwell. The diagnosis was bad - a dangerous swelling in her breast. They took her to hospital in Kuntsevo, where she suffered one and a half years. It is still hard for me to speak of this. In any case, visitors could only enter the hospital with a special pass. In one of the wards, with the same ailment, lay Olga Nikolayevna Androvskaya - People's Artist of the Soviet Union. Additionally, there lay Aleksander Trifonovich Tvardovsky, who was suffering from a fatal disease. He was one of the first to praise me for my work as a writer, publishing my early novels in his journal "The New World". Thus, every time I went to see Byubyusara at the hospital, I also made a call on him. In spite of strenuous efforts by the doctors, he nevertheless passed away.

Byubyusara equally, with each passing day, began to fade away. She no longer had the physical strength to raise herself in bed, and lost her natural colour. The light from her caressing eyes growing weaker and weaker. Obviously, when I knew her end was near, the ground dropped away from beneath my feet.

During her last few days, they moved her to Frunze. As for me, I knew no rest. I could not work anymore. Again and again I walked round the hospital, alone and hopeless. But, I had to face the fact she was dying. Byubyusara smiled weakly each time I appeared before her - trying somehow to cheer me up. She was my guardian angel. Nonetheless, on the 11th May, 1973, my beloved Byubyusara left this world behind her.

SHAKHANOV. Witnesses say at the funeral reception you wept, and cried out in your sorrow. One of the leaders of the Republic lost all patience, and ordered "Get him out of here!"

It was strange, even impossible, for those men in authority to watch human sorrow!

They wouldn't have shed a tear, I suppose, even at the funeral of their own wives, in case they were accused of "weakness" and censored.

Yet your feelings were strong. How could they be otherwise? However, you were starting to be known as a writer, occupying a high position in communist social affairs, so you were expected to stem your tears in front of such people - even when mourning the death of a beloved woman!

I remember how, when speaking with one of the greatest Kirghizian poets, Suyumbai Eraliyev, he spoke about this: "Byubyusara was the most wonderful person, in her there were woven beauty of body, and strength of mind, as well as all the characteristics of a Kirghizian girl. In my time, I like all other poets, dedicated verses to her. The unfortunate end she met shook all the Kirghizian people, and especially those who valued her talent. I was told many times that her union with you was a great pure love. At the burial of Byubyusara, you was dressed in black, and went with lowered eyes, not hiding tears. Everywhere one heard murmurs: He should be ashamed of himself, as a married man, and the father of a family! I stood and thought with pride in you both. "How great is Chingiz in literature, and how great also in sincere standing, as he sees his beloved woman off on her last journey to the grave!"

AITMATOV.   I thank you, dear friend, for those kind words. How could people know, that in losing Byubyusara, I additionally lost myself?

SHAKHANOV.   When they celebrated the thousandth anniversary of "Manas" in the centre of Bishkek, there was ceremoniously uncovered a monument - "The eagle" - the work of Turgenbai Sadikov. That memorial took the form of an eagle with the wings spread wide. It bore in them many Kirghizian sons and daughters to the heights of glory. On one side of the memorial you stand in deep meditation. On the other the inimitable Byubyusara stands, as a white swan, majestically flying in the skies of Kirghizian ballet art. Whether that happened by chance, or whether it was the fantasy of the sculptor, who knows. Either way, it represented a pair of humans who were not united in earthly life, but are joined in Eternity.

At the unveiling of that memorial - which became a great event in the cultural life of the Republic - I saw you gazing on her with love and pride.

AITMATOV. Soon after Byubyusara's death, I was invited to Italy. At night, on the steamer, we sailed to Sicily. However, the open sea and bright night seemed distant. The light cool breeze somehow foreign. Astoundingly, as the multi-coloured lights of a great city blinked behind us, I heard a piece of music which Byubyusara and I both loved to listen to. Those around me on the deck began to dance, but I stood on one side, leaning on a railing, not able to hold back my tears - and not trying to. Sea, night, stars, moon, a deserted island, but all accompanied by a feeling of complete isolation.

Even now, when I hear this music, I remember Byubyusara, and become agitated again. That said, I think words will not be enough to explain such things to you. Let me try a scenario instead. In the novel "Tavro of Kassandra" there is an episode when my hero (as a member of a delegation) is sailing to Japan on a steamer. It is the same picture, the exact emotions caused by the melody. A picture, seen in the ocean and engraved on my mind by a marine trip to Italy. This combination of events becoming a literary symbol of my yearning for her.

SHAKHANOV. In the middle of the seventies we met in Moscow, and you invited me to your hotel room. There you introduced me to your wife, Mariam, sitting beside you. Inwardly I was very happy that fate had presented you with such a woman, with her pleasant features and her pure soul. She not only respected your work deeply, but had a good influence on the production of new projects. As such, she is a woman of judgement, of high culture, and full of talent. As I recall, she wrote a film script about mindless zombies based on your novel "The day lasts longer than an age". The Turkmenian Film Studio shot the film, and so it was seen on the silver screen. All demonstrating that there is great happiness when one has beside oneself someone who understands ones spiritual world - as a comrade and a thinker.

AITMATOV. After Byubyusara's death, I could not refill the emptiness in my soul.

You see, my dear Mukhtar, fate brought love into my life: at first with hope, then with absence and torment. In those latter, very difficult, times it happened that I met Mariam. Thankfully, with the passing of the years, my torment subsided and life grew more normal. Nowadays, Mariam and I have two hopes, two supports - our daughter Shirin, and our son Eldar. Indeed, my wife and I dream that whatever professions they choose, they will grow up to be worthy and honest people.

SHAKHANOV.   I am certain this it will be the case. Just recently your young daughter made me very happy. It was when we accompanied you and your family to the airport in Alma-Ata, on your way to Brussels. Interestingly, Shirin whispered something softly in my ear, so you would not hear it.

"Uncle Mukhtar, papa is suffering from sugar diabetes. If he comes to you as a guest, you must watch he won't eat too many sweet things. I beg you, keep an eye on him!"

AITMATOV.   You and I spent a good deal of time together then. Therefore she asked you to look after her father, you see.

SHAKHANOV.   The journalist Zhanibek Zhanizak collected material on his Dictaphone regarding women in your life, inquiring into whom you had met and made friends with. He even wrote a short book entitled "Aitmatov's women" - and got it published. I have seen it lying around on shelves in bookshops across various districts.

AITMATOV.   To glance into a soul completely strange to you, is like peeping through a key-hole - a very low occupation indeed. If someone likes doing that, well, let him. Who can control the pen-pusher whose pen flies as lightly and swiftly as borzoi hunting dogs?

Kerez was my first wife. From student days together, she and I progressed to difficult, but nonetheless attractive days. She had lived with my deceased mother Nagima, side by side (like a real daughter), for several years. Kerez bore me two sons - Sanzhar and Askar. God be praised, both of them are now mature men with their own view of the world, Moreover, they are already working.

As far as Tattibubi Tursunbayeva is concerned, in her day she held an honourable place in my life. Also, she was an extraordinary personality: born to enrich the Kirghizian theatrical arts.

At different twists and turns of fate other women were found in my life, about whom, God be thanked, no idle scribbler has written! Finally, I must admit I am a thousand-fold blessed by destiny, since it introduced me to women who served Muses. Allowing me to live starry hours in creative bliss.

SHAKHANOV.   In those years of living in Kirghizia, as a representative of the association "Rukhaniyat", a party was arranged for me wherein I could recite my work as a poet. An evening scheduled to take place in the grand hall of the Toktogul Philharmonic Society. Towards its end, a young woman came tripping up to me, and slightly nervously began to speak:

"Mukhtar, my dear, you scarcely know me. I am Kerez, the first wife of your friend Chingiz ..." she trailed off confused.

I too was a little upset, because I had never previously met her and felt forced to make pleasantries about her health, and everyday affairs ...

"Chingiz did much to strengthen bonds between the Kirghizians and the Kazakhs. We are glad you too tread this same path. Your Chingiz is the type of person born once a century. The years I spent with him were the best in my life" so she told me, agitatedly.

AITMATOV. "Thank you, Mukhtar. To liven up our converse a little, recite, please, your ballad wherein you say three years spent with a loved one is worth more than three millennia without. Anyone who reads, or hears, these verses is compelled to start thinking deeply.

SHAKHANOV.   The ballad starts off "You said that life was very short" but it is called "Legend about long life". This is how it goes:

LEGEND ABOUT LONG LIFE

You have said life is short enough,
Like the flight of a blinded moth.
There was a time when on one's palm

Centuries dreamed, without alarm.
People lived for three thousand years,
Knew no passion, no pain, no fears.
Though they blossomed out very slow,
Later slowly they lost their glow,
And fell into a happy dream-sleep ...
Young ones, who knew not seven-hundred years,
 Could not marry, despite their tears.
 Full of prosperity people were found,
But one day a rumour ran round,
Just like flames which run through dry grass:
Not having reached two hundred years,
Boy and girl had.. . Oh, my poor ears!
That young lad to his father said:
"Father. I shall soon be wed!"
But his father to him replied:
"You will shame us, break laws beside.
Then I shall curse you!" thus said he.
"Why in such a haste must you be?
Take a look at your sister!" he exclaimed,
"She's not married - a thousand years old!
May you rot, and decayed dust taste –
No more words on you shall I waste!
Wait another five-hundred years –
Then get married, despite all your fears,
Take twenty wives!"- my tale runs so.
"No, dear father!" the son said, "no, no!"
Though you kill me, I won't do so,
Though I die, pardon me", said he,
"But a husband I now must be!"
Father stood silent, like a stone.
One day silent, two days alone.
But those lovers an oath then swore:
"Even death will part us no more!"
 Off they ran then, hand in hand,
To snowy mountains, a distant land.
There they caught them, and set them apart

For a hundred years at the start.
Still to God they prayed:
"Understand".....
People can't live in such a land –
One hundred years –
And not know love?
Where's the sense in it, God above?
Give us steppeland, and let us fly!
Give us three days - and then let us die!
But let us blaze with living love,
Mid loveless people - let us live!"
Heavy was God's hand, you see ...
He gave Time such a blow - one, two, three –
Time was compressed to a thirtieth part,
* Life was torn to the very heart...*
Now a century one moment stays.
Who said life is short anyways?..

AITMATOV.   *But did the poet who wrote those verses climb up to the height of love's Everest?*

SHAKHANOV.   *In my early youth something happened, that not for one single day has passed from my memory, and every night I dreamt of it again .....*

AITMATOV.   *I have heard about your life story here and there, but mainly from your colleagues. Once or twice I thought I would ask you to tell me personally ... Yes, now the time has come. We, as a pair of fellow-thinkers shall exchange thoughts on things nearest and dearest to our souls, freely and frankly.*

If you can, be quite open, I shall try not to break the thread of your innermost secret reminiscences.

SHAKHANOV.   *At that time we youths had high ideas and ideals. My friend Asan, and I, agreed to help at least one person every day, doing some little good deed. Inspired by this thought, we roamed round (in our spare time) and looked for people in Shimkent who needed aid. Of course, there* *were* many people on the streets, each one hurrying about his business. Not every day, however, dies one meet old people who need helping across the road, or find someone who needs their baggage carried. But as they say: "An agreement is worth more than gold!" So every day we went to the bazaar, where there were many old people. How glad, and how thankful they were, when we offered to help them. Unsurprisingly, rumours went round that we earned a rouble or two as porters! Hence, we had to stop it!

Those trips to the bazaar, along with our efforts to help people who needed assistance, led me into the wonderful world of poetry. By the way, the newspaper "Lenin's Way" that published your novel "Dzhamilya" devoted almost a whole column to a selection of my poems. Back then, I was only sixteen, and worked as a coupler for a tractor driver - like your hero "Kemel" in the story "The camel's eye". They also published my photo in an old greasy cap, along with a warm article about my work - by the up-and- coming young journalist Minbay Ilesov. It was hard to imagine how glad that sun-tanned and ragged young tractor-coupler Shakhanov was, and how proud he was of his picture in the paper. After that I began to storm newspapers and journals with my immature verses, and they began to publish them.

One fine day I was invited to take part in a poetry recital in the Shimkent Pedagogical Institute. There I met many other young poets, just beginning to write verses. We went up onto the stage one by one, and read our poems. I read a few, and returned again to my place - and there she was, waiting for me. A beautiful young girl with lovely dimples on her cheeks, looking like a young deer. Nervously, she held out her note-book, and asked for my autograph. Her eyes were gleaming like blackcurrants, while ger smoothly-combed black hair, neatly tied in a knot on the nape of her slender neck, looked altogether lovely. Her note-book was new and clean, with its shiny cover. I opened it, and saw my photograph there, cut out of the newspaper. Beside it there were my verses, neatly glued into the place, and all outlined in coloured-pencils! From the sheer surprise of this all, I felt awkward. I couldn't even utter a word!

She, I was told, was Kulyanda. I wrote something, rather clumsily, and signed my name. This was my first public signature!

In that way, by chance, I met Kulyanda. All marking an evening which introduced pure love to me. From her lips I first heard my poems recited, although I didn't think of becoming a real poet in those days.

Yet, Kulyanda often assured me: "You will be a great poet!" Those words of hers were an elixir for my heart, and gave me confidence.

Shimkent back then was not like it is today. In the western part of the town's outskirts there was a large forest, bushes sprouting all round. Not far from this area of woodland, Kulyanda lived in a five-storey block of flats, with her elder brother's family. When studies were over at the Institute, I accompanied her home.

We waited patiently for Saturdays and Sundays. Every weekend, we took a bus out of town away from the hustle and bustle, and used to walk back home.

Kulyanda knew all about wild grasses and herbs, and their healing qualities. For the first time I heard of the wonderful effect of curative herbs, such as mint-leaves, and St John's wort. In her books and notes (pressed among the leaves), one could always find dried herbs - which had not lost their fragrance.

Once, by the side of the road we saw a dead skylark. "Ah! What a pity" she quietly whispered to me. "Why did he die, poor thing? Did a snake hypnotize it, or have some boys chased it? Well, we'll have to bury it!"

I settled down beside her, and with a broken branch lying nearby, I was able to make a hole. Solemnly, we laid the dead lark in it. In those young days we did not think of things dying at any moment. We did not know that butterflies last only six days!

For my part, I had grown up in a village, in nature's embrace, and saw various birds and beasts around me. I wandered in the dense grass, up to my waist, and frequently lay down and slept there. Watching the play of the flying clouds. However, I had not heard of, or learned so much about nature as Kulyanda. Thanks to her I began to look at the world around me with other eyes.

She appreciated very much my idea of doing at least one good deed every day. "Great deeds grow from little ones" she, thoughtfully murmured once. If people stop doing good, stop making each other good, the world will be darker and colder.

Kulyanda could call up many examples of this from literature and from the real lives of great people. We often thought about the story of

Don Quixote and Sancho Panza. Once she repeated a phrase (I can't remember whose it was) but it had wings and flew like this:

"A man who loses all shame can no longer be called a man!" Then she added: "Yes, losing all shame, we lose everything. It is one of the greatest problems of our society ... Many of our girls wear miniskirts, baring their thighs high above the knees. Yet, what can be more frightening than greedy, groping eyes? How can we stop such things?"

Those words of Kulyanda I remember till today! Curiously, she never called me by my personal name, but just "you" each time. On my request she should use my name, a nick-name, or even "dear" she replied: "My granny till this day calls old grandad "you". But the town-folk use nick-names and diminutive ones, thereby breaking old traditions down!"

I was very touched by her modesty, and was delighted with her general attitude towards people and life. How could I know those happy days would fly away so quickly, like a dream?

Tulegen Aibergenov, was an outstanding Kazakh poet, one of those who first gave the hand of friendship to me: our meeting was a rare gift for me.

He passed away at the early age of twenty nine. All the same, he managed to bring into our poetry a new breeze. He was five years my senior. After publication in the newspaper of my first poems, he sought me out, and tried to make my acquaintance. Curly-headed, with a high brow, and open look, he at once began to please me.

"Have you got a girl, then?" he asked on one occasion.

I told him about Kulyanda.

"Introduce me to her, sometime!" he requested politely.

"Very well. The day after tomorrow, July 2nd, is my birthday. I shall invite her along with you, and introduce you. Otherwise she will be too shy, and will not come to meet a strange man.

"Agreed! I was going away tomorrow, but now I'll stay for your birthday and hope to make her acquaintance without scaring her!"

Two days later we three all met, and left town together. Out in the fresh air, we opened some old newspapers, and spread them on the grass. Afterwards, I took special provisions from my bag, cooked by my mother for the occasion, and also I produced lemonade and beer bottles. Tulegen congratulated me on my birthday, and gave me two books - as I remember, one was "Birds of Zailisk Alatau" by Kovshar and the other "Tortoises".

I thanked him, and jokingly said:

"Tulegen, haven't you got me mixed up with one of your veterinary students, by chance?

"But why not?" he replied, "To be a real poet one must know a great deal of the world around us, otherwise you will win no success or respect!"

Kulyanda supported his point of view in this matter:

"I equally want to present you with a book. Its author is the famous Kirghizian writer, Chingiz Aitmatov.

He was born in the village of Sheker, and graduated from the Zhambil Agricultural Technikum." She handed me a weighty volume, in Russian, entitled "Stories of the mountains and steppelands" which I was very pleased to receive.

So you see, I first got acquainted with you through Kulyanda at a time when my feelings first awoke! On that day much poetry was heard. Then Tulegen dedicated a poem of eight lines to Kulyanda, and wrote it in her red exercise book ... I also wrote her eight lines, as follows:

"In your eyes I saw happiness, with its moistened light.
But only for us two was that secret bright.
My song, like a moment of gladness, grew suddenly sweet,
When fate predestined that we - a young pair - should meet!
One thing though, I fear - the cruel thought try to hide –
As fate once united us, so can it also divide.
Time's wind may try to wipe out our meeting's trace
But powerless now are harsh years to bring us disgrace!"

That evening we accompanied Tulegen to the Chimkent Bus-Station. Once there, he took me to one side and whispered in my ear: "I congratulate you! You have captured an extraordinary bird. Don't let her go! Such a girl could be a real helpmate in the life of a great poet!"

So we were left with Mama alone. She often fell sick in those years and we hoped that nothing serious would happen. Personally, I began to think more often about getting married, the more so since Kulyanda was near me.

One day she asked me out straight: "Do you believe in dreams?"

"No!" I replied. She waited some time before responding:

"Probably we cannot remain together for long" she added with a drooping head. "You said the truth in your poem –

> *"One thing though, I fear - the cruel thought try to hide –*
> *As fate once united us, so can it-also divide!"*

Later, when Kulyanda's life ended, so tragically broken off, I accused myself - and those accursed lines - written in her note-book. Afterwards reading that Boris Pasternak once warned Yevtushenko: "Don't foretell anything in verses about your possible tragic end. The power of words can, without your notice, take effect on you, and lead you to what you have foretold".

But I digress. Kulyanda was going with her girl-friend to visit her parents one weekend. They got seats on the Moscow - Alma-Ata train. At that time I was in Alma-Ata on business connected with the publishing of one of my books. The train which (previously) always stopped for one or two minutes at the Tyulkubas halt, did not do so on that day. The conductor, let him be accursed, forgot to warn the passengers about this change in schedule. The girls, therefore, were so agitated when the train did not stop, they threw their bags out of the door, and tried to jump out. Her friend fell, and broke her leg, and she, Kulyanda, dropped onto the rails, beneath the wheels ...

That unexpected tragedy was a bitter blow for me, and nearly broke my heart. In early spring, when the snow-drops are appearing, and in autumn when the geese and cranes - with throaty cries - quit their native land, I feel an inexplicable grief. The sight of Shimkent, where Kulyanda and I used to roam together on short, sleepless nights, still scorches my breast. In such minutes I do not wish to see or hear anything. The mist hangs around ... For two years I could not find myself again.

One day, early in the morning, I got on a bus and set off to the place where Kulyanda was buried. It was a lovely spring morning. The skylarks were singing, like silvery mountain streams. Having collected some wild flowers on my way, the kind which Kulyanda specially loved, I came to her grave, on the outskirts of the village. Long-restrained feelings suddenly burst forth, and I found myself in tears. Weeping with bitter sobs, as though left entirely alone in a huge, bare world. I lay on the green grass for several hours - breathing in the fragrance of the bitter wormwood, and other herbs about me. After mid-day, an elderly shepherd with his herd nearby, came up and gave me some tea from his flask, but asked me nothing. Obviously guessing all, looking in my eyes, swollen with tears. I didn't say a word, but nodded my head as a sign of thanks to him for his tea, and his silence. He left me soon after having murmured a prayer for the souls of the dead.

So short was the life of that girl who left an indelible mark on my fate, a girl with the soul of an angel, and one who valued you, my dear Chingiz, above all other writers.

AITMATOV.   You have moved me deeply…

SHAKHANOV.   In my life there was one other woman, about whom only two or three of my closest friends know. I myself never even met her in person, though from the beginning of the seventies I regularly got letters from her. She knew all my poems from newspapers and periodicals, and far earlier than others rejoiced at my success. Indeed, she was the first person to help, if I stumbled. In one of her letters she said: "Most likely you would like to know my name, and get acquainted with me, but I have decided to be your friend at a distance!"

All I know of her is her handwriting. Once at the Palace of Sport in Alma-Ata, holding five thousand spectators, a party for my poetry was organized. It lasted three and a half hours. It was shown on TV several times. Among other poems, I read these lines:

> "*Where there are dreams, the flower of manliness blooms.*
> *The flame of Love in my breast my heart consumes.*
> *There is no love without torment, nor bitter woe.*
> *Without them love is empty, its song can't flow.*
> *But he who groans "There's no love!" - don't believe in him —*
> *In the light of day he's sunk in darkness grim!*
> *And don't believe him who thinks that if he's wed,*
> *He'll be the possessor of truest love instead!*"

Afterwards, the T.V. producer showed me a close-up shot of a very lovely young woman, with eyes full of tears. The moment I saw that face I thought this is her! The one who writes me so many nice letters! Maybe I was mistaken. Men are always looking for lovely women!

Perhaps she was an unfortunate woman, suffering incurable sickness - who knows? However, I am still endlessly grateful to this woman – still an unknown person: my un-met friend. In one outstanding letter she even wrote: "When you are sixty, surrounded by friends at your jubilee, this will be the time when I shall come with a bunch of flowers, and tell you that it is me who for many years has been sending all those letters!" All making me think and wonder: "When I am sixty shall I really see this woman, so near to me, at last?"

In another letter she said: "The strength of nightingales lies in their song, the strength of falcons lies in their wings, and claws. Your calling is to write poetry. Why do you waste your strength on unnecessary activities and cares? They are like snowmen and snow-houses which children build in the winter - today they stand, but on the morrow they fade away." With serious concern for me she used to write, and criticise the amount of time I spent on social and political activities, apart from other everyday duties.

AITMATOV. It is a remarkable thing that among a multitude of voices crying: "You must belong to me alone" there is heard one which is concerned with your fate, and speaks with sincere and selfless concern for you.

SHAKHANOV. In the first years after Kulyanda's death I lost all interest in women. By day and by night, only her image shone in my dreams, and softly whispered into my ears. Her smile, her gentle soft laughter never failed nor faded. But one can't wed a dream, and in time, even the deepest wounds heal over. Thus, I began to look for somebody like her, both in body and soul. Maybe those dreams were the cause of unhappiness in my later life.

I only know one thing, whether that's good or bad - in the moment of deepest need and distress, I often sought support in a woman rather than a man. Not always were these expectations justified, I now honestly admit. Before I met Kanshaim, a woman of exceptional purity, whose word and action always coincided, there were others, such as Kizilkul and Rosalinda in my life - who left me many pleasant memories. Although, even they were not the only ones. Several others, whose concern for me was real, and who sympathised with my hopes, tried to take me under their sheltering wings, and refresh my soul with the elixir of really sincere tenderness. In the most difficult years of my life, they were a true source of support.

I frequently hear words such as these spoken of me: "How is it that he who sings so beautifully of love in his poems, mistakes the way himself? I, of course, am not "pure water, whiter than milk" though I know those women who knew me cannot accuse me, or reproach me, with a lack of generosity and justice.

Since childhood I have been accustomed not to return evil for evil. Spite, whether justified or not, once it settles in your soul, kills all other feelings - except revenge. No matter how hard it was, I tried not to give way to vengeful feelings, because I knew I could lose more - I could lose the purity of my poetic conscience.

To accept a woman as the object of one's delight and to discover qualities of the highest order, such as goodness, nobility of soul, and faithfulness - this is my conception of a relationship which will last over a long period of years. My own fate, my happiness and satisfaction, is tied up with that point of view. I shall always treat everyone, who suits my strict taste in moments of joy and sadness, with great respect. I shall always treat them with thankfulness, until my last moments on this earth.

AITMATOV.   You, in many things, are a man of hard fortunes, like me. But notwithstanding all this, I say thank you to the past - and to all it has brought me: good or bad. Let's hope both you and I will still have a fruitful future before us. Your wife Kanshaim is a woman of silken character, and respects our customs and ways. She loves and respects you. There is nothing artificial in her, she is natural. Even to you, as our forebears did, she still says "you", with utmost simplicity.

When the festival of the thousandth anniversary of "Manas" was about to take place, a daughter was born to you both. We, my wife Mariam and I, became her god-parents, I myself named the little lassie with the same name as the bride of the great Manas - Aichurek, so that she may know happiness in life, which none can dim, nor take!

SHAKHANOV.   I thank you, my dear Chingiz! Now, if you agree, let us get back to the secrets of love between men and women!

In the Kazakh town of Turkestan, which in the fourteenth century was counted a a pearl of Central Asia, a second Mecca, there stands a wonderful old piece of architecture -the mausoleum of Khodzha Akhmed Yasavi. That palace was built on the order from a great military leader of those days, Amir Temur, This majestic and noble home still reflects the light of the sun and moon in its blue cupolas. Yet, one uncompleted architectural configuration strikes ones eye. An insufficiency in architecture forming the basis of an old legend about unrequited love - that I once put into verse.

Amir Temur gave orders to gather the best architects from the four corners of the earth, along with the best building craftsmen, to erect a mausoleum in honour of Khodzha Akhmed Yasavi. Now, the leader of the sculpting and engraving section of workers was a bold young man - who had no equal anywhere in his mastery of clay-moulding. Furthermore, he was a handsome fellow to look at, with a fine, healthy body. Another gift he had from God was a wonderfully musical and harmonious voice.

Every evening, when the sun had run its day, and the architects and other masters had finished their work, and rested a little, they gathered by the half-built walls of the tomb, and began to sing. Then his voice rang out, and re-echoed across the silent steppe, recalling for other workers from foreign parts their own homeland, along with things near and dear to them.

Every time when his song began to ring around the camp, as well as above the silken doors of Temur's personal yurta, there would flutter a beautiful maiden named Marzia: the sister-in-law of Temur. For a long time she stood motionless and listened to the wonderful sound of his voice.

In order to point out the Amir's evaluation of the masters' work, Marzia herself brought the workers water to drink every noon. In time, the young master and Marzia (hiding her face behind a veil), fell in love. Once he could restrain himself no longer, and flicked back the fine veil from her brow. To chance witnesses of this, it seemed as if the light of day faded in the presence of such blazing beauty. Others stood aghast at the unheard of liberty which the young master had taken, in daring to offend a noblewoman. As for Marzia, she only gave a short, sweet smile, and ran back into the tent.

Slaves encircled the young man, enquiring "Do you want to be your own worst enemy, and get your head cut off?" One added: "Tomorrow Temur returns from campaign, and his sister-in-law will tell him all, of course, about your daring action. The Amir may severely punish you for this, and maybe us too for letting you get away with it!"

The young master began to tremble, and bowed his head sorrowfully.

"What can I do now, what can I do?" he begged in a cold sweat.

"We must all run away tonight" one suggested: "We must save ourselves from execution when Temur hears of this!"

On the following day, the overseers did not find the usual numbers of architectural workers, builders, and decorative artists at their stations. Thus, they sent out a party to look for these absentees. Once caught, they were thrown into prison.

That morning Marzia wrote the scared young master a letter.

"In one short day all bounds to lay waste
Within your soul you made such needless haste,
That you, O actor, caused your courage to fade!
At first I liked your daring manner displayed,
And was attracted
By your pureness of heart.. . What made you take such a liberty at the start?
I could not breathe for passion, did you not see?
With its hot flood it swept my feet from me!
Did you not note it, not read it in my eyes?
Desire, from which all fear and death ever flies!
Your work was fine - I could not look away.
Your songs were like wine, in the heavens their echoes play!
But strange it was, that succeeding in work and song,
Your will, unchecked, and daring, did Allah wrong!
So now all's been wiped out, and burned to dust?!
What can one do?
My own feelings I dare not trust.
I fear not your death - for the Mausoleum I grieve,
Which will not now be finished, if young masters leave.

The master's work is dearer to me than the man!
Where do you lurk?
Why not finish what you began?
Without its stones can a stream yet further flow?
Without its goal, how far can manliness go?
He who is scared cannot "beloved" be named!
Who loses heart cannot for love be famed!

AITMATOV.   That excellent and very instructive legend opens before us the simple truth. The teller of the story gives the young master attractive features, bestows on him a handsome form and a wonderful voice, and it would seem that he had all he needed to fulfil his will. But in the needful hour, he could not find the courage necessary to succeed. In other words, all he possessed, lost its value. Hence, he took flight, and the Mousoleum was left incomplete. How well you showed where there is a lack of valour, love can never find its true place! Sometimes love seems to me like some computer apparatus. Of one little detail goes wrong (invisibly) inside, all the rest turns into confusion.

SHAKHANOV. Once Rasul Gamzatov and I were walking together in Moscow from the Kremlin to the Hotel Moscow, when a voice rang out:
"Oh, my goodness! Is that really you, Rasul Gamzatov?"
We both turned round and saw a beautiful Russian woman, with her little son beside her. Her whole appearance aroused delight and pleasure. Looking back at a bus-queue she then called:
"Peter! Come here quickly. See who we have met by chance!"
From the queue there stepped a tall blonde fellow, who hurried towards us, smiling as he came, with a pleasant look.
"Peter was the first one who acquainted me with your poems!" She nodded her head at her husband. "Every time we met he used to read new poems: tender, penetrating and sometimes puzzling pieces at first look". Again she turned towards Rasul and added: "How pleased I was then to think that I should become the wife of a young poet! How proud I was after marriage, when he went on reciting those poems to me, and how surprised I was when he finally told me that you had written them all! If it had not been for those lovely verses drawing us together, I don't think I should have married as I did ... Therefore we

both stand eternally in your debt, Rasul Gamzatovich. We dreamed of seeing you one day, and of expressing our gratitude to you, and our deepest respect for your poetry".

Gamzatov stood confused at first, and then took a quick look at his watch, intimating that we had little time to spare:

"No, no, please! Just one minute you can spare us!" she said, and led us aside from the crowd. Then she began quietly to recite:

> *"Where are you happiness? Where's your bright face!"*
> *"I rest on the summit, which you have not seen!"*
> *"Where are you happiness? I've found that place!"*
> *"I am in streams, where you've not yet been!"*
> *"Where are you then? I've swum hundreds of streams!"*
> *"I am in songs which you sing, so it seems!"*
> *"Where are you then? Have I sung songs for you?"*
> *"I'm on ahead. I am waiting for you!"*

Peter immediately took up the strain, and continued:

> *"The people all round say in love did I fare.*
> *The people all round say oft courting I've been.*
> *With one here, they say, with another one there.*
> *"You've sinned!" they all say, More than once you were seen!"*
> *"Don' t believe! 'Twas not I! I knew not how to sin!*
> *As far as I now can recall, all to win,*
> *Twas you, and you only I loved and desired,*
> *Although I don' t know if by passion you're fired!"*

People gathered around. Rasul started to thank the couple, but just then a tottering drunkard came with a bristly chin, and began beating himself on the breast with his fist:

"There's no such thing as love. I tried it out too, in my time. But she betrayed me, that woman I loved! All talk about true love is just fizzy fuss and fiddle-faddle!" He tried to clutch Rasul by the arm, but Peter quietly pushed him to one side: gently, but resolutely.

"We have you to thank for everything!" smiled the woman, looking straight at Rasul, before finally leaving for the bus-queue again.

At the entrance to the Moscow Hotel, Rasul Gamzatov jokingly said:

"You see, we have just met the two opposite poles of love in one place!" This was true. Two who believed in love, and one who did not!

Before we turn to another topic, Chingiz, I must recite you a poem which I wrote while I was a very young man.

AITMATOV.   I shall listen with pleasure. Please go on;

SHAKHANOV.   First of all, I want to say a few words about how it came to be written. I think you will find its history interesting. In one of our newspapers, I read at the Hamburg Legal Court of Justice about a certain woman, suing for a divorce. She would not accept the advice given by the jury to make things up with her husband, and withdraw her case. She replied: "During seventeen years of family life, my husband used three phrases only. At dawn he said "Good morning!" In the late evening, returning from work he said: "What have we got to eat?" and when the clock pointed to 11 p. m. he said: "It's time to go to bed!" On hearing this the judge found the woman's complaint was justified.

> *"You weep, that love has now played out its parts.*
> *You're still in love, but he's no longer kind.*
> *And love, just as a song of loving hearts,*
> *Is heard by them,*
> *And only by them, you'll find!*
> *Don' t weep - but see*
> *That love is a magic spell.*
> *Forgetting this is of no service there.*
> *To live with no song,*
> *As if in the dark, means hell;*
> *As if in the waste, or a crater cold and bare.*
> *Love sings,*
> *And then the most unhappy pair*
> *Stay silent, love's gift lost in the air!*

AITMATOV.   I understood. You have drawn us to the problem of an unequal spirituality between men and women. I thought about this long ago. Here are some tentative conclusions - although it may be better to call these cogitations the story of a mature young fellow, and a young girl still in her teens. Anyway, let's begin! Both of them are handsome, pleasant young people. They have got to know one another, and found much in common. Certainly, after sweet discussions, they spent sleepless nights thinking of each other. Moreover, their decision to get wed was supported by their friends and parents. Indeed, their marriage went through, with feasting, shouting, singing and dancing for three days. All causing talk about their love in the parks and garden where they used to stroll. However, the problems of family life soon arose. Firstly, these young lovers began to understand that they looked at the world from differing angles. Soon people around them began to notice it too. Secondly, their baby was not enough to hold them together, and could not heal the split between them. All stemming from a failure to converse spiritually, and share sacred things! Each word uttered only served to increase the tension. Each gesture only began to agitate them more and more. Even sitting at one table was torment for them both. What could they do now? One of them needed to find enough courage to end their hellish relations as man and wife. Yet, they equally dreaded the resultant loneliness, the gossiping tongues and the twisted chitter-chatter. Maybe they should pretend to be contented together, and at the same time begin to hate life? Who can say?

SHAKHANOV.   Dear Chingiz, I also have a story similar to the one you have just told. In mine, a young girl met a lad and they truly thought they loved each other. Thus, they decided to marry. Months flew by, then years flew by too. It was all a semi-conscious whirl. Once, however, as guests of some well-known friends, lively discussions about politics, furniture, new flats and the like abounded. In general the usual kind of everyday chatter. Soon the men separated - most of them going to play cards. With them, the husband of our girl went along.

That evening, having nothing better to do, she started listening to a man already going grey. Quickly noticing he didn't speak like others, she became aware that his remarks held wisdom and conviction - an independent point of view.

Suddenly, chance cries were heard from the card-players. Provoking, one supposes, the women to animatedly whisper gossip among themselves.

Yet, our heroine continued to sit on the divan beside the grey-haired man. Soon, a very serious talk started between them. Not only deep judgements, but the tone of voice and attentive looks, attracted the attention of the others. She, for her part, was evidently moved by what he was saying. Finding sensible answers to questions which had long bothered her. Furthermore, he became more and more interesting in her. And so the evening ended. Later on, of course, they met again. Then a second and a third time. Afterwards feeling they needed each other. "Why didn't I meet you before? Everything could have turned out so differently", she found herself confessing. Clearly, they both felt this within their souls. Yet, were they to blame for the feelings growing between them? Who can say?

AITMATOV.   The answer to such a question, I, tried to give in my own way, and put into the form of Dzhamila. Indeed, there is nothing more tormenting than a spirituall gap between spouses.

SHAKHANOV.   I remember in my youth, I read in the diary of a young girl the following words: if the boyfriend whom you love begins to lose interest in you, remember, therein lies your own fault" Yes, to be a real woman is an art, or rather a science, I should say. Remember how Pasternak puts it

> "To become a woman's a very great stride;
> To send a man crazy - heroic pride?

I'll even risk saying there should be one more role on a woman. What, you may ask? Well, it is excellent to love, but no less important to be loved. Often one hears women complaining to each other: "I love him more than anything else in the whole world. So, why doesn't he respond to me with just such a love?"

If born a woman, I say, - thank Fate! After all, women differ from men in their tenderness, in the depth of their feelings, in their ability to forgive, and in their own vulnerability. Men live by unwritten laws, albeit completely compulsory ones, which make it a matter of honour for them to submit to women and their wishes, and to protect them too!

Therefore one is obliged, if a woman, to not merely be beautiful, but to nourish in oneself all the spiritual riches of ones people. A duty which has come down through the centuries in the form of nurturing traditions and customs, as well as the historical wisdom of past ages. Fundamentally, in actions, manners, ways of laughing, expressing joy, and also sorrow, feminine gentleness overcomes all. Truly, there are many who dress in a feminine way, wearing earrings and rings, even though they do not cultivate in themselves the qualities of a real Woman.

Once, when speaking to me of this, Yevgeny Yevtushenko remarked: "Mukhtar, as I see things, women who are in love stand much higher than we men. It they love truly it means the end of everything. The world revolves on its axis, though they do not notice it".

AITMATOV.   Yes, I agree with the words of Yevgeny Yevtushenko. Either the world will come to an end, or it must be reborn.

SHAKHANOV.   I, in my turn, do my best to express such a point of view.

> *Aspiration's fire having changed, in the light of truth,*
> *To Everest's peak, which scarcely could be seen,*
> *Few men were able to attain, forsooth,*
> *Of thousands born on earth - though bold and keen.*
> *Yes, noble Everest to high love is like!*
> *Its crags alarm the skies, the very clouds;*
> *Its peak seems near to the Sun,*
> *As though' twould strike,*
> *And, like a falcon, mounts high heaven's shrouds ...*
> *"All comes to an end.*
> *By a blast of wind is torn*
> *All hope from one's soul, and hurled into the gloom.*
> *Don' t change into a laughing-stock folk scorn!"*
> *Thought brave Tranzei.*
> *"Fear not your final doom!*
> *Tranzei,*

Who was condemned by harshest law,
And must today, indeed,
 Put an end to his life.
In Nero's day, patricians were struck on the raw,
And found no way of escaping from the strife.
 See, here's his dagger,
Shining cunningly now,
As if t'were teasing him: "Well then, my friend,
Has not the hour now come to strike, somehow,
Which will unite us,
Then divide, in the end?..
Outside the window, on the road back home,
The people are crowding,
Quietly there they speak:
"Be quick, and in the name of sacred Rome,
Now stab yourself!
Or is Nero's law too weak?"
The walls stand dismal.
Life and Death in their fight
Are motionless. Tormented stays the hand,
Does not stretch out to the dagger, cold and bright,
 For Life's still warm, resilient, and grand,
And firmly holds to him with tight embrace,
 And at that moment is ready to burst in bloom ...
But fear begins in its shameful dance to chase,
A-crumpling will-power, trampling honour in gloom.. .
And at that moment,
 In garments snowy white,
Arria came in, as slender and sweet as could be,
And how her tender eyes were shining bright!
And to Tranzei there these words said she:
"God made you a man, and riches he heaped on you,
 And happiness gave you too.
But your hour has struck!
It's time to part with all you have, that's true –
Or do you wish a coward's name on you stuck?

If you desire to keep your manly name,
Which you have borne so well until this day,
Then why grieve so?
Just look! More great the pain
Of mockery, shame, and ridicule, I say!
Believe me, there is nought in death to fear!
Take up your dagger!
Let force in your hand not fade!
Without this test you'll trust in nothing here –
Not in hard will, nor in your steely blade!
And will such happiness,
Which of itself drew near,
Tell us the moment when it has to go?
Let this be your last great achievement here!
Well, copy my motion after me.

Strike so!

Not breaking off her gaze from her Tranzel,
That loving look,
Those eyes with coral dressed,
That tender smile, Arria struck straightway
Her small, sharp dagger, in her beating breast ...
So he struck too, cast off all fear and doubt.
They stretched their hands to each other once again,
And in a moment all movement faded out,
And just two corpses
Before the crowd lay slain.. .
And love, which even in one inclined to fear,
His worthiness and honour thus far raised!
Yes, glory be! If it is needed here,
The summit of mountains for their height be praised!"

AITMATOV.   There is an expression by Stendhal which goes like this:
"Say, what is greater than the courage of a woman fighting for love?"
You have rightly shown in your poem that the height of spirit needs no
extraneous praise.

If we wish to make permanency the basic measure of love, then we need to be mindful that in olden days people regarded love within a framework of inner understanding, and from a religious point of view. In ancient calendars, on cliff-drawings, on ornamental manuscripts, on stone sarcophagi taken out of the earth, we can see a multitude of representations, where women burnt themselves - of their own will - in order to leave for another world with their dead husbands.

Such a terrifying custom was widely spread across all corners of this earth. For example, dwellers on the island of Hainan, in China, covered a dead husband with a silk sheet, or a tiger-skin, while beside him lay his living wife (bound hand and foot) so both may be burned together on the funeral pyre. They believed, leaving this world together, they would live together reincarnated in the next one.

Many other surprising facts, analogous to those just given, can be found in the writings of Herodotus and other famous historians of those times. If some wealthy lord died, then the doors to the next world must be opened together with his favourite wife - and she was laid beside him in funeral rites.

This led to different excesses. For example, friends of a wealthy Shah (during his lifetime), always knew who his most beloved wife was! When her name was announced he became happy beyond words! All meaning, of course, she was mortified and buried near to him upon his passing. Curiously, his other wives suffered due to the fact it was a disgrace to remain alive after their husband's death.

Moreover, young women of some tribes - in the event of their future husband's death - would put a permanent noose around their necks, as a sign of continuing maidenhood.

On the island of Suleiman (in the event of a local lords death), those who arranged the funeral throttled his wife, then drank some poisonous juice to made themselves inebriated, following which each put a noose around their neck and hung themselves - in a mood of high ecstasy. They believed a famous person must not be sent alone into the next world.

Furthermore, it is claimed that on the island of Fiji, when the lord of the local Somo-somo tribe, Ra-Mbiti, drowned in the ocean, his seventeen widows were also killed.

Additionally, such "evidence of love", was widely spread among ancient tribes in Scythia, Greece, and Lithuania.

SHAKHANOV. Here, most likely, we must speak not so much of "love", as of a mystical conservatism and a blindness of souls. Until quite recent times, in parts of Africa, there was a wide-spread custom of burying slaves with a dead lord, as well as his wife. This was counted a strict religious duty. Occasionally some Europeans met and witnessed such ceremonies. They even tried to stand in defence of the slaves, but were howled down by the furious participants of the funeral ceremony: "Who will feed and serve our lord n that next world" they asked?

A very interesting and original form of family life was kept up by members of the ancient Indian tribe of Naiars. A young couple, having taken part in their own marriage ceremony, still did not live together under one roof. The young husband continued to live at home, and the young woman stayed with her relations. Interestingly, his wife had the right to live for with her husband for only a few days a year. Moreover, this law was upheld even following the birth of their children. Frequent meetings were equally forbidden – and was considered to be the height of shamelessness. All their lives these wedded couples lived alone. Strangely, divorces were rare. Maybe, because their rare meetings turned out to be real love festivals? Either way, lives broken by unhappy hearts have been hidden from untold millions of eyes.

Unusually wedding and divorce traditions of the Daiaks (as recorded by the ethnographer Pier Pfeffer), seem to have reached an egalitarian level. As such, he wrote: "Women can be the initiators of divorce alongside of men. And the Daiaks see no problem in it."

AITMATOV. When in love, each one acts individually, according to his outlook - and his attitude towards love itself. But man is so made that he frequently errs, in taking for real love some puny, passing passion. Sincere love is a long-standing torment.

It seems a very rare event when spiritually rich and talented people find one another and unite. I should like to propose the formation of a world-wide "Encyclopaedia of Love', within which one might find noble qualities, achievements: and occurrences born of love itself.

SHAKHANOV. People are unhappy, but not because they are really stupid. Once, several years back, at one of my poetic parties in Moscow, I answered a question from the audience and remember myself saying:

"If in the enormous city of Moscow, with its ten million citizens, one could find a thousand pairs of really happy people, enriching each other as partners, near and dear to each other in their world outlook - it would be a great achievement!" Afterwards I thought the figure was too high! True love is a precious rarity in this world. This is without any doubt.

I would like to divide humanity into two groups - those who are capable of really and truly loving, and those who are cut off from such a possibility.

When one famous ruler of India (coming from a branch of the Mogols), Zakhan-Shah, lost his beloved wife Mumtaz, he felt totally alone in the Universe! Neither treasures, nor beauties - with the tender eyes of gazelles - could help him forget his lost love. Then, this great Shah understood only a temple, which had never been seen before beneath the Moon, could give him consolation. So, in memory of the woman who had loved him for nineteen years, and given him nine children, he erected a lovely temple, the Taj-Mahal, in the seventeenth century. That snowy-white temple is still a wonder of the world, and stands to this day as an enduring symbol of majestic Love. Inspiring its visitors with an airy spiritual elegance and perfection of line. After all, love has no predetermined formula, even though there are many noble memorials raised in its honour.

AITMATOV.   At the end of the seventies, Mariam and I were in Moscow, and stayed in a hotel there. Hearing of this, you came one evening to see us - and then you read us a poem about the great love of a Kazakh composer, Estai. I think this composition of yours would be a splendid illustration to our present conversation.

SHAKHANOV.   It is called "The Ballad of the Bright Pain". I will be glad to recite it to you, and will begin with a short introduction:

The poet Estai, who composed the poem "Khorlan", so loved by the folk, at the age of seventy two felt his approaching end. Thus, he called his faithful friend Nurlibek. This poor man had been thrown from his horse, and had both legs broken, but hearing the call of his old friend had travelled the whole day by a cart to pay him a visit.

Raising his trembling hand, on which an old golden ring shone - polished as it was by time - the poet said: "Tell my elders to bury me with this ring on my hand, given to me by Khorlan, my love. I have worn it for fifty one years. Let it stay with me". Then he wept: "0h, my beloved, how could you put all your love and feeling into such a little ring?"

A woman came to me, complained of woe ...
Her speech flowed on - a bitter burning fate:
"What can I do with my daughter, ailing so,
My beloved girl who melts like a candle of late?
For years I've led her, like an unseen sail,
Her fate, her hopes, her dreams, and her desires,
So at the moment when she meets her mate,
He'll know no beauty which better his soul inspires!
She's grown up now, not chafing, not making a fuss,
Her minds bright,
Her soul is good and kind.
Among her girl-friends she's a wonder thus,
Like a flower in Spring, no purer blossom you'll find!
But grief and gladness are as like as chicks,
And in my soul they have a crowded nest.
And so misfortune early on her picks –
And love so deeply wounded her in the breast!
Until this day, no deep grief have we known,
And so her wound I feel too, as my lot.
Now I'm on guard against sorrow, not my own.
The moon of hope above our home shines not.
Three years - that's long enough for any pain!
One cannot measure pleasure in numbered years;
One artist there was, so merry, and not in vain –
Within her soul, his music raised her tears.
Well, married is he, and has six children, forby!
Alas, they seem impossible, only to me!
Year after year I grieve, and want to cry,
But she affirms she's happy as she can be!
How bold men are

I scarcely can make clear!
She turned them down with a smile on her lips, a stare.
She's like
A senseless, flighty, light-legged deer,
Which seeks for verdure on burnt-out pastures bare!!!
I assure myself that all is possible still,
That life and happiness may be found, no jest,
But in my soul, still grieved, and fearing ill,
The blizzard blows ...
The blizzard in my breast ...
For her
Is none desirable more than he!
She cries at night, as sad as a waning moon.
But when dawn comes again, a new day, see,
She still insists she's happy, or will be soon!
Her soul is tenderer than first light of day..
How can I save her garden, that scarce will bloom?
Give me advice –
Poetic words now say –
Pronounce your line,
With warm heart rout my gloom!..
Then mother left, her features full of woe.
In her own sorrowful way was partly right.
Her words recalled to my mind her daughter so,
And I devised some comments to set things right ...
I thought to myself:
We've centuries at our backs,
But how many folk though raised by fate, it seems,
Don't understand this life,
Don't notice those tracks
Which lead to summits high, but chase their dreams.
And only poets sang of loving pains,
So that the folk recalled those lovers too.
Estai warmed up my soul with his live airs,
And thus recalled all those whose love was true.
When he, worn out by sickness, and ill fate,
Could hear death through the rustling of the page,

He called to himself his one and only mate,
And thus he spoke
The last request of old age:
"Hey, Nurlibek,
How many years with you,
How many days went flying upon one rein?
I still don't give up life with no fight, it's true,
But death is strong —
I breathe with difficult pain.
You alone understand a poet, as you should,
So hear me now, as my last behest I make:
Here on the borders of light and dark, for good
Remember friend, this truth, which I found no fake:
Life's made of days, by true love only warmed,
And lacking love, the soul of man is dead.
Of this the "stupid" poets are well-informed,
And pass their wisdom on to others ahead.
The language of streams,
And of the mountain heights
Is known to me, and with them I've conversed.
A half a century since we met, with delight,
Like a day has passed.
Khorlan I loved from the first.
That means I lived …
I lived then, not in vain.
With dreams of her
I slept,
With dreams arose.
And I was happy, hour after hour again,
Although I suffered each hour, each year, my woes.
The world I forgot
Was all with love aflame,
But still my pain was beautiful and bright.
My tears were envied by other lovers the same,
Whose youth had also only just come in sight.
Though fate, it's true, to me was more severe,
What pain

Is harder to bear than being apart?
Though paths divide, I still repeat quite clear –
I might survive,
 Just thinking of her warm heart.
Khorlan's bright ring for half a century gleamed.
With that on my hand, I conquered any storm.
My wife could not for fifty years, it seemed,
Take away her eyes
From my hand where it shone warm.
To that old custom of forebears
I stand true,
 So kindly now obey
My last request –
Khorlan's gold ring leave on my finger too,
Accompanying me to the shadow-land, to rest.
 I leave for that land
As happy as before,
And in death's hour, with love still shining bright,
I shall stay true to one hope alone, not more,
That to Khorlan my road will lead aright.
This is no dream –
All which in life we attain.
My dream
Is immortality's sister true!
Khorlan's with me, and I protect her name!"
He closed his eyes,
And sighed "It's time - adieu!"
When our Khorlan had heard of this and that,
She then exclaimed to me:
"I know Estai –
He loved and sang until they laid him flat!
A proven poet - at last he came to die!"
So saying Khorlan began to wail and weep.
The shawl around her shoulders
 Shone like the moon.
But still her words
Their strength indeed could keep,

Which they received from love, from love alone!
So, years passed by.. .
To death then giving way,
But overcoming briefly the pains of hell,
She suddenly asked to hear Estai's last lay,
About how tender were eyes he loved so well.
And truly, tenderness then filled her eyes.
She whispered, breathing heavily once more:
"My love is boundless
As ocean waves which rise.
I haste to you!"
. . . she died on the heavenly shore!
So don' t blame lovers for loving - that won' t do!
To love be true - that's an achievement grand!
More fearful the fate of those whose love falls through,
Who are not given to wander hand in hand!
O mother, say, why should we add to their scars
Which fate on them so generously has poured, -
Though folk who're drunk with hate, which all things mar, ,
Cannot forgive heart's love, in bosoms stored.
And even if two lived for long far apart,
Alone to them is given love's flame so bright,
To those who bore the stamp of truth on each heart,
And who both prayed to one and the same bright light.
I beg of you, do not distress true love,
With tears and words no living warmness flout,
For vulnerable are love's wings, stretched out above!
Love's soul is sacred, don' t try to rout it out!
But wish them tenderness, and flaming joy,
More powerful than time, and worrying woes.
For even death itself cannot destroy
Those hearts, where love immortal flowers and flows!

AITMATOV. I would like to bring one or two stories to your attention. I read them in childhood, but till today still remember them very well. One is a story of love and constancy about Jeremiah Bentham, the great thinker - it is a poem. In his youth he fell in love with a young girl, made her a proposal of marriage, but was refused. However, as the years passed by, Bentham continued to love her. Thus, at the age of sixty, he wrote her a letter informing her of his enduring love – only to receive a further refusal. They say when speaking of her he could not restrain his tears. Finally, when he was eighty, he wrote his beloved a farewell letter: "I am still alive, my dear soul! The feeling I had for you at sixteen, when I presented you with my first bunch of flowers is still flaming in me! I love you, and bless fate which gave me such a love! Farewell!"

As a great English Colonel, the Duke of Wellington, also experienced a wonderful, but unhappy, love. Indeed, his beautiful Catherine attracted many suitors, but responded to the Duke's love alone. This was probably why they spent innumerable happy days together and took an oath to love each other forever. However, Lord Longford, Catherine's father, was against their marriage. A situation further complicated when Wellington went off on military service to India. Nevertheless, Catherine waited nine years for his return, although on getting home her lover did not recognize her. Sadly, the woman who had filled Wellington's dreams day and night needed to veil her face due to small-pox. That however did not dismay the "Iron Duke" and he arranged a luxurious wedding-feast to celebrate their reunion. Following which, they lived happily together.

SHAKHANOV. The term "sexual revolution" was born in the sixties in Western Europe, and spread throughout the world. This dangerous disease killed shame in a man, thus robbing him of one of his most precious and persistent qualities. "Sexual freedom", under the banner of open and unrestrained sexual relationships, scorned all limits and became part of "modern culture". Someone said of it, rather poisonously, but nonetheless precisely: "Pornography means impotent love in a morgue!"

Truly, according to the assertions of scientific specialists, in order to preserve a healthy organism, along with psychological stability, three things are needed, First - comes nourishment; second - sound sleep; third - intimate love-relations. Without proper food man loses his strength. Without sufficient sleep he becomes ill. Without intimate relations, his character is weakened. He becomes touchy, loses his personal power, and finally suffers ennui. Hence, wise men have advocated regular intimate relationship in every country: as a health-giving and stabilizing activity, and acting as a panacea against many ailments. Yet, that feeling of intimate relationship must not be merely physical, but also spiritual.

People all over the world speak in various tongues, but all yearn and grieve, rejoice, and confirm their love in one language - the heart's language. If I am not mistaken, among people of one tribe on the shores of the Amazon, it is highly indecent to dine when sitting facing one another. In all other matters, there are no moral prohibitions. Maybe the ideologists of the "sexual revolution" have borrowed this idea from that Amazon tribe? However, any attempt to drive out of our lives a sense of morality and shame is the greatest crime of the last century.

At present, researchers take two opposing views. While one regrets that the epoch of great and noble love has passed permanently away from our lives, the others look with optimism to the future, asserting this loss is temporary only, and that we shall return to a belief in true love as the source of man's greatness and nobility.

I shall recite an excerpt from a new poem of mine "Erring eyes" which is devoted to this very problem:

> *"And every time his beloved girl*
> *The poet praised up to the skies,*
> *And he affirmed, his head in a whirl;*
> *"There is none other maid likewise,*
> *More lovely,*
> *Attractive,*
> *More like the dawn,*
> *Than any other maid on earth.*
> *That's my beloved, just like a fawn,*
> *Incomparable, of highest worth!"*
> *Intrigued by the bard's poetic word,*
> *The ruler thirsted to see the maid,*
> *To look on her beauty, of which he'd heard.*
> *But when on her he later gazed,*
> *He was surprised at the poet's praise,*
> *For she was just an ordinary lass,*

In no way different in form nor face,
In no way magnificent, more than the mass;
No better than any servant she seemed,
No brighter than this kitchen cook,
Who day and night in white apron gleamed
Among the cauldrons, to take a look!
With clever cooking, many she dazed,
And even won their hearts, it's true!
The King, tormented, and much amazed,
Then called the poet to him, and cried:
"D'you call her a beauty, in your haste?
Although you're a poet, known far and wide,
You have no deep seeking in your taste".
The poet then proudly made reply:
"Don't be offended, 0 gracious King!
You are all-powerful, reigning high,
But there's one feeling, one great thing
Which does not fall beneath your role.
Take one more look at this maiden here,
And read her most unusual soul,
All woven out of nobility clear.
But look on her with my poet's eyes,
And with my poet's eyes alone,
Or you will never realize
The laws of love - she is my own!
Now through a whole millennium of years,
Which stormed with passions of every kind,
And slightly tormented by fears,
By loss of blood, and by noble mind,
Sometimes irresolute, with no heart,
Sometimes quite dissolute, morals put by,
But technically, clever, and very smart,
And like dark night, with a darker eye,
In the form of a proud and pompous man,
Towards us steps with powerful pride,
The 21st century,
Dead on plan!

O god! What else will happen beside?
It seems its eyes are out of place,
And people say they have fallen so,
And now lie lower, beneath its waist
And even lower still may go!
And, maybe, from its pocket tight
A 21st century poet may rise,
To know and evaluate love aright.
In new conditions, and newer guise,
Proposing to look, as a poet can,
Into the eyes of a man or a maid..
What should we try now? What loving plan?
Where can we look, and not be betrayed?

....

I do not know - that's a frightful plight!
But there's no going back, that's clear.
One does not wish to return to the night,
Where thunder's alarms already we hear. ..
I'm sorry for that poor daughter of mine,
If the 21st century can't raise its eyes,
And put them back on a higher line,
Where they'll see love's truth, and not its lies!

AITMATOV.   Yes, the twentieth century allowed man to witness two World Wars, not to mention untold localized bloodshed. On one hand, our conquest of the cosmos and the rapid progress of technology stand proud, while on the other, an unprecedented lowering of spiritual and moral standards prevails. Such a magnificent feeling as mutual love - which protects and moves all life - is now being mocked and trampled by youth. Its place given to pornography, prostitution and parasitical passion. As I see things, all this is as dangerous as the threat of a nuclear war. Inventing so many new things, we have lost far more valuable ones - spiritual and moral principles, which from ancient times have supplied and supported man's existence on earth.

I have no doubt at all this was what the poet Andrey Voznesensky had in mind, when he said: "All progress is reactionary, if it destroys mankind!" and how right he was! Now I should like to ask you to read your poem "The Fifth Man", which made a deep impression on me. The more especially as we came to conclude of our conversation.

SHAKHANOV.   I am glad you found it interesting, and hope that others will too. Also, I hope it marks a befitting conclusion to our discussion on women, and their nature-given noble qualities, seen in all mothers.

FIFTH MAN

In my ancient city of Otrar,
Of er which the banner of honour flew high,
One bold young rider, no coward was he,
With his whole-hearted valour, forby,
Once saved his native land from woe.
The Almighty wished a reward to make,
Proposed to him three riches so –
But only one of them he might take.
The first was a wide and masterly mind,
Which would delight all around in its flight.
But loneliness therein he might find,
So he must consider, and choose aright.
The second was beauty, found in the flesh,
Which with its brilliance might easily blind,
But that might breed envy which all would enmesh,
And little content and calm would he find.
The third was a wide and generous soul,
As spacious as native steppeland wide.
And thus would turn foes into friends, on the whole,
And bring men as brothers to one's side
The young man thought and thought, then replied:
"All-Highest, I am thrilled by this choice,
But rather give me one wife by my side,
Where those three gifts would all find a voice!
For I'm a man, like a swift stream in Spring,
Which can overflow, and lose its course,

And this can flood with mud everything –
Yes, I am a man of considerable force.
But I'm still a man, a great burden I bear,
I'm kind at heart, and responsive too.
I'm trusting, and proud, and believe easy there,
And sometimes I thus am deceived, it's true!
I need a good wife, as the joy of my life,
A woman devoted, believing in me,
An understanding, forgiving wife,
Who for my work inspiration would be!
Without such a woman, I soon should die!"
Many centuries passed ...
And still thousands of men,
A-hunting for such a good woman now fly,
And hope she'll be willing to give herself then.
To one had been given these qualities three:
Wise reason,
And beauty,

And generous ways,

But weakness of will was a hindrance, you see;
Another just lost his path in a maze.
His wild, hot impatience there led him astray,
And he, poor devil, got properly caught,
Just chased the first skirt which crossed his way,
And so he lost everything, more than he ought.
The third was a man blindly trusting in strength,
Who lived and believed in such force alone,
But such men lose all tender feelings at length,
Like trees in deep winter, when all leaves have flown.
The fourth, when the final decision came,
Could not find the courage the last risk to take,
And so he destroyed his own love, just the same,
And no further efforts he later could make.
And only the fifth man was left to believe

That, come the next day, he'd get level with fate,
And for his long-suffering dream did receive
This beloved ideal woman to take as his mate!
Success to him then! Let us wish him success!
I must say, long since I've not seen such a pair!
Long since I've not been, will not be, I guess,
At the wedding of such a true happy man there!"

AITMATOV. Well then, who is destined to be fifth man? Just look, for millions of years, since the creation of earth, all humans have hunted after Love, in the hope of catching her. For a real man, the fundamental aim of existence was, is, and will be, to find that predestined woman, suited to him in her character, looks and actions. To love truly is always evidence of great spiritual talent in people. In life there are many untalented folk, and in love too. That is why the "Everest peak" of feelings can be conquered only by a few of them.

Since the time of Adam and Eve that magical force known as love, which inspires everyone, and makes one weep, has existed on earth. None can foretell it, but all must experience it in their own lives. Now we have spoken openly, trying to solve this great problem, remembering those women we met in our life-road, who shared our secret.

Of some things we have not spoken. Some of our thoughts have not found the words they needed. When dealing with sacred things, sometimes we cannot put them into words, they are so ethereal, and fly so swiftly.

"There, where friendship disappears, society falls to pieces: there where love disappears, our successors will suffer!"- so said the great Prophet Mohammed.

Our years have passed unreturning by, like the obstinate waves on a windy day, rushing forward and breaking on the cliffs and crags. Now our years remind us of more peaceful waters, quietly lapping the shores, and slowly swirling around boulders and stones.

After us comes a new, wide-winged generation, which turn their bowsprits again towards the beating waves of the ocean, the waters of life, ever moving, never ceasing.

May God grant that those mountain cliffs which seemed so high and unassailable, may become accessible to us, and that our days and nights of doubt and despair may all the same let our ships pass into the shallows safely, avoiding the reefs, and making for the harbor - so that our undying, unconquerable hopes should become real landmarks throughout all our lives!

THE OLIVE-BRANCH OF IMMORTALITY
(EPILOGUE)

"I believe in the purifying strength of History"
Daisaku Ikeda
Japanese thinker

This fantastic happening was told to me by a well-known artist. Roaming in search of something to draw from nature, in the simple surroundings of some deserted hamlet in the Urals, he suddenly stopped. Here was a wonder! As if by magic, before him there appeared an unusual forest, in which grew heavenly blue pines. Then, further on, something unimaginable happened, in which you, the reader, may not be able to believe (and I also had my doubts). He had barely, with an outburst of brotherly tenderness embraced one pine, when in the flash of an eye it melted into a grey mist, and disappeared into the heavens. The forest, which from a distance looked alive, was dead. Lifeless and motionless as a corpse ...

I know scientists would put this down to some strange kind of radiation, while psychiatrists would name it hallucination. Why not use that true story as a metaphor? This is what I thought - maybe it is possible to revive something which existed before, and call it back to life again? Only we do not, for some reason, feel this, and do not see it. Is that not very likely because, in the words of the French film-director Alan Rene, "The subject is dead, if the living glance concentrated upon it disappears". If we listen carefully, if we understand how vitally necessary for our spiritual health is the warning of Teilhard de Chardin, the outstanding philosopher-humanist, (without which we are simply predestined not to survive!) "Try to see more, and better - that is not a caprice, not mere inquisitiveness, not a luxury, but a necessity! See, or perish!"

So, the problem of "seeing", is all the sharper and sicker, because the twentieth century changed so swiftly, on the crest of a scientific-technological and social revolution, and has carried humankind out of its usual routine of existence. The majority of people have "awoken", as it were, in a strange new world, on an unknown planet, in a new era. If we wish to be real people and live a life of full value, we must discover it all over again, we must open it up, striving with all our strength to find an answer to the eternal question, which endlessly torments us with its seemingly unanswerable enquiry - "From whence do you come, and whither are you now going?"

> *"From one soul to the other no path they lay.*
> *Not understood - no curse with crueller ends!*
> *The road from soul to soul's like a duel, let's say.*
> *What a steep sharp slope - the path to a circle of friends!"*
> M.SHAKHANOV.

There can be no doubt that this dialogue-testament between an outstanding writer of the twentieth century, Chingiz Aitmatov, and one of the greatest poets of Asia, Mukhtar Shakhanov, under the title of "The Plight of a Postmodern Hunter" was born of the unquenchable thirst to meet someone of a similar nature, a relative of the spirit. Maybe the drama of human existence, its great unhappiness, is simply not meeting a similar soul. What is worse - not recognizing such a needed conversationalist, someone with whom you are best able to speak your innermost thoughts, and pass him by, not guessing that this moment could change the very roots of your life.

That is why, dear reader, I hope that having this book in your hands, will gift joy- first of all — then delight, through this diaiogue between two unusually interesting people. The greater their power, the more it will interest you with its truth, and with its poetry, with the heightened level of their conversations, which arises not as a result of high-flying rhetorical skills, nor the wish to show themselves wise. The unusual, warm, almost family atmosphere of their dialogue is the result of their careful wording, of their clear and precise contemplations about the reality of the world, and about the true history of mankind - seemingly of an everyday nature, but suddenly showing a wise philosophy of existence - understandable and accessible to all who can listen and respond to it. For that reason the thoughts of D. Ikedi, one of which heads these remarks of mine, are so important as a matter of principle.

He further says: "The need to speak in a humane language, is it not there, in the depth of things, the sense of spiritual rebirth?"

Spiritual revival ...

Is it by chance that the problem of the revival of the spirit now sounds truly tragic? It is like an S.O.S. Save our souls! To whom is this signal of all-humanity addressed? To humanity, and to himself, of course. To all knowledge and consciousness existing only in man. Truly, no matter how sorrowful, if a man places all hopes in himself as the crown of Nature, he will not succeed. What are we, then? Who are we? Better than worse, more like executives, volunteer sprites, having robbed ourselves of memory, having blinded ourselves with fear before the unknown, and not believing we can possibly be born again..

This is because we do not know that to be born again, according to the revelation of the Holy Metropolitan Antonio, means to see this world as God created it. Or, on the contrary, nonetheless guessing that we shall only see "hell", into which the once blossoming Garden of Eden was turned, we therefore in every way oppose the ghastly nightmare of enlightenment. We prefer already to see the end of history - that is the role of a "zombie" - a spirit without memory.

Look up in the dictionary for the meaning of "zombie", and you see it is literally taken as "one raised from the dead". Among African tribes thus were named those unfortunate ones whose psyche was so programmed with the aid of psychological means, "bio-robots" simply terrified all those around them, by whom they were seen.

I should like to believe, dear reader, that the chapter in this book entitled "Crime, throughout the Ages, or the Marquis de Sade, Donenbai, and the poison of African two-fanged fish" - shook you as it shook me, not because we knew nothing about that phenomenon (we had heard about it!) but just because in the general subject of their conversation lay its fundamental idea - our responsibility for life, and for the future. Often people do not notice what is happening to them, they become involuntarily victims of "irradiation" of pseudoculture. It poisons the human psyche with TV and horror films, public pornography, and open sex, with the propaganda of crude violence, and an implanted life-style, foreign to natural traditions and customs. Finally, all of this condemns a man to historical forgetfulness. By the way, among ancient peoples there was a saying "History is the mother of real truth". So then, whom do we reject? From the slavish serving of false ideals, and chasing after lying dreams. Is it not that which first gives birth to estrangement, and later to scorn for the wise codex of the "Steppeland Academy", in full accordance with which people lived, and contempt for yourself, as it were some barbarian, blindly agreeing to wear the feudal Bey's chains of prejudice? Scorn for a sacred attachment to Mother Earth, and to the understanding of righteousness, kindness, wisdom, glory and honour.

"And what did all that give us?" Putting that question, our modern companion with unconcealed envy gazes on foreign idlers, counting them the highest and decisive measure of a "correct" civilization.

But it never comes into his head, that bitter thought of the poet also, by the way our comtemporary, A. Voznesensky, who said: "All progress is reactionary, if it destroys a man".

The problem of conscience, as a condition of free choice is the fundamental problem of the dialogue "Testament at the Edge of the Century". A lasting problem, and the context is crammed full of it, is the aspiration of all mankind toward a spiritual knowledge of the world and his destruction on the road to the third Millennium, which demands a conscientious opposition to the most terrifying evil that is possible - the loss of the taste for life itself.

Do you love life? Do you love those around you? Absence of love, if you experience that feeling, dear reader, (and about that you know better than anybody else) is a symptom of sickness of a soul. The absence of love towards your dear one is the same as the absence of care for yourself. I do not speak of egoistic self-love, the love of your personal comfort, and personal possessions which the majority of folk around despairing struggle for, because that is mere survival. All that is hypocrisy, self-deceit, which unfailingly displays itself to one's heart with pain. Buddha has said: "Do not take that which does not belong to you, for it will destroy you".

What belongs to you at birth? Freedom. But at once the question arises - freedom from something, or for something? You take a step, and you make a blunder, if that question is not strictly observed.

One thing is clear: the authors of this book lead the reader onward to a complicated and tormenting problem which nonetheless must stand before any man quite clearly if he wishes (and who can doubt that he does) to be a modern man. That means not to feel himself like a grain of sand, lost in the cosmos, but a thinking person in the expanses of space and time. If we do not feel this, then what are we? What are people not ready to do anything for the sake of it? Only for that are we created: "I wish to live, to think, to suffer ..."

Sometimes to think, at other times to lament, sometimes to be a real man. That is a cunning dodge! Thanks to that, some uselessly think that they, and only they, have the right to decide for people how they should live, and to what degree should feel themselves free. The psychology of totalitarianism still sits in the consciousness of society, but ... who can say how the things will develop?

The first seeds of democracy are sown already. Whether they ripen and bear fruit or not depends upon us. On you, dear reader! A moment of enlightenment when a person may, and must make his own individual decision, and choose independently, is given once to everyone. In that opportunity lies the highest justice of our existence. Only do not let that moment pass - take it as God's gift, as a commission, as your fortune in this swiftly-changing world of ours.

Is it not on the strength of this that many people live beyond their strength sometimes? Is the burden too heavy? The dialogue between Chingiz Aitmatov and Mukhtar Shakhanov is soaked with a boundless faith in Man. That is not an abstract belief, not a mere pat on the shoulder, but a truly passionate aspiration to set an example, as historical persons, such as our contemporaries, let's say Mukhtar Auezov, or Dmitri Shostakovich, or maybe say, the Presidents of new sovereign governments, or even as they say, the simple folk, and to show that man's happiness lies in the service to his people, and that this is his call throughout life.

The more one acts for the good of all, the more one fully exists. To be fully existent, one needs to be responsible for all. To accept the past, to work for the present and the future, not daring to show indifference, nor sophisticated doubts about "What can one man do?" or "How much depends on me?" That is the miserable philosophy of the "little man", and it is just what both authors equally cannot accept, and heatedly reject. That is only to be expected. Both Aitmatov and Shakhanov do not change the essence of their artistic creation by one iota, and do not forsake their justly humanitarian ideals, which mainly consist of the belief that the meaning of life lies in spiritual heroism. Wider still - in their belief in the history of mankind, which shows such great attainments - the history of kind actions and love for others, which despite cruelty towards those who oppose them, hopelessly, or maybe because of this, light up an inextinguishable fire in the darkness, rousing the mass, and helping them to live on a higher spiritual level.

Aitmatov's "Dzhamila" and the excellent poem by Shakhanov, "The theory of mutual understanding" are echoes of eternity. The delicate wonderful thoughts, or more truly, observations, made by Aitmatov, speak about the one single foundation of poetry, which are confirmed in the poem by Shakhanov, and by its ties with ancient Armenian poetry, and especially that of Narekatsi.

"What is more unjust", asks that modern poet, "than to be a woman and not be beautiful?" Nine centuries ago that Armenian poet turned to God with a mourning cry, and a challenge:

"Do not make me groan, and sad tears shed,
Do not send me pangs, and no new-born head,
Nor make me a cloud, whence no rain-drops have sped ..."

Here is no similarity with the external method, but a striving by man towards the fulfilment of his calling and predestination - a calling towards liberation and incarnation. That is the great drama of human existence, which should not scare us.

Just the opposite. Preparedness for life, for the conquering of phantoms and fantastic visions which are formed often artificially through involuntary slavery, all that disperses if one looks ahead with a bright and fearless eye. Do we not really agree with the ancient Greeks, such as Epictetus, who once said: "Only educated people are free". There it is - wisdom, a lesson, a way for the modern man, frightened and bullied and sent out of his senses by various prophetical misanthropes of the inevitable Apocalypse, and simply standing in awe before life. It must be that spiritual perception, with all its soulshaking complications, is a many-rhythmed and divine secret.

Truly, mankind in these days, in the presence of all these new unique technical breakthroughs, experiences the "sickness of the dead-end". I am not surprised, however, paradoxical it may seem, that if we were to set up a referendum on the theme "Is the world round?" we could find not a few who would be convinced of the opposite! The true reality of this world is the never subsiding and unfailing problem of our times.

The dialogue of Chingiz Aitmatov and Mukhtar Shakhanov. "The Plight of a Postmodern Hunter" is reading material far from usual, and far from simple, but nonetheless in not distracting, but attracting, goes still further. For these authors are interested in ancient and modern history, in the origins of traditions and folk customs, in the world-views and flights of thought of many representatives of the "mysterious" East. This book is unique because it makes great demands on the efforts of the soul of the reader. But it is just that which is of great importance to the reader! In any case, to a reader, who, as Rolland says, not just reads a book, but who searches for himself in it.

Vladimir Korkin.

HERTFORDSHIRE PRESS

Title List

Igor Savitsky:
Artist, Collector, Museum Founder
by Marinika Babanazarova (2011)

Since the early 2000s, Igor Savitsky's life and accomplishments have earned increasing international recognition. He and the museum he founded in Nukus, the capital of Karakalpakstan in the far northwest of Uzbekistan. Marinika Babanazarova's memoir is based on her 1990 graduate dissertation at the Tashkent Theatre and Art Institute. It draws upon correspondence, official records, and other documents about the Savitsky family that have become available during the last few years, as well as the recollections of a wide range of people who knew Igor Savitsky personally.

Игорь Савитский: художник, собиратель, основатель музея

С начала 2000-х годов, жизнь и достижения Игоря Савицкого получили широкое признание во всем мире. Он и его музей, основанный в Нукусе, столице Каракалпакстана, стали предметом многочисленных статей в мировых газетах и журналах, таких как TheGuardian и NewYorkTimes, телевизионных программ в Австралии, Германии и Японии. Книга издана на русском, английском и французском языках.

Igor Savitski: Peintre, collectionneur, fondateur du Musée (French), (2012)

Le mémoire de Mme Babanazarova, basé sur sa thèse de 1990 à l'Institut de Théâtre et D'art de Tachkent, s'appuie sur la correspondance, les dossiers officiels et d'autres documents d'Igor Savitsky et de sa famille, qui sont devenus disponibles dernièrement, ainsi que sur les souvenirs de nombreuses personnes ayant connu Savistky personellement, ainsi que sur sa propre expérience de travail a ses cotés, en tant que successeur designé. son nom a titre posthume.

LANGUAGE: **ENG, RUS, FR**   ISBN: **978-0955754999**   RRP: **£10.00**
AVAILABLE ON **KINDLE**

Savitsky Collection Selected Masterpieces.
Poster set of 8 posters (2014)

Limited edition of prints from the world-renowned Museum of Igor Savitsky in Nukus, Uzbekistan. The set includs nine of the most famous works from the Savitsky collection wrapped in a colourful envelope. Selected Masterpieces of the Savitsky Collection.

[Cover] BullVasily Lysenko 1. Oriental Café Aleksei Isupov 2. Rendezvous Sergei Luppov 3. By the Sea. Marie-LouiseKliment Red'ko 4. Apocalypse Aleksei Rybnikov 5. Rain Irina Shtange 6. Purple Autumn Ural Tansykbayaev 7. To the Train Viktor Ufimtsev 8. Brigade to the fields Alexander Volkov This museum, also known as the Nukus Museum or the Savitsky

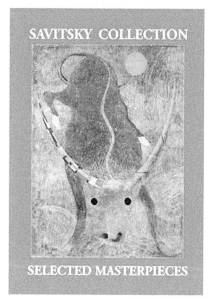
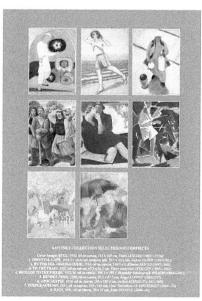

ISBN: **9780992787387**
RRP: **£25.00**

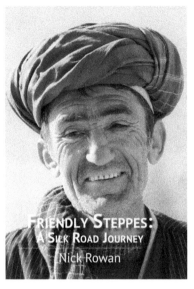

Friendly Steppes. A Silk Road Journey
by Nick Rowan

This is the chronicle of an extraordinary adventure that led Nick Rowan to some of the world's most incredible and hidden places. Intertwined with the magic of 2,000 years of Silk Road history, he recounts his experiences coupled with a remarkable realisation of just what an impact this trade route has had on our society as we know it today. Containing colourful stories, beautiful photography and vivid characters, and wrapped in the local myths and legends told by the people Nick met and who live along the route, this is both a travelogue and an education of a part of the world that has remained hidden for hundreds of years.

HARD BACK ISBN: **978-0-9927873-4-9**
PAPERBACK ISBN: **978-0-9557549-4-4**
RRP: **£14.95**
AVAILABLE ON **KINDLE**

Birds of Uzbeksitan
by Nedosekov (2012)

FIRST AND ONLY PHOTOALBUM
OF UZBEKISTAN BIRDS!

This book, which provides an introduction to the birdlife of Uzbekistan, is a welcome addition to the tools available to those working to conserve the natural heritage of the country. In addition to being the first photographic guide to the birds of Uzbekistan, the book is unique in only using photographs taken within the country. The compilers are to be congratulated on preparing an attractive and accessible work which hopefully will encourage more people to discover the rich birdlife of the country and want to protect it for future generations

HARD BACK
ISBN: **978-0-955754913**
RRP: **£25.00**

Pool of Stars
by Olesya Petrova, Askar Urmanov,
English Edition (2007)

It is the first publication of a young writer Olesya Petrova, a talented and creative person. Fairy-tale characters dwell on this book's pages. Lovely illustrations make this book even more interesting to kids, thanks to a remarkable artist Askar Urmanov. We hope that our young readers will be very happy with such a gift. It's a book that everyone will appreciate. For the young, innocent ones - it's a good source of lessons they'll need in life. For the not-so-young but young at heart, it's a great book to remind us that life is so much more than work.

ISBN: **978-0955754906   ENGLISH**   AVAILABLE ON **KINDLE**

«Звёздная лужица»

Первая книга для детей, изданная британским издательством Hertfordshire Press. Это также первая публикация молодой талантливой писательницы Олеси Петровой. Сказочные персонажи живут на страницах этой книги. Прекрасные иллюстрации делают книгу еще более интересной и красочной для детей, благодаря замечательному художнику Аскару Урманову. Вместе Аскар и Олеся составляют удивительный творческий тандем, который привнес жизнь в эту маленькую книгу

ISBN: **978-0955754906   RUSSIAN**
RRP: **£4.95**

Buyuk Temurhon (Tamerlane)
by C. Marlowe, Uzbek Edition (2010)

Hertfordshire based publisher Silk Road Media, run by Marat Akhmedjanov, and the BBC Uzbek Service have published one of Christopher Marlowe's famous plays, Tamburlaine the Great, translated into the Uzbek language. It is the first of Christopher Marlowe's plays to be translated into Uzbek, which is Tamburlaine's native language. Translated by Hamid Ismailov, the current BBC World Service Writer-in-Residence, this new publication seeks to introduce English classics to Uzbek readers worldwide.

PAPERBACK
ISBN: **9780955754982**
RRP: **£10.00**
AVAILABLE ON **KINDLE**

Kairat Zakiryanov

Under the Wolf nest.
Turkic Rhapsody

Көкжал белгісімен. Түркі рапсодиясы

Under Wolf's Nest
by KairatZakiryanov
English –Kazakh edition

Were the origins of Islam, Christianity and the legend of King Arthur all influenced by steppe nomads from Kazakhstan? Ranging through thousands of years of history, and drawing on sources from Herodotus through to contemporary Kazakh and Russian research, the crucial role in the creation of modern civilisation played by the Turkic people is revealed in this detailed yet highly accessible work. Professor Kairat Zakiryanov, President of the Kazakh Academy of Sport and Tourism, explains how generations of steppe nomads, including Genghis Khan, have helped shape the language, culture and populations of Asia, Europe, the Middle East and America through migrations taking place over millennia.

HARD BACK
ISBN: **9780957480728**
RRP: **£17.50**
AVAILABLE ON **KINDLE**

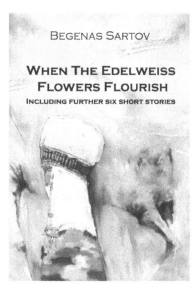

BEGENAS SARTOV

WHEN THE EDELWEISS
FLOWERS FLOURISH
INCLUDING FURTHER SIX SHORT STORIES

When Edelweiss flowers flourish
by Begenas Saratov
English edition (2012)

A spectacular insight into life in the Soviet Union in the late 1960's made all the more intriguing by its setting within the Sovet Republic of Kyrgyzstan. The story explores Soviet life, traditional Kyrgyz life and life on planet Earth through a Science Fiction story based around an alien nations plundering of the planet for life giving herbs. The author reveals far sighted thoughts and concerns for conservation, management of natural resources and dialogue to achieve peace yet at the same time shows extraordinary foresight with ideas for future technologies and the progress of science. The whole style of the writing gives a fascinating insight into the many facets of life in a highly civilised yet rarely known part of the world.

ISBN: 978-0955754951   PAPERBACK   AVAILABLE ON **KINDLE**

Mamyry gyldogon maalda

Это фантастический рассказ, повествующий о советской жизни, жизни кыргызского народа и о жизни на планете в целом. Автор рассказывает об инопланетных народах, которые пришли на нашу планету, чтобы разграбить ее. Автор раскрывает дальновидность мысли о сохранение и рациональном использовании природных ресурсов, а также диалога для достижения мира и в то же время показывает необычайную дальновидность с идеями для будущих технологий и прогресса науки. Книга также издана на **кыргызском языке**.

ISBN: **9780955555754951**
RRP: **£12.95**

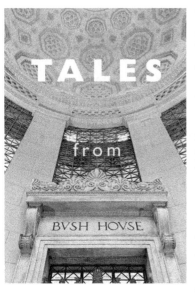

Tales from Bush House
(BBC Wolrd Service)
by Hamid Ismailov
(2012)

Tales From Bush House is a collection of short narratives about working lives, mostly real and comic, sometimes poignant or apocryphal, gifted to the editors by former and current BBC World Service employees. They are tales from inside Bush House - the home of the World Service since 1941 - escaping through its marble-clad walls at a time when its staff begin their departure to new premises in Portland Place. In July 2012, the grand doors of this imposing building will close on a vibrant chapter in the history of Britain's most cosmopolitan organisation. So this is a timely book.

PAPERBACK
ISBN: **9780955754975**
RRP: **£12.95**
AVAILABLE ON **KINDLE**

Chants of Dark Fire
(Песни темного огня)
by Zhulduz Baizakova
Russian edition (2012)

This contemporary work of poetry contains the deep and inspirational rhythms of the ancient Steppe. It combines the nomad, modern, postmodern influences in Kazakhstani culture in the early 21st century, and reveals the hidden depths of contrasts, darkness, and longing for light that breathes both ice and fire to inspire a rich form of poetry worthy of reading and contemplating. It is also distinguished by the uniqueness of its style and substance. Simply sublime, it has to be read and felt for real.

ISBN: **978-0957480711**
RRP: **£10.00**

Kamila
by R. Karimov
Kyrgyz – Uzbek Edition (2013)

«Камила» - это история о сироте,
растущей на юге Кыргызстана.
Наряду с личной трагедией Камилы и ее
родителей, Рахим Каримов описывает
очень реалистично и подробно местный
образ жизни. Роман выиграл конкурс
"Искусство книги-2005" в Бишкеке
и был признан национальным
бестселлером Книжной палаты
Кыргызской Республики.

PAPERBACK
ISBN: **978-0957480773**
RRP: **£10.00**

Galina Dolgaya

THE GODS
OF THE MIDDLE WORLD

Gods of the Middle World
by Galina Dolgaya (2013)

The Gods of the Middle World tells the story of Sima, a student of archaeology for whom the old lore and ways of the Central Asian steppe peoples are as vivid as the present. When she joints a group of archaeologists in southern Kazakhstan, asking all the time whether it is really possible to 'commune with the spirits', she soon discovers the answer first hand, setting in motion events in the spirit world that have been frozen for centuries. Meanwhile three millennia earlier, on the same spot, a young woman and her companion struggle to survive and amend wrongs that have caused the neighbouring tribe to take revenge. The two narratives mirror one another, and Sima's destiny is to resolve the ancient wrongs in her own lifetime and so restore the proper balance of the forces of good and evil

PAPERBACK
ISBN: **978-0957480797**
RRP: **£14.95**
AVAILABLE ON **KINDLE**

Jazz Book, poetry
by Alma Sharipova , Russian Edition

Сборник стихов Алмы Шариповой JazzCafé, в котором предлагаются стихотворения, написанные в разное время и посвященые различным событиям из жизни автора. Стихотворения Алмы содержательные и эмоциональные одновременно, отражают философию ее отношения к происходящему. Почти каждое стихотворение представляет собой законченный рассказ в миниатюре. Сюжет разворачивается последовательно и завершается небольшим резюме в последних строках. Стихотворения раскрываются, как готовые «формулы» жизни. Читатель невольно задумывается над ними и может найти как что-то знакомое, так и новое для себя.

ISBN: 978-0-957480797
RRP: £10.00

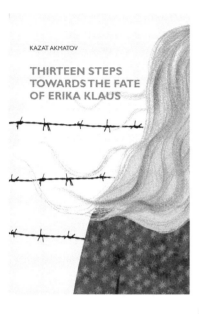

KAZAT AKMATOV

THIRTEEN STEPS
TOWARDS THE FATE
OF ERIKA KLAUS

13 steps of Erika Klaus
by Kazat Akmatov (2013)

The story involves the harrowing experiences of a young and very naïve Norwegian woman who has come to Kyrgyzstan to teach English to schoolchildren in a remote mountain outpost. Governed by the megalomaniac Colonel Bronza, the community barely survives under a cruel and unjust neo-fascist regime. Immersed in the local culture, Erika is initially both enchanted and apprehensive but soon becomes disillusioned as day after day, she is forbidden to teach. Alongside Erika's story, are the personal tragedies experienced by former soldier Sovietbek , Stalbek, the local policeman, the Principal of the school and a young man who has married a Kyrgyz refugee from Afghanistan . Each tries in vain, to challenge and change the corrupt political situation in which they are forced to live.

PAPERBACK
ISBN: **978-0957480766**
RRP: **£12.95**
AVAILABLE ON **KINDLE**

The Modernization of Foreign Language Education: The Linguocultural - Communicative Approach
by SalimaKunanbayeva (2013)

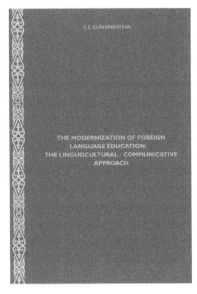

Professor S. S. Kunanbayeva - Rector of Ablai Khan Kazakh University of International Relations and World Languages This textbook is the first of its kind in Kazakhstan to be devoted to the theory and practice of foreign language education. It has been written primarily for future teachers of foreign languages and in a wider sense for all those who to be interested in the question (in the problems?) of the study and use of foreign languages. This book outlines an integrated theory of modern foreign language learning (FLL) which has been drawn up and approved under the auspices of the school of science and methodology of Kazakhstan's Ablai Khan University of International Relations and World Languages.

PAPERBACK
ISBN: **978-0957480780**
RRP: **£19.95**
AVAILABLE ON **KINDLE**

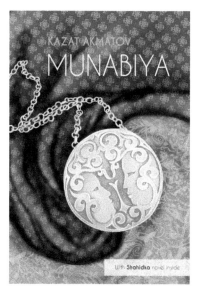

Shahidka/ Munabia
by KazatAkmatov (2013)

Munabiya and Shahidka by Kazat Akmatov National Writer of Kyrgyzstan Recently translated into English Akmatov's two love stories are set in rural Kyrgyzstan, where the natural environment, local culture, traditions and political climate all play an integral part in the dramas which unfold. Munabiya is a tale of a family's frustration, fury, sadness and eventual acceptance of a long term love affair between the widowed father and his mistress. In contrast, Shahidka is a multi-stranded story which focuses on the ties which bind a series of individuals to the tragic and ill-fated union between a local Russian girl and her Chechen lover, within a multi-cultural community where violence, corruption and propaganda are part of everyday life.

PAPERBACK
ISBN: **978-0957480759**
RRP: **£12.95**
AVAILABLE ON **KINDLE**

Howl *novel*
by Kazat Akmatov (2014)
English –Russian

The "Howl" by Kazat Akmatov is a beautifully crafted novel centred on life in rural Kyrgyzstan. Characteristic of the country's national writer, the simple plot is imbued with descriptions of the spectacular landscape, wildlife and local customs. The theme however, is universal and the contradictory emotions experienced by Kalen the shepherd must surely ring true to young men, and their parents, the world over. Here is a haunting and sensitively written story of a bitter -sweet rite of passage from boyhood to manhood.

PAPERBACK
ISBN: **978-0993044410**
RRP: **£12.50**
AVAILABLE ON **KINDLE**

KAIRAT ZAKIRYANOV

THE TURKIC SAGA
OF GENGHIS KHAN
AND
THE KZ FACTOR

The Turkic Saga
of Genghis Khan and the KZ Factor
by Dr.Kairat Zakiryanov (2014)

An in-depth study of Genghis Khan from a Kazakh perspective, The Turkic Saga of Genghis Khan presupposes that the great Mongol leader and his tribal setting had more in common with the ancestors of the Kazakhs than with the people who today identify as Mongols. This idea is growing in currency in both western and eastern scholarship and is challenging both old Western assumptions and the long-obsolete Soviet perspective. This is an academic work that draws on many Central Asian and Russian sources and often has a Eurasianist bias - while also paying attention to new accounts by Western authors such as Jack Weatherford and John Man. It bears the mark of an independent, unorthodox and passionate scholar.

HARD BACK
ISBN: **978-0992787370**
RRP: **£17.50**
AVAILABLE ON **KINDLE**

Alphabet Game
by Paul Wilson (2014)

Travelling around the world may appear as easy as ABC, but looks can be deceptive: there is no 'X' for a start. Not since Xidakistan was struck from the map. Yet post 9/11, with the War on Terror going global, could 'The Valley' be about to regain its place on the political stage? Xidakistan's fate is inextricably linked with that of Graham Ruff, founder of Ruff Guides. Setting sail where Around the World in Eighty Days and Lost Horizon weighed anchor, our not-quite-a-hero suffers all in pursuit of his golden triangle: The Game, The Guidebook, The Girl. With the future of printed Guidebooks increasingly in question, As Evelyn Waugh's Scoop did for Foreign Correspondents the world over, so this novel lifts the lid on Travel Writers for good.

PAPERBACK
ISBN: **978-0-992787325**
RRP: **£14.95**
AVAILABLE ON **KINDLE**

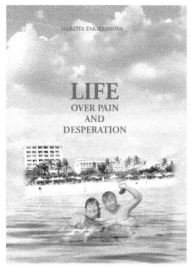

Life over pain and desperation
by Marziya Zakiryanova (2014)

This book was written by someone on the fringe of death. Her life had been split in two: before and after the first day of August 1991 when she, a mother of two small children and full of hopes and plans for the future, became disabled in a single twist of fate. Narrating her tale of self-conquest, the author speaks about how she managed to hold her family together, win the respect and recognition of people around her and above all, protect the fragile concept of 'love' from fortune's cruel turns. By the time the book was submitted to print, Marziya Zakiryanova had passed away. She died after making the last correction to her script. We bid farewell to this remarkable and powerfully creative woman.

HARD BACK
ISBN: **978-0-99278733-2**
RRP: **£14.95**
AVAILABLE ON **KINDLE**

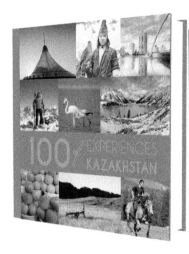

100 experiences of Kazakhstan
by Vitaly Shuptar, Nick Rowan
and Dagmar Schreiber (2014)

The original land of the nomads,
landlocked Kazakhstan and its expansive
steppes present an intriguing border
between Europe and Asia. Dispel
the notion of oil barons and Borat and be
prepared for a warm welcome into a land
full of contrasts. A visit to this newly
independent country will transport you
to a bygone era to discover a country
full of legends and wonders. Whether
searching for the descendants of Genghis Khan - who left his mark on this
land seven hundred years ago - or looking to discover the futuristic
architecture of its capital Astana, visitors cannot fail but be impressed
by what they experience. For those seeking adventure, the formidable Altai
and Tien Shan mountains provide challenges for novices and experts alike

ISBN: 978-0-992787356
RRP: £19.95

Dance of Devils , Jinlar Bazmi
by AbdulhamidIsmoil
and Hamid Ismailov
(Uzbek language),
E-book (2012)

'Dance of Devils' is a novel about the life of a great Uzbek writer Abdulla Qadyri (incidentally, 'Dance of Devils' is the name of one of his earliest short stories). In 1937, Qadyri was going to write a novel, which he said was to make his readers to stop reading his iconic novels "Days Bygone" and "Scorpion from the altar," so beautiful it would have been. The novel would've told about a certain maid, who became a wife of three Khans - a kind of Uzbek Helen of Troy. He told everyone: "I will sit down this winter and finish this novel - I have done my preparatory work, it remains only to write. Then people will stop reading my previous books". He began writing this novel, but on the December 31, 1937 he was arrested.

AVAILABLE ON **KINDLE**
ASIN: B009ZBPV2M

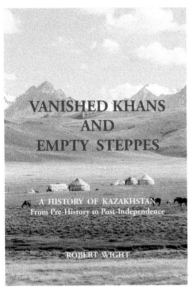

Vanished Khans and Empty Steppes
by Robert Wight (2014)

The book opens with an outline of the history of Almaty, from its nineteenth-century origins as a remote outpost of the Russian empire, up to its present status as the thriving second city of modern-day Kazakhstan. The story then goes back to the Neolithic and early Bronze Ages, and the sensational discovery of the famous Golden Man of the Scythian empire. The transition has been difficult and tumultuous for millions of people, but Vanished Khans and Empty Steppes illustrates how Kazakhstan has emerged as one of the world's most successful post-communist countries.

HARD BACK
ISBN: **978-0-9930444-0-3**
RRP: **£24.95**

PAPERBACK
ISBSN: **978-1-910886-05-2**
RRP: **£14.50**
AVAILABLE ON **KINDLE**

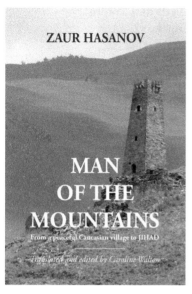

Man of the Mountains
by Abudlla Isa (2014)
(OCABF 2013 Winner)

Man of the Mountains" is a book about a young Muslim Chechen boy, Zaur who becomes a central figure representing the fight of local indigenous people against both the Russians invading the country and Islamic radicals trying to take a leverage of the situation, using it to push their narrow political agenda on the eve of collapse of the USSR. After 9/11 and the invasion of Iraq and Afghanistan by coalition forces, the subject of the Islamic jihadi movement has become an important subject for the Western readers. But few know about the resistance movement from the local intellectuals and moderates against radical Islamists taking strong hold in the area.

PAPERBACK
ISBN: **978-0-9930444-5-8**
RRP: **£14.95**
AVAILABLE ON **KINDLE**

Silk, Spice, Veils and Vodka
by Felicity Timcke (2014)

Felicity Timcke's missive publication, "Silk, Spices, Veils and Vodka" brings both a refreshing and new approach to life on the expat trail. South African by origin, Timcke has lived in some very exotic places, mostly along the more challenging countries of the Silk Road. Although the book's content, which is entirely composed of letters to the author's friends and family, is directed primarily at this group, it provides "20 years of musings" that will enthral and delight those who have either experienced a similar expatriate existence or who are nervously about to depart for one.

PAPERBACK
ISBN: **978-0992787318**
RRP: **£12.50**
AVAILABLE ON **KINDLE**

Finding the Holy Path
by Shahsanem Murray (2014)

"Murray's first book provides an enticing and novel link between her adopted home town of Edinburgh and her origins form Central Asia. Beginning with an investigation into a mysterious lamp that turns up in an antiques shop in Edinburgh, and is bought on impulse, we are quickly brought to the fertile Ferghana valley in Uzbekistan to witness the birth of Kara-Choro, and the start of an enthralling story that links past and present. Told through a vivid and passionate dialogue, this is a tale of parallel discovery and intrigue. The beautifully translated text, interspersed by regional poetry, cannot fail to impress any reader, especially those new to the region who will be affectionately drawn into its heart in this page-turning cultural thriller."

В поисках святого перевала – удивительный приключенческий роман, основанный на исторических источниках. Произведение Мюррей – это временной мостик между эпохами, который помогает нам переместиться в прошлое и уносит нас далеко в 16 век. Закрученный сюжет предоставляет нам уникальную возможность, познакомиться с историейи культурой Центральной Азии. «Первая книга Мюррей предлагает заманчивый роман, связывающий между её приемным городом Эдинбургом и Центральной Азией, откуда настоящее происхождение автора.

RUS ISBN: **978-0-9930444-8-9**
ENGL ISBN: **978-0992787394**
PAPERBACK
RRP: **£12.50**

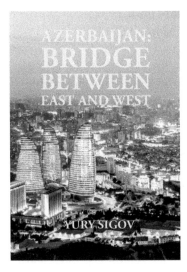

Azerbaijan:
Bridge between East and West
by Yury Sigov, 2015

Azerbaijan: Bridge between East and West, Yury Sigov narrates a comprehensive and compelling story about Azerbaijan. He balances the country's rich cultural heritage, wonderful people and vibrant environment with its modern political and economic strategies. Readers will get the chance to thoroughly explore Azerbaijan from many different perspectives and discover a plethora of innovations and idea, including the recipe for Azerbaijan's success as a nation and its strategies for the future. The book also explores the history of relationships between United Kingdom and Azerbaijan.

HARD BACK
ISBN: **978-0-9930444-9-6**
RRP: **£24.50**
AVAILABLE ON **KINDLE**

Kashmir Song
by Sharaf Rashidov
(translation by Alexey Ulko, OCABF 2014 Winner). 2015

This beautiful illustrated novella offers a sensitive reworking of an ancient and enchanting folk story which although rooted in Kashmir is, by nature of its theme, universal in its appeal.

Alternative interpretations of this tale are explored by Alexey Ulko in his introduction, with references to both politics and contemporary literature, and the author's epilogue further reiterates its philosophical dimension.

The Kashmir Song is a timeless tale, which true to the tradition of classical folklore, can be enjoyed on a number of levels by readers of all ages.

COMING SOON!!!
ISBN: 978-0-9930444-2-7
RRP: £29.50

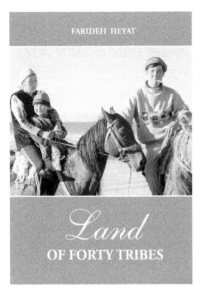

Land of forty tribes
by Farideh Heyat, 2015

Sima Omid, a British-Iranian anthropologist in search of her Turkic roots, takes on a university teaching post in Kyrgyzstan. It is the year following 9/11, when the US is asserting its influence in the region. Disillusioned with her long-standing relationship, Sima is looking for a new man in her life. But the foreign men she meets are mostly involved in relationships with local women half their age, and the Central Asian men she finds highly male chauvinist and aggressive towards women.

PAPERBACK
ISBN: **978-0-9930444-4-1**
RRP: **£14.95**

Terror: events, facts, evidence.
by Eldar Samadov, 2015

This book is based on research carried out since 1988 on territorial claims of Armenia against Azerbaijan, which led to the escalation of the conflict over Nagorno-Karabakh. This escalation included acts of terror by Armanian terrorist and other armed gangs not only in areas where intensive armed confrontations took place but also away from the fighting zones. This book, not for the first time, reflects upon the results of numerous acts of premeditated murder, robbery, armed attack and other crimes through collected material related to criminal cases which have been opened at various stages following such crimes. The book is meant for political scientists, historians, lawyers, diplomats and a broader audience.

PAPERBACK
ISBN: **978-1-910886-00-7**
RRP: **£9.99**
AVAILABLE ON **KINDLE**

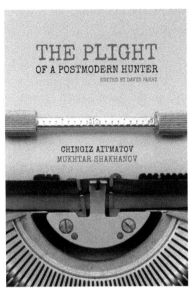

THE PLIGHT OF A POSTMODERN HUNTER
Chlngiz Aitmatov.
Mukhtar Shakhanov
(2015)

"Delusion of civilization" by M. Shakhanov is an epochal poem, rich in prudence and nobility – as is his foremother steppe. It is the voice of the Earth, which raised itself in defense of the human soul. This is a new genre of spiritual ecology. As such, this book is written from the heart of a former tractor driver, who knows all the "scars and wrinkles" of the soil - its thirst for human intimacy. This book is also authored from the perspective of an outstanding intellectual whose love for national traditions has grown as universal as our common great motherland.

I dare say, this book is a spiritual instrument of patriotism for all humankind. Hence, there is something gentle, kind, and sad, about the old swan-song of Mukhtar's brave ancestors. Those who for six months fought to the death to protect Grand Otrar - famous worldwide for its philosophers and rich library, from the hordes of Genghis Khan.

HARDBACK
LANGUAGES ENG
ISBN: **978-1-910886-11-3**
RRP: **£17.50**

Raushan Burkitbayeva – Nukenova

edited by David Parry

The Wormwood Wind
Raushan
Burkitbayeva- Nukenova (2015)

A single unstated assertion runs throughout The Wormwood Wind, arguing, amid its lyrical nooks and crannies, we are only fully human when our imaginations are free. Possibly this is the primary glittering insight behind Nukenova's collaboration with hidden Restorative Powers above her pen. No one would doubt, for example, when she hints that the moment schoolchildren read about their surrounding environment they are acting in a healthy and developmental manner. Likewise, when she implies any adult who has the courage to think "outside the box" quickly gains a reputation for adaptability in their private affairs – hardly anyone would doubt her. General affirmations demonstrating this sublime and liberating contribution to Global Text will prove dangerous to unwary readers, while its intoxicating rhythms and rhymes will lead a grateful few to elative revolutions inside their own souls. Thus, I unreservedly recommend this ingenious work to Western readers.

HARD BACK
LANGUAGES ENG
ISBN: **978-1-910886-12-0**
RRP: **£14.95**

"The true story of immigration"
— Paul Wilson is a long-time writer on the Silk Road —

CRANES
IN
SPRING

TOLIBSHOHI DAVLAT

The best work in the literary competition
"Open Central Asia Book Forum and Literature Festival - 2014"

"Cranes in Spring"
by Tolibshohi Davlat
(2015)

This novel highlights a complex issue that millions of Tajiks face when becoming working migrants in Russia due to lack of opportunities at home. Fresh out of school, Saidakbar decides to go to Russia as he hopes to earn money to pay for his university tuition. His parents reluctantly let him go providing he is accompanied by his uncle, Mustakim, an experienced migrant. And so begins this tale of adventure and heartache that reflects the reality of life faced by many Central Asian migrants. Mistreatment, harassment and backstabbing join the Tajik migrants as they try to pull through in a foreign country. Davlat vividly narrates the brutality of the law enforcement officers but also draws attention to kindness and help of several ordinary people in Russia. How will Mustakim and Saidakbar's journey end? Intrigued by the story starting from the first page, one cannot put the book down until it's finished.

COMING SOON

LANGUAGES ENG / RUS
HARDBACK
ISBN: **978-1-910886-06-9**

The Hollywood Conundrum or Guardian of Treasure
Maksim Korsakov
(2015)

In this groundbreaking experimental novella, Maxim Korsakov breaks all the preconceived rules of genre and literary convention to deliver a work rich in humour, style, and fantasy. Starting with a so-called "biographical" account of the horrors lurking beneath marriages of convenience and the self-delusions necessary to maintain these relationships, he then speedily moves to a screenplay, which would put most James Bond movies to shame. As if international espionage were not enough, the author teases his readers with lost treasure maps, revived Khanates, sports car jousting, ancient aliens who possess the very secrets of immortality, and the lineal descendants of legendary Genghis Khan. All in all, an ingenious book, as well as s clear critique of traditional English narrative convention.

LANGUAGES ENG / RUS
PAPERBACK
ISBN: **978-1-910886-14-4**
RRP: **£24.95**

My Homeland, Oh My Crimea
by Lenifer Mambetova
(2015)

Mambetova's delightful poems, exploring the hopes and fates of Crimean Tartars, are a timely and evocative reminder of how deep a people's roots can be, but also how adaptable and embracing foreigners can be of their adopted country, its people and its traditions.

COMING SOON
LANGUAGES ENG / RUS
HARDBACK
ISBN: **978-1-910886-04-5**

Lightning Source UK Ltd.
Milton Keynes UK
UKHW011903041221
395001UK00003BA/164